THE NEW GROVE
LATE ROMANTIC MASTERS

THE NEW GROVE
DICTIONARY OF MUSIC AND MUSICIANS

Editor: Stanley Sadie

The Composer Biography Series

BACH FAMILY

BEETHOVEN

EARLY ROMANTIC MASTERS 1

EARLY ROMANTIC MASTERS 2

HANDEL

HAYDN

HIGH RENAISSANCE MASTERS

ITALIAN BAROQUE MASTERS

LATE ROMANTIC MASTERS

MASTERS OF ITALIAN OPERA

MODERN MASTERS

MOZART

NORTH EUROPEAN BAROQUE MASTERS

SCHUBERT

SECOND VIENNESE SCHOOL

TURN OF THE CENTURY MASTERS

WAGNER

THE NEW GROVE®

Late Romantic Masters

BRUCKNER   BRAHMS
DVOŘÁK   WOLF

Deryck Cooke
Heinz Becker
John Clapham
Eric Sams

W. W. NORTON & COMPANY
NEW YORK   LONDON

First published in
The New Grove Dictionary of Music and Musicians®,
edited by Stanley Sadie, 1980

The New Grove and *The New Grove Dictionary of Music and Musicians*
are registered trademarks of Macmillian Publishers Limited, London

First published in UK in paperback with additions 1985 by
PAPERMAC
a division of Macmillan Publishers Limited
London and Basingstoke

First published in UK in hardback with additions 1985 by
MACMILLAN LONDON LIMITED
4 Little Essex Street London WC2R 3LF
and Basingstoke

British Library Cataloguing in Publication Data
Late romantic masters.—(The Composer
biography series)
1. Music—Europe—History and criticism
2. Composers
I. Cooke, Deryck   II. The new Grove
dictionary of music and musicians   III. Series
780'.92'2   ML240

ISBN 0–333–39025–3 (hardback)
ISBN 0–333–39026–1 (paperback)

First American edition in book form with additions 1985 by
W. W. NORTON & COMPANY
New York and London

ISBN 0-393-01697-8 (hardback)
ISBN 0-393-30101-X (paperback)

Printed in Great Britain

Contents

List of illustrations

Cover: Johannes Brahms: portrait (1881) in pastels by Ludwig Michalek, (Staats- und Universitätsbibliothek, Hamburg)

Illustration acknowledgments

General abbreviations

A	alto, contralto [voice]	*Jb*	Jahrbuch [yearbook]
acc.	accompaniment, accompanied by	Jg.	Jahrgang [year of publication/volume]
Ag	Agnus Dei		
Anh.	Anhang [appendix]	K	Köchel catalogue [Mozart]
ant	antiphon	Ky	Kyrie
appx	appendix		
aut.	autumn	lib	libretto
B	bass [voice]	movt	movement
Bar	baritone [voice]		
bn	bassoon	n.d.	no date of publication
Bs	Benedictus		
BWV	Bach-Werke-Verzeichnis [Schmieder, catalogue of J. S. Bach's works]	ob	oboe
		off	offertory
		orch	orchestra, orchestral
		orchd	orchestrated (by)
c	circa [about]	org	organ
c.f.	cantus firmus	ov.	overture
cl	clarinet		
collab.	in collaboration with	PO	Philharmonic Orchestra
conc.	concerto	posth.	posthumous(ly)
corr.	corrected	pubd	published
Cz.	Czech		
		qnt	quintet
D	Deutsch catalogue [Schubert]	qt	quartet
d	died	*R*	photographic reprint
db	double bass	recit	recitative
dbn	double bassoon	repr.	reprinted
ded.	dedication, dedicated to	rev.	revision, revised (by/for)
		S	soprano [voice]
edn.	edition	San	Sanctus
		Sp.	Spanish
facs.	facsimile	str	string(s)
frag.	fragment	sum.	summer
		sym.	symphony, symphonic
Gl	Gloria		
grad	gradual	T	tenor [voice]
		timp.	timpani
hn	horn	tpt	trumpet
Hung.	Hungarian	transcr.	transcription, transcribed by/for
inc.	incomplete	trbn	trombone
inst	instrument, instrumental	Turk.	Turkish

U.	University	WoO	Werke ohne Opuszahl [works without opus number]
v, vv	voice, voices		
va	viola	ww	woodwind
vc	cello		
vn	violin		

Symbols for the library sources of works, printed in *italic*, correspond to those used in *Répertoire International des Sources Musicales*, Ser. A.

Bibliographical abbreviations

SM	*Studia musicologica Academiae scientiarum hungaricae*
SMw	*Studien zur Musikwissenschaft*
SMz	*Schweizerische Musikzeitung/Revue musicale suisse*
SovM	*Sovetskaya musïka*
ZfM	*Zeitschrift für Musik*
ZMw	*Zeitschrift für Musikwissenschaft*

Preface

This volume is one of a series of short biographies derived from *The New Grove Dictionary of Music and Musicians* (London, 1980). In its original form, the text was written in the mid-1970s, and finalized at the end of that decade. For this reprint, the texts have been re-read and modified. The material on Wolf and Dvořák has been amended by the original authors. The Brahms article has been amended by its author, too, with the assistance of Margit McCorkle, who also has taken responsibility for the revision of the work-list. The author of the Bruckner text is the late Deryck Cooke; minor emendations have been made to his text and work-list with the assistance of Hans-Hubert Schönzeler, and Richard Evidon has updated the bibliography (originally supplied by Leopold Nowak).

The fact that the texts of the books in the series originated as dictionary articles inevitably gives them a character somewhat different from that of books conceived as such. They are designed, first of all, to accommodate a very great deal of information in a manner that makes reference quick and easy. Their first concern is with fact rather than opinion, and this leads to a larger than usual proportion of the texts being devoted to biography than to critical discussion. The nature of a reference work gives it a particular obligation to convey received knowledge and to treat of composers' lives and works in an encyclopedic fashion, with proper acknowledgment of sources and due care to reflect different standpoints, rather than to embody imaginative or speculative writing about a composer's character or his music.

It is hoped that the comprehensive work-lists and extended bibliographies, indicative of the origins of the books in a reference work, will be valuable to the reader who is eager for full and accurate reference information and who may not have ready access to *The New Grove Dictionary* or who may prefer to have it in this more compact form.

S.S.

ANTON BRUCKNER

Deryck Cooke

Leopold Nowak

Life

I   Early years

Anton Joseph Bruckner was born in Ansfelden, near Linz, on 4 September 1824. He was the eldest of five surviving children of the Ansfelden schoolmaster and organist, Anton Bruckner (*b* 1791), and his first acquaintance with music was when he was taken to Mass by his mother, who sang in the church choir. He received his first musical tuition from his father, learning to play hymn tunes on a miniature violin at the age of four, and soon afterwards finding their harmonies on the family spinet; by the age of ten he was already able to deputize for his father as organist at the church services. At this time his parents would sometimes take him to the nearby Augustinian monastery of St Florian where, amid the splendours of its Baroque architecture, he heard far more impressive services, accompanied by the majestic sound of the great organ. His first lessons in music theory came at the age of 11, when he was sent to the nearby small town of Hörsching, to stay with his 21-year-old cousin and godfather Johann Baptist Weiss, who was schoolmaster and organist. Weiss was a local composer of some repute, and Bruckner learnt harmony from him, chiefly by the old traditional method of playing the organ from a figured bass; he also heard a Mozart mass for the first time, as well as Haydn's oratorios *The Creation* and *The Seasons*, and he perhaps made his own first attempts at composition.

The following year, the fatal illness of Bruckner's father necessitated his return to Ansfelden to deputize in the schoolhouse and the church and as fiddler at the village dances. But when his father died in 1837, his mother refused to allow the 13-year-old boy to lose his education by supporting the family; she moved with her four other children to cheap lodgings in another village, and secured from Michael Arneth, the kindly prior of St Florian, his admission as a chorister. The monastery was to be his home for the next three years, and his spiritual home for the rest of his life. As a chorister there, he pursued his education and music studies, taking further organ lessons from Anton Kattinger, the St Florian organist; he was eventually allowed to deputize for him at the less important services. He worked hard at theory, devoted much of his time to organ improvisation and also renewed his violin lessons, so that in 1839, when his voice broke, he was able to stay on for a further year as a violinist. But the time was approaching when he had to make his own way in the world, and with a surprising lack of self-confidence he decided to rely on the minimal security of his father's profession of school-master–organist, rather than brave the hazards of a purely musical career.

To take his teacher-training course, Bruckner had to spend a year in Linz, the capital of Upper Austria, and since the post of schoolmaster was associated with that of organist, music played a large part in the curriculum. He studied music theory with the author of a standard and expert book on the subject, August Dürrnberger, while in the cathedral he heard some more of Mozart's masses and first encountered those of Joseph and

Michael Haydn. Much more important, however, was the fact that, as a 16-year-old provincial product of the organ loft, he first came into contact with metropolitan and international concert music: overtures by Weber, and particularly Beethoven's Fourth Symphony, gave him a glimpse of an entirely new world. After this experience his appointment to the humble post of assistant schoolmaster at the little village of Windhaag (near Freistadt), satisfactory as it was for supporting his family, could only be the more unpalatable to him. He took up the post in 1841 at the age of 17, and he also persevered with his own interests: he copied out Bach's *Art of Fugue*, as well as fugues by Albrechtsberger; he played the fiddle at the local dances; and he began composing again, with a small-scale Mass in C for alto solo, two horns and organ, written for a singer in the church choir. But the village was remote from his native district, his salary was pitiful, his superior was unsympathetic to his musical preoccupations, and his duties included farm labouring, even down to muck-spreading.

Bruckner was relieved when, after some 15 months, his St Florian mentor Michael Arneth arrived on a tour of inspection. There was no vacancy at St Florian, but Arneth found him a position as assistant schoolmaster in the village of Kronstorf (near Steyr), within his own native area. Although Kronstorf was even smaller than Windhaag, the situation was much more congenial: his salary was higher, his superior acted as a father towards him, and he made many close friends who took part with him in music-making. The horizon was also less limited: he could now visit St Florian whenever he had the time; he was able to take theory lessons once more, with the main choirmaster in the town of Enns, who based his teaching on Bach's chorales and the '48'; and he could play a large organ again, that of the Steyr parish church. He had acquired more fluency as a composer, and he wrote a number of modest works during his three-year stay at Kronstorf, the most successful being another small-scale mass (for Maundy Thursday) for four-part unaccompanied choir.

II St Florian

At last, in 1845, the post of first assistant teacher at St Florian fell vacant, and Bruckner, at the age of 21, was able to return to the place he loved. He remained there for the next ten years, still regarding himself as a schoolmaster rather than a musician, though he continued studying and composing music. He pursued his course in Bach's music with the choirmaster in Enns; he attended Bach organ recitals in Linz, also encountering the music of Mendelssohn at concerts there; he formed a male-voice quartet with some friends, and composed the first dozen or so of his numerous pieces for the medium, as well as a few cantatas for particular occasions. He also enjoyed the luxury of playing on a Bösendorfer grand piano belonging to a friend, Franz Sailer, his brother's godfather; when Sailer died in 1848 he bequeathed the instrument to Bruckner, who composed at it for the rest of his life. It was Sailer's death that motivated Bruckner's first notable work, the Requiem in D minor for soloists, chorus, orchestra and organ, which was first performed at a memorial service in St Florian the following year. In 1848 he had been appointed provisional organist at St Florian, after the transfer of Kattinger to Kremsmünster, and in 1851 he was given the full appointment, an event which marked the beginning of his slow transformation from school-master to full-time musician. 1854 brought the death of another, closer friend, Michael Arneth, and for the funeral he wrote two impressive short pieces, both in F minor – a male-voice chorus with three trombones, *Vor Arneths Grab*, and a *Libera me* for mixed choir, three trombones and organ, to be performed at the end of the Requiem Mass. Also in 1854 he produced another notable large-scale composition, the *Missa solemnis* in B♭ minor for soloists, chorus, orchestra and organ, which was heard for the first time that year at the induction service in St Florian for Arneth's successor, Friedrich Mayr. This work finally made it clear that Bruckner was a highly gifted and skilled composer; but even so, it was suggested to him by a visiting organist–composer that he should gain absolute mastery by taking a correspondence course in strict harmony and counterpoint with Sechter at the Vienna Conservatory. Bruckner was to take this advice the following year – another step in the direction of becoming a full-time musician; in the meantime he took two examinations (in high-school teaching, and in organ playing and improvisation), gaining two diplomas that would ensure him a senior position if he should ever have to fall back on the profession of schoolmaster–organist.

When Bruckner went to Vienna in July 1855 to ask Sechter to accept him as a private pupil, he was nearly 31 (the age at which Schubert had gone to Sechter in November 1828, only to die before the end of the month). He took with him his *Missa solemnis*, and Sechter was impressed enough by his talent to accept him unhesitatingly. But Sechter also advised him to leave the seclusion of St Florian, and on his return he

5

applied for the vacant post of cathedral organist at Olomouc (secretly, for fear of offending Mayr). When Mayr learnt of this clandestine application, he reprimanded Bruckner severely, and when the post of cathedral organist at Linz fell vacant later the same year, Bruckner was afraid to apply at all. His friends were amazed when they discovered that he was not in Linz on the day of the test, since he was the obvious man for the job; but they managed to get him there. Dürrnberger took him into the cathedral and finally, when the other two candidates had done badly, into the organ loft. He won the post easily, and in December 1855 he moved to Linz, where he was to spend the next 13 years.

III Linz

Although Bruckner had always been fanatically industrious, his period in Linz, which occupied the whole of his 30s, was the busiest time of his life. As cathedral organist he also had to officiate at the parish church; he still worked hard at perfecting his already prodigious organ technique; to improve his financial position (he was still supporting his family) he took a number of piano pupils; and as a lover of choral music he took an active part as a singer in (and later as conductor of) the principal Linz choral society, the *Liedertafel* Frohsinn. All this activity continued while he was pursuing his arduous correspondence course with Sechter in Vienna, working seven hours a day on exercises in strict harmony and counterpoint, and going once a year to undergo a severe examination with Sechter to ratify his progress. In fact even Sechter, a notorious taskmaster, was worried by Bruckner's amazing assiduity; one day, on receiving 17 manuscript books crammed with solutions of difficult problems, he wrote advising him not to drive himself so, or his mental health would suffer. Fortunately, one of Sechter's immutable rules was that his pupils should refrain entirely from free composition while studying theory with him; and just as fortunately, Bruckner's inherent unquestioning obedience obliged him to comply with this stipulation (there is an almost complete gap in his output between the years 1856 and 1861). Thus he was spared (perhaps unwillingly) a burden of creative work which might well have brought him to the verge of a nervous breakdown. He was also lucky to be sustained through this gruelling time by a new mentor, the Bishop of Linz, Franz Josef Rudigier, who, though an iron-willed political prelate, was a great music lover and admirer of Bruckner as musician and man.

The course with Sechter ended in 1861 with a handsome testimonial that gladdened Bruckner's heart, though after so much study of the bare bones of music, he confessed that he felt 'like a watch-dog that has broken his chain'. Nevertheless he felt compelled to apply to the Vienna Conservatory for a diploma qualifying him as an instructor in harmony and counterpoint in music academies. He was examined by a number of eminent musicians, including Sechter, and passed with distinction. The climax was his improvisation of an organ fugue on a submitted theme, after which Johann Herbeck (conductor of the concerts of the Gesellschaft der Musikfreunde and a teacher at the conservatory) was moved to say: 'He should have examined us! If I knew one tenth of what he knows, I'd be happy'. Bruckner had finally mastered all that he could be taught of organ playing, theory, harmony, counterpoint and im-

1. Anton Bruckner in 1863

provisation; but then, at the age of 37, this eternal student decided that (his masses for chorus and orchestra notwithstanding) he had still to acquire a full command of symphonic form and orchestration. This time he chose for his teacher a practical musician, Otto Kitzler, principal cellist and occasional conductor at the Linz Municipal Theatre, who based his tuition less on established textbooks than on the practice of the new 19th-century composers, primarily Beethoven, but also on more recent figures, including Mendelssohn.

Though Bruckner could not have realized it at the time this was the turning-point in his creative life; he regarded it as merely a matter of completing his studies, but in fact this new departure changed his whole orientation. Hitherto he had been an old-fashioned provincial composer, a master craftsman producing well-wrought but stylistically anonymous works, for the church and for local choral societies, based on a thorough knowledge of the techniques of the past – of Mozart, Haydn and Bach, and of the pure harmony and counterpoint of the old polyphonic composers as systematized by later theorists. During his few remaining years at Linz, he became aware of and a part of what was happening to music in his own time, expressing himself in an entirely individual way by absorbing the new methods into his solid base of traditional technique. After this he was to move to Vienna to become one of the most prominent and controversial figures of the period.

At first Bruckner simply studied orchestration and form (sonata form in particular) with Kitzler, and during 1862 he produced, as part of his exercises, four pieces for orchestra and the String Quartet in C minor, his first, practically featureless, orchestral and chamber works. Bruckner's belated and unforeseen transformation was not brought about so much by Kitzler's tuition, invaluable though that was in providing the necessary technical means, as by a revelation that came to him after he had been with Kitzler about a year: his first encounter with Wagner's music. Towards the end of 1862, Kitzler decided to mount the first Linz performance of *Tannhäuser*, and he studied the score with Bruckner, who attended the first performance on 13 February 1863. Bruckner was completely overwhelmed by a work which showed that a composer could break many of the rules insisted on by Sechter, use harmonic progressions not admitted by him and in spite or even because of this, create music of towering genius. During this period he composed two further orchestral exercises, the Symphony in F minor and the Overture in G minor; these, reflecting not Wagner's style but something of his unconventional approach to composition, show considerable vitality and individuality, though they are as yet hardly stamped with Bruckner's own musical personality. A step forward was taken in 1863–4 with the D minor Symphony which, despite its prophetic opening, he rejected at the end of his life by dubbing it 'die Nullte'. The real breakthrough came later in the year with the Mass in D minor for soloists, chorus, orchestra and organ, in which the mature Bruckner suddenly stands revealed. It is some measure of Bruckner's ingrained conservatism and lack of self-confidence, and of the stimulus given to him by Wagner's revolutionary approach, that his comment on the bold new style of this mass was 'I didn't dare before'. Now that he had dared, however, he had no more qualms.

Nevertheless, Bruckner did not regard himself as a revolutionary: he had simply decided that Wagner was the latest 'master', one whose example he ought to follow. His long, traditional training saved him from becoming a mere slavish imitator of Wagner's style, to which he was now much exposed. The following year he was invited to Munich for the first performance of *Tristan und Isolde*; there he made Wagner's acquaintance, but was too awestruck to show him what he had written of his First Symphony. In Linz, in 1868, with Wagner's permission, he conducted the *Liedertafel* Frohsinn and a large orchestra, with a baritone soloist, in the first performance of the closing section of *Die Meistersinger*, two months before the première of the opera. Also, during these years, he attended the Linz productions of *Lohengrin* and *Der fliegende Holländer*, and with the departure of Kitzler he studied further with Ignaz Dorn, a violinist and composer whose musical gods were Wagner, Berlioz and Liszt. But all this, much as it stimulated him to strike out firmly along his own path, left no more than a few marks on the style of the three further masterpieces he composed during those years, the Symphony no.1 in C minor (1865–6) and the masses in E minor (1866) and F minor (1867–8).

In 1867 Bruckner, who had always suffered from intermittent fits of depression, had a nervous breakdown and was obliged to spend four months in a sanatorium at Bad Kreuzen. His illness was probably brought on by the vast amount of study, professional activity and creative work on which he had been engaged during the previous 12 years, and by hopes deferred and disappointments in love. Ironically, it was at this time that he was beginning to make his mark as an important com-

poser: his Mass in D minor had received its first performance in Linz Cathedral in 1864 and had been given in
the imperial chapel in Vienna under Herbeck in 1867,
and he was to conduct the first performance of his
Symphony no.1 in Linz in 1868. In September 1867,
after his recovery, he heard of Sechter's death, which left
unoccupied the post of professor of harmony, counterpoint and organ at the Vienna Conservatory, and that of
organist at the imperial chapel. His thoughts now turned
to Vienna. He applied for the organ post at the imperial
chapel, but was rejected, and a similar fate befell his
application to the University of Vienna in connection
with the creation of a new lectureship in harmony and
counterpoint.

Bruckner probably did not have a high enough opinion of himself as a pedagogue to apply for the professor-
ship at the Vienna Conservatory, and so should have
been overjoyed to discover that the influential Herbeck,
himself a teacher there, regarded him as Sechter's
natural successor and began urging him to put in for the
post. But he was overcome with indecision, since the
salary at the conservatory was somewhat less than the
amount he was able to earn from his multifarious
activities in Linz. Not until the summer of 1868 was he
persuaded by his friends to accept the post, which was
now actually being offered to him. Herbeck had
managed to get the salary raised, to secure him the
provisional organ post at the imperial chapel (though
the official appointment with full salary was not made
until ten years later), and to obtain for him a government grant to assist him in 'the composition of major
symphonic works'.

IV Vienna

In 1868, at the age of 44, Bruckner took up his duties in Vienna, the city in which he was to be living for the remaining 28 years of his life (though he did spend much time visiting Upper Austria). At first, the future looked bright: although only the provisional organist at the imperial chapel, he almost immediately extended his fame as a performer and improviser beyond the bounds of his native country. In 1869 he was chosen to represent Austria in a public competition of famous European organists at Nancy, to inaugurate the new organ in the church of St Epvre. He made such an impression there that he was invited to Paris to play the new organ at Notre Dame, where he was acclaimed a master by Franck, Saint-Saëns and Gounod. In 1871 he took part in a similar competition in London, on the organ of the Royal Albert Hall; this time he was invited to stay and give a series of recitals on the organ of the Crystal Palace, where he received tremendous ovations from vast audiences. His recitals consisted largely of his own, reportedly magnificent, improvisations, either on themes taken from the few Classical works he chose to play, or on themes of his own, and it was as much his creative genius that enthralled his audiences as his masterly organ technique. Regrettably this ready command of improvisation led him to neglect actual organ composition, so that he left only a few short and insignificant pieces for the instrument.

Bruckner's financial position was further improved by his appointment in 1870 as teacher of theory, organ and piano at the teacher-training college of St Anna, and these early years in Vienna saw extremely successful

*2. Anton Bruckner taking snuff with Richard Wagner: silhouette
by Otto Böhler*

performances of the E minor and F minor masses. The short, liturgical E minor, dedicated to Bishop Rudigier and performed at the dedication of the new votive chapel of Linz Cathedral in 1869, had a great local success; but the large symphonic F minor, given in 1872 under Bruckner's own direction in the Augustinerkirche in Vienna, had wider repercussions. Herbeck compared it with Beethoven's *Missa solemnis*, it received a favourable notice from Hanslick and made a considerable impression on Liszt.

Bruckner continued composing church music in Vienna, though he wrote only a few short, concentrated graduals and offertories except for the large-scale *Te Deum* completed in 1884 and the setting of Psalm cl of 1892. Practically the whole of his creative energy went into the composition of symphonies, nos.2–5 between 1871 and 1876, nos.6–8 between 1879 and 1887 and no.9 from 1889 to his death in 1896, when it remained unfinished. But in turning from the mass to the symphony, he immediately faced three different problems, which arose successively in connection with each of his first three symphonies, and continued practically throughout his life.

In the first place, the Vienna Philharmonic Orchestra set a pattern by promptly rejecting his Symphony no.1 for its 'wildness and daring'. Then, in 1872, after playing it through they dismissed no.2 as 'nonsense' and 'unplayable', although it had been praised by Liszt, and were only persuaded to play it the following year under Bruckner, when Herbeck found a patron to finance the performance (which received a standing ovation from both the audience and the orchestra). And in 1875, again after a trial playing, they dismissed no.3 as 'unperformable', and were only persuaded to perform it, two years later, by the intervention of a cabinet minister who was one of Bruckner's supporters. The performance, directed by Bruckner, was an utter fiasco, no doubt owing to the orchestra's lack of belief in the work; there was whistling and catcalling, the audience dwindled rapidly, and at the end only 25 young musicians (including the 17-year-old Mahler) remained to applaud and congratulate the composer. This antipathy of the Vienna PO meant that during his first ten years in Vienna Bruckner found it hard to get a hearing. And the situation continued: although no.4 (completed in 1880) was given a very successful première in 1881 by the Vienna PO under Hans Richter, no.5 (1876) had to wait until 1894, two years before Bruckner's death, for its première in Graz; only two movements of no.6 (1881) were performed during his lifetime.

A second source of trouble was that Bruckner's friends, colleagues and pupils, dismayed by the failure of his symphonies, suggested improvements to make them more palatable to orchestras, conductors and audiences. Already, after the Linz première of no.1, Hanslick and others had been bewildered by the work's complexities and advised Bruckner to write more simply; after the première of no.2 Herbeck took advantage of his position as Bruckner's champion to persuade him to make alterations to it for the second performance in 1876. These alterations, which Bruckner undertook with the greatest reluctance, were mainly cuts intended to reduce the considerable length of the work, though one involved reorchestration of the music to make it easier to play. This set the pattern for what followed. By the time of no.4 two of Bruckner's favourite pupils, Franz Schalk and Ferdinand Löwe, were ready to continue where Herbeck left off, and by the time of no.7 Schalk's brother Josef, another favourite pupil, was taking part as well.

The humble Bruckner, after his determined stand against Herbeck's interference, became a victim of self-doubt, and proved largely amenable to the suggestions of these sophisticated young Viennese musicians (not without genuine misgivings); and they, realizing this, produced versions of their own without his permission, which became the accepted texts: heavily cut, and retextured and reorchestrated in Wagnerian manner. Their laudable motive was the promotion of their revered master's symphonies; indeed, so intent were they on getting the works heard that, in the absence of orchestral performances, they gave public performances of them on two pianos. But the result, nonetheless, was that the symphonies appeared before the public without essential parts, making them shorter, but also formally much less intelligible; and lack of form was a criticism often levelled at Bruckner's symphonies, based on performances of these mutilated versions.

A critic was the third source of trouble, the redoubtable Hanslick. He had been friendly towards Bruckner in Linz, giving him useful advice and guidance, and had mentioned in the Viennese press the Linz première of his First Symphony, adding a few lines recommending him as Sechter's successor at the Vienna Conservatory. He continued this attitude during Bruckner's first five years in Vienna, encouraging him to attend the organ competition in Nancy, and writing a favourable review of the première of the F minor Mass, and a fairly favourable one of the première of the Second Symphony. But a devastating change came with Hanslick's scathing review of the 1877 première of the Third Symphony: 'A vision of how Beethoven's Ninth befriends Wagner's *Walküre* and finds itself under her horse's hooves ... That fraction of the audience which remained to the end consoled the composer for the flight of the rest'. This review, coupled with the fiasco of the performance, did Bruckner untold harm; it was four years before he was granted another hearing.

Unfortunately Bruckner, without foreseeing the cost, had calmly proclaimed himself a Wagnerian. In 1873 he had nerved himself to show the scores of his Second and Third Symphonies to Wagner, who had been greatly impressed with no.3 and had accepted Bruckner's proposed dedication of it to him. In consequence, Bruckner called it his 'Wagner Symphony'; in a Viennese musical world given over to internecine strife between the followers of Wagner and those of Brahms, this amounted to a *casus belli*. In the phrase of Erwin Doernberg: 'Bruckner strayed into the battlefield and became the only casualty'. He became known as 'the Wagnerian symphonist', and was not helped by the excesses of the Wagnerians, who were delighted to have a composer of symphonies to pit against Brahms. Hanslick, a dedicated classicist who detested the new Romantic emotionalism of Wagner's music dramas, upholding against them Brahms's unswerving devotion to the absolute forms of symphonic and chamber music, continued to hold Bruckner's symphonies up to ridicule; and since the other Viennese music critics took their cue from him, Bruckner was assured, on the rare occasions when his symphonies did get a hearing, of a chorus of vituperation in the press.

Early in 1874, Bruckner found himself once more in financial difficulties, having resigned from his post at the teacher-training college of St Anna; he immediately applied once more to the University of Vienna to be appointed lecturer in harmony and counterpoint. Hanslick, as dean of the music faculty, forgot his earlier recommendation of Bruckner to the Vienna Conservatory, and placed every possible obstacle in his way; only when it became obvious that Bruckner had most of the professors' support did he give way. The appointment, made late in 1875, was at first a purely honorary one, but from 1877 onwards it included a fixed salary. That year, in spite of the débâcle of the Third Symphony's première, Theodor Rättig demonstrated his faith in the work by offering to publish it; his edition came out the following year – the first of any Bruckner symphony and the only one for the next eight years.

Bruckner's relationship with Wagner became closer from the time of his visits to Bayreuth for the premières of the complete *Ring* (1876) and of *Parsifal* (1882). On this last occasion, Wagner is reputed to have said 'I know of only one composer who measures up to Beethoven, and that is Bruckner'. He also reputedly promised to conduct all Bruckner's works, and was prevented from doing so only by his death, an event which the deeply moved Bruckner commemorated in the elegiac coda of the Adagio of his Seventh Symphony.

It was the Seventh Symphony that brought Bruckner, at 60, his first real taste of public success and the beginning of his belated fame, though not in Vienna. Arthur Nikisch conducted its première in Leipzig, uncut, at a Gewandhaus concert on 30 December 1884; the applause lasted for a quarter of an hour and the reviews were wholeheartedly enthusiastic. Nikisch himself said 'Since Beethoven there has been nothing that could even approach it. . . . From this moment I regard it as my duty to work for the recognition of Bruckner'. And a few months later, when Hermann Levi conducted the Munich première of the work, there was a great ovation, an enthusiastic press and another conductor who was willing, henceforward, to champion Bruckner's music. The Vienna PO decided to perform the work, only to receive a letter from Bruckner begging them not to, giving as his reason 'the influential Viennese critics, who would be only too likely to obstruct the course of my dawning fame in Germany'. He was proved right. Although the String Quintet in F (1879), Bruckner's only important chamber work, had had a brilliant success in Vienna at its first public performance in January 1885, when the Viennese première of the symphony was given, in 1886 under Richter, Hanslick wrote: 'Like every one of Bruckner's works, the symphony contains ingenious inspirations, interesting and even pleasant details – here six, there eight bars – but in between the lightnings are interminable stretches of darkness, leaden boredom, and feverish over-excitement'. However personally wounding Bruckner may have found this abuse, it came too late to obstruct the course of his dawning fame. Hanslick had to admit that 'most certainly, it has never happened that a composer has been called out four or five times after each movement'. The tide had turned; Bruckner's symphonies began to be acclaimed in Vienna as well as Germany, and also in Holland, England and the USA.

Contemporaneously with the Seventh Symphony Bruckner composed his setting of the *Te Deum*, which soon became very popular; but his troubles as a composer were by no means over. When he completed his Eighth Symphony, in 1887, he sent it to Hermann Levi, his newly found champion, hoping for an early performance; but Levi was bewildered by it, and asked Josef Schalk to persuade Bruckner to revise it. Bruckner, who was utterly cast down by this unfavourable verdict from his 'artistic father' (as he called Levi), made a thorough revision of the symphony over the next three years. Then he entered a new period of self-doubt. During this time he made unnecessary revisions of some of his earlier works, recomposing Symphonies nos.1 and 3 (the latter in collaboration with Franz Schalk), revising no.2, and retouching the F minor Mass. This labour, undertaken in his mid-60s when his health was beginning to fail, explains why the Ninth Symphony, begun in 1889, was left unfinished at his death seven years later.

However, Bruckner's last years were sweetened by belated recognition through the increasing number of performances of his symphonies and publication of most of them (in both cases, unfortunately, in the unauthentic versions), by grants, awards and honours, and by the nationwide and international celebration of his 70th birthday in 1894. From 1889 he received a regular grant from a group of Austrian industrialists, and from 1890 another grant from the Austrian government; in 1886 the emperor bestowed on him the Order of Franz Joseph, and in 1891 he was awarded an honorary doctorate by the University of Vienna. At a gala reception to celebrate this award, attended by 3000 people, the rector of the university, Dr Adolf Exner, concluded his address with these words: 'Where science must come to a halt, where its progress is barred by insurmountable barriers, there begins the realm of art, which knows how to express that which will ever remain a closed book to scientific knowledge. I, *rector magnificus* of the University of Vienna, bow humbly before the former assistant teacher of Windhaag'.

During 1895 and 1896 Bruckner was occupied with the finale of his Ninth Symphony, but though he left some 200 pages of sketches, he had not the strength to complete it; he was still working on it the morning he died, 11 October 1896 in Vienna. His funeral, in the Karlskirche, was attended by many famous people. According to a request expressed in his will, his body was embalmed and buried in the crypt beneath the great organ in his beloved St Florian.

V Character

Bruckner's character, as a man as well as an artist, was really fundamentally formed by his origins in one of the most primitive and lowly strata of European society – the Austrian peasantry, rooted to the land, unquestioningly obedient to the state and to the Roman Catholic Church. His ancestors had lived for more than five centuries within the narrow horizon of the same small rural area of Upper Austria, first as serfs, then as small farmers or innkeepers, and finally – in the two generations preceding Bruckner – as village schoolmasters. Even the post of village schoolmaster was a humble one, since the duties rewarded by the small salary often included help with labour on the land. However, it did involve contact with Austrian culture,

3. Anton Bruckner in 1894

and especially with music, since another duty, in most cases, was that of acting as organist at the village church; and Austrian musical culture, particularly the ecclesiastical side, was deeply rooted, extending right down from Vienna, through lesser cities such as Linz and monastic establishments such as St Florian, to villages as small as Ansfelden.

In this, his early environment, Bruckner was as simple, naive, trustful, deferential and pious as a man could only be who had grown up in a small village in Metternich's time, ruled by a conservative and authoritarian government. It was not that he was in any way simple-minded, as is popularly supposed: his letters, in spite of the old-fashioned deference of those addressed to 'notabilities', reveal a perfectly normal and even lively intelligence; and his company was apparently enjoyed during many convivial evenings by the prelates of St Florian and Linz, by his sophisticated friends in their homes, and by his quick-witted pupils in the alehouses. Had he not been musically gifted, he would simply have remained and been accepted as a typical countryman with a fund of homespun wisdom, though perhaps one easier than most on which to play a practical joke.

What remained puzzling about Bruckner was that he did not change with the changing times or with his changing environment. When Austria became more liberal, under Franz Joseph, and even when he arrived in the less narrow orbit of Linz, and later in the far more sophisticated atmosphere of Vienna, he still adhered to his old-fashioned rural manners and customs. He retained his baggy country clothes, his broad Upper Austrian dialect, and his habit of deferring to any authority. There are many anecdotes concerning his endearing *faux pas*: how he once tipped Richter a thaler after a rehearsal that had particularly pleased him, how he reacted to an offer of assistance by the emperor by begging him to stop Hanslick from writing his damaging reviews, and so on. His inability to acquire even a little sophistication may to some extent indicate a retarded psychological development, caused by having spent his youth and his 20s in the monastic atmosphere of St Florian. It certainly had something to do with an unworldliness arising from his religious faith, which, though a legacy from his ancestry, he in no way took for granted; it became the centre of his whole life. But in addition to the understandable gaucherie of a simple and pious villager who unwillingly became a controversial figure in a big city and found himself out of his social depth, there was a fundamental, entirely personal sense of insecurity in Bruckner's character, which seems to have had its roots in the loss of his father and his original home when he was 13. From then on he was always seeking and finding father figures to help him – Arneth, Dürrnberger, Rudigier, Wagner, Herbeck; and even at the age of 63 he was calling Levi, his junior by 15 years, 'my artistic father'. And it was only due to the fatherly insistence of Dürrnberger and Herbeck that he overcame his reluctance to take the two crucial steps in his life – the move to Linz and then to Vienna.

This insecurity was basic to Bruckner's life, and explains certain strange, unconsciously motivated features of his personality. His numeromania, the counting of things, such as cathedral gables, until he got the number absolutely right, was a compulsion to reduce a worrying

25

multiplicity to order by accounting for it exactly. It even had a musical repercussion: in the autographs of the symphonies, the bars are numbered carefully throughout, in groups of four, eight etc. Then his attitude to women must be mentioned, which neatly ensured that he should never have to enter into a real relationship, with its possible threats to what little security he did possess. So pious a man could not contemplate any sexual relationship not sanctified by the bonds of holy matrimony, and he was always seeking a wife – 'a suitable dear girl', as he put it. His search practically always consisted of his infatuation with a pretty teenager he hardly knew, and apart from the fact that he was too old for her, he put her off completely by making his first serious approach a kindly but formal request for her hand in marriage. The bewildered answer was usually 'But Herr Bruckner, you are too old!'. He undoubtedly suffered many disappointments of this kind, but each was soon swept away by his absorption in creative work.

Another aspect of Bruckner's insecurity was his mania up to the age of about 40 for taking examinations and gaining diplomas or testimonials. For all his technical mastery he could never be convinced that his knowledge was sufficient without the official confirmation of some expert or authority. This lack of self-assurance concerned, not his ability as a composer and improviser, but his thorough knowledge of his craft, of the rules of strict harmony, counterpoint, fugue etc. The conception of the creative musician as simply a master craftsman, though already outmoded, was still an unquestioned reality for the old-fashioned and provincial Bruckner. And finally, there was the strangest of all his obsessions, his insistence whenever possible on having a close look at dead bodies: those of Beethoven and Schubert when they were exhumed for reburial, the charred remains of the many victims of a fire in the Ringtheater, and the body of the assassinated Emperor Maximilian when it was brought back from Mexico to be reinterred in Vienna. This, combined with the fact that he left provision for his own dead body to be embalmed, awakens the suspicion that Bruckner's sense of insecurity even extended into eternity – perhaps he thought the 'resurrection of the body' of Catholic dogma was unlikely to happen to a body destroyed by fire or natural corruption.

None of these things adversely affected Bruckner the self-confident creative musician. In 1868, when he was asked to play at a concert of the Academic Choral Society in Vienna, he wrote to a friend saying that it would depend on the quality of the organ and asking him to inspect the instrument, adding:

Further, it is no longer possible for me to perform other people's compositions . . . I should have to restrict myself to my own fantasies, to improvised fugues. In any case, there are plenty of people in Vienna who can play other people's compositions. I believe that only my own style can characterize me.

The same insistence that he be accepted on his own terms applied to Bruckner the composer. In Vienna, where so many great composers had worked, he took up the challenge, and encouraged by Wagner's example in opera added to his first mature symphony eight more, the last seven of which were unprecedentedly vast in scale and unorthodox in structure. In spite of continued opposition and criticism, and many well-meaning exhortations to caution from his friends, he looked neither to right nor left, but simply got down to work on the next symphony. He is reputed to have said:

They want me to write in a different way. I could, but I must not. Out of thousands, God gave talent to me . . . One day I shall have to give an account of myself. How would the Father in Heaven judge me if I followed others and not him?

The act of composing was to Bruckner part of his indestructible religious life; as well try to persuade him that there was no God in Heaven as criticize the scope and structure of his symphonies, which belonged to that God. There is no evidence that he himself had doubts about any of his symphonies once finally completed – not even no.8, which was actually improved in the recomposition following Levi's negative reaction to the original score.

After Bruckner had completed a symphony, however, his well-meaning friends would soon point out that it stood a much better chance of being performed and well received if cut and made to sound more attractive by toning down the starkness of its orchestration and adding one or two 'effective' touches. The result of such advice was to reawaken immediately all the insecurity in the non-musical part of Bruckner's personality. The score in whose composition he had felt absolute confidence now became one more troublesome object in the confusing everyday world – something to get performed and of which to fear criticism. Lacking all self-assurance in such matters, he felt obliged to bow to the opinions of his friends, 'the experts', to permit the revisions and even to help make them in some cases (though he may have hoped to control thereby the extent of the alterations).

How deeply this affected him is shown by the fact that at one stage he began examining his scores for faults which he must have known to be illusory. After Herbeck had forced on him alterations to the Second Symphony for the second performance of 1876 and after the catastrophic première in 1877 of the Third ('Wagner') Symphony, the prospect in 1878 of Rättig's publication of one of his works may have impelled Bruckner to make sure that all his scores were free from blemish. Whatever the reason, he asked Friedrich Klose, one of his pupils, to help him track down all the consecutive unisons and octaves in his scores, including the heavily scored tutti passages where they would naturally appear as doublings. When Klose eventually gave up in dismay, saying that any number of such consecutive perfect intervals could be found in Wagner's scores, Bruckner replied that Wagner, the master, was permitted these things, but not Bruckner, the schoolmaster. One is tempted to detect a note of irony in Bruckner's attitude; but irony was not part of his personality, whereas unrealistic self-doubt certainly was.

That this self-doubt never really shook Bruckner's faith in his definitively completed scores is revealed by the obstinate reservations he continually made about the revised versions. In 1876 he fought tenaciously against the alterations to no.2 suggested by Herbeck, who had to resort to the same bullying persuasion that he had used earlier to get Bruckner to go to Vienna. In 1887, when Löwe and Franz Schalk drew up their own cut and reorchestrated version of no.4, Bruckner allowed it to be published as the first edition, but registered a secret veto by refusing to sign the printer's copy and making a fair copy of his own definitive score of 1880. In 1888, when the Schalk brothers advised him to revise no.3, Mahler assured him, to his delight, that a revision was quite unnecessary, and he stopped work on it immediately; unfortunately the Schalks' advice prevailed in the end. In 1891, when Weingartner was rehearsing no.8 in Mannheim (for the projected first performance, which did not materialize there), Bruckner wrote him a letter revealing his reason for allowing massive cuts and alterations to his works: 'I do recommend you to shorten the finale severely, as indicated. It would be much too long, and is valid only for later times and for a circle of friends and connoisseurs'. And in another letter: 'Please submit to the wishes of the orchestra. But I do implore you not to alter the score; also, it is one of my most burning desires to have the orchestral parts printed without alterations'. Evidently, he regarded the unauthentic revisions as makeshifts, useful only in that they suited the taste of his own time; he had his eye on posterity for the vindication of his own scores. But during these last years of his life, when his symphonies were being performed more frequently – always in these unauthentic revisions – he even began to fear that posterity might let him down. During 1892–3 he had all his definitive manuscripts bound and packed in a sealed parcel, and in his will, made in 1894, he provided for them to be sent to the Vienna Court Library for safe-keeping and eventually to be delivered to a certain publishing firm if requested. His fears were not groundless. That year in Graz Franz Schalk conducted the first performance of no.5 from a cut and reorchestrated version of his own (Bruckner was too ill to be present) which became the first edition of the work in 1896 (when Bruckner was on his deathbed). And no.9 suffered a similar fate at the hands of Löwe in 1903, seven years after Bruckner's death. It was not until 1927 that the International Bruckner Society was founded, against strong opposition from Löwe and Franz Schalk, and in 1931 it began the long business of publishing Bruckner's own definitive scores for the first time. At last the ghost of his insecurity was laid; by sheer pertinacity he had succeeded posthumously in having his own way in the only issue that really mattered.

CHAPTER TWO

Works

I The versions of the symphonies

The first editions, published 1880–1903 (1924, if one includes 'no.0'), have been utterly discredited by the International Bruckner Society editions and are almost never used. The extreme cases are nos.4, 5 and 9, of which Franz Schalk and/or Löwe drew up their own scores with cuts and with different orchestration; furthermore they did not hesitate to alter note values and bar periods and even the actual notes. In no.4 they made the Scherzo's first ending *pianissimo* (instead of *fortissimo*) with an attendant removal of most of Bruckner's texture; Schalk changed the melodic line in the last bars of the slow movement of no.5 and altered the falling-octave motif of the finale's introduction from crotchets to quavers; and Löwe altered the climactic dissonance of the slow movement of no.9 from a chord containing all seven notes of the harmonic minor scale to a simple diminished 7th. The other first editions, though they retain Bruckner's own texture and orchestration almost unchanged, also lack authenticity owing to altered phrasing, dynamics, expression and tempo markings, and in some cases to cuts.

When the International Bruckner Society decided to rectify the situation by publishing Bruckner's own scores the task was entrusted to Robert Haas; between 1934 and 1944 eight of the symphonies were issued under his general editorship: nos.1–2 and 4–8 edited by him and no.9 edited by Alfred Orel. Fritz Oeser's edition of no.3, though not commissioned by the society and published by a different firm in 1950, was accepted as conforming entirely to the society's ideals. Each of its editions was labelled 'original version', which was in some cases a misnomer: for example, Bruckner's original version of no.4 (1874) was only an attempt on the way to a definitive score (1880) which he then stood by and which the society published in 1936. The society would have done better to label each of the scores 'first definitive version': they are (except for no.1 and no.8) the scores finally arrived at by Bruckner himself, which he revised only on the persuasion of others, and are therefore simply 'the Bruckner symphonies'.

Other works were issued under the Haas regime, including the E minor and F minor masses, and the society's work continued in the aim of creating a complete critical edition. However, in 1945 Haas was replaced by Leopold Nowak, who, in addition to publishing the D minor Mass and other works, issued between 1951 and 1965 new editions of all nine symphonies, which were clearly intended as corrections and replacements of the Haas regime's editions. Nos.1, 4, 5, 6, 7 and 9 are entirely reprinted from the earlier plates with only a few slight alterations in detail that are almost unnoticeable in performance; only in no.4 is there also a structural change (the return, in the finale's last few bars, of the first movement's opening theme) and in no.7 some tempo changes restored from the first published edition of 1885. In no case is there a *Revisionsbericht*, and this makes it impossible to assess the validity of the alterations. More important is that Symphonies nos.2, 3 and 8 were issued by Nowak in their revised versions, with the intention of replacing the Haas editions. These revised versions, though they are known to have been influenced by others, especially in the matter of cuts, are entirely in Bruckner's own handwriting, and Nowak believed that they must therefore be accepted as his final definitive versions.

This would be unquestionably the case with a composer obeying nothing but the dictates of his own self-criticism, but it does not take into account Bruckner's deep sense of insecurity in the face of others' criticism or his agonized submission to 'expert opinion' on the one hand, and his insistence that his own complete scores should be preserved, on the other. The cuts he was advised to make are simply the result of putting a blue pencil through essential parts of the structure. Those in the Herbeck-influenced revision of no.2 reduce the carefully proportioned double codas of the first and last movements by half and give the second theme of the slow movement no time to establish itself properly before the first theme returns. Nowak admitted that Bruckner could not possibly have wanted these changes, writing in the preface to his edition: 'We know that it was only with the greatest reluctance that Bruckner accepted these suggestions'.

The case of no.3 is different, since Bruckner actually recomposed it; but he did so at the persuasion of Franz Schalk, and there is evidence that Schalk played a large part in mutilating the finale, as Nowak again admitted in the preface to his editions:

The finale . . . was copied by Franz Schalk in a shortened version of his own, which was approved by Bruckner and used by him as the basis for

his revision. Two of Schalk's shortened passages were accepted by the
master ... Bruckner approved those changes not made by himself ...
Josef [Schalk] wrote to his brother 'Your cuts and transitions, by the
way, were adhered to'.

A good deal of psychological qualification is necessary
to understand this use of the words 'approved' and
'accepted'.

The case of no.8 is different again, since Bruckner not
only recomposed it, after Levi's unfavourable verdict,
but greatly improved it in a number of ways (though not
the ways suggested by Levi, who seems simply to have
been bewildered by it). This is the one symphony that
Bruckner did not fully achieve in his first definitive
version, to which there can be no question of going
back. However, Josef Schalk interfered this time, suggesting to Bruckner that the symphony should be cut as
well as recomposed. For example, he persuaded
Bruckner to excise a vital part of the second group in the
finale, since he thought the passage contained an unfortunate reminiscence of the first movement of Symphony
no.7; Bruckner did so in the recapitulation but apparently forgot to cut the equivalent bars in the exposition.
And so, to quote Nowak again, from the preface to his
edition of this version:

Josef Schalk wrote to Max von Oberleithner [who saw the 1892 edition
through the press], saying that he wanted this abbreviation [the cut in
the exposition], since the reminiscence of the Seventh Symphony seemed
quite unfounded to him. He was not quite wrong, because the abbreviation before letter Oo [the cut in the recapitulation], made by Bruckner
himself, eliminated the same passage in the reprise. Thus the balance of
motifs in the revision is disturbed. Nevertheless, following Bruckner's
decisions, nothing is to be changed.

Here, it is the word 'decisions' that needs qualification: a
pupil of Bruckner persuaded him to excise an essential
14-bar theme from his score; that pupil then cut it in the

exposition when the confused Bruckner disturbed 'the balance of the motifs' by cutting it only in the recapitulation; and a later editor restored the lack of balance by accepting the cut in the recapitulation because it is in Bruckner's hand and ignoring that in the exposition because it was only made on the pupil's orders. All this presents an appalling picture of the kind of muddled, amateurish and senseless desecration of Bruckner's scores brought about by his pupils' tampering. It was no doubt for this reason that Haas in his edition of the symphony did something which, from a purely musicological point of view, is indefensible: he accepted the manifest compositional improvements of Bruckner's 1890 revision, but restored the material which had been cut on Josef Schalk's persuasion from the third and fourth movements of the 1887 first definitive version, including the 14-bar theme in question in the finale's exposition and its 16-bar variant in the recapitulation. As Nowak said in the preface to his edition of the 1890 revision, 'different sources, according to the principles of the working out of a complete critical edition, can never be intermingled', and he has backed this with the publication in 1973 of the 1887 version. Thus both of Bruckner's scores are now in Nowak's collected critical edition, and the problem can be studied by comparing them. But Haas was thinking of a conductor's score that would be in constant use, and his edition stands as a conjectural restoration of what Bruckner's revision would have been like without Josef Schalk's interference.

The case of no.1 is different again, since Bruckner's 1891 recomposition of his 1866 score was undertaken and carried out entirely on his own; Levi actually advised him against this revision, a unique reversal of the usual state of affairs. Yet it was made during his final phase of self-doubt, after the revisions of nos.3 and 8 forced on him by others; most scholars prefer the 1866 version, feeling that, as with the recomposition of no.3, the intrusion of Bruckner's later style into one of his earlier scores obscures the bold lines of the original. Both the Haas and the Nowak editions are of the 1866 version and are practically identical; Haas also published a study edition of the 1891 score, without parts. Nowak has not made his own edition of this single Bruckner revision which is known not to have been influenced by anyone. Summing up, it can be said that the scores of the nine symphonies published by the International Bruckner Society under the Haas regime represent, as far as may be, Bruckner's own intentions, free from the influence of his friends, colleagues and pupils.

II   The music

The large quantity of music that Bruckner composed before the age of 39, which amounts to at least as much as what he wrote afterwards, contains only one or two premonitions of his eventual stature; had he died at that age, it would certainly have been forgotten. To categorize it appropriately is difficult; 'academic' applies only to two of the works composed deliberately as exercises for Kitzler in 1862 – the four orchestral pieces and the String Quartet. *Gebrauchsmusik* is perhaps better – music written with devotion by a professional craftsman for use in church and by choral societies, in the only idiom known to him and them, the outmoded Classical style. Inside the narrow limits of

Bruckner's early musical horizons, those of a monastery musician and a provincial organist and choirmaster, tradition reigned in the form of the Austrian Classical church music of Mozart and Joseph and Michael Haydn. The music of Beethoven, Schubert and Schumann, not to mention Berlioz, Liszt and Wagner, might never have existed; but Mendelssohn's music became familiar enough to contribute to the style of some of Bruckner's numerous male-choir compositions. His training, until he met Kitzler, was thorough but old-fashioned: as late as 1854 (in the *Missa solemnis*) he was still writing a figured bass part for the organ. Yet Bruckner's best music of these years is never dull; it is often engaging, sometimes moving, and must have served its purpose well, that of satisfying the musically conservative society for which it was written. All it lacks is the strong individuality which alone enables music to outlast its own time. Even when Bruckner achieved something like mastery of the choral and orchestral forms of Classical church music, in his Requiem of 1848–9 and his *Missa solemnis* of 1854, the music, though occasionally exhilarating, rarely goes beyond its models. This mastery without originality can be glimpsed in ex.1, a passage from the Gloria of the *Missa solemnis*, written at the age of 30, just before he gave up composing for six years to study with Sechter.

There are one or two faint portents in the Requiem Mass, but nothing from which anyone could have foretold the sudden emergence of Bruckner's mature musical personality at its most intense, in ex.2, the opening bars of the Mass in D minor, completed in 1864. The revelation brought by his first acquaintance

Ex.1

with Wagner's music gave Bruckner the courage to release his own pungent individuality, but the music does not owe anything to Wagner's style, only to his principle of harmonic independence. Its anguished D minor chromaticism is built up over a tonic pedal by bold polyphonic imitation of a single point (an ascending diminished 5th and a descending semitone), the parts entering successively on the degrees of the ascending scale of D major. But it is hard to believe that style as potent and original as this can materialize from nowhere when a composer is 40 years old. It must be, as Robert Simpson has suggested, that Bruckner had gradually evolved a personal idiom in the ephemeral, safe sphere of organ improvisation, but had never dared to use it in his written-out compositions for fear of being criticized as an iconoclast. When he did use it, it was already enriched by his study of Wagner.

Ex.2   Alla breve

In this mass, and the even finer one in F minor of 1868, Bruckner still adhered to the symphonic structures of the Haydn and Mozart masses and to their fugal idiom, which he had used earlier in the *Missa solemnis*. But by now his actual style had moved away from Haydn and Mozart – not only in its uncompromising chromaticism but also in its massive choral effects with freely modulating triadic harmonies, and its dramatic use of unexpected key changes. As a result the structures are expanded and used with much greater freedom and self-assurance. These two masses stand with the greatest settings of the 19th century.

At the opposite pole from these large choral and orchestral works, more suitable for the concert hall than the church, is the shorter E minor Mass of 1866, for eight-part choir with sparing use of a small wind band, representing the other, liturgical side of Bruckner's mature musical personality and revealing a renewal of the harmonic and contrapuntal style of the Renaissance. It was inspired by the ideals of the Cecilians, the group of 19th-century Catholic ecclesiastics who advocated that church music should abandon the path taken by Romantic music, with its attendant pitfalls of sentimentality and diffuseness, and return to the strength and purity of Palestrina; and its polyphonic Sanctus is actually built on a theme adapted from Palestrina's *Missa brevis*.

The remaining church music of Bruckner's maturity belongs to one or other of these two worlds. The massive *Te Deum* of 1884, and Psalm cl of 1892, share the Romantic grandeur of the D minor and F minor masses. The antiphons, graduals and offertories are in the Renaissance-based liturgical style of the Mass in E minor; two of them – the *Pange lingua* of 1868 and the *Os justi* of 1879 – are entirely in old church modes, the Phrygian and the Lydian respectively. And yet most of these concentrated miniatures, which are for choir unaccompanied or accompanied by trombones, organ or both, combine the two sides of Bruckner's musical personality in a microcosm of his whole style. Alongside real plainsong, plainsong-type melodies and modal progressions of root position triads are found strange chromaticism, unusual key changes and unorthodox

41

juxtapositions of triadic harmonies. In the *Ecce sacerdos* of 1885, for example, a piece of unison plainsong is followed by a refrain using successive root position chords of E major, C minor, G major, E♭ minor, B♭ major, F♯ minor, D major, A major, F major and C major. On the other hand, the simple *Locus iste* of 1869 is an exquisite personal distillation of Mozart's church style. Of Bruckner's secular choral pieces, only two are worthy to stand by the church compositions: the fiercely patriotic *Das deutsche Lied* for male chorus and brass (1892), and his last complete work, the barbaric *Helgoland*, for male chorus and full orchestra (1893).

Turning to the symphonies is not to enter an entirely different world, since the two large masses and the *Te Deum* are themselves symphonic, and the inspiration of all Bruckner's major works was religious. Some of the symphonies actually draw on material from the church compositions, notably no.2, whose slow movement and finale quote respectively from the Benedictus and Kyrie of the F minor Mass, and no.7, whose slow movement contains a blazing climax based on an important passage in the 'Non confundar in aeternum' of the *Te Deum*. But more generally, it is not specific music but types of material which are common to the symphonies and the church compositions. For example, the liturgical character of some of the chorale themes in the symphonies arises out of their simultaneous melodic and harmonic reliance on the archaic church progression from tonic to subdominant and back. The most notable examples are the chorale theme in the finale of no.5 and the second theme of the second group of the Adagio of no.8 (see ex.3). Moreover the 19th-century tonal language is often

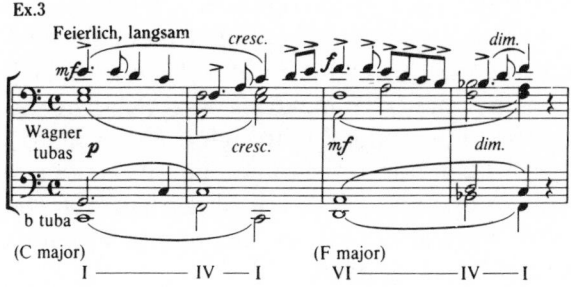

Ex.3

shot through with ambiguous melodic and harmonic inflections deriving from the old church modes: in all four movements of no.6, for example, the brightness of the symphony's basically major tonality is continually clouded over by the dark degrees of the Phrygian scale – its flat 2nd, 6th and 7th. Such modal inflections, ubiquitous in the symphonies, find a new life amid their alien 19th-century surroundings, and are one of the foundations of Bruckner's timeless style.

At the other end of the spectrum is the 19th-century chromaticism which Bruckner mastered at the beginning of his first mature work, the D minor Mass (ex.2). This element, in a more extreme form, found its way into the beginning of the slow movement of his Symphony no.1, his next important work. Lacking the pedal point of ex.2, the tonality remains entirely obscure for 20 bars before the tonic key of A♭ is clearly established. Both these passages were written before Bruckner heard *Tristan*, but after absorbing that exploration of extreme chromaticism he wisely shunned further excursions into the idiom, which could only have led him away from a personal style into slavish imitation of Wagner. Yet at the end of his life he began the last movement he was ever to complete, the slow movement of no.9, with an intensely personal main theme (ex.4) that carried the chromaticism of *Tristan* to the edge of the crisis in tonality culminating with Schoenberg. The passage continues modally through triads of D major, B minor and F♯ minor to the tonic triad of E major, which the opening one-and-a-half-bar phrase suggests, but for eight slow beats after that opening phrase all sense of an established key disappears.

Ex.4

Between these two extremes are other features shared by the symphonies and the church compositions, such as the surprising mediant and submediant key shifts developing further the implications of certain procedures of Schubert; forthright themes based on falling octaves, from 18th-century models like the openings of Mozart's Symphonies nos.29 and 35; original treatments of pure triadic harmonies in unorthodox juxtapositions or in unexpected modulations; and the original use of hammering ostinatos and murmuring tremolando.

Yet it would be facile to describe the symphonies as masses without words. Certain elements shared by the two genres were used much more subjectively in the symphonies: if ex.3 would be almost as much at home in a mass as in a symphony, ex.4 is too full of a peculiarly personal anguish for Bruckner to have used in a liturgical context. There is also a good deal of profound nature feeling peculiar to the symphonies, bound up inextricably with religious feeling, and naturally the scherzos contain such manifestly secular elements as dance-tunes and hunting music. And in the finale of the Third Symphony there is a polka in counterpoint with a chorale. Such things are in no way incompatible with the overall religious inspiration of the symphonies – the religion of a truly devout person embraces all aspects of life; but for Bruckner they would have been incompatible with the idea of music for worship in church.

The most crucial difference between the symphonies and the church compositions is that the former seem to go beyond religious beliefs to express the more fundamental, primitive stratum of feeling that gave these beliefs birth – a sense of the awe-inspiring, born of the naked wonder, fear and delight of elemental humanity confronted by the mysterious beauty and power of nature and the vast riddle of the cosmos. Bruckner understood this feeling in his conscious mind, of course, as worship of the incomprehensible God of his religion; but his utter lack of sophistication admirably fitted him to be the unconscious channel of this more primeval feeling, and in acting as this channel he found it necessary to essay more far-reaching symphonic structures than those of any previous music except Beethoven's Ninth Symphony and the music dramas of Wagner.

This realization did not come to Bruckner all at once. The first two symphonies are original mainly in their materials and in their preference for varied rather than exact restatements in the recapitulations. His essential style and foreshadowings of his later methods are present, but the proportions are not yet large enough to allow them to expand to their full grandeur. These first two symphonies invite comparison with those of the early Romantics, and from this point of view Bruckner emerges as a new and strikingly original creator. But with no.3 he erected for the first time the huge framework he was to cultivate for the rest of his life, the task being so difficult that he needed three attempts at both this symphony and no.4, and even so, traces of the struggle are still evident in the outer movements of no.3 and in the finale of no.4 (which in neither case really detract from the magnificence of the whole). From no.5 onwards he found no further difficulty in working with his immense designs.

From Beethoven's Ninth Bruckner derived his four main movement types – the far-ranging first movement, the big adagio built from the varied alternation of two themes, the sonata form scherzo and the huge cumulative finale – as well as the tendency to begin a symphony with a faint background sound, emerging almost imperceptibly out of silence. From Wagner he derived his expanded time scale, based on slow-moving harmonic processes, his frequent reliance on the full brass for weight of utterance and his use of intense and long-drawn string cantabile for depth of emotional expression.

What Bruckner did not take over was Wagner's greatly expanded orchestra and extremely sophisticated orchestration. He began with a modest orchestra of double woodwind, four horns, two trumpets, three trombones, timpani and strings. From no.3 on he added a third trumpet, from no.4 a bass tuba, from no.7 four Wagner tubas and from no.8 triple woodwind instead of double. In nos.7 and 8 he used cymbals and triangle (in both cases only at the climax of the slow movement) and a harp only in no.8 (in the slow movement and the trio section of the Scherzo). He asked for mutes (on the strings and on a solo horn) only in the slow movement of no.4; and nowhere did he call on any of the special woodwind instruments, piccolo, english horn, E♭ and bass clarinets, double bassoon (though in the first version of no.8 he did specify a piccolo in the last two movements and a double bassoon in the finale, accessories which vanished in the revision) or on any percussion instrument apart from cymbals and a triangle. Moreover, his scoring for this remarkably chaste orchestra was mainly of a quite un-Wagnerian simplicity, with the various sections sharply demarcated, as opposed to Wagner's subtle doublings and mixings; yet the resultant sonorities have an entirely individual beauty and grandeur, out of all proportion to the comparatively modest means employed. At the end of no.5 he could achieve, without Wagner tubas and with only double woodwind, the utmost fullness and clarity of sound in the final majestic *fortissimo* combination of fugue and chorale (a passage for which Franz Schalk, in his own totally rescored version of the work for practically the same orchestra, found it necessary to co-opt an extra brass band).

Despite its general debt to Beethoven and Wagner, the 'Bruckner Symphony' is a unique conception, not only because of the individuality of its spirit and its materials, but even more because of the absolute origin-

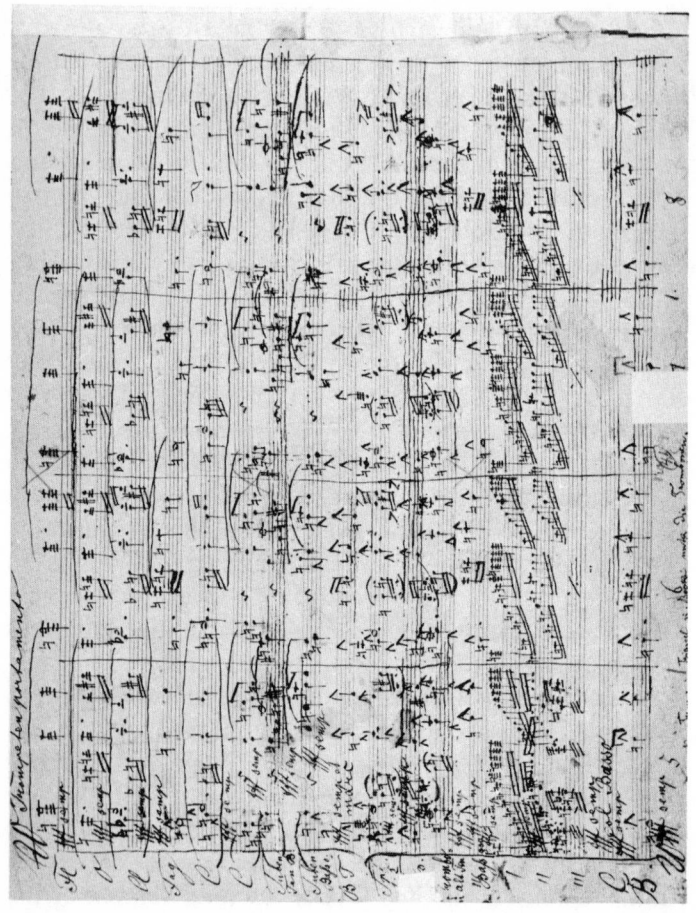

4. Autograph MS of part of the second movement of Bruckner's Symphony no.7, first performed in Leipzig on 30 December 1884; it is disputed whether or not the instruction to the timpani, triangle and cymbals to play at the climax is in Bruckner's hand

ality of its formal processes. At first, these processes seemed so strange and unprecedented that they were taken as evidence of sheer incompetence: Bruckner's symphonies were widely regarded as spectacular mishandlings of the symphonic form established by Beethoven, or as misguided and disastrous attempts to compose 'Wagnerian symphonies'. Now it is recognized that Bruckner's unorthodox structural methods were inevitable: the presentation of huge blocks of material often isolated from one another, the extended pauses followed by unexpected continuations, the long ascents that break off sharply when a climax seems imminent, the persistent sequences and the remorseless reiteration at the ends of sections or movements of a single motif to the same harmony over periods of 16, 32 or even 64 bars – all these are essential elements of the conception. Bruckner created a new and monumental type of symphonic organism, which abjured the terse, dynamic continuity of Beethoven, and the broad, fluid continuity of Wagner, in order to express something profoundly different from either composer, something elemental and metaphysical.

In consequence, the apparent sonata shapes of Bruckner's first and last movements are illusory and misleading. His first movements do consist of an exposition (nearly always built on three subject groups rather than two, as in Schubert's Ninth Symphony), a development (which often begins with the most hushed, slow-moving, serene music of the whole movement), a recapitulation (which always, as so frequently with Haydn, includes further stages of development) and a coda; and he no doubt saw himself organizing his materials according to the sonata procedures he studied so diligently with Kitzler. However his extraordinary attitude to the world, and the nature of his materials which arose from this attitude, dictated an entirely unorthodox handling of traditional formal procedures. Sonata form is a dynamic, humanistic process, always going somewhere, constantly trying to arrive; but with Bruckner firm in his religious faith, the music has no need to go anywhere, no need to find a point of arrival, because it is already there. The various stages of the formal process are not offered as dynamic phases of a drama, but as so many different viewpoints from which to absorb the basic material. The stance is not Romantic, but medieval: indeed, the mentality of the Austrian Catholic peasantry, which Bruckner to a very large extent retained, was essentially a survival from the Middle Ages. Experiencing Bruckner's symphonic music is more like walking round a cathedral, and taking in each aspect of it, than like setting out on a journey to some hoped-for goal.

Hence Bruckner's music is always leisurely, even on the few occasions when a really fast tempo is specified, and this leisureliness is enhanced by the slow-changing harmony. There are characteristics of his symphonies, especially the aforementioned reiterations of a single motif to the same harmony over many bars at the end of a section or movement, which at first hearing seem to demand from the listener too great a naivety and patience to be accepted as main pillars of a symphonic structure; but they are essential to the scale of the conception, even if at odds with the quick-thinking modern mind. No more than a medieval cathedral will Bruckner's symphonies reveal their majesty and gran-

5. Anton Bruckner in 1894

deur to the sophisticated or the impatient. Yet the elements of simplicity in the structure should not be overstressed, since they are complemented by the extraordinary subtlety of the tonality and harmony: the opening of no.8 in C minor, for example, is in B♭ minor, a conflict between two keys that is the main basis of the first movement and is only resolved in the finale. The opening of no.9 in D minor is also in that key, but by the 26th bar the music has reached D♭ major and continues immediately in E major; another striking treatment of tonality is the beginning of the Adagio (ex.4).

Bruckner's slow movements, which are placed second except in nos.8 and 9, where they follow the scherzo, are the heart of his symphonies and possess a quite incomparable sublimity. Their formal basis is nearly always the varied alternation of two long-drawn themes, the final statement of the first being surrounded by swirling string figurations and rising to a tremendous climax; and the purity and breadth of the themes themselves, at the extremely slow tempo, build up to something uniquely massive and overwhelming, whether the mood is ecstatic, as in most of the symphonies, or tragic, as in no.9.

No generalization can be made about Bruckner's scherzos, which are more varied than those of any other composer except Mahler. All are based on 3/4 dance rhythms (except for the 2/4 hunting scherzo of no.4), but the tempos differ enormously, and the movements are not really dances at all – or at least, not human dances, but rather dances of the elements (nos.5, 6 and 7), or perhaps of frightening, gigantic, supernatural figures (nos.8 and 9). The trios, too, are extremely diverse, from the childlike ländler in no.4 and the bright, aphoristic 2/4 trio in no.5, to the rapid and sinister 3/8 trio in no.9.

The finales, like the first movements, are built on Bruckner's non-dynamic type of three-subject sonata form. Except in no.7, they are larger and more discursive, but not because they act as illuminations and resolutions of all that has gone before or as a breakthrough into a new world, as often with Mahler; they avoid the Romantic view of the finale as the culminating highpoint of the symphony and simply ratify the world of the first three movements on a larger scale. This is true even of the huge last movement of no.5, which, weaving chorale and fugue into sonata form, is undoubtedly Bruckner's greatest finale. From no.3 on, the final act of ratification takes the form of bringing back the opening theme of the whole work; but this is not an example of cyclic form as it is commonly understood. Since Bruckner's style is so homogeneous and his formal processes are so non-dynamic, the opening theme of the symphony returns at the end as a natural conclusion, not as a saviour or a *deus ex machina*.

Bruckner was the first symphonic composer to take up the metaphysical challenge of Beethoven's Ninth (which had been so completely ignored by Mendelssohn, Schumann and Brahms) by absorbing the new symphonic methods demonstrated by Wagner's music dramas. His vast forms, however, were so adventurously original that they could no longer be related to Beethoven's, while the complex 'Wagnerian' music with which he filled them expresses a personal world of feeling at the opposite pole from that of Wagner. Perhaps the task he set himself was so Herculean that he could not always succeed in every detail; there are certainly awkwardnesses in some of his movements, but such small, partial failures are overshadowed and dwarfed by the greatness of the whole.

WORKS

Detailed list, including lost and doubtful attributions, in R. Grasberger: *Werkverzeichnis Anton Bruckners* (Tutzing, 1977) [WAB]
Editions: *A. Bruckner: Sämtliche Werke*, i–ii, iv–viii, xiv–xv, ed. R. Haas (Vienna, 1930–49); xiii, ed. R. Haas and L. Nowak (Leipzig, 1940); iii, ed. F. Oeser
(Wiesbaden, 1950); ix, ed. A. Orel (Vienna, 1934) [H/Oe/Or]

Anton Bruckner: Gesamtausgabe, i–xix, ed. L. Nowak, xx/6, ed. F. Grasberger (Vienna, 1951–) [N/Gr]
Chorwerke aus dem Nachlasse Anton Bruckners, ed. V. Keldorfer (Vienna, 1911) [K]
A. Göllerich and M. Auer: *Anton Bruckner: ein Lebens- und Schaffensbild* (Regensburg, 1922–37) [G]
(*printed works published in Vienna unless otherwise stated; MS collections in A-KR, LIm, SF, Wgm, Wn, Wst*)

Numbers in the right-hand column denote references in the text.

ORCHESTRAL

* – original, unedited score   † – two editions virtually identical

WAB	Title	Date	First performance	Remarks	Publication	Complete edition	
115	Apollo March, E♭, military band	c1862	Vöckalbruck, 14 Sept 1924	doubtful	arr. pf by A. Stradal, G iii/2, 22	—	31, 32–7
96	March, d	1862	Klosterneuburg, 12 Oct 1924		ed. A. Orel (1934)	—	9, 37
97	3 pieces, B♭, e, F	1862	Klosterneuburg, 12 Oct 1924		ed. A. Orel (1934)	—	9, 37
	Overture, g	1862–3	Klosterneuburg, 8 Sept 1921		ed. A. Orel (1921)	—	
	Symphony, f (Study Symphony)	1863	Klosterneuburg, 18 March 1924 [1st, 2nd, 4th movts], 12 Oct 1924 [3rd movt]		ed. (1913) [2nd movt]	N x	10
116	March, E♭ military band	1865			facs., G iii/2, 225		
—	Scherzo, g	1865		intended for Sym. no.1 rev. 1869	facs., G iii/2, 234; ed. J. Wöss (1924)		
—	Symphony no.0 'Die Nullte', d	1863–4	Klosterneuburg, 17 May 1924 (3rd, 4th movts), 12 Oct 1924 (all 4 movts)			N xi	10
	Adagio, A♭	1865–6		orig. version of 2nd movt, Sym. no.1	arr. pf by Auer, G iii/2, 125		15, 21, 28, 32–7, 42, 45–7, 52–3

WAB	Title	Date	First performance	Remarks	Publication	Complete edition	
101	Symphony no.1, c Linz version	1865–6	Linz, 9 May 1868			H i, N i/1	11, 12, 15, 16, 17, 33, 43
	Vienna version	1890–91	Vienna, 13 Dec 1891	1866 score recomposed	ed. (1893) frags., facs., G iv/1, 112	H i, N i/2	21, 36–7
142	Symphony, B♭	1869		sketch of 1st movt			
102	Symphony no.2, c original version	1871–2	Vienna, 26 Oct 1873		ed. (1892)	H ii	15, 17, 18
	revised with J. Herbeck	1875–6	Vienna, 20 Feb 1876	slight rev. 1877, 1890		N ii [incl. 1877 rev.]	16, 21, 29, 34, 42
103	Symphony no.3, d 1st definitive version	1873–7	Vienna, 16 Dec 1877	composed 1872–3, 1874, 1876–7	ed. (1878)	*Oe iii, N iii/1 (1873 version); N iii/1 suppl. (Adagio, 1876 version)	15, 18, 19, 29
	recomposed with F. Schalk	1888–9	Vienna, 21 Dec 1890		ed. F. Schalk (1890)	*N iii/3	21, 30, 34
104	Symphony no.4 'Romantic', E♭ original version	1874	Linz, 12 Dec 1909 (Scherzo), 20 Sept 1975 (complete)			N iv/1	33
	definitive version	1878–80	Vienna, 20 Feb 1881	with new scherzo and finale	version by F. Schalk and F. Löwe (1889)	H iv [incl. orig. finale], N iv/2	16, 29, 32
	revised version	1887–8	Vienna, 22 Jan 1888	slight rescoring of 1880 version			
105	Symphony no.5, B♭	1875–6	Munich, 20 Oct 1935; Graz, 8 April 1894 (Schalk version)	rev. 1887–8	version by F. Schalk (1896)	†H v, N v	16, 30, 32, 42
106	Symphony no.6, A	1879–81	Vienna, 11 Feb 1883 (2nd, 3rd movts), 26 Feb 1899 (complete)		ed. C. Hynais (1899)	†H vi, N vi	16, 43

WAB	Title	Date	First performance	Publication	Remarks; Complete edition	
107	Symphony no.7, E	1881–3	Leipzig, 30 Dec 1884	ed. Schalk and Löwe (1885)	*H vii, N vii [1885 edn.]	17, 19, 20, 35–6, 42, 48
108	Symphony no.8, c 1st definitive version	1884–7	BBC broadcast, 2 Sept 1973		N viii/1	21
	recomposed with J. Schalk composite version	1887–90	Vienna, 18 Dec 1892	ed. J. Schalk, 1892	*N viii/2	21, 28, 30, 33, 35, 42
				1890 score with 1887 material restored	H viii	
—	Trio, F	1889	Vienna, 5 July 1939	composed for Scherzo of Sym. no.9 unfinished	Or ix	
109	Symphony no.9, d	1887–96	Munich, 2 April 1932; Vienna, 11 Feb 1903 (Löwe version)	version by Löwe (1903)	†Or ix, N ix	21, 30, 32, 44
143	Symphony no.9, finale	—	—	—	Or ix (sketch)	22

LARGE SACRED

WAB	Title	Date	First performance	Publication	Remarks; Complete edition	
25	Mass, C, A solo, 2 hn, org	c1842	? Windhaag, 1842	G i, 173	for Maundy Thursday; incl. grad, off, but no Ky, Gl	3
9	Choralmesse, F, 4vv	1844	—	G i, 258	Ky, San, Bs, Ag only; San as in WAB9	4
146	Mass, 'Kronstorfer', d	1884	St Florian, 1 Dec 1974	—	lost	
133	Requiem, male vv, org	1845	—	—	Ky sketch only	
140	Missa pro Quadragesima, g, 4vv, 2 trbn, org	1843–5	—	facs, G ii/2, 84		
39	Requiem, d, S, A, T, B, 4vv, orch, org	1848–9	St Florian, 15 Sept 1849	H xv, 1931; N xiv	rev. 1892	4, 38
139	Mass, E♭, 4vv, 2 ob, 3 trbn, org	c1846	St Florian, 1 Aug 1854	facs, G ii/2, 86	Ky sketch only	
24	Magnificat, B♭, S, A, T, B, 4vv, orch, org	1852		G ii/2, 99		
34	Psalm xxii, E♭, 4vv, pf	c1852	St Florian, 11 Oct 1921	facs, G ii/2, 119		

WAB	Title	Date	First performance	Publication	Remarks; Complete edition	
36	Psalm cxiv, G, 5vv, 3 trbn	1852	Linz, 1 April 1906	facs., G ii/2, 154	H xv, N xv	5, 38, 40
29	Missa solemnis, b♭, S, A, T, B, 4vv, orch, org	1854	St Florian, 14 Sept 1854	facs., G ii/2, 189–228	in *A-Wgm*	
37	Psalm cxlvi, A, for S, A, T, B, 4vv, 4vv, orch	1860	St Florian, 14 Dec 1861	excerpts, G iii/1, 71		
35	Psalm cxii, B♭, 4vv, 4vv, orch	1863	Vöcklabruck, 14 March 1926	ed. J. Wöss (1926) (Innsbruck, 1892)		10, 12, 33, 38, 41, 43
26	Mass no. 1, d, S, A, T, B, 4vv, orch, org	1864; rev. 1876, 1881–2	Linz, 20 Nov 1864	(1896)	N xvi	11, 15, 33, 41
27	Mass no.2, e, 8vv, ww, brass	1866; rev, 1876, 1882, 1885, 1896	Linz, 29 Sept 1869		Nxvii/1 (1866 version) H xiii, N xvii/2 (1882 version)	11, 15, 17, 21, 33, 40, 41, 42
28	Mass no.3, f, S, A, T, B, 4vv, orch, org	1867–8; rev. 1876, 1877, 1881, 1890–3	Vienna, 16 June 1872	Vienna, 1894	H xiii, N xviii	15, 21, 41, 42, 325
141	Requiem, d, frag.	1875		G iv/1, 361	18 bars; H xv	
45	Te Deum, C, S, A, T, B, 4vv, orch. org	1881–4	Vienna, 10 Jan 1886	(1885)	N xix	15, 41
38	Psalm cl, C, S, 4vv, orch	1892	Vienna, 13 Nov 1892	(1892)	Gr xx/6	15, 41

SMALL SACRED WORKS
(for SATB chorus unless otherwise stated)

WAB		
31	Pange lingua, C, chorus, 1835–43, G ii/1, 228; rev. 1891, facs., G ii/1, 230	
136	Domine ad adjuvandum me, chorus, str, 1835, sketch	
—	Pange lingua, C, chorus, c1842, G i, 202	
21	Libera me Domine, F, chorus, org. c1843, G i, 243	
32	Pange lingua (Tantum ergo), D, chorus, 1843 (1914)	
134	Salve regina, 1844, lost	
132	Litany, chorus, ww, c1844 or c1858, lost	
144	Herz Jesu-Lied, B♭, chorus, org, c1845, G ii/2, 11 [doubtful]	
145	O du liebes Jesu Kind, F, T, org. c1845, facs., G ii/2, 13 [doubtful]	
3	{ Asperges [no.1], Aeolian mode, chorus, org, 1843–5, G ii/2, 67 { Asperges [no.2], F, chorus, org, 1843–5, G ii/2, 74	4, 15, 41
41	4 Tantum ergo, 1846, rev. 1888 (Innsbruck, 1893): E♭, C, B♭, A♭, all 4vv	
42	Tantum ergo, D, 5vv, org	
12	Dir, Herr, dir will ich mich ergeben, chorale, A, chorus, 1858–68, G ii/2, 114	
17	In jener letzten der Nächte, chorale, f, chorus, c1848, G ii/2, 97	
43	Tantum ergo, A, chorus, org, 1848 or 1849, G ii/2, 116	
14	Entsagen (O. von Redwitz), cantata, B♭, S/T, SATB, org/pf, c1851, facs., G ii/2, 141	
47,48	2 Totenlieder, E♭, F, mixed vv, 1852, G ii/2, 141	
44	Tantum ergo, B♭, chorus, 2 vn, 2 clarini, 1854 or 1855, G ii/2, 255	

22 Libera me, f, SSATB, 3 trbn, vc, db, org, 1854, in *Meisterwerke kirchlicher Tonkunst in Österreich*, ed. V. Goller (Vienna, 1922) — 5

53 Vor Arneths Grab (Marinelli), f, TTBB, 3 trbn, 1854, G ii/2, 184 — 5

15 St Jodok spross aus edlem Stamm: Festgesang (cantata), C, S, T, B, SATB, pf, 1855, facs., G ii/2, 241

5 Ave Maria, F, chorus, vc, org, 1856 (Innsbruck, 1893)

1 Afferentur regi, off, F, chorus, 3 trbn, org ad lib, 1861 (1922) [orig. 4vv, org]

2 Am Grabe (Marinelli), f, TTBB, 1861, ed. (1924) [same text as Vor Arneths Grab, 1854]

6 Ave Maria, F, SAATTBB, 1861 (Vienna, 1887)

16 Preiset den Herrn (M. Pamesberger), festival cantata D, Bar, TTBB, ww, brass, timp, 1862, facs., G iii/2, 197

49 Trauungslied (F. I. Proschko), F, TTBB, org, 1865, facs., G iii/2, 220

4 Asperges me, F, chorus, c1868, G iii/2, 140

33 Pange lingua (Tantum ergo), Phrygian mode, chorus, 1868, ed. F. Witt, *Musica sacra*, xviii (1885), music suppl., 44 — 41

19 Inveni David, off, f, male vv, 4 trbn, 1868, facs., G iii/2, 240

18 In St Angelum custodem (Iam lucis orto sidere) (R. Riepl), hymn, Phrygian mode, SSBB, 1868 (Linz, 1868)

23 Locus iste, grad, C, chorus, 1869 (1886) — 42

46 Tota pulchra es, ant, Phrygian mode, T, chorus, org, 1878 (1887)

54 Zwei Herzen haben sich gefunden (Zur Vermählungsfeier) (Mattig), D, TTBB, 1878, ed. J. Kluger, *Jb des Stiftes Klosterneuburg*, iii (1910), 133

30 Inveni David, chorale on c.f., 1v, org, 1879 [orig. for WAB30]

30 Os justi, grad, Lydian mode, SSAATTBB, 1879 (1886) — 41

10 Christus factus est, grad, d, SSAATTBB, str, 3 trbn c1879, rev. 1896 (1886); version for unacc. chorus, 1884 (1886)

7 Ave Maria, F, A solo, org/harmonium, 1882, ed. in *Neue Musikzeitung*, xiii (1902), suppl.

11 Christus factus est, chorus, 1884 (1886)

40 Salvum fac populum, ant, chorus, 1884, facs., G iv/2, 496 — 42

13 Ecce sacerdos magnus, ant, a, SSAATTBB, 3 trbn, org, 1885, K viii

52 Virga Jesse floruit, grad, e, chorus, 1885 (1886)

8 Ave regina, chorale on c.f., 1v, org c1886, ed. J. Kluger, *Jb des Stiftes Klosterneuburg*, iii (1910), 132

51 Vexilla regis, hymn, Phrygian mode, chorus, 1892, *Album Wiener Meister* (Vienna, 1892)

50 Veni Sancte Spiritus, chorale on c.f., F, G iv/1, 524 [discovered by R. Trüttinger, 1931]

ACCOMPANIED SECULAR CHORAL

93 Vergissmeinnicht (E. Marinelli), cantata, D, S, A, T, B, SSAATTBB, pf, 1845, facs., G i, 283 [2 earlier versions entitled Musikalischer Versuch nach dem Kammer-Styl]

137 Wie des Bächleins Silberquelle, G, sketch, 2 S, pf, c1845, facs., G ii/2, 65 [v parts only]

61 Auf, Brüder, auf zur frohen Feier! (Marinelli), cantata, D, SATTBB, 3 hn, 2 tpt, b trbn, 1852, G ii/2, 131, facs., G ii/1, 115; rev. 1857 as Heil, Vater, Dir zum frohen Feste (Marinelli) and Heil Dir zum schönen Estlingsfeste (B. Pirlinger)

76 Lasst Jubeltöne laut erklingen (A. Weiss), Eb, TTBB, 2 hn, 2 tpt, 4 trbn, c1854, G ii/2, 161 [orig. text: Dir holde Heimat soll erklingen (A. A. Naaf)]

60 Auf, Brüder, auf! und die Saiten zur Hand! (Marinelli), cantata, D, 4 male vv, male SATB, chorus, 2 ob, 2 bn, 3 hn, 2 tpt, 3 trbn, 1855, G ii/2, 230

70 Germanenzug (A. Silberstein), d, TTBB, brass, 1863 (Ried, 1865)

89 Um Mitternacht (R. Prutz), 1st setting, f, A, TTBB, pf, 1864 (Vienna, 1911), K ii

73 Herbstlied (F. von Sallet), f♯, 2 S, TTBB, pf, 1864, K i

80 Mitternacht (J. Mendelssohn), Ab, T, TTBB, pf, 1870 (1903)

74 Das hohe Lied (H. von der Mattig), Ab, 2 T, Bar, 8 male vv: 1st version, org acc., 1876 (1922), 2nd version, orch acc., 1877–9 (1902)

88 Trösterin Musik (A. Seuffert), c, TTBB, org, 1877, K iii [orig. text: Nachruf (Mattig)]

57 Abendzauber (Mattig), Gb, Bar, TTBB, 3 yodellers, 4 hn, 1878, K iv

63 Das deutsche Lied (E. Fels), d, TTBB, brass, 1892, K vii — 42

71 Helgoland (Silberstein), g, TTBB, orch, 1893 (1899) — 42

UNACCOMPANIED SECULAR CHORAL

59 An dem Feste (A. Knauer), Db, TTBB, 1843, G i, 231 [rev. 1843 as WAB67 and 1893 as WAB86]
67 Festlied (L. Kraus), D, male vv, 1843 (Augsburg, 1928)
78 Das Lied vom deutschen Vaterland, Db, TTBB, 1845?, G ii/2, 14
84 Ständchen, G, TTBB, c1846, facs., G ii/2, 61
77 Der Lehrerstand, Eb, TTBB, c1847, G ii/2, 16
85 Sternschnuppen (Marinelli), F, TTBB, 1848, G ii/2, 94
83 2 mottos, D, A, for TTBB, 1851, G ii/2, 145
65 Das edle Herz (Marinelli), 1st setting, A, TTBB, c1851, G ii/2, 111
69 Die Geburt, Db, TTBB, 1851, G ii/2, 147
62 Des Dankes Wort sei mir gegönnt (Marinelli), T, B, male vv, 1855
64 Du bist wie eine Blume (Heine), F, SATB, 1861, facs., G iii/2, 193
94 Anheben lasst uns all zusamm': Volkslied (J. Winter), C, TTBB, c1861, facs., G iii/2, 191; arr. lv, pf, facs., G iii/2, 192
66 Das edle Herz (Marinelli), 2nd setting, A, SATB, 1861, G iii/2, 13
55 Der Abendhimmel (Zedlitz), 1st setting, Ab, TTBB, 1862, G iii/2, 18
135 Zigeuner-Waldlied (?Silberstein), male vv, 1863 [lost but incl. in Germanenzug, c1863]
56 Der Abendhimmel (Zedlitz), 2nd setting, F, TTBB, 1866 ed. (1902)
91 Vaterländisches Weinlied (Silberstein), C, TTBB, 1866, as Vaterländisch in Wiener Componistenalbum (1892)
92 O könnt ich dich beglücken (Vaterlandslied) (Silberstein), Ab, T, Bar, male vv, 1866 (Vienna, 1902)
95 [Das Frauenherz (K. Kerschbaum), motto, A, mixed vv, 1868, G iii/2, 158
   [Des Höchsten Preis (A. Mittermayr), motto, C, TTBB, 1868, G iii/2, 159
148 2 mottos (J. K. Markus), C, d, male vv, 1869, facs., Z/m, Jg.106 (1939), 256

147 Freiner Sinn und froher Mut, motto, D, male vv, 1874
82 Sängerbund (?Mattig, Kerschbaum), C, TTBB, 1882, K v
90 Um Mitternacht (Prutz), 2nd setting, f, T, male vv, 1886, facs., Strassburger Sängerhaus (Strasburg, 1886), 13, K vi, rev. 1887
87 Träumen und Wachen (Grillparzer), Ab, T, male vv, 1890 (rev. 1892)
86 Tafellied, Db, TTBB, 1893, G i, 231

SONGS
(all for 1v, pf)
138 Mild wie Bäche (?Marinelli), c1845, inc. sketch, facs., G ii/2, 59
68 Frühlingslied (Heine), T, 1851, G ii/2, 44
58 Amaranths Waldeslieder (Redwitz), T, Oct ?1858, ed. in Die Musik, i (1901–2), suppl. [following p.1619]
75 Im April (E. Geibel), for A, 1868, ed. (1898)
79 Mein Herz und deine Stimme (A. von Platen), T, 1868, G iii/2, 144
72 Herbstkummer (Ernst), T, 1868, G iii/2, 151

CHAMBER
114 Aequale, c, 3 trbn, 1847, G ii/2, 83
149 Aequale, c, 3 trbn, 1847
111 String Quartet, c, 1861–2, N xiii/1   9, 37
110 Abendklänge, e, vn, pf, 1866, facs., G i, 104
112 Quintet, 2 vn, 2 va, vc, F, 1878–9 (1884), N xiii/2
113 Intermezzo, d, 2 vn, 2 va, vc, 1879 (1913), N xiii/2 [intended as new Qnt scherzo]   20

ORGAN
128 4 preludes, Eb, ?1837, G i, 97
127 Prelude, Eb, ?1837, ed. in M. Auer (1931, 6/1966), appx, 3
130 Prelude, d, c1846 or c1852 (Augsburg, 1927)
126 Postlude, d, c1852 (Augsburg, 1927)
131 Prelude and Fugue, c, 1847, G ii/2, 77
125 Fugue, d, 1861, ed. in F. Gräflinger (1911, rev., enlarged 2/1927)
129 Prelude, C, 1884 (1926)

BIBLIOGRAPHY

CATALOGUES AND SOURCE STUDIES

O. Keller: 'Anton Bruckner-Literatur', *Die Musik*, xiv (1914–15), 158, 217

Katalog der Anton Bruckner Gedächtnisaustellung im O.-Ö. Landesmuseum (Linz, 1935)

L. Nowak, ed.: *Anton Bruckner und Linz: Ausstellungskatalog* (Vienna, 1964)

L. Nowak: 'Das Bruckner-Erbe der Österreichischen National-bibliothek', *ÖMz*, xxi (1966), 526

A. D. Walker: 'Bruckner's Works: a List of the Published Scores of the Various Versions', *Brio*, iii/2 (1966), 4

F. Grasberger, ed.: *Anton Bruckner zum 150. Geburtstag: eine Ausstellung im Prunksaal der Österreichischen Nationalbibliothek 29. Mai bis 12. Oktober 1974* (Vienna, 1974)

R. Grasberger: *Werkverzeichnis Anton Bruckners* (Tutzing, 1977)

W. Kirsch: 'Die Bruckner-Forschung seit 1945: eine kommentierte Bibliographie', *AcM*, liii (1981), 157; liv (1982), 208–61; lv (1983), 201–44; lvi (1984), 1

ICONOGRAPHY

C. Almeroth: *Wie die Bruckner-Büste entstand* (Vienna, 1899) [on the busts by Tilgner]

F. Gräflinger: *Anton Bruckner: Leben und Schaffen* (Berlin, 1927)

A. Orel: *Anton Bruckner 1824–1896: sein Leben in Bildern* (Leipzig, 1936)

M. Auer: 'Bruckner-Bilder', *Deutsche Musikkultur*, v (1940–41), 138

W. Abendroth: *Bruckner: eine Bildbiographie* (Munich, 1958)

J. Lassl: *Das kleine Brucknerbuch* (Salzburg, 1965, 2/1972)

H. Schöny: 'Anton Bruckner im zeitgenössischen Bildnis', *Kunstjahrbuch der Stadt Linz 1968*, 45–84; pubd separately as *Bruckner-Ikonographie* (Vienna, 1968)

L. Nowak: *Anton Bruckner: Musik und Leben* (Linz, 1973)

H. C. Fischer: *Anton Bruckner: sein Leben* (Salzburg, 1974)

W. Wiora: 'Über die Würdigung Anton Bruckners durch eine Bildbiographie', *Mf*, xxvii (1974), 281

LETTERS AND DOCUMENTS

O. Kitzler: *Musikalische Erinnerungen* (Brno, 1904) [incl. Bruckner letters]

O. Keller: 'Anton Bruckner-Literatur', *Die Musik*, xiv (1914–15), 217

F. Gräflinger, ed.: *Anton Bruckner: gesammelte Briefe* (Regensburg, 1924)

Bibliography

M. Auer, ed.: *Anton Bruckner: gesammelte Briefe*, new ser. (Regensburg, 1924)

R. Lach: *Die Bruckner-Akten des Wiener Universitäts-Archivs* (Vienna, 1926)

F. Schalk: *Briefe und Betrachtungen* (Vienna and Leipzig, 1935)

A. Orel: *Ein Harmonielehrekolleg bei Anton Bruckner* (Vienna, 1940)

K. Gudewill: 'Das neue Bruckner-Schrifttum', *Deutsche Musikkultur*, v (1940–41), 145

E. Schwanzara, ed.: *Anton Bruckner: Vorlesungen über Harmonielehre und Kontrapunkt an der Universität Wien* (Vienna, 1950)

A. Orel, ed.: *Bruckner-Brevier: Briefe, Dokumente, Berichte* (Vienna, 1953)

E. N. Waters: 'Variations on a Theme: Recent Acquisitions of the Music Division', *Library of Congress Quarterly Journal*, xxvii/1 (1970), 51–83 [Bruckner's harmony and counterpoint exercises]

O. Biba: 'Bruckner-Neuerwerbungen des Archivs der Gesellschaft der Musikfreunde in Wien', *Mitteilungsblatt der Internationalen Bruckner-Gesellschaft*, xvii (1980), 20

GENERAL BIOGRAPHY, MEMOIRS

F. Brunner: *Dr Anton Bruckner* (Linz, 1895/R1974)

H. Rietsch: 'Anton Bruckner', *Biographisches Jb und Deutscher Nekrolog*, i (Berlin, 1897); pubd separately (Berlin, 1898)

C. Hruby: *Meine Erinnerungen an Anton Bruckner* (Vienna, 1901)

J. Kluger: 'Schlichte Erinnerungen an Anton Bruckner', *Jb des Stiftes Klosterneuburg*, iii (Vienna, 1910), 107–37

F. Gräflinger: *Anton Bruckner: Bausteine zu seiner Lebensgeschichte* (Munich, 1911, rev., enlarged 2/1927)

E. Decsey: *Bruckner: Versuch eines Lebens* (Berlin, 1920, 3/1930)

F. Eckstein: *Erinnerungen an Anton Bruckner* (Vienna, 1923)

G. Krenn: 'Jugenderinnerungen an Meister Bruckner', *Linzer Tagespost* (1924), no.264

F. Klose: *Meine Lehrjahre bei Bruckner: Erinnerungen und Betrachtungen* (Regensburg, 1927)

J. Gruber: *Meine Erinnerungen an Dr Anton Bruckner* (Einsiedeln, 1929)

F. Klose: *Bayreuth: Eindrücke und Erlebnisse* (Regensburg, 1929), 61ff

G. Engel: *The Life of Anton Bruckner* (New York, 1931)

M. von Oberleithner: *Meine Erinnerungen an Anton Bruckner* (Regensburg, 1933)

F. Grüninger: *Der Ehrfürchtige: Anton Bruckners Leben dem Volk erzählt* (Freiburg, 1935, 6/1953)

W. Wiora: 'Anton Bruckner', *Die grossen Deutschen*, ed. W. Andreas and W. von Scholz, iv (Berlin, 1936, rev. 2/1959)

E. Refardt: *Brahms, Bruckner, Wolf: drei Wiener Meister des 19. Jahrhunderts* (Basle, 1949)

O. Wessely: 'Anton Bruckner und Linz', *Jb der Stadt Linz 1954*, 201–82

F. Linninger: 'Orgeln und Organisten im Stifte St Florian', *Oberösterreichische Heimatblätter*, ix (1955), 171

N. Tschulik, ed.: *Anton Bruckner im Spiegel seiner Zeit* (Vienna, 1955)

O. Wessely: 'Beiträge zur Familiengeschichte Anton Bruckners', *Jb des oberösterreichischen Musealvereines*, c (Linz, 1955), 143

A. Kellner: *Musikgeschichte des Stiftes Kremsmünster* (Kassel, 1956)

W. Schulten: *Anton Bruckners künstlerische Entwicklung in der St Florianer Zeit* (diss., U. of Mainz, 1956)

Felix von Kraus: *Begegnungen mit Anton Bruckner, Johannes Brahms, Cosima Wagner*, ed. Felicitas von Kraus (Vienna, 1960), 11ff

W. Schulten: *Über die Bedeutung der St Florianer Jahre Anton Bruckners (1845–1855)* (Aachen, 1960)

H.-M. Plesske: 'Anton Bruckner in der erzählenden Literatur', *Kunstjahrbuch der Stadt Linz 1961*, 63

A. Orel: 'Bruckner und Wien', *Hans Albrecht in memoriam* (Kassel, 1962)

H. Schöny: 'Neues zu Anton Bruckners Vorfahren', *Jb des oberösterreichischen Musealvereines*, cviii (Linz, 1963), 251

C. F. Wehle: *Anton Bruckner im Spiegel seiner Zeitgenossen: sein Lebensroman in Tatsachen* (Garmisch-Partenkirchen, 1964)

H. Winterberger: *Anton Bruckner in seiner Zeit* (Linz, 1964)

K. A. Hartmann and W. Wahren: 'Briefe über Bruckner', *NZM*, cxxvi (1965), 272, 334, 380

R. Quoika: *Die Orgelwelt um Anton Bruckner* (Ludwigsburg, 1966)

E. Kroll: 'Anton Bruckner und die Berliner Philharmoniker', *Orchester*, xv (1967), 241

L. Nowak: 'Anton Bruckner und München', *Die Münchner Philharmoniker: 1893–1968*, ed. A. Ott and E. Faehndrich (Munich, 1968), 47

F. Grasberger: 'Anton Bruckners Auslandsreisen', *ÖMz*, xxiv (1969), 630

D. Kerner: *Krankheiten grosser Musiker*, ii (Stuttgart, 1969)

——: 'Anton Bruckner', *Hessisches Ärzteblatt*, xxx (1969), 336 [medical history]

H. J. Busch: 'Anton Bruckners Tätigkeit als Orgelsachverständiger', *Ars organi*, xix (1971), 1585

In Ehrfurcht vor den Manen eines Grossen: zum 75. Todestag Anton Bruckners (Linz, 1971) [incl. studies by R. Altmüller, R. Gottfried, R. Haase, T. Hofer, J. Lassl, L. Nowak, F. J. Plash, H. Stadlmayr, H. Wopelka, O. Wutzl, F. Zamazal, H. Zappe]

C. van Zwol: *Op reis door 't land van Bruckner* (Amersfoort, 1974)

Bibliography

F. Grasberger: 'Adalbert Stifter und Anton Bruckner', *Stifter-Symposion Linz 1978*, 48

T. Antonicek: *Anton Bruckner und die Wiener Hofmusikkapelle*, Anton Bruckner: Dokumente und Studien, ed. F. Grasberger, i (Graz, 1979)

F. Grasberger, ed.: *Anton Bruckner in Wien: eine kritische Studie zu seiner Persönlichkeit*, Anton Bruckner: Dokumente und Studien, ed. F. Grasberger, ii (Graz, 1980) [incl. studies by M. Wagner, J.-L. Mayer, E. Maier, L. M. Kantner]

E. Maier and F. Zamazal: *Anton Bruckner und Leopold von Zenetti*, Anton Bruckner: Dokumente und Studien, ed. F. Grasberger, iii (Graz, 1980)

LIFE AND WORKS

R. Louis: *Anton Bruckner* (Berlin, 1904)

——: *Anton Bruckner* (Munich, 1905, 3/1921, ed. P. Ehlers)

M. Morold: *Anton Bruckner* (Leipzig, 1912, 2/1920)

A. Westarp: *Anton Bruckner: l'homme et l'oeuvre* (Paris, 1912)

J. de Marliave: 'Anton Bruckner', *Etudes musicales* (Paris, 1917)

F. Gräflinger: *Anton Bruckner: sein Leben und seine Werke* (Regensburg, 1921)

J. Marnold: 'Anton Bruckner', *Musique d'autrefois et d'aujourd'hui* (Paris, 1921)

K. Grunsky: *Anton Bruckner* (Stuttgart, 1922)

H. Tessmer: *Anton Bruckner* (Regensburg, 1922)

A. Göllerich: *Anton Bruckner: ein Lebens- und Schaffensbild*, i (Regensburg, 1922/*R*1974); ii–iv, ed. M. Auer (1928–37, 2/1938/*R*1974)

M. Auer: *Anton Bruckner: sein Leben und Werk* (Vienna, 1923, 6/1967)

R. Wetz: *Anton Bruckner: sein Leben und Schaffen* (Leipzig, 1923)

J. Daninger: *Anton Bruckner* (Vienna, 1924)

G. Gräner: *Anton Bruckner* (Leipzig, 1924)

K. Kobald, ed.: *In memoriam Anton Bruckner* (Vienna, 1924) [incl. studies by G. Adler, M. Auer, E. Decsey, F. Eckstein, W. Fischer, A. Göllerich, M. Graf, F. Gräflinger, R. Holzer, J. Kluger, K. Kobald, F. Löwe, V. O. Ludwig, F. Moissl, F. Müller, A. Orel, M. Springer]

E. Kurth: *Anton Bruckner* (Berlin, 1925/*R*1971)

A. Orel: *Anton Bruckner: ein österreichischer Meister der Tonkunst* (Altötting, 1926)

R. Haas: *Anton Bruckner* (Potsdam, 1934)

W. Paap: *Anton Bruckner: zijn land, zijn leven en zijn kunst* (Bilthoven, 1936)

K. Laux: *Anton Bruckner: Leben und Werk* (Leipzig, 1940, 2/1947)

65

L. van Vassenhove: *Anton Bruckner* (Neuchâtel, 1942)

A. Machabey: *La vie et l'oeuvre d'Anton Bruckner* (Paris, 1945)

R. W. Wood: 'Anton Bruckner', *The Music Masters*, ii, ed. A. L. Bacharach (London, 1950)

F. Blume: 'Bruckner, Josef Anton', *MGG*

H. F. Redlich: *Bruckner and Mahler* (London, 1955, rev. 2/1963)

P. Benary: *Anton Bruckner* (Leipzig, 1956)

A. Basso, ed.: *Anton Bruckner simposium* (Genoa, 1958) [incl. studies by S. Martinotti, A. Machabey, A. Basso and E. D. R. Neill]

E. Doernberg: *The Life and Symphonies of Anton Bruckner* (London, 1960/*R*1968)

L. Rappoport: *Anton Bruckner* (Moscow, 1963)

M. Lancelot: *Anton Bruckner: l'homme et son oeuvre* (Paris, 1964)

L. Nowak: *Anton Bruckner: Musik und Leben* (Vienna, 1964)

F. Grasberger, ed.: *Bruckner-Studien: Leopold Nowak zum 60. Geburtstag* (Vienna, 1964) [incl. studies by W. Boetticher, K. G. Fellerer, K. Geiringer, F. Grasberger, W. Hess, H. Jancik, E. Jochum, A. Kellner, F. Kosch, H. Kronsteiner, J. Kronsteiner, F. Racek, H. F. Redlich, H. Sittner, E. Tittel, W. Waldstein, A. Weinmann]

S. Martinotti: *L'approdo musicale*, xxiv (1967) [special Bruckner number]

H.-H. Schönzeler: *Bruckner* (London and New York, 1970, Ger. trans., 1974; rev. 2/1978)

J. Gallois: *Bruckner* (Paris, 1971)

M. Moroianu: *Anton Bruckner* (Bucharest, 1972)

O. Wessely, ed.: *Bruckner-Studien* (Vienna, 1975) [incl. studies by T. Antonicek, O. Biba, G. Brosche, R. Flotzinger, F. Grasberger, E. Hilmar, E. Maier, S. Martinotti, G. K. Mitterschiffthaler, L. Nowak, W. Pass, E. Schenk and G. Gruber, K. Schütz, M. Wagner, E. Werner, O. Wessely]

D. Watson: *Bruckner* (London, 1975)

M. Wagner: *Bruckner* (Mainz, 1983)

PERSONAL AND MUSICAL CHARACTER STUDIES

A. Knapp: *Anton Bruckner: zum Verständnis seiner Persönlichkeit und seiner Werke* (Düsseldorf, 1921)

E. Schwebsch: *Anton Bruckner: ein Beitrag zur Erkenntnis von Entwickelungen in der Musik* (Stuttgart, 1921, 2/1923)

O. Lang: *Anton Bruckner: Wesen und Bedeutung* (Munich, 1924, 3/1947)

A. Orel: *Anton Bruckner: das Werk, der Künstler, die Zeit* (Vienna, 1925)

F. Grüninger: *Anton Bruckner: der metaphysische Kern seiner*

Bibliography

Persönlichkeit und Werke (Augsburg, 1930)

——: *Wege zu Anton Bruckner: Erinnerungsblätter zu seinem 40. Todestag* (Karlsruhe, 1936)

A. Köberle: *Bach, Beethoven, Bruckner als Symbolgestalten des Glaubens* (Berlin, 1936, 4/1941)

W. König: *Anton Bruckner als Chormeister* (Linz, 1936)

W. Abendroth: *Deutsche Musik der Zeitwende: eine kulturphilosophische Persönlichkeitsstudie über Anton Bruckner und Hans Pfitzner* (Hamburg, 1937, 2/1941)

O. Loerke: *Anton Bruckner: ein Charakterbild* (Berlin, 1938, 3/1943)

H. J. Moser: 'Bruckner und Mozart', *Programmbuch der Berliner Kunstwochen 1940* (Berlin, 1940)

W. Furtwängler: *Johannes Brahms, Anton Bruckner* (Leipzig, 1942/R1963)

W. Wolff: *Anton Bruckner: Rustic Genius* (New York, 1942)

D. Newlin: *Bruckner, Mahler, Schoenberg* (New York, 1947, 2/1947; Ger. trans, 1954; rev. 3/1979)

L. Nowak: *Te Deum laudamus: Gedanken zur Musik Anton Bruckners* (Vienna, 1947)

A. Knab: 'Bach, Beethoven, Bruckner', *Musica*, iii (1949), 316

G. Gavazzeni: 'Intorno ad Anton Bruckner', *Il suono è stanco* (Bergamo, 1950)

E. Schenk: *Um Bruckners Persönlichkeit* (Vienna, 1951)

W. Furtwängler: 'Anton Bruckner', *Ton und Wort* (Wiesbaden, 1954, 7/1959) [1939 essay]

M. Dehnert: *Anton Bruckner: Versuch einer Deutung* (Leipzig, 1958)

A. Liess: 'Anton Bruckners Gestalt und Werk', *Universitas*, xvi (1961), 31

L. Nowak: *Reden und Ansprachen* (Vienna, 1964)

F. Eymann: *Von Bach zu Bruckner* (Berne, 1968)

F. Grasberger: 'Das Jahr 1868', *ÖMz*, xxiii (1968), 197

H. Pflugbeil: 'Omnia ad maiorem Dei gloriam – Anton Bruckner', *Credo musicale . . . Festgabe zum 80. Geburtstag . . . Rudolf Mauersberger* (Kassel, 1969), 63

P.-G. Langevin: *Le siècle de Bruckner: essais pour une nouvelle perspective sur les maîtres viennois du second âge d'or* (Paris, 1975) [special issue of *ReM*, nos.298–9]

O. Wessely: 'Anton Bruckner und Gustav Mahler', *ÖMz*, xxxii (1977), 57

C. C. Röthig: *Studien zur Systematik des Schaffens von Anton Bruckner auf der Grundlage zeitgenössischer Berichte und autographer Entwürfe* (Kassel, 1978)

C. Floros: *Brahms und Bruckner: Studien zur musikalischen Exegetik* (Wiesbaden, 1980)

EDITORIAL PROBLEMS

M. Auer: 'Der Streit um den "echten" Bruckner im Licht biographischer Tatsachen', *ZfM*, ciii (1936), 538, 1191

F. Klose: 'Zum Thema "Original und Bearbeitung bei Bruckner" ', *Deutsche Musikkultur*, i (1936–7), 222

A. Orel: 'Original und Bearbeitung bei Bruckner', *Deutsche Musikkultur*, i (1936–7), 193

M. Auer, R. Pergler and H. Weisbach: *Anton Bruckner: wissenschaftliche und künstlerische Betrachtungen zu den Original-Fassungen* (Vienna, 1937) [with discussion by several distinguished conductors]

E. Wellesz: 'Le versioni originali delle sinfonie di Bruckner', *RaM*, x (1937), 13

F. Wohlfahrt: 'Der Ur-Bruckner', *Deutsche Musikkultur*, ii (1937–8), 144

F. Oeser: *Die Klangstruktur der Bruckner-Symphonie: eine Studie zur Frage der Original-Fassungen* (Leipzig, 1939)

E. T. A. Armbruster: *Erstdruck oder 'Originalfassung'?* (Leipzig, 1946)

W. Hess: 'Die Urfassung von Bruckners dritter Sinfonie und das Problem der Gesamtausgabe', *SMz*, lxxxviii (1948), 453

L. Nowak: ' "Urfassung" und "Endfassung" bei Anton Bruckner', *Kongressbericht: Wien Mozartjahr 1956*, 448

A. D. Walker: 'Bruckner Versions', *Gramophone*, xliii (1965–6), 289

D. Cooke: 'The Bruckner Problem Simplified', *MT*, cx (1969), 20, 142, 362, 479, 828

F. Grasberger, ed.: *Die Fassungen: Bruckner-Symposion Linz 1980*

SYMPHONIES
(general studies)

A. Halm: *Die Symphonie Anton Bruckners* (Munich, 1914, 2/1923)

R. Wickenhauser: *Anton Bruckners Symphonien: ihr Werden und Wesen* (Leipzig, 1926–7)

W. Abendroth: *Die Symphonien Anton Bruckners: Einführungen* (Berlin, 1940, 2/1942)

F. Wohlfahrt: *Anton Bruckners symphonisches Werk* (Leipzig, 1943)

R. Simpson: 'Bruckner and the Symphony', *MR*, vii (1946), 35

G. Engel: *The Symphonies of Anton Bruckner* (New York, 1955)

I. Krohn: *Anton Bruckners Symphonien: Untersuchung über Formenbau und Stimmungsgehalt* (Helsinki, 1955–7)

A. Basso: 'Introduzione alle sinfonie di Bruckner', *Anton Bruckner simposium*, ed. A. Basso (Genoa, 1958), 70

S. Martinotti: 'Aspetti e caratteri del sinfonismo di Anton Bruckner', *Anton Bruckner simposium*, ed. A. Basso (Genoa, 1958), 177–228

S. Vestdijk: *De symfonieën van Anton Bruckner en andere essays over muziek* (Amsterdam and The Hague, 1966)

Bibliography

P.-G. Langevin, ed.: *Anton Bruckner, apogée de la symphonie* (Lausanne, 1977)

P. Barford: *Bruckner Symphonies* (London, 1978)

(*special studies*)

M. Morold: 'Das Brucknersche Finale', *Die Musik*, vi (1906–7), 28

M. Bauer: 'Zur Form in den sinfonischen Werken Anton Bruckners', *Festschrift Hermann Kretzschmar* (Leipzig, 1918), 12

E. Kurth: *Romantische Harmonik und ihre Krise in Wagners Tristan* (Berlin, 1919, 2/1923)

H. A. Grunsky: *Das Formproblem in Anton Bruckners Symphonien* (Augsburg, 1929)

——: *Formenwelt und Sinngefüge in den Bruckner-Symphonien* (Augsburg, 1931)

R. von Tobel: *Die Formenwelt der klassischen Instrumentalmusik* (Berne, 1935)

K. Grunsky: *Fragen der Bruckner-Auffassung* (Stuttgart, 1936)

K. Schiske: *Zur Dissonanzverwendung in den Symphonien Anton Bruckners* (diss., U. of Vienna, 1940)

J. H. Wilcox: *The Symphonies of Anton Bruckner* (diss., Florida State U., 1956)

F. Grasberger: 'Form und Ekstase: über eine Beziehung Haydn–Schubert–Bruckner in der Symphonie', *Anthony van Hoboken: Festschrift zum 75. Geburtstag* (Mainz, 1962), 93

S. Martinotti: 'Ricognizione del sinfonismo di Bruckner', *Convegno musicale*, i (1964), 45

E. Werner: 'The Nature and Function of the Sequence in Bruckner's Symphonies', *Essays in Musicology in Honor of Dragan Plamenac* (Pittsburgh, 1969), 365

E. Voss: 'Bruckners Sinfonien in ihrer Beziehung zur Messe', *Schallplatte und Kirche*, v (1969), 103

K. Wöss: *Ratschläge zur Aufführung der Symphonien Anton Bruckners* (Linz, 1974)

M. Bushler: *Development in the First Movements of Bruckner's Symphonies* (diss., City U., New York, 1975)

W. Wiora: 'Über den religiösen Gehalt in Bruckners Symphonien', *Studien zur Musikgeschichte des 19. Jahrhunderts*, li (1978), 157

O. Wessely, ed.: *Die österreichische Symphonie nach Anton Bruckner: Bruckner-Symposion Linz 1981*

W. Notter: *Schematismus und Evolution in der Sinfonik Anton Bruckners* (diss., U. of Freiburg, 1983)

(*individual studies*)

H. Kretzschmar: *Anton Bruckner: 3. Symphonie* (Leipzig, 1898)

Bruckner

——: *Anton Bruckner: 4. Symphonie* (Leipzig, 1898)
K. Grunsky: *Anton Bruckner: 9. Sinfonie in D moll* (Leipzig, 1903)
G. Staub-Schlaepfer: 'Neue Glossen zu Bruckners 8. Sinfonie', *SMz*, xc (1905), 12
H. Grunsky: *Anton Bruckner: 1. Sinfonie C moll* (Berlin, 1907)
——: *Anton Bruckner: 6. Sinfonie A dur* (Berlin, 1907)
W. Niemann: *Anton Bruckner: 5. Symphonie* (Leipzig, 1907)
A. Knab: *Bruckner: 5. Symphonie* (Vienna, 1922)
H. Unger: *Anton Bruckner und seine 7. Symphonie* (Bonn, 1944)
R. Simpson: 'The Seventh Symphony of Bruckner', *MR*, viii (1947), 178
H. F. Redlich: 'Bruckner's Forgotten Symphony (No. "0")', *Music Survey*, ii (1949), 14
——: 'The Finale of Bruckner's Ninth Symphony', *MMR*, lxxix (1949), 143
E. Schwebsch: *Anton Bruckners VI. Symphonie* (Stuttgart, 1953)
L. Nowak: 'Das Finale von Bruckners VII. Symphonie: eine Formstudie', *Festschrift Wilhelm Fischer* (Innsbruck, 1956), 143
——: 'Anton Bruckners Formwille, dargestellt am Finale seiner V. Symphonie', *Miscelánea en homenaje a Monseñor Higinio Anglés* (Barcelona, 1958–61), ii, 609
F. Grasberger: 'Anton Bruckner und Richard Wagner: zur Herausgabe der III. Symphonie (Fassung von 1889) in der Bruckner-Gesamtausgabe', *ÖMz*, xiv (1959), 524
S. Martinotti: *Guida alla settima sinfonia di Anton Bruckner* (Genoa, 1960)
P. Dawson-Bowling: 'Thematic and Tonal Unity in Bruckner's Eighth Symphony', *MR*, xxx (1969), 225
J. Tröller: *Anton Bruckner: III. Symphonie d-moll* (Munich, 1976)
M. Wagner: *Der Wandel des Konzepts: zu den verschiedenen Fassungen von Bruckners Dritter, Vierter und Achter Sinfonie* (Vienna, 1980)

SACRED MUSIC
S. Ochs: *Anton Bruckner: Te Deum* (Stuttgart, 1896)
A. Göllerich: 'Anton Bruckners 114. Psalm', *Die Musik*, vi (1906–7), 36
A. Heuss: *Te Deum von Anton Bruckner* (Leipzig, 1908)
P. Griesbacher: *Bruckners Te Deum: Studie* (Regensburg, 1919)
W. Fischer: 'Zur entwicklungsgeschichtlichen Wertung der Kirchenfuge Bruckners', *In memoriam Anton Bruckner*, ed. K. Kobald (Vienna, 1924), 60
K. Singer: *Bruckners Chormusik* (Stuttgart, 1924)
W. Kurthen: 'Liszt und Bruckner als Messenkomponisten', *Musica divina*, xiii/2 (1925), 44

70

Bibliography

M. Auer: *Anton Bruckner als Kirchenmusiker* (Regensburg, 1927)

F. Munch: 'La musique religieuse d'Anton Bruckner', *Le ménestrel*, xc (1928), 69, 81, 93

K. J. Perl: *Christliche Musik und Anton Bruckner* (Strasbourg, 1937)

W. Kirsch: 'Anton Bruckners Motetten der Wiener Zeit', *Musik und Altar*, xi (1958–9), 56

H.-G. Scholz: *Die Form der reifen Messen Anton Bruckners* (Berlin, 1961)

S. Martinotti: *L'opera sacra di Anton Bruckner* (diss., U. of Milan, 1962)

L. Nowak: 'Probleme bei der Veröffentlichung von Skizzen dargestellt an einem Beispiel aus Anton Bruckners Te Deum', *Anthony van Hoboken: Festschrift zum 75. Geburtstag* (Mainz, 1962), 115

S. Martinotti: 'La musica sacra di Bruckner', *Convegno musicale*, ii (1965), 65–111; pubd separately (Turin, 1965)

L. Nowak: 'Der Name "Jesus Christus" in den Kompositionen von Anton Bruckner', *Wissenschaft im Dienste des Glaubens: Festschrift . . . Hermann Peichl* (Vienna, 1965), 199

A. Schmitz: 'Anton Bruckners Motette "Os justi": eine Erwägung zur Problematik der kirchenmusikalischen Restauration im 19. Jahrhundert', *Epirrhosis: Festgabe für Carl Schmitt*, i (Berlin, 1968), 333

A. C. Howie: *The Sacred Music of Anton Bruckner* (diss., U. of Manchester, 1969)

——: 'Traditional and Novel Elements in Bruckner's Sacred Music', *MQ*, lxvii (1981), 544

EARLY WORKS

A. Orel: *Unbekannte Frühwerke Anton Bruckners* (Vienna, 1921)

L. Böttcher: 'Ein bedeutsamer Brucknerfund', *Neue Musik Zeitschrift*, iii (1949), 177 [pf works]

——: 'Unbekannte Klavier-Werke von Anton Bruckner', *Das Musikleben*, ii (1949), 236

OTHER MUSIC STUDIES

E. Wellesz: 'Anton Bruckner and the Process of Musical Creation', *MQ*, xxiv (1938), 265

O. Lang: 'Die Thematik Anton Bruckners', *Deutsche Musikkultur*, iv (1939–40), 64

A. A. Abert: 'Die Behandlung der Instrumente in Bruckners Streichquintett', *Deutsche Musikkultur*, v (1940–41), 133

W. Vetter: 'Das Adagio bei Anton Bruckner', *Deutsche Musikkultur*, v 1940–41), 121

B. Walter: 'Bruckner and Mahler', *Chord and Discord*, ii/2 (1940), 3

H. F. Redlich: 'Bruckner and Brahms: Quintets in F', *ML*, xxxvi (1955), 253

W. Kirsch: *Studien zum Vokaltsil der mittleren und späten Schaffensperiode Anton Bruckners* (diss., U. of Frankfurt am Main, 1958)

P. Benary: 'Gedanken zur Bruckner-Interpretation', *SMz*, cii (1962), 296

L. Nowak: 'Symphonischer und kirchlicher Stil bei Anton Bruckner', *Festschrift Karl Gustav Fellerer* (Regensburg, 1962), 391

C. Dahlhaus: 'Bruckner und der Barock', *NZM*, cxxiv (1963), 335

W. F. Korte: *Bruckner und Brahms: die spätromantische Lösung der autonomen Konzeption* (Tutzing, 1963)

L. Nowak: 'Form und Rhythmus im ersten Satz des Streichquintetts von Anton Bruckner', *Festschrift Hans Engel* (Kassel, 1964), 260

U. Duse: 'Bruckner e il suo caso', *Musica e cultura: quattro diagnosi* (Padua, 1967), 13

G. Gentilucci: 'Attualità del caso Bruckner', *Rassegna musicale Curci*, xx (1967)

R. Simpson: *The Essence of Bruckner: an Essay towards the Understanding of his Music* (London, 1967)

K. Unger: *Studien zur Harmonik Anton Bruckners: Einwirkung und Umwandlung älterer Klangstrukturen* (diss., U. of Heidelberg, 1969); summary, *Mf*, xxv (1972), 87

B. McIntyre: *Conductorial Decisions in Bruckner's Symphonies nos.8 and 9* (diss., Indiana U., 1970)

K. Wagner: 'Bruckners Themenbildung als Kriterium seiner Stilentwicklung', *ÖMz*, xxv (1970), 159

M. Wagner: *Die Melodien Bruckners in systematischer Ordnung* (diss., U. of Vienna, 1970)

O. Wessely: 'Zur Geschichte des Equals', *Beethoven-Studien*, ed. E. Schenk (Vienna, 1970), 341 [derivation of brass chorales in Bruckner's syms.]

P. Grant: 'Bruckner and Mahler: the Fundamental Dissimilarity of their Styles', *MR*, xxxii (1971), 36

H. Federhofer: 'Heinrich Schenkers Bruckner-Verständnis', *AMw*, xxxix (1982), 198

O. Wessely, ed.: *Bruckner-Interpretation: Bruckner-Symposion Linz 1982*

——: *Johannes Brahms und Anton Bruckner: Bruckner-Symposion Linz 1983* (Linz, 1984)

SPECIAL PERIODICALS

Organon: Zeitschrift für geistliche Musik (Munich, 1924–34) [of the Deutsche Bruckner-Gemeinde]

Bruckner-Blätter: Mitteilungen der Internationalen Bruckner-Gesellschaft (Vienna, 1929–37); renamed *Mitteilungen der*

Bibliography

Deutschen Bruckner-Gesellschaft (1939–40)

Chord and Discord (New York, 1932–41, 1947–) [journal of the Bruckner Society of America]

Mitteilungsblatt der Internationalen Bruckner-Gesellschaft (Vienna, 1971–)

Bruckner-Jb (Linz, 1980–)

Musik-Konzepte, xxiii–xxiv (1982)

JOHANNES BRAHMS

Heinz Becker

Life

I Early years

Johannes Brahms was born in Hamburg on 7 May 1833. On his father's side he came of farming and artisan stock in the Dithmarschen area of Holstein, where his grandfather Johann Brahms (1769–1839) was an innkeeper in the town of Heide. His father Johann Jakob Brahms (1806–72), the first of the family to take up music as a career, met with opposition but in 1826 moved to Hamburg, where he started as a street and dance musician, later joining the Hamburg city orchestra as a double bass player. In 1830 he was granted citizenship of Hamburg and on 9 June that year he married his housekeeper, Johanna Henrika Christiane Nissen (d 1865), who was 17 years older than him and came from a respectable but impoverished bourgeois family.

Johannes was their second child, and two years later they had a third, Fritz, also a musician, who worked for a while as a music teacher in Venezuela and died in Hamburg on 5 November 1885. Johannes probably received his first musical training from his father, but at the age of seven he became a pupil of Otto F. W. Cossel, a piano teacher of some renown in the city, under whom he quickly became a proficient pianist. When he was warmly applauded at a public concert in 1843, an American agent tried to engage him for a tour of the

USA as a child prodigy; but his teacher had the good sense to prevent this. When Cossel noticed the boy's eagerness to compose, he spoke to his own teacher Eduard Marxsen (1806–87), a former pupil of Ignaz Seyfried who was highly regarded in Hamburg both as pianist and composer and who in 1846 undertook Johannes's training in music theory. As his parents had only a modest income, the young Brahms took advantage of many opportunities to recommend his father as a musician for public and private functions. As composer and arranger for the small Alster Pavilion orchestra in which his father played, he soon gained experience in arranging music for small ensembles. Far from restricting his artistic development, this helped to train his sense of musical effect and developed his talent for improvisation. This background was to have a lasting impact on Brahms. Elements of light music, including salon music, were to come to the fore in his later works. Having been familiar with this popular idiom from his childhood, Brahms always accepted it and he had no reason to look down on it; his occasional evocations in later works, like the Paganini Variations, of the bittersweet sound of coffee-house music show that he never forgot this style.

On 21 September 1848 Brahms gave his first solo concert as a pianist, and a second followed on 14 April 1849. At that time he was mainly studying the works of Bach and Beethoven as well as those of contemporary virtuosos including Thalberg and Herz. He was also composing intensively, and at Marxsen's suggestion sent a parcel of his compositions to Robert Schumann for his opinion; it came back unopened.

It has been suggested that Brahms was the composer

of a *Souvenir de la Russe* and some paraphrases of favourite themes from operas by Meyerbeer and others, issued under the name of G. W. Marks by the publisher Cranz of Hamburg, but this attribution has not been established. For a private recital at least, however, he is known to have used the pseudonym Karl Würth.

When the Austrians and Russians suppressed the Hungarian uprising in summer 1848 a stream of insurgents passed through Hamburg on their flight to North America, and some of them stayed on, bringing their music with them and starting a craze for all things Hungarian, which was exploited both for commercial reasons and in order to show sympathy for the rebels. So it was that Brahms perforce came in contact with the *csárdás* and the *alla zingarese* style which were mistaken in Germany for original Hungarian folk music, and thus early in his artistic development encountered the strange world of irregular rhythms and the feeling for triplet figures that were to make such an impression on his later work. Among the refugees was one of the most important interpreters of this music, the Hungarian violinist Eduard Hoffmann (1828–98), known by the name of Reményi (the Hungarian equivalent for 'Hoffmann'), who had studied in Vienna. In 1850 he gave a concert in Hamburg that captivated the 17-year-old Brahms whom, on his return from the USA three years later, he persuaded to accompany him on a concert tour; Brahms learnt at first hand from Reményi how to play *alla zingarese* and to use rubato in ensemble playing.

Their tour began on 19 April 1853 and took them (by way of several stops) first to Hanover, where Brahms met the violinist Joseph Joachim at the end of May. Joachim

6. *Johannes Brahms, c1850*

at once recognized his exceptional creative gifts and established a lifelong friendship with him. His description of the young Brahms was 'pure as diamond, soft as snow'. Early in July Brahms and Reményi travelled to Weimar, where Liszt entertained them at the Altenburg. Here Liszt played Brahms's E♭ minor Scherzo op.4 at sight from the manuscript.

Brahms soon realized that his musical world was diametrically opposed to the artistic strivings of Liszt and the 'New German School'. According to Heuberger he was very critical of them in letters to his parents at this time. He gave Heuberger a summary of his impressions:

First of all I stayed with Liszt, but I soon discovered that I was of no use there. This was just at his most successful time when he was writing the 'symphonic poems' and all that stuff, and soon it all came to horrify me. After all, I was a determined fellow then and I knew what I wanted. I left a couple of weeks later, and whenever we have met since, although we have outwardly seemed to be on perfectly friendly terms, it has been as though a barrier has sprung up between us.

Kalbeck suggested that Brahms spent barely more than 'two or at the most three weeks' with Liszt at the Altenburg. Probably the visit lasted little more than 12 days. Later he justified his abrupt departure with the explanation that he 'should have had to lie, and that was impossible'. After also parting from Reményi, who remained with Liszt and became one of his intellectual disciples, Brahms returned to Joachim in Göttingen. Joachim encouraged his young friend in his artistic ideals and suggested that he visit Robert Schumann, with whom he had just become acquainted. Brahms first went on a long walking tour in the Rhineland, making the acquaintance of several musicians (including Joseph Wasielewski, Ferdinand Hiller and Franz Wüllner) and then familiarizing himself with Schumann's music during a stay at the country estate at Mehlem owned by Deichmann, a financier in Cologne. Finally, at Wasielewski's insistence, he summoned the courage to visit Schumann in Düsseldorf on 30 September 1853. Schumann, deeply impressed both with Brahms's compositions and with his unusually expressive piano playing,

81

greeted this 'young eagle' with the famous and prophetic article entitled 'Neue Bahnen' in the *Neue
Zeitschrift für Musik*. In fact this exaggerated com-
mendation created more opposition than support for
the young Brahms, who at the time was still unknown;
it was not representative of Schumann's genuine vision.

Although Brahms had become accustomed to flattery
and encouragement whenever he appeared in public,
recognition from such an authoritative source
represented both a duty and a burden to him. He
returned to Hamburg, but when he heard of Schumann's
nervous breakdown the following February his friendship for the family sent him back to Düsseldorf to help
them. On this visit his devotion to Clara Schumann,
who was 14 years his senior, grew into a romantic
passion. Clara was not to see her husband again until
immediately before his death at the end of July 1856.
She fell into financial difficulties and soon, in desperation, had to give public concerts to support herself.
Brahms took charge of her household during this
period, and his close contact with the woman he so
admired brought him into a highly precarious situation.
He maintained his relationship with Schumann and
sorted through his library; he also adopted the artistic
thinking and designs of the older composer. The 16
Variations in F♯ minor op.9, which date from this tense,
depressing time, are rooted in Schumann's intellectual
world; Brahms chose a theme from his *Bunte Blätter*
op.99 and added to the autograph the suggestive dedication 'Variationen über ein Thema von Ihm – Ihr
zugeeignet'. The work is filled with enigmatic references.
Brahms seems to be poised silently between the theme
and the dedication, with the music as the only means of

expressing his feelings. He later called this period his 'Wertherzeit', thus indicating the emotional upheavals that he was experiencing over Clara. Each separation from her brought him new anguish and heartbreak. On 31 May 1856, two months before Schumann's death, he wrote to her exultantly: 'My beloved Clara . . . You are so infinitely dear to me, dearer than I can say. I should like to spend the whole day calling you endearing names and paying you compliments without ever being satisfied . . . Your letters are like kisses'.

After Schumann's death, on 29 July 1856, Brahms went through a period of desperate calf-love for Clara (playing Werther to her unwitting Charlotte), to which he himself cautiously referred later in life. At first he buried himself in technical composition studies, but the following year he apparently declared his love to Clara. When she moved to her mother's house in Berlin in September 1857 Brahms returned to Hamburg, where he was to live for the next few years; on the way he spent four months in Detmold (a visit which he repeated in the autumns of the two following years), working as court pianist, chamber musician and conductor of the court choir. He also found many opportunities to conduct the court orchestra, consisting of about 45 players, and so learnt the rudiments of orchestral technique: his two orchestral serenades opp.11 and 16 represent the outcome. He spent March and April of 1858 in Berlin, so as to see Clara Schumann again, but in the summer of that year in Göttingen he met and fell in love with Agathe von Siebold, a professor's daughter, and seriously considered marriage. This came to nothing, but it helped Brahms to recover from his earlier passion, and Agathe inspired him to write a number of deeply felt compositions, including the lieder in folksong style opp.14, 19 and 20. Later, with the three calls of *A–G–A–(T–)H–E* in the second theme group of the first movement of his G major Sextet, he ensured that her name would go down to posterity.

II Hamburg, 1859–62

Brahms settled in Hamburg in 1859 and that year founded a women's chorus; it could be augmented to 40 voices when necessary and it continued until his departure from Hamburg. He arranged folksongs and wrote original compositions for these ladies and also for a smaller women's chorus of 12 voices. On 30 April 1860 Brahms jokingly gave his chorus a set of ancient statutes, the style of which betrays his intensive study of Mattheson's old treatises on music theory in the city library. When Clara Schumann went to Hamburg to give three guest concerts, on 15 and 16 January and 16 November 1861, a group from Brahms's women's chorus performed with her. Brahms attached little importance to his work with this group, in spite of the pleasurable companionship it gave, or to the arrangements he made for it. He later revised and published a number of the original works – 12 Songs and Romances op.44 – and in 1894 rewrote some others for solo voice and piano.

In 1858 Brahms completed his Piano Concerto in D minor op.15, which was begun as early as 1854 and had since then undergone much revision. His first performance of it in Hanover on 22 January 1859 was a *succès d'estime*, but when he repeated it five days later in Leipzig, where everyone was eagerly awaiting the young virtuoso, it was a striking failure. As a result the first

Hamburg performance (24 March 1860), with Brahms's father playing the double bass and his family sitting in the stalls, was all the more welcome as a personal and financial success for the young composer. At this time Brahms entertained justifiable hopes for his artistic future, but he did not realize how difficult a path he had chosen by not enlisting the support of the musical establishment.

In 1857 he and Joachim had declared their opposition to the policies of the New German School. When the Allgemeine Deutsche Musikverein was founded, the circle around Liszt and Brendel became a closely knit, powerful and influential party whose members resented Brahms's aloofness the more since they regarded him as by far the strongest creative talent. When he was in Leipzig for the disastrous performance of his D minor Piano Concerto, he avoided visiting Liszt and Brendel, although this was expected of him. The *Neue Zeitschrift für Musik* nevertheless very properly rebuked the Leipzig public, thereby making it possible for Brahms to relent; but in March 1860 he, Joachim, J. O. Grimm and Bernhard Scholz signed a 'declaration' dissociating themselves completely from the artistic and aesthetic principles of Liszt and his circle. They thus chose the more honourable path, but also a thornier one, as Brahms was soon to discover. In summer 1860 he offered Breitkopf & Härtel the publication of his Piano Concerto, both serenades, the *Begräbnisgesang* and *Ave Maria*, but all were refused except for the first serenade. Rieter & Biedermann in Winterthur took the other works, and Simrock simultaneously brought out the second serenade. Brahms was now in need of public recognition, for he had his heart set on succeeding

Friedrich Wilhelm Grund as conductor of the Hamburg Philharmonic Concerts when the latter was expected to retire in October 1860, on the occasion of his 70th birthday. To this period belong the B♭ Sextet (completed in 1860), the Variations on a Theme by Handel and the four-hand Variations on a Theme by Schumann, the first two parts of the *Magelone* song cycle and the renewal of work on the *German Requiem*, which he had started during his stay in Düsseldorf in 1857.

In his D minor Piano Concerto op.15 Brahms sought to reconcile the symphonic and concerto principles; the piano part, rather than always taking the foreground, is integrated into the orchestral texture. The concerto thus seems to demonstrate Brahms's rejection of Liszt's concerto style more effectively than his signature on the public declaration against the 'New Germans'. In reply to the scathing review in the *Leipziger Signale*, Carl G. P. Grädener explained in the *Neue Berliner Musikzeitung* (29 June 1859) that Brahms had written a 'symphony-concerto', a 'symphony with obbligato piano', without a 'hint of a virtuoso or salon manner'.

In June 1862 Brahms attended the Rhine Music Festival in Cologne, combining with this a visit to Clara Schumann in Münster am Stein. Here he began work on the F minor Quintet, which he completed in 1864. By July he was back in Hamburg. Growing appreciation spurred him on to creative effort, and the prospects of succeeding Grund seemed favourable. In order to avoid possible official misgivings over a local appointment, he decided impulsively but wisely to go to Vienna, since there, in the musical capital of Europe, he could establish an unassailable artistic reputation that would enable the Hamburg senate to summon him back from beyond their city walls. On 8 September 1862 he left his native city in good spirits, little suspecting that he would never again live there.

III First years in Vienna

After his arrival in Vienna, Brahms found several old friends from his Hamburg days and met others through Clara Schumann's introductions. He was soon accepted into artistic circles and won new friends through his music, especially the G minor and A major piano quartets. Among these were Julius Epstein and Joseph Hellmesberger, who was enthusiastic about Brahms's compositions and performed many of them with his quartet. Brahms's first public appearance on 16 October 1862 met with only limited success, which, however, turned into friendly acknowledgment at his own concert on 29 November. An important factor in his later development was his acquaintance with Otto Dessoff, director of the Philharmonic Concerts, whose orchestral work and conducting technique Brahms took as his model. His meeting and friendship with Carl Tausig inspired the composition of his Variations on a Theme by Paganini, both an artistic gesture and one of professional respect to an already established musician.

Brahms's hopes for the Hamburg post, however, were not fulfilled. On 6 March 1863, at his last concert, Grund publicly handed his baton to the young singer Julius Stockhausen, who on 6 May sponsored a charity concert at which he sang and conducted, thereby ensuring a decision in his favour. On 1 May Brahms had left Vienna to celebrate his 30th birthday with his family, but when news of the situation in Hamburg reached him he retreated to the suburb of Blankensee to work on the cantata *Rinaldo*. Before the month was out he was recalled to Vienna to succeed Ferdinand Stegmayer, who had died on 6 May, as director of the Vienna Singakademie; he accepted the position, although elected by only 39 votes to 38.

On 28 September 1863 Brahms held his first rehearsal as director. As funds were low he had to confine himself to *a cappella* works, and began on a course of study of early music by composers such as Eccard, Schütz, Gabrieli, Rovetta and Bach, without neglecting more recent works by, for example, Beethoven and Mendelssohn. Without any initiative on his part, he was drawn into the long-standing rivalry with the Vienna Singverein and its director Johann Herbeck, a match for Brahms as a conductor if not as a composer. To enhance his reputation, Brahms put on a concert on 17 April of his own works – choral music, the B♭ Sextet, the Sonata for two pianos (the first version of the F minor Quintet) – which, as it consisted entirely of new compositions, did not meet with wholehearted applause. It did however serve to introduce Brahms to the Viennese public as a powerful creative artist, and above all it clearly showed the directions in which his musical future lay. Growing difficulties in his new post, not least its considerable administrative burden, caused him to relinquish it after only one season.

More out of kindness than because of financial pressure, he started giving piano lessons; and through them he made some lifelong friends, among them Freiherr von Stockhausen's daughter Elisabeth. Later, when she married, Brahms unselfishly helped the career of her husband Heinrich von Herzogenberg, a composer.

Brahms became acquainted with Wagner through

Cornelius and Tausig. According to the account in Wagner's autobiography, the two composers first met late in 1862, probably on several occasions, when Brahms was involved in preparing performing material for Wagner's concerts on 26 December that year and 1 and 11 January 1863 (this is confirmed by a written instruction from Wagner to Tausig, now in the Bayreuth Archive). Wagner was apparently struck by Brahms's extremely retiring manner. Their meeting on 6 February 1864 (mentioned by Kalbeck) seems to have been their last; this took place at Penzing near Schönbrunn, where Wagner had rented Baron von Rochow's country house. In 1869, fearing Brahms's rivalry in the field of opera, Wagner attacked him in a periodical article 'Über das Dirigieren' with such vehemence that he set up insurmountable barriers between them; only Brahms's restraint prevented open conflict. In mid-June 1864 he returned to Hamburg to try to save his parents' marriage which, not least because of the great difference in their ages, was threatening to break up; but his efforts were in vain. A few weeks later in Baden-Baden he met the young Hermann Levi, then Kapellmeister in Karlsruhe, and became one of his closest friends for a time. In the following years Levi was to be one of the most important and effective promoters of Brahms's compositions. Their association came to an end in 1875 when Levi, in his capacity as a conductor, was acting increasingly as a champion of Wagner's works. In exchange Brahms won the friendship and support of Hans von Bülow, who was deeply disillusioned with Wagner and was turning his back on him.

On 31 January 1865 Brahms's mother died, and he attended her funeral; he commemorated her in the sombre

Adagio mesto of the Horn Trio op.40 with the allusion from the folksong *Dort in der Weiden steht ein Haus*. In October of the same year his father announced his marriage to Caroline Schnack, a widow 18 years his junior, who had a son of her own. Brahms remained on good terms with her all his life, and after his father's death provided for her and for her sickly son.

Brahms's stay in Vienna was frequently interrupted by concert tours – alone, or with Joachim and Julius Stockhausen, though this kind of music-making was little to Brahms's taste – which took him not only to Germany and Austria but to every town of musical importance in Hungary, Switzerland, Denmark and the Netherlands. After 1868, the year he settled permanently in Vienna, Brahms restricted his tours to performances of his own works. If he still nursed a secret hope for the Hamburg appointment, the fact that he had been passed over once again in 1867, when Stockhausen's successor was named, must have destroyed it for good. He had meanwhile become a composer of European standing; and though he made no serious attempt to secure the Hamburg post, it must have hurt him that he was not even consulted over the appointment. In April 1894 he was offered the post of conductor of the Philharmonic Concerts in succession to Bernuth, but this was only a shamefaced gesture of reparation to a man who was already a freeman of Hamburg. He refused, and did not conceal his disappointment with his native city.

That he was still keen to obtain an official appointment is clear from his interest in succeeding Ernst Rudorff at the Cologne Conservatory, and his inquiries about the nature of Max Bruch's duties as

Hofkapellmeister in Sondershausen when the latter left in 1870. An established position was closely bound up in his mind with the idea of being a 'decent, middle-class citizen', as he wrote to Klaus Groth, and this he felt was a prerequisite for a happy marriage and family life; and so he tried once more to obtain one, though obviously he found it hard to do so. When Herbeck resigned from the Vienna Gesellschaftskonzerte in 1870, Brahms was immediately considered as a successor on the orchestral side; but he declined the nomination, and not until nearly three years later, in September 1872, was he persuaded to change his mind, on condition that he would also conduct the chorus. His father had died on 11 February 1872, and his realization that the last real link with Hamburg had gone may have prompted this decision. The fact that he was also moving into new lodgings, at Karlsgasse no.4, indicates that he had resolved to make Vienna his permanent home. He was to stay in this humble two-roomed flat for the remaining 25 years of his life.

IV Middle years in Vienna

Brahms used this post, like the previous one, to introduce great Baroque works to the Viennese public, and embarked on a course of concerts of music by Bach and Handel without, however, arousing great enthusiasm in his audience. When he conducted his first concert on 10 November 1872, there were no amateurs in the orchestra, as there had been formerly: he now had at his disposal the court opera orchestra, a professional body led by Joseph Hellmesberger. At first he proved brilliant as a conductor, but his choices of programme had a mixed reception. Though he did not neglect contem-

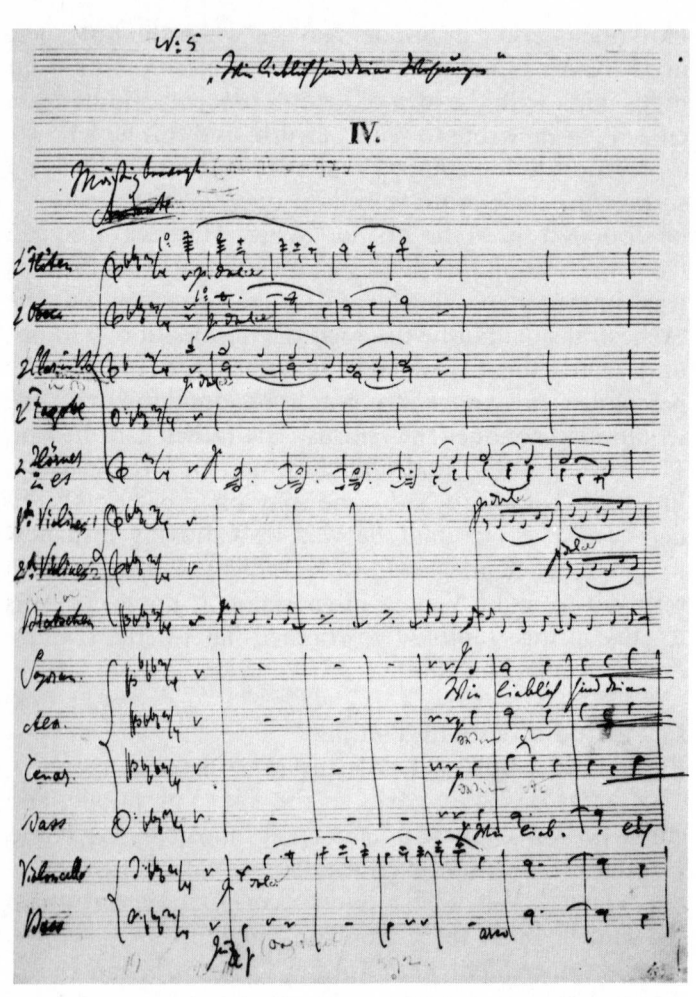

7. Autograph MS of the opening of 'Wie lieblich sind deine Wohnungen' from Brahms's 'German Requiem' composed 1857–68

porary works, Brahms was particularly enthusiastic in presenting early music by such composers as Handel, Bach, Eccard and Isaac. Hanslick commented sneeringly: 'Here, as little as anywhere else, they present concerts with the express purpose of having themselves buried first in the Protestant manner and then in the Catholic manner'. In spite of his thoroughly successful work as conductor of the Gesellschaftskonzerte, Brahms was conscious that he was not qualified to hold such a post permanently. There followed struggles behind the scenes, with concealed animosities and veiled criticisms, particularly from his predecessor, Herbeck, who was now a member of the artistic advisory board. Brahms resigned from his post in 1875, more relieved than disappointed, giving as his reason simply Herbeck, who he said had deliberately hindered the development of his career (see Kalbeck). He took his leave on 18 April with a performance of Bruch's *Odysseus* and never took up a permanent appointment again. Brahms was wise to resign: he had not failed through his conducting ability, his choices of programme, or the intrigue, but simply because the age had passed when a composer could also succeed as a conductor. Composer–conductors could no longer hold their own in the rising generation of virtuoso conductors, which included Hans Richter, Hermann Levi, Felix Mottl and Franz Muck.

Brahms's decision to resign from the Gesellschaftskonzerte was no agonizing step; rather, it corresponded with his most intense longing: to compose. By now he was internationally famous, with over 60 opus numbers, including many major works, to his credit. In 1868 his real choral masterpiece, the *German Requiem* op.45, was finished. It had been begun in 1857 as the idea for a concerto in D minor, and had passed through various stages of development during 1860 and 1861. The real impetus to finish it came out of Brahms's shock at the death of his mother, and in February 1865 he had taken up the work again and finished the first five movements while staying in Karlsruhe, Winterthur and Zurich. He completed it in Zurich and Baden-Baden in August 1866, but added another movement (later inserted as the fifth) in Hamburg in May 1868. While early performances of parts of the *Requiem*, such as that of three movements conducted by Herbeck in Vienna on 1 December 1867, had a deep effect on the public, the completed *Requiem* was acclaimed as a work of heroic, monumental stature when it was performed in 1871 in Bremen, Cologne, Wiesbaden and Karlsruhe, and its composer was hailed by the public as a patriot. Brahms confirmed this opinion by composing the 'patriotic' Lieder op.41 in 1861 and the *Triumphlied* op.55, completed in summer 1871 in commemoration of the Franco-Prussian War and dedicated to the emperor.

In summer 1873, on the Starnberger See, Brahms completed his most popular work, the Variations on a Theme by Haydn op.56. In its orchestral version, it was rapturously applauded at its première, and from then on Brahms suffered no more serious artistic setbacks. He was also financially secure, living on the revenue from his concerts and amassing a considerable capital from the growing royalties on his compositions. Fritz Simrock, Brahms's main publisher, had become sole head of his firm on his father's death in 1868, and when in 1870 he moved to Berlin he tried to persuade Brahms to enter into a lifelong contract with him. But the composer was circumspect enough to foresee the implications of such a long-term commitment, and refused: although he could well have lived off his compositions, he was unwilling to submit to the dictates of a monopolizing publisher, even one who was a personal friend. Simrock would never agree to pay him according to the sales of his works instead of with a lump sum.

Honours began to pour in from abroad. In May 1876 G. F. Cobb proposed to the senate of Cambridge University that Brahms and Joachim, among others, should be given honorary doctorates in music; but Brahms refused, and did so again when Cambridge renewed the offer in 1892. Joachim, however, accepted on 7 March 1877, and when he went to Cambridge to receive his degree that year he took with him the score of Brahms's First Symphony in C minor op.68 and conducted it at the ensuing celebrations; the resemblance between the finale's horn theme and the 'Cambridge Chimes' of Great St Mary's was remarked. Work on this symphony had started in 1855, but the first movement was not finished until 1862 and the others were not completed until the summers of 1874, 1875 and 1876, in Rüschlikon, Zeigelhausen, Sassnitz, Hamburg and Lichtenthal. The première on 4 November 1876 in Karlsruhe under Dessoff, and Brahms's own repeat performance in Mannheim, became a miniature festival as many musicians had come from a distance to attend the events. The Munich public was much more reserved, accustomed as it was to the works of Lachner and Rheinberger, and thus unable to follow Brahms's symphonic writing. Vienna received the symphony kindly, however, when Brahms conducted it there on 17 December as a guest of the Gesellschaftskonzerte, of which Herbeck was again the director.

In 1876 the authorities in Düsseldorf opened serious negotiations with Brahms over their projected music academy; they had hoped to appoint a person of note as city music director in the place of the mediocre Julius Tausch, who had been head of the Musikverein there since Schumann's death. In the end, Brahms declined, partly because the terms of the appointment were not sufficiently well defined and partly because of his former unfortunate experiences with official posts.

The years 1877–9 were among Brahms's most productive. In January 1877 he gave concerts in Leipzig, where the Herzogenbergs had settled in 1872: the group of faithful Brahms enthusiasts they had gathered round them were supported by the devoted and reliable Carl Reinecke, who had come to Leipzig as conductor of the Gewandhaus orchestra in 1860 and (on 18 February 1869) had conducted the first complete performance of the *German Requiem*. The reunion with his adored Elisabeth von Herzogenberg, whose singing Brahms greatly admired, may have released the great 'spring of song' of 1877, when he composed in the ensuing weeks no fewer than 18 songs of opp.69–72. The summer months of these three years found him in Pörtschach on the Wörthersee, where he composed the greater part of the D major Symphony and the motet *Warum ist das Licht gegeben*, in 1877–8 five of the eight piano pieces of op.76, in 1878 the Violin Concerto, in 1878–9 the G major Violin Sonata and in 1879 the Two Rhapsodies op.79. Between the spring of 1878 and 1893 he made eight journeys to Italy, accompanied each time by close friends; but although he adored the country, he was never drawn to compose in any Italian style.

On 11 March 1879 Brahms received an honorary doctorate from the University of Breslau. The wording of his citation 'Artis musicae severioris [!] in Germania nunc princeps' ('First among contemporary masters of serious music') brought a direct attack from Wagner in his article 'Über das Dichten und Komponieren', which Brahms ignored. Once again he did not attend the degree ceremony, but thanked the university with his slightly mocking Academic Festival Overture op.80, the première of which he conducted there on 4 January 1881. In the late summer of 1878 he was invited to the 50th anniversary celebrations of the Philharmonic Society in Hamburg, where his Symphony no.2 was enthusiastically received, and had the satisfaction of being fêted in his native city as a leading contemporary composer.

Brahms composed his Violin Concerto op.77 at Pörtschach in summer 1878, taking advice from Joachim on the technique of the solo violin part. The stature of this work matches the great models by Beethoven and Mendelssohn. Although Brahms spoke explicitly of the 'orchestral accompaniment', he succeeded in reconciling symphonic and concerto structures and in blending the solo and orchestral writing into a homogeneous texture; in spite of all its extended idiomatic passages and its immense technical difficulties, the solo part never acquires the character of a virtuoso display. When Clara Schumann heard the first movement in a private performance, she wrote that the orchestra and soloist were 'thoroughly blended' in the work. The première in Leipzig on 1 January 1879, which Brahms himself conducted, prompted respect rather than enthusiasm, however, and the Vienna performance on 14

97

January 1879 was similarly received with only polite applause. Even Brahms's friend Hanslick called the work a 'somewhat brittle invention' with the composer's 'imagination sailing at half-mast, so to speak'. It was not until the performance at Crystal Palace, London, on 22 February 1879, that the concerto was able to find acceptance and hold its own.

Brahms had by now established a routine of giving concerts in the winter and composing in the summer, but the number of works that he began in the winter months show that even he did not live to a schedule. In March 1880 he began work on piano trios in C major and E♭, but completed only the former, in Bad Ischl in June 1882. On 2 and 3 May 1880 he was in Bonn for the unveiling of the Schumann Memorial, the work of the sculptor Adolf Donndorf, and there met Clara Schumann, who had been a piano professor at the Frankfurt Conservatory since 1878. As he could no longer evade his lady admirers in Pörtschach, he spent the summer of 1880 in Bad Ischl, and from 1889 it was his favourite resort. There in 1882 he wrote the Quintet in F major op.88 and the *Gesang der Parzen* op.89. To Ischl also belong his Three Motets op.110, the Quintet in G major op.111 and all his works from the Clarinet Trio in A minor op.114 (1891) to the 11 Chorale Preludes op.122 (1896), with the exception of the *Vier ernste Gesänge* op.121, which he composed in Vienna in early May 1896.

V Meiningen and Vienna

1881 was important in Brahms's private life. His deep friendship with Clara Schumann had been troubled with minor misunderstandings, and now came a break with

Joachim; for Brahms, seeing his friend tormenting his wife with jealous and unfounded accusations, openly took her part. The rift was healed in 1887, but the old warmth never existed between them again. In February 1881 Bülow, who had been Intendant in Meiningen since 1 October of the previous year, performed Beethoven's last piano sonatas in Vienna, and his playing won him Brahms's instant friendship. Bülow offered Brahms the famous Meiningen court orchestra as a 'rehearsal orchestra', which Brahms immediately accepted. Towards the end of 1881 he went to Meiningen, and the concert of his works given there on 27 November, repeated in January 1882 at the Berlin Singakademie, started the Meiningen court orchestra's famous Brahms tradition. Bülow was not only important to Brahms as a colleague who could help to publicize his works and develop an authentic style of interpretation; he was also a worthy successor to Hermann Levi, who after meeting Wagner had joined his camp. While Levi felt drawn principally to Brahms's chamber works and less to his symphonic music, Bülow immediately recognized his First Symphony as the point of spiritual contact with the line of development from Beethoven's work that was eventually to lead to the Second Viennese School.

Brahms spent the next spring in Vienna, where the opp.84–6 lieder were published; and in Bad Ischl that summer he finished the C major Trio, as well as the F major Quintet and the *Gesang der Parzen* for chorus and orchestra, with which he thanked Duke Georg von Meiningen for bestowing an order on him. His acquaintance with the duke and duchess deepened into a close friendship that was to last for the rest of his life. A plan to spend summer 1883 in Bad Ischl was abruptly changed when the inspiration to compose his F major Symphony came to him during a trip to the Rhine at Whitsun. He rented accommodation in Wiesbaden, near his friends the Beckeraths, and after some preliminary drafts wrote the whole work without a pause. In Wiesbaden he met the young contralto Hermine Spies, and his interest in her both as an artist and as a woman resulted in a rich output of songs.

The security of knowing that in Meiningen he could work peacefully and privately with a first-rate orchestra may have contributed to his embarking on his last Symphony, in E minor, in summer 1884. After a peaceful stay as guest of the Duke of Meiningen in the Villa Carlotta at Cadenabbia on Lake Como, he returned to Mürzzuschlag near the Semmering Pass, where he wrote the first two movements, completing the remaining ones the next year. In October 1885 he rehearsed his new symphony privately in Meiningen, and immediately afterwards took the orchestra on tour through Germany and the Netherlands, performing the work in many towns.

The summer of 1886 was the first of three which Brahms spent at Hofstetten on Lake Thun. This was a summer of chamber music. The Vienna performance of his Cello Sonata in E minor op.38 by Robert Hausmann on 7 March 1885 spurred him into writing a second cello sonata, in F major (op.99), which he committed to paper at Lake Thun in August 1886; and in the same months he wrote the violin sonatas opp.100 and 108 and the Trio in C minor op.101. In 1887, after much hesitation (and with reservations), Brahms and Clara Schumann returned the letters they had written to each

8. *Johannes Brahms with Allgeyer and Hermann Levi*

other. At first Clara wanted to extract from Brahms's letters 'everything relating to his artistic or private life': 'I would put all this together, and then let him have the letters to destroy. But he would not hear of it, and so today I handed them over to him with tears' (Clara's diary, 16 October 1887). To that summer's compositions belong the *Zigeunerlieder* and the Double Concerto in A minor op.102, which had a critical, but not popular, success at its première in Cologne on 18 October. As in Pörtschach, the curiosity of the tourists spoilt the peace of this holiday for Brahms, and after the summer of 1888 (when he composed very little) he abandoned Hofstetten too. In Berne he met Hermine Spies again; they parted, with mutual affection.

From 1889, Brahms spent each summer in Ischl, where he entertained many of his friends and acquaintances. Two years earlier Kaiser Wilhelm had awarded him the 'Pour le Mérite' of the Order of Peace and now the Austrian emperor, passing over the lower grades, created him Commander of the Order of Leopold. Through the Bürgermeister, Dr Carl Petersen, Hamburg belatedly recognized his genius by making him a freeman of his native city. Brahms replied by dedicating to Hamburg his *Fest- und Gedenksprüche* op.109, which he conducted there on 14 September at the musical celebrations for the Hamburg Exhibition of Trade and Industry.

Brahms had by now privately resolved to lay aside his pen. In October 1890 he wrote to Simrock that 'on leaving Ischl' he had 'thrown a lot of torn-up manuscript paper into the Traun' once he had finished the Quintet op.111, and had gone no further with his plans to compose a fifth symphony on his journey to Italy in the

spring. He put his house in order, destroying everything
unusable and dealing with incomplete or abandoned
works; from this clearance came the 13 Canons op.113
(of which nos.1, 2, 8, 10, 11 and 12 had appeared in the
music books of his Hamburg women's chorus), the 51
piano studies (first drafted in 1863) and the 49 German
folksongs.

In 1891 Brahms met the clarinettist Richard
Mühlfeld, whose performances of one of Weber's concertos and Mozart's Clarinet Quintet so moved him that
he spent hours listening to him practising and studied all
the potentials and limitations of his instrument. During
summer 1891 in Ischl he wrote, very rapidly, the
Clarinet Trio in A minor and the Clarinet Quintet in B
minor. By November Joachim and Mühlfeld were able
to play the trio with him in Meiningen and on 12
December both pieces received their premières at the
Berlin Singakademie, with Joachim's quartet (it was on
this occasion that A. von Menzel made his famous ink
drawing of Mühlfeld). Two years later, in summer 1894,
Brahms added to these works the pair of clarinet sonatas
in F minor and E♭ op.120, and with these four works
for 'Fräulein Klarinette', as he called it, ended instrumental composition. Even at this late stage the connection
with Meiningen elicited from him some of his most
valuable instrumental works. He must have been aware
of the place he held in the estimation of his contemporaries when Fritz Steinbach compiled programmes for
the Meiningen Music Festival of 27–9 September 1895
consisting solely of works by Bach, Beethoven and
Brahms – the highest possible tribute to a living composer.

In spring 1896 Clara Schumann, who had been suf-

fering from increasing deafness for some years and had
had two strokes, lay dying. When Brahms heard of her
death on 20 May, he left Ischl at once for Bonn to attend
her funeral and follow her coffin. Perhaps the first drafts
of the *Vier ernste Gesänge* were inspired by his emotions over her illness; but he dedicated them to Max
Klinger. In June Brahms's friends noticed a change in his
complexion. He himself thought it was due to a passing
attack of jaundice, and the doctors kept from him the
true diagnosis of cancer of the liver, the illness that had
also caused his father's death. He went to Karlsbad in
September for treatment, but in vain, and by 26 March
1897 he had deteriorated noticeably and was bedridden,
cared for by Frau Celestine Truxa. He died in Vienna
on 3 April, at 8.30 a.m. On 6 April he was buried in
the central cemetery in Vienna, amid crowds of mour-
ners and messages of sorrow from all over Europe, especially Germany. In Hamburg all the ships lowered their
flags to half-mast.

VI   Character and personality
Brahms could treat his fellow men with the most sensitive consideration and wound his closest friends with
callous disregard. Even though he presented himself as a
sociable, convivial person, his true nature was revealed
only in the solitude that he so vitally needed; when he
was alone and unobserved he could overcome those
innate inhibitions that he disguised with jests and light-
heartedness in company. 'Brahms was basically very
reserved indeed. His deepest feelings were his own and
no one else's. Anything which smacked of sentiment he
abhorred, and said so'; thus Rosa Lumpe characterized
him to Helene von Vesque. Clara Schumann, who knew

him more intimately than anyone else, remarked to Max Kalbeck in 1880: 'To me he is as much a riddle – I might almost say as much a stranger – as he was 25 years ago.' When he dedicated the *Vier ernste Gesänge* to Max Klinger and not to Clara, whose final illness inspired their composition, he betrayed his deep-rooted reluctance to reveal his inner self, a reluctance also manifested towards the end of his life in the rigorous destruction of manuscripts and notes. It is possible that the ambivalence of Brahms's character also governed his thinking as an artist, expressing itself in conflicts often inexplicably intense; but it is certain that his achievements as a composer are not made accessible by detailed knowledge of his biography. Extraneous events and spiritual encounters did in fact occasionally influence his compositions and his creative genius; but in no way could he be called a self-centred programmatic composer, one who wrote into his work the soul-felt emotions of his life as an artist. When Peter Cornelius noted in his diary in 1864 that Brahms was a 'quite egotistical, self-satisfied man', he was not wrong, but had grasped only one thread of the fabric of Brahms's personality. How, as a matter of course, he took over his parents' household when their marriage foundered, the selflessness with which he looked after his stepmother and her son to the end of his life without making any fuss, the generosity with which he helped friends and strangers alike and the willingness to further the careers of younger musicians (such as Dvořák) are enough to contradict such a one-sided view.

Although he always ended by acting on his own decisions, Brahms constantly asked friends such as Joachim, Clara Schumann and Elisabeth von

Herzogenberg for artistic advice: he needed their opinions through which to arrive at his own conclusions. Artistic failures may have disappointed him, but they never threw him off course. One advantage he had over his friends, and not only those in Vienna, was his 'misspent youth', as Billroth once described it. His first-hand knowledge of the underworld in the port of Hamburg gave him another pair of eyes through which to view the world about him. He himself once described the significance of these youthful impressions: 'Anything which was dear to me in my youth has remained so ever since, and I have never been able to consider or judge it differently'. Brahms was by origin a man of the people; perhaps he never did succeed in truly breaking down the barriers that guarded the elegant society into which he entered lightly and easily – this he had in common with Beethoven. The casual remark, 'A fellow who pleases the aristocracy is bound to be a good-for-nothing', is not contradicted by his dedicating the *Triumphlied* to Emperor Wilhelm. People and patriotism were to him the same thing; this attachment to his country also explains his love not only of German but of all folk music.

Brahms was unquestionably a fanatic champion of justice, a quality which occasionally dulled his insight. He always felt himself obliged to behave chivalrously, according to a personal code of honour that he placed even above friendships and which also helps to explain his blind patriotism. His reverence for Bismarck was so ingrained that he used his adages almost as daily precepts.

Although Brahms had basically a reserved nature, this did not prevent him from expecting to be at the

9. Johannes Brahms with Alice Barbi in the Ringstrasse, Vienna, 1892

centre of any group and to enjoy that position. The so-called 'Brahms faction' was forced to submit to him, as he shunned anyone who disrupted his train of thought with contradictory viewpoints; but he was a peaceable man at heart, and he always found the strength to resolve differences with those he knew were personally devoted to him. Nevertheless, he remained the absolute master of his world.

Brahms was never 'religious', in the strict sense of the word, but in the humane sense he was a Christian. The habits which outlasted his childhood included reading from the children's Bible he was given in the year of his birth and from which he compiled the texts for his sacred choral works. He read it constantly; to the end of his life it remained his book of books, and his correspondence is astonishing for its subtle grasp of problems in the scriptures. His personal religious viewpoint was logically thought out, as shown in his confessional *German Requiem*, which suppresses the eschatological objectives of the Christian faith in favour of a pious orientation to this world. 'Life steals more from one than does death', he remarked once about himself. K. M. Rheintaler tried to persuade him to add an appropriate movement to bring the *Requiem* nearer the spirit of Good Friday; Brahms politely but firmly refused, and the final passages of the work are dominated not by a vision of merciless death but by comfort for those who are left to mourn.

Only some unknown youthful trauma can explain Brahms's attitude to women. At 20 he had the 'face of a child which any girl could kiss without a blush' (as Hedwig von Holstein put it) but was already that object of feminine passion and curiosity that he was to be – and enjoy being – throughout his life. His veneration for Clara Schumann was undoubtedly a deep emotion which was reciprocated, to judge by her jealousy of Elisabeth von Herzogenberg, who was 28 years her junior, many years later. Brahms's tempestuous love for a woman 14 years older than himself mellowed with the years into a calmer and eventually cooler friendship that Brahms respected most chivalrously. His flight from

Düsseldorf was symbolic of this aspect of his life, for he also abandoned Agathe von Siebold at a decisive moment and literally fled from Elisabeth von Herzogenberg, to whom he had lost his head when she was only 16. He eventually lost touch with Agathe but his friendship with Elisabeth continued until his death. She alone represented a real and serious threat to his relationship with Clara Schumann. Characteristically he was surer of himself in the company of married women, with whom he could act more freely and without risking involvement – ultimately a sign of his inner insecurity. The same applies to his first Viennese sweetheart Bertha Porubszky, with whom (when she was Frau Faber) he remained friendly all his life; he spent every Christmas eve with her family until, in his last years, Maria Fellinger took over this loving task. Apart from Clara Schumann, all the objects of his adulation were singers – Agathe, Elisabeth, Bertha and even his idol of the 1880s, Hermine Spies, for whose affections he competed with Klaus Groth. Hermine's letters show how she longed for Brahms to declare himself, but he withdrew. He recovered relatively quickly from these attachments, and Alice Barbi, another singer, who was the sweetheart of his last years, played only an ephemeral role in his affections; by this time Brahms was beyond good and evil.

Works

I Piano music

Brahms's output of instrumental music is not as great as his output of vocal works but it spans his entire creative life, from the Scherzo in E♭ minor op.4 in 1851 to the Two Clarinet Sonatas op.120 of 1894. The piano was his starting-point, as the list of his works clearly shows. First came the E♭ minor Scherzo, the three piano sonatas, the Schumann Variations op.9 and the Four Ballades op.10; these were followed by the Scherzo for violin and piano in 1853 and the B major Piano Trio (all his few early chamber works include the piano). This contention is of course based on only the works which have survived. In 'Neue Bahnen' (1853) Robert Schumann mentioned songs and string quartets, but even these could not disturb the balance among his early works in favour of piano compositions.

After the Waltzes op.39, composed in 1865, there followed a break of seven years during which Brahms composed only vocal music. His composing for the piano in fact ceased soon after he moved to Vienna; for a full 15 years he wrote no music for solo piano, unless during those years he was making drafts of some of the pieces which form the late piano collections opp.116–19. In 1879 he completed the op.79 rhapsodies, and between 1891 and 1893 the fantasias, intermezzos, capriccios, romance, ballade and rhapsody of opp.116–

19. Brahms's piano music, then, seems to encircle his life's work rather than permeate it.

His three piano sonatas opp.1, 2 and 5 were all written before the artistic departures of 1853, and thereafter he wrote only variations, rhapsodies, fantasias, intermezzos or, quite simply, piano pieces; the term 'sonata' was otherwise used only in conjunction with a solo instrument, as for instance the violin sonatas (1879, 1886 and 1888), the cello sonatas (1865 and 1886) and the clarinet sonatas (1894). These later instrumental sonatas were inspired by extraneous circumstances, so that the assumption is justified that he had little further interest in sonata form as an abstract musical concept. That he took to writing ballades, intermezzos (the fourth movement of his F minor Sonata is also an intermezzo) and fantasias showed that he was moving towards freer forms, though not towards formlessness; it was no whim of youthful genius that made him abandon the piano sonata in 1854. The influence of Schumann, who preferred the tone poem or *Fantasiestück* to the sonata, doubtless played a part in what was mainly a reflection of the artist's sensitivity to changing taste. Sonata form was to Brahms more a framework for his music than, as with Beethoven, a structure that not merely contained but actually expressed the music. Where Beethoven preferred the presentation of two themes whose nature and contrast provided the material for the musical action in which the essence of the movement resided, Brahms was content to allow his themes to be varied even in the exposition, as if the essence of the music lay in them rather than in the structure they brought about. In spite of his addiction to taut forms, he was no apologist for Goethe's 'disciplined imagination'. The fact that the slow movement of op.1 is based on a folksong, *Verstohlen geht der Mond auf*, is a significant comment on Brahms's conception of a cyclical work. It was no coincidence that in his ballades and rhapsodies he was developing two different genres of music that belonged to the beginning of musical Romanticism and were used as more or less identical descriptions for works that could not be strictly classified as sonatas or overtures. They were primarily the opposite of the Classical sonata and seemed mainly to represent to Brahms an unregimented music, committed to no particular system. The terms 'balladic' and 'rhapsodic' in Brahms's sense do not mean haphazard but untrammelled – without pattern or arbitrary form.

The real instrumental ballade, particularly the piano ballade, can be linked to the prototype of the *Lied ohne Worte* or perhaps more significantly to the piano rhapsody as developed by Tomášek in 1813. There is in fact no sharp dividing line between ballade and rhapsody, and Brahms's Two Rhapsodies op.79, though they flirt with sonata form, are rightly regarded as the spiritual successors of his early piano ballades. Chopin was the first composer to make the piano ballade a respectable genre; his last, in F minor op.52, is regarded by many as his greatest work. Chopin's ballades are not introverted and self-consuming, but embrace the listener, whereas the audience is not essential to Brahms's ballades (although they are excellent recital pieces) – sound, but not elegant, piano music. The four ballades of op.10 are so basically different from one another that one wonders whether they should share one opus number. By comparing the tune of the first one, *Edward*, with the poem that inspired it, one sees that Brahms was wholly attracted by the poetic structure of his literary pattern without imitating it in detail. All four are in ternary form, but not structurally alike, though in each the component parts are clearly contrasted through tempo changes and other techniques of piano music. The second ballade, in D, is in five separate sections – lyric, dramatic, bucolic, dramatic, lyric. The third is sub-titled 'Intermezzo' and, in spite of its contrasting middle section, is in fact built on a single theme. The fourth is not in song form, but is built on a tripartite *ABC* structure, with only an apparent reference to the opening section just before the third. This scheme is characteristic of all ballades, but within it the constituent parts must be well-knit and closely constructed. Brahms varied the individual sections and decorated their motifs and themes with technical skill, but always left their essential form untouched, whereas in sonata technique the elaboration of individual elements features independently of the cohesive whole.

Brahms first used the term 'rhapsody' in 1869 for a vocal work, the Alto Rhapsody op.53; by the time he used it again in 1879 (for the two piano works) it was already outdated, and served him simply as a way out of a dilemma. Immediately before the piano rhapsodies he wrote his Eight Piano Pieces op.76 – four capriccios and four intermezzos – and here too he encountered difficulties. When he sent them to Simrock for publication he wrote in desperation 'Can you think of a title?' 'Capriccio' may well be the best name for the second of this collection, which is a piquant and sparkling piece such as Brahms rarely wrote. 'Intermezzo' is actually nothing more than an umbrella term under which Brahms could collect anything which was neither capricious nor passionate. In his F minor Sonata the term 'intermezzo' is justified, as this movement is in the truest sense interpolated, as a tranquil, almost tender, reminiscence; in op.76 the best examples of the true intermezzo are nos.3 and 4.

Brahms originally wanted to call the B minor rhapsody 'Capriccio', showing how loosely he used such terms. Both rhapsodies are thrilling pieces, marked respectively 'agitato' and 'passionato' (terms Brahms also used for his capriccios), and closer study shows that only their emotional thematic content justifies their title. In spite of their different structures they adhere fairly strictly to sonata form, as witness not only the secondary passages in the dominant which, in textbook manner, appear in the tonic in the recapitulation, but above all the middle sections which are interspersed with developmental passages.

Perhaps the most important technique of development in Brahms's work is the variation. The art of extracting more and more variations out of given melodic material derives from traditional folklore, when this was a subject for musical competition; but joining a succession of variations to a cyclical whole and to a new and independent form is a comparatively recent development, deriving particularly from Brahms, in whose works one can distinguish both types – independent and integrated. All his piano variations belong to the former group – opp.9, 21, 23, 24, 35 and 56*b* (for two pianos) – and he also used the variation principle in the slow movements of his first two piano sonatas; but as he inserted extra passages and fanciful extensions, he could not describe these movements as variations. In the early variations, melody predominates over all other characteristics, so that little in the way of new thematic material appears. Even in op.21 the melody still reigns supreme; it is taken up by the bass, presented in a variant, its intervals are diminished and then augmented, but it always provides the substance for each variation.

The Schumann Variations op.9 betray Schumann's influence on Brahms from their meeting in 1853. His variation technique changed strikingly as his Classical models gave way to a freer conception of form, from which emerged fantasias that he did not call variations but which resemble the 'fantasia variation' in his op.1. In contrast to this early movement, even the tune in op.9 is often reproduced with alterations: the bass as well as the treble is prominent in some of the variations, but harmony is of secondary importance. Brahms wrote op.9 as a faithful disciple of Schumann, but his intensive research into the potentialities of the variation later gave him a very divergent conception. He rejected the free variation only tenuously connected to the theme, and by taking as his models Bach's Goldberg Variations and Beethoven's technique of thematic modification, he came to realize that the type of variation Beethoven developed did not arise from clinging to the melody and rhythm of the theme, but from its transformation into something new, based on its phrase structure and harmony. In the Variations on an Original Theme op.21 no.1, the essence of the theme is brought out in a different way in its individual mutations from that in which it is presented in op.9. Digressive changes of form and fanciful interpolations have gone. The phrase structure is more strictly adhered to and the harmony is as important as the melody. The bass has grown in importance, not only as a melodic line (as in op.9) but also as a harmonic bass. The same principle applies to the slow movement of the Sextet op.18. Brahms's insistence on the variation as an integral cycle is shown in the final sections of a variation movement, which always extends into its own independent chain of variations with a content equivalent to that of the preceding episodes.

For his Handel Variations op.24, Brahms chose a long fugue as a conclusion appropriate to his theme. This work, like the Paganini Variations op.35 no.1, was written specifically for the concert hall and both, especially the latter, are technically highly exacting; but in spite of this similarity, the two works present significant contrasts. For the Handel Variations Brahms chose a striking theme from the first suite in B♭ from the *Suites de pièces de clavecin* (1733); each variation contains its own transformation, but at the same time has a distinct character, such as the Baroque canon (no.6), the Hungarian rhapsody (no.13), the siciliano (no.19) and the chromatic fantasia (no.20). For the Paganini Variations he chose a stiff, stereotyped theme with a strong, incisive rhythm. He wrote this work under the influence of Tausig's playing, and called it 'studies for the piano', which shows that he intended it as the didactic, technical work which in fact it is.

II Chamber music without piano

Brahms could express himself easily on the piano but he hesitated to plunge into an unfamiliar medium; he asked Joachim for an opinion of his string compositions before rehearsing them thoroughly and finally committing them to print. His horror of immature work resulted in his public image as an accomplished composer from the

116

start. The earliest work, a Scherzo in C minor for violin
and piano, has no opus number and was withdrawn
from publication, indicating that Brahms was not
prepared to acknowledge it. The first chamber music
work he published was the Piano Trio in B major op.8
(1853–4), one of the few early works that he later revised.
A comparison of the two versions shows that the
original was indeed more youthful, more vigorous or
'wilder', as he described it, but certainly no less artis-
tically accomplished than the revised version of 1889.
In 1853 Schumann encouraged his young friend to publish some manusci ipt trios, but Brahms refused, for he saw
them simply as studies. 20 years passed before Brahms,
after countless attempts, was ready to give the public his
first string quartets. Meanwhile he remained faithful to
the piano.

After many false starts with string quartets, he turned
to the string sextet. The success of his first sextet, op.18 in
B♭, encouraged him a few years later to embark on a
second, op.36 in G major; probably because of the ter-
mination of his relationship with Agathe von Siebold,
he did not even take Clara Schumann into his confidence over the composition of this work. The B♭
Sextet sounds more straightforward and technically less
complex, while the G major work with its
contrapuntally intertwined structure seems lost in
gloomy meditation. Op.18 starts with a revolving,
cantabile theme, while the main subject of op.36 covers
the ground in great strides; but both opening movements
have a similar formal structure. The finale of op.18 is a
smiling, leisurely *allegretto* rondo, whereas op.36 ends
with a turbulent, complex blend of rondo and sonata
movement. It is basically a monothematic work, with all

four movements returning to the same thematic core – the combination of two identical intervals a 2nd apart, that is, the 5th and its inversion, the 4th.

After the failure of the string quintet version (with two cellos) of op.34, Brahms waited over 20 years before writing another quintet for strings, and this time, having learnt from experience, scored it in the conventional manner with two violas. The Quintet in F major op.88 was written very rapidly in 1882 at Bad Ischl and seems to have been inspired by the mood of springtime in Vienna, for the second theme of the first movement is based on a Viennese waltz. It has, curiously, only three movements, for the middle one is a blend of slow movement and episodic scherzo. The Adagio, whose theme comes from a study for a sarabande written in 1855, appears three times and the Scherzo, a siciliano, returns once in a modified form, making the movement a five-part rondo. This lively quintet was greeted with enthusiasm at its première in Frankfurt.

Brahms intended his Quintet in G major op.111, which has the same scoring, to be his last composition, but it is no mournful cry of farewell. The beginning of the first movement is based on drafts he made in Italy for his projected fifth symphony and the cello theme retains its symphonic impetus. In spite of the 'profound, concise Adagio', as Joachim called it, which follows Brahms's favourite form, the variation, unclouded gaiety pervades the work. Delightful reminiscences of the *csárdás* in the final movement and of the waltz in the first betray its Austro-Hungarian origins; rarely has a man in his late 50s sounded as youthful as Brahms did in this quintet.

On 11 December 1890 Brahms sent his publisher

Simrock an alteration to the finale of his Second String
Quintet op.111, adding casually: 'With this note you can
take leave of my music, because it is high time to stop'.
But he did not stop. His meeting with Richard Mühlfeld
in 1894 inspired him to write four chamber works with
clarinet, in which the stimulating effect of instrumental
sound is heightened. The Clarinet Quintet in B minor
op.115 has only one worthy forerunner, Mozart's, and
together with the Clarinet Trio it introduces the last
phase of Brahms's work. Hanslick called the quintet a
work for connoisseurs. In spite of the delicately
moulded scoring, its warmth of tone is undeniable. The
slow movement consists of two cantabile sections
enclosing a lively *alla zingarese* that sounds like an
intermezzo from a concerto with percussive effects and
a solo wind instrument. In the last two movements
Brahms resolved the problems of thematic transformation and variation in different ways. In the finale the
main theme appears in four guises and the coda refers
back to the beginning of the opening movement, bringing the thematic structure full circle.

The two string quartets op.51 are the result of 20
years' work towards mastery of strict four-part counterpoint. It is known from Brahms's own lips, in descriptions to his friends, that he made at least 20 trials at
quartet writing during these years. As early as 1865
Joachim asked how the C minor Quartet was
proceeding and in 1869 Brahms sent Clara Schumann
the two outer movements; but in spite of his friends'
encouragement he was dissatisfied. He rehearsed each
movement privately, altering and polishing indefatigably,
and only completed the score in 1873 at Tutzing on the
Starnberger See.

Although these quartets appeared together they are quite different in character. The C minor Quartet seems to be modelled after Beethoven's great Razumovsky quartets, while the A minor work more resembles Schumann's graceful style. The grand but pliant A♭ theme of the Romance (the second movement of the C minor Quartet) shows the influence of Beethoven, but the pretty, dancing scherzo with its lively waltz trio follows the best Viennese tradition. The formal, taut but weighty finale contains a theme related to the principal ideas of the first movement.

The main theme of the A minor Quartet is based on the motif *F–A–E*, after Joachim's motto, 'frei aber einsam', which suggests that Brahms originally intended to dedicate it to Joachim; in spite of various changes of mood it extends over 20 bars. The violin duet of the second subject is particularly impressive. The third movement, 'quasi menuetto', is in Brahms's favourite Slavonic triple metre which is combined with a canon in the middle section. The last movement, though not strictly a *csárdás*, is definitely inspired by the musical traditions of south-east Europe.

Although when Brahms wrote these two quartets he seemed to have overcome his difficulties with the genre, he wrote only one more, the Quartet in B♭ op.67 (1876), in the final movement of which he turned to the variation form once more. The cantabile theme undergoes eight ingenious transformations that represent a highpoint in Brahms's use of the form. In the last two passages he used the vigorous, leaping theme of the first movement contrapuntally, and so united the four movements in one intellectual whole.

III   Chamber music with piano

The three piano quartets opp.25, 26 and 60 were written at the same time but are very different in character. Op.25 in G minor may resemble Beethoven's music in its thematic material and development, and the more poetic op.26 in A major might seem to have been inspired by Schubert, but these comparisons rest only on individual features. The effective and thrilling *alla zingarese* finale of the former, which Brahms composed before he heard a Hungarian *csárdás*, shows clearly the influence of the Hungarian refugees. It is as far from the spirit of Beethoven as the scherzo of op.26 is close to it. Whereas Beethoven no more than alluded to the Magyar idiom (for instance in the finale of his quartet op.132), Brahms sometimes refined it (for example in the Hungarian dances) and sometimes, as in the slow movement of the Clarinet Quintet op.115, presented the idiom in stylized form. The C minor Quartet op.60 was originally conceived before the two Hamburg quartets and is derived from a quartet in C♯ minor that Brahms laid aside in April 1856. He made use of parts of his original draft when composing the final version, but thoroughly revised and reorganized them (see Webster, 1980). The original version was evidently destroyed. From Brahms's conversations we know that this work is strongly autobiographical, describing the strivings of a lonely man in an insoluble dilemma, and its emotional ambivalence is therefore not surprising: it is among the intellectually most pretentious chamber works he ever wrote. The usual sunny mood is missing, and a darker, more sombre atmosphere prevails. The slow movement, in E major (a key that indicates a connection with the

121

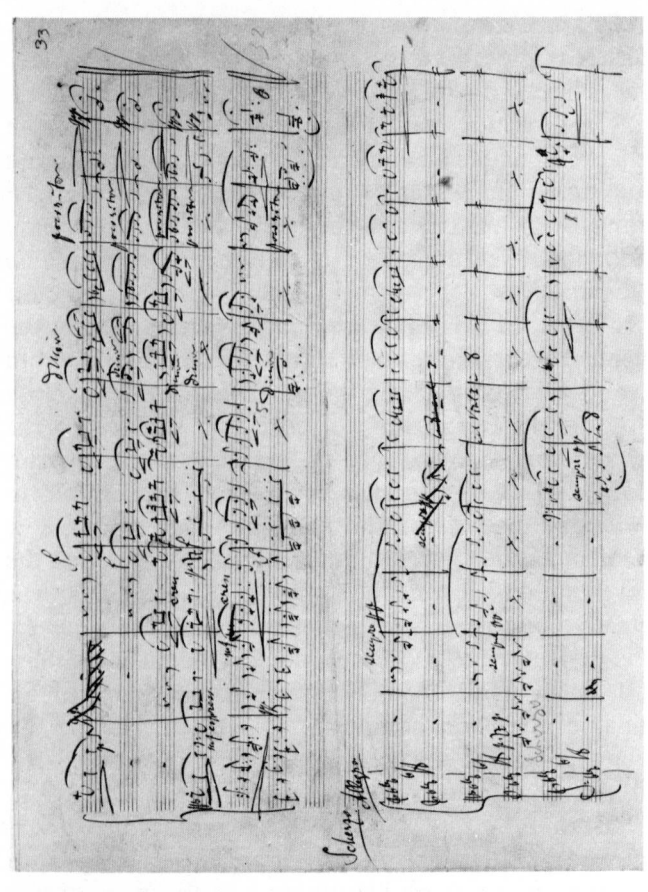

10. Autograph MS of the end of the second movement and opening of the third of Brahms's Piano Quintet in F minor, composed in 1861–4

original C♯ minor work), is deeply felt and has been regarded, probably rightly, as a declaration of love.

The Piano Quintet in F minor op.34 (see fig.10) is exceptional among Brahms's works, both in its scoring and also in the complicated history of its composition. It was first written as a string quintet with two cellos, and Brahms, who was usually only too ready to discard his failures, laid it aside after Joachim had criticized it adversely: after many unsuccessful corrections he eventually made it a sonata for two pianos, which he performed publicly with Tausig in a concert at the Gesellschaft der Musikfreunde on 17 April 1864. This version met with little success and Brahms, contrary to his usual practice, took the advice of Clara Schumann, who had liked the first version, and turned the sonata into a piano quintet. Surprisingly, in view of all these transformations, this work shows no trace of being a belated 'arrangement'. In general Brahms tended to put his weightier material into his outside movements, but here the third movement, a scherzo, is the most impressive by virtue of its unconventional form and rich vein of imagination. The entry of the majestic theme after the tautly rhythmic introduction is one of Brahms's most effective ideas. Though the finale is basically a Classical rondo it is a contemplative movement, and the usual mood of gay abandon is absent.

Brahms first sketched out his Trio in B major op.8 in 1853 and completed it the next January, shortly before Schumann's nervous breakdown. In 1889 he revised it completely, which shows that it contained the seeds of hitherto unexpressed ideas; in particular he altered the second theme groups in the first, second and fourth movements, which 'answer' the main theme groups, and he shortened the development section and omitted the fugue in the first movement, so that only the Scherzo remained essentially unchanged. Nearly 30 years passed before Brahms wrote another work for the same instrumentation. The Horn Trio was composed in 1865, but although it allows for the substitution of a cello it does not belong among his piano trios, just as the two clarinet sonatas with their optional viola parts may not be counted as primarily viola music.

The opening movements of both the opp.87 and 101 piano trios begin with vigorous, incisive themes that set their vehement and energetic mood. The Scherzo of op.101 precedes the slow movement, but there is no indication of why Brahms decided on this arrangement. Clara Schumann thought the Lombard rhythm of the Andante con moto in op.87 'popular', and certainly the theme (which resembles that of the Scherzo of op.101 in its note sequence) does have a balladic quality and served Brahms as a basis for a most ingenious set of variations. Even more 'popular' is the C major Andante from op.101, with its effortless interchange of triple and duple time, and in particular its use of triplets, betraying its Magyar origin.

Brahms wrote the Horn Trio in E♭ op.40 in 1865 in Lichtenthal, near Baden-Baden, and its première was on 28 November that year. The popularity of the horn as a serenade instrument may have caused him to write the first movement as a rondo, in which a taut second theme appears twice, alternating with a main theme that develops from a dominant 7th chord. The sorrowful Adagio mesto in E♭ minor was written shortly after the death of Brahms's mother, and the reference to the folksong *In den Weiden steht ein Haus* recalls his youth in his parents' home. In the Clarinet Trio in A minor op.114, the first fruit of his collaboration with Richard Mühlfeld, Brahms grasped the opulent range of the instrument with complete assurance, using its cantilena potentiality and sparkling fluency while avoiding the danger of turning his work into a miniature chamber concerto. He avoided the bucolic associations of the clarinet even in the Scherzo, whose trio is characterized by effects of melodic anticipation.

The seven instrumental sonatas with piano accompaniment are spread unevenly over a period of 32 years. The Cello Sonata op.38 was begun in 1862, the 'Regenlied' Violin Sonata op.78 16 years later, the three Thun sonatas opp.99, 100 and 108 in 1886 and the two sonatas for Mühlfeld op.120 in 1894. Brahms's fundamental love of variation is even reflected in the character of his works: of the cello sonatas, the elegiac and pastoral op.38 contrasts with the passionate op.99. Of the violin sonatas, op.78 in G major with its 'Regenlied' theme in the third movement, derived from the solo song op.59 no.3, pairs with op.100 in A major, written on Lake Thun while Brahms was 'awaiting the arrival of a dear friend' (Hermine Spies) and containing many song quotations; contrasting with both of these is op.108, which by reason of its virtuoso piano part is more suited to the concert hall than the salon.

The common opus number of the two clarinet sonatas, on the other hand, suggests that they belong together, and there is little contrast between them. Lyrical, pastoral and epic passages abound, and the passionate and pathetic character of the instrument is only tentatively exploited, while the bucolic and ironic high register is ignored. Brahms assessed the acoustical possibilities of the clarinet very carefully. His preference for variation form is confirmed by the fact that it is not the F minor sonata with its playful rondo finale, but the E♭ work with its final variation movement that brought his work in this vein to a close.

IV Orchestral music

Brahms began composing orchestral music between 1857 and 1859 when he had the opportunity of working with the Detmold orchestra, though in Düsseldorf he had previously made a full and thorough study of the techniques of instrumentation. The two serenades, op.11 in D and op.16 in A, show how strictly he worked to a plan while familiarizing himself with the new medium. The First Serenade was originally drafted as an octet, then adapted for chamber orchestra and finally after various experiments arranged for full orchestra. It bears little individual stamp and is strongly Classical in its derivation. Whereas from his earliest piano compositions Brahms seemed to be virtually a mature personality, his early orchestral works show that he also had to learn gradually. The Second Serenade, finished in 1859 and revised in 1875, is a most original work, scored without violins. Brahms chose the simple suite form for both works, so that he could practise orchestral effects without adding the complications of symphonic form; both are essentially studies.

The work on the D minor Piano Concerto op.15 represents another step away from the confines of chamber music. Brahms first wrote it as a sonata for two pianos, revised it unsuccessfully as a concerto in 1854 and only after his experiences in Detmold worked on it seriously, incorporating one movement from the 1854 revision. He seemed to dismiss its failure, his first real artistic setback, but its effect was to stop him offering to the public any more orchestral work for the next 14 years.

When the Symphony no.1 was already far advanced, Brahms wisely tested his orchestral technique once more on a familiar form and wrote his Variations on a Theme by Haydn op.56a. Only then did he seem confident enough to finish the symphony, on which he had been working since 1855. He had finished the first movement in 1862, though it still lacked the slow introduction, but was dissatisfied with it and laid it aside until the summer of 1874. After writing the Haydn Variations he resumed work on the symphony and finished it in September 1876, but shortly before its première in Karlsruhe under Dessoff (4 November) he felt compelled to make cuts in the inside movements. He had taken 15 years to summon the courage to present a work along Classical lines to a public conditioned to programmatic symphonies; but now that he had overcome his fears, he began almost at once on his second symphony in Pörtschach in the late summer of 1877, and finished it in barely four months. The première in Vienna under Hans Richter (30 December 1877) was a success. Five and a half years later Brahms began his third symphony; and this again he completed in less than four months (though it seems to incorporate ideas from earlier sketches). And, like the Second Symphony, the fourth followed its predecessor within the year, being written mostly during his two summer holidays in 1884 and 1885 in Mürzzuschlag in Styria.

It can be taken either as a statement of fact or as a reproach to observe that Brahms used sonata form, depending how much one is referring to the external structure. He did not in fact adhere to a traditional method of development but modified it deliberately in accordance with his own ideas, though refraining from breaking away into a revolutionary and uncontrollable unknown. At a time when the status of a progressive musician could be measured by the way he constructed, or linked, the movements of a programmatic symphony, Brahms was still working with clear divisions and lucid articulation; yet his themes are wonderfully intertwined, not with the obvious identity of leitmotifs but with an inner harmony of ideas. He did, however, cultivate an artistic technique of variation, alienation and transformation of thematic material in development passages, which he used even in the expositions.

Stress on the outer movements is characteristic of Brahms. All four symphonies work from a weighty opening movement through loosely connected inner movements to a monumental finale. With the exception of the Symphony no.4, all the inner movements are in three-part song form, with monothematic first and last sections and harmonically and thematically contrasted central sections. He followed the Classical tradition of putting the slow movement second, unlike Mendelssohn and Schumann who sometimes reversed the second and third movements; but he never called the third movement a scherzo (though he did use this term in his chamber music, and the two serenades both contain scherzos, clearly distinguished from minuets). The third movements of his symphonies can themselves refute the accusation that Brahms was clinging to outmoded forms: they cannot be defined as scherzos, minuets or even as dance movements, but rather are anonymous, original creations in which the features of scherzo, minuet and Austrian ländler meet and blend. The third movement of the Fourth Symphony is in sonata form without a development section. Brahms indicated the end of the exposition in the opening movements of all but his last symphony with the conventional repeat sign. The second subjects serve the first as explanatory or auxiliary thoughts. Brahms liked to add elaborate passages to his main themes and used his secondary themes as digressions, so that the idea of 'thematic contrast', in a Classical sense, is replaced by variation and transformation.

Brahms's adherence to strict form led him to choose the rigid ostinato form of the chaconne, which he handled with astonishing discretion, for the Haydn Variations (the first example of variation form in his orchestral music) and the finale of the Symphony no.4. Although the theme of the finale, which embraces a 5th with an octave stride at the cadence, appears 30 times, it hardly penetrates the listener's consciousness. Brahms took it from Bach's Cantata no.150, extended it to double its original length and made its diatonic intervals more poignant by adding a chromatic passing note.

Brahms made orchestral composition harder for himself by rejecting the pictorial instrumentation prevalent in the works of his contemporaries and immediate predecessors. The sensuous sound of the english horn, the swelling ripple of the harp and the full-bodied attack of a percussion section form no part of his orchestration. He could have written banally effective orchestral music without abstaining for so long from symphonic composition, but he set himself the task of inventing an instrumental formula suited to his own

11. Johannes Brahms, c1856

style of composition, including lucid scoring of the inner parts. He could not use a strongly coloured, compact sound for his polyphonically constructed type of movement, with its frequent switches of melodic weight from the outer to the inner parts, because it would have obliterated the finely drawn lines of his composition. In fact he found the right medium for his symphonic sound in the so-called Classical orchestra, with double woodwind. Concentration on essentials, absence of exuberant gestures and moderation in the choice of his medium define Brahms more as a renovator of tradition than as a reactionary symphonist.

V Concertos

Brahms composed his concertos with specific interpreters in mind, and he knew the performer and the character-istics of his playing before he started writing. He wrote both piano concertos for himself, as shown by the robust and inelastic solo part, the Violin Concerto (a surprisingly late work) for Joachim, and the Double Concerto for Joachim and Robert Hausmann.

The Piano Concerto in D minor op.15 is based on themes from three movements written for an early son-ata for two pianos in 1854, which Albert Dietrich later recognized in the concerto; the scherzo of this sonata was used in the second movement of the *Requiem*. The first movement of the concerto, completed in 1856 but changed again the following year, is a far-reaching adap-tation of a movement from the sonata. The Adagio, a 'portrait' of Clara Schumann, was written at the end of 1856, and the first version of the rondo finale somewhat earlier. Brahms's correspondence with friends, and entries in Clara Schumann's diary, give a fairly accurate, though incomplete, account of the genesis of this work. At the first performance, in Hanover on 22 January 1858, it gained reserved approval from the critics. That its second performance in Leipzig was a disaster may have made Brahms cautious of writing another concerto too soon, and only after his first Italian journey in 1878 did he make sketches for his second concerto, in B♭ major. He then laid it aside in favour of the Violin Concerto until after his second trip to Italy in 1881, when he must have finished it without interruption, for the complete score was ready by 11 July. The first performances were in Budapest on 9 November and Stuttgart on 22 November with Brahms as soloist. Theodor Billroth, Brahms's surgeon friend and a keen amateur violist, said that this concerto's relationship to the earlier one was the same as that of adulthood to youth. It is the longest Brahms wrote and one of the longest ever written. Against all tradition, it has four movements (though this does not make it a 'piano symphony') and probably includes the scherzo originally sketched for the Violin Concerto. The Second Concerto brings in the solo instrument at the very beginning of the first movement, whereas in the earlier concerto Brahms chose the alternative method and introduced it after the orchestral exposition; he also chose different solutions for the transitional section between the two theme groups.

The D minor Concerto has more in common with Beethoven's Ninth Symphony than its key. Brahms's youthful impetuosity led him to strain the limits of his capacity for expression and the first movement is a daring work of heightened passion. The B♭ Concerto is more benevolent and its slow movement, which includes a cello solo, is outstandingly emotional. Neither of these concertos is a rewarding virtuoso work to play, because the phrases do not lie easily for the pianist's fingers – they are awkward, impracticable and unwieldy. Their interpreter needs more physical strength and stamina than elegance and technical accomplishment.

The Violin Concerto, written in the summer of 1878 in Pörtschach, has the same spirit as the D major Symphony. Brahms first composed it in four movements, but later cut out the middle movements and rewrote the Adagio. It was first performed on 1 January 1879 at the Leipzig Gewandhaus with Joachim, to whom it was dedicated, as soloist. The rondo finale has a slightly Hungarian touch to it, in honour of Joachim's country of origin.

Brahms himself described the Double Concerto op.102 for violin and cello as a 'strange flight of fancy'. It is one of the products of his preoccupation with Baroque music, for it explores the potentialities of the concerto grosso in a 19th-century idiom. Its predominantly polyphonic structure also recalls older techniques, and it is more remarkable for its complex technical agility than for its creative imagination. Brahms composed it in the summer of 1887 on Lake Thun, hoping that it would effect a reconciliation with Joachim; possibly for this reason he used the cello as a mediator.

VI Choral works

The *German Requiem* (see fig.7) is not only unquestionably Brahms's greatest vocal work, but it is also the central work of his career. With it, in 1868, he made a decisive breakthrough. It was, of course, not his first attempt to combine vocal and instrumental music – the

Ave Maria op.12, the *Begräbnisgesang* op.13 and a setting of Psalm xiii op.27 precede it – but it is the first work that combines a mixed chorus, solo voices and full orchestra. It is in seven sections, which distinguishes it from the five-part Roman Catholic Requiem, and its text, which Brahms chose himself from his constant reading of the Bible, is non-denominational, centring on faith in the Resurrection rather than fear of the Day of Judgment. The first, second, fourth and final movements are purely choral, the third and sixth for baritone solo and the fifth for soprano; this last was added at the suggestion of his old teacher Marxsen whose advice Brahms sought repeatedly while he was composing it (see Blum, p.74). Each section has its own character, emphasized by Brahms's subtle instrumentation. For instance, as in his Second Serenade, there are no violins in the first movement, which sets a dark and heavy mood, while both movements for baritone end with a fugue. One cannot comprehend the *Requiem* on the basis of 19th-century choral tradition alone (in this respect Brahms was not a direct descendant of Schumann and Mendelssohn). Rather, it reflects Brahms's interest in the polyphonic vocal music of the previous three centuries, and indeed parts of the same text were also chosen by Schütz for his *Cantiones sacrae* (1625) and *Geistliche Chor-Musik* (1648). Handel was undoubtedly his model for choral technique in the *Requiem* as well as in the *Schicksalslied* and the *Triumphlied*.

The *Schicksalslied* op.54 comes nearest to the spirit of the *Requiem*. It was composed at Baden-Baden in May 1871 as a setting of Hölderlin's poem *Hyperions*

Schicksalslied, to which Brahms was first introduced by a friend at Wilhelmshaven in 1868 and which appealed to him so immediately that he made the first drafts on the spot. It is a restrained work, in three movements that form a dynamic arc like that of the *Requiem*, but its Romantic, Hellenistic character links it more closely to the Alto Rhapsody op.53 and the *Gesang der Parzen* op.89.

The Rhapsody for alto, male chorus and orchestra (known as the Alto Rhapsody), written in 1869, is a setting of part of Goethe's *Harzreise im Winter*, as its sub-title indicates. It is one of Brahms's most shattering and deeply personal works. He wrote it as a wedding song for Julie Schumann, Clara's daughter, but it seems to express Brahms's own plight as one condemned to a solitary life. As with opp.53 and 54, the choice of text for his op.89 – Goethe's *Gesang der Parzen* from Act 4 of his *Iphigenie auf Tauris* – shows that works of universal human relevance appealed to him most. Opinion of it is sharply divided, and to this its imprecise form has certainly contributed. Brahms used an almost ascetic musical language with no florid sound-effects to capture the Mycenean gloom of the ancient world.

The last of Brahms's works based on classical sources is *Nänie* op.82, on a text by Schiller, written as a dirge for his friend Anselm Feuerbach, to whose mother it is dedicated. The wind opening recalls the *Schicksalslied* but the delicate structure of the motifs in *Nänie* distinguishes it from the earlier work. The text is divided into three parts, of which the first consists of four couplets, the second two and the last only one. It is polyphonic, sometimes fugal, and is also built in an arc, with the

135

orchestral introduction to the first section recurring at the opening of the last. The penultimate hexameter is repeated at the end.

The *Triumphlied* for eight-part chorus and full orchestra op.55 was Brahms's patriotic contribution to the victory of Sedan. It is less complicated and more superficial than *Nänie* and is a clear example of the composer's capacity for both spontaneous inspiration and also artistic insight, for once the first impetus had been satisfied and the initial euphoria had subsided he abandoned this patriotic 'occasional' work in favour of his *Schicksalslied* and a more genuine and profound creative urge. He found it very hard to complete the *Triumphlied* when he resumed work on it nearly two years later. The piece was originally intended for Bismarck, but he eventually dedicated it to the Kaiser. Though its dotted rhythms are more incisive than is usual in his works, the *alla marcia* mood is not predominant. Brahms had learnt from Handel how well choral polyphony lends itself to massive festive or triumphal works. The choice of a double chorus shows that he had always intended to exploit Baroque antiphony in this kind of late Romantic *Te Deum*. It is in three movements and develops through spaciously and majestically unfolding phrases.

Brahms wrote the Alto Rhapsody for the same instrumentation as his early cantata *Rinaldo* op.50, in which he first used a male chorus, though with a solo tenor. A setting of Goethe's *Torquato Tasso*, which makes use of its eponymous poet's *Gerusalemme liberata*, it is the only example of Brahms's working with dramatic material. He began it in Hamburg on his first return from Vienna in 1863, and the fact that he never tried to write such a work again shows that he was only persuaded to write it because of the competition organized by the Aachen Liedertafel for a work for large male chorus. However, he did not complete it by the 1 October deadline, and when he returned to Vienna he actually left the unfinished score behind. Only when the *Requiem* was completed, five years later in the summer of 1868, did he finish *Rinaldo* in Bonn, though this was more from a sense of tidiness than inner compulsion. Perhaps on account of this interruption he gave up his original plan to make it *durchkomponiert*, and added a final section, 'Auf dem Meere'. Though he tried to imbue this work with a dramatic spirit he only managed to strike theatrical poses, which partly explains its limited success.

Brahms's choral works with piano or instrumental ensemble accompaniment occupy an intermediate position between his choral works with orchestra and *a cappella* music. Among the quartets with piano accompaniment the *Zigeunerlieder* op.103 (of which he arranged eight for solo voice) and the *Liebeslieder* waltzes opp.52 and 65 most appealed to popular taste. Both works honour in their own way Brahms's chosen homeland, the Austro-Hungarian Empire on the Danube. In op.52 the piano accompaniment for four hands is more important than the vocal line, but the reverse is true of op.65. In these waltzes, Brahms revived the old dance-song in a new idiom, resulting in Schubertian Viennese ländler rather than Straussian waltzes. Spontaneous Viennese charm underlies the first collection, but the second is full of Magyar passion and bitterness, similar to the mood of the *Zigeunerlieder*.

Brahms had met Hungarian gypsy music in his youth

*12. Johannes
Brahms with
Adele Strauss*

138

and had learnt the thrill of interpreting it through his own intensity and power on his early tours with Reményi. All his life he wrestled with this style, sublimating it in his own, related idiom. Between 1852 and 1869 he composed 21 Hungarian dances for piano solo and duet (he later orchestrated nos. 1, 3 and 10); in 1857 he wrote the Variations on a Hungarian Song op.21 no.2, in 1861 the smouldering Rondo alla zingarese of the Piano Quartet op.25, in 1887 the 11 *Zigeunerlieder* op.103 (written in Thun and Vienna) and in 1891 four of the op.112 quartets, settings of Hugo Conrat's translations of gypsy poems. In Hungarian, words are always accented on the first syllable, so that upbeats do not as a rule exist in the music. Brahms imitated this stylistic idiosyncrasy: not one of his gypsy songs begins on an upbeat. Research has established beyond doubt that Brahms went back to the original tunes in Zoltán Nagy's 1887 collection, but modified and refined their national idiom, never once using the gypsy scale.

Apart from the choral works with instrumental accompaniment, Brahms composed 13 motets (opp.29, 37, 74, 109 and 110), 46 *a cappella* songs (opp.22, 41, 42, 44, 62, 93*a* and 104) and 20 canons. The large quantity of pure *a cappella* music in his work explains his commitment to the musical needs of his time, as a study of 19th-century choral music reveals most clearly the transition from the courtly musical traditions of the 18th century to the bourgeois musical culture of the 19th. For the generation of Mendelssohn, Schumann, Marschner and Loewe, to name only a few of Brahms's immediate predecessors, *a cappella* music was both a new experience and an expression of an individual modernity. At the beginning of his creative career, in the

139

middle of the 19th century, Brahms encountered the climax of this entirely new movement in choral music, although the Baroque choral tradition, as exemplified by the Handel cult in England, had not yet completely died. Brahms's choral technique owed less to the great choral works of his century, such as Beethoven's Choral Fantasy and *Christus am Oelberge* or Mendelssohn's *Elijah* or *St Paul*, than to his study of the strict contrapuntal music of the early Baroque period, both in the Hamburg city library and in Schumann's private library in Düsseldorf. Contrapuntal structure, especially the canon, therefore, gave the initial impulse to his *a cappella* works, and he proudly wrote to Clara Schumann that he had actually mastered all types of canonic technique. The justification for this statement lies in his numerous works which contain canons at all possible intervals, for example, canon at the 2nd above, the 9th below (op.30), the 9th above (op.55 no.2) and the 7th above (op.52 no.10), the double canon (*Zu Rauch*, without opus number), the canon 'per arsin et thesin' (*O bone Jesu* op.37 no.1), the circle canon (*Mir lächelt kein Frühling*, composed in 1881) and the canon 'per augmentationem' (op.29 no.1). This strict vocal polyphony left its mark on his later instrumental music, too, with its consciousness of strict form. In the Schumann variations op.9 he used no fewer than seven different canonic constructions. For Brahms canons and canonic technique were not a means of convivial music-making, but of compression of form. His inclination towards imitation in pairs, as in op.74 no.1, came from his study of Netherlands polyphony; and his assured handling of counterpoint allowed him to deviate from the norm when necessary. The conventional reply at the

5th only features in passing in his fugues in which, as in his canons, he worked with varied intervals, and in his later compositions he favoured the 4th as the standard interval for his fugal answers.

Brahms's later choral movements essentially avoid the homophony and homorhythm of the early choruses for women's voices written for a particular group; in the later works, all intended for publication, he chose a polyphonically fragmented style which recalls most strikingly the early Baroque madrigal. He had a sensitive feeling for the intrinsic value of each part, and though the lower parts rarely establish their independence from the descant, they frequently contribute complementary rhythms.

Brahms did not follow tradition in his vocal writing as a fleeting concession to contemporary taste, but because it corresponded to his essential position as an artist. This is illustrated by his motet writing, which extended throughout his creative life, from op.29 in 1860 through op.74 in 1877 to the Three Motets op.110 written in 1889. Next to these last motets, and of particular importance, stands the *Fest- und Gedenksprüche* op.109, a work for double chorus that strikingly exemplifies his liking for the stately style of the old Venetian motets of homage. He intended these memorial verses as general festival hymns for national days of commemoration and not just for the occasion when he became a freeman of the city of Hamburg, although they are dedicated to the lord mayor.

One cannot be sure what Brahms intended to define when using the term 'motet'. The *Fest- und Gedenksprüche* op.109 are not called 'motets', although they certainly belong in that category. Perhaps their official nature deterred Brahms from using historical nomenclature. The Sacred Choruses for female voices op.37, in strict canonic form, must be called motets, but among the Three Motets op.110 the chorus 'Ach, arme Welt' has a formal diction which in no way justifies the name 'motet'. Brahms used the most varied forms of the motet, as for instance the choral motets op.29 no.1 and op.74 no.2 and the epigrammatic motet op.29 no.2. In the earlier ones he was still accustomed to introducing passages in canon, for instance 'Verwirf mich nicht' in op.29 no.2. In his middle period his canons are less strict, for example op.74 no.1, and the parts are treated freely. In his late motets he actually abandoned strict canonic treatment in favour of the Venetian multiple-chorus model, with resultant layers of choral effect.

Brahms's conception of the cadence was very different from that of his contemporaries. He liked to avoid the Classical tonic–dominant harmonies, but it is difficult to subscribe to the view that in his vocal writing he adopted progressions from music in the church modes, which his preference for plagal harmonies might suggest. He loved to 'loosen' a phrase, either by using 2nds or the minor key with a diminished 7th. This must not be mistaken either as Aeolian or as an inverted 2nd, but rather as an exciting discord, as with the added 6th in a major triad. When Schoenberg called Brahms 'the progressive' it was chiefly the harmony that he had in mind. Brahms never flinched from bold harmonies in his choral works with orchestra, although most of them yield to linear analysis. Pure triadic motion in the Palestrina style is exceptional, but a fine example of it is the last section from op.62 no.7, *Vergangen ist mir*

Glück und Heil, which J. H. Wetzel justifiably described as a 'study in the effectiveness of the pure triad'.

VII   Lieder

From 1851 to 1896 Brahms published 31 volumes containing 196 solo songs, six of duets and five of solo quartets with piano accompaniment. These are spread unevenly, for certain years saw an intensive output, others few or only a single song and still others no songs at all. The question of external influence is entirely relevant to Brahms's song composition, but with few exceptions cannot be answered convincingly. Certainly the 15 songs written in 1858 express his feelings about Agathe von Siebold, and the significant output of 1877 (19 songs) was an echo from Vienna of his reunion with Elisabeth von Herzogenberg; and his friendship with the singer Rosa Girzick and infatuation with Hermine Spies certainly inspired him to creative effort.

Brahms's texts cover a broad spectrum, for he chose them simply for their musical value and let them inspire him freely. He did, however, choose many poems by Goethe, two by Schiller – *Abend* and *Nänie* – and few by Storm and Heine. He showed a marked preference for second-rate poets such as Klaus Groth, Gustav Freytag, Count von Schack, Georg Friedrich Daumer, Herrmann Lingg and Adolf Frey.

It is possible to break down his output of songs chronologically by form. Until 1860 he wrote purely strophic songs or variation songs, that is, with repeated but modified tunes. His op.32 in 1864 was a decisive turning-point, for the pure stanza song gave way to *Durchkomponierung* or stanzas with changing melodies, while the variation song held its own. From 1873 on the *durchkomponiert* type gradually faded out, and had disappeared completely by 1877 with op.69, while simple stanzas once more dominated. The variation song survived throughout Brahms's creative span and he made it very much his own. He followed Goethe's principle of adapting the melody to suit the changing content of each stanza, while maintaining its basic character. He used the artificial method of repeating the melody of the first stanza note for note in the last, to give the listener the feeling of a return after the variations of the middle verses.

The influence of folksong on Brahms's lieder is a cause of his predominantly diatonic handling of melody. (Striking exceptions are the eight *Lieder und Gesänge* op.57 to texts by Daumer.) Even his basses mostly move diatonically, and chromatic movement is present only in the inner parts. The rhythmic pattern of the first lines is maintained even in the melodic variations, while more complex rhythmic techniques are reserved for the instrumental accompaniment. Though Brahms was not against the idea of clarification by means of tone-colours, he did not use this method. His song accompaniments are expressive, but not 'plastic'. He did not like massive piano preludes and postludes, but started straight into the song (also a characteristic of the folksong). 'Songs today have gone so far astray that one cannot cling too closely to one's ideal, and that ideal is the folksong', he wrote to Clara Schumann.

Brahms's greatness as a lieder composer appears most strongly in serious songs. Banter, archness and the lightly draped muse were not for him, and though he did use these moods occasionally, he dismissed them as trivial. The first song with which he introduced himself to his new friends in Düsseldorf was, predictably, a love-lament – *Liebestreu* (op.3 no.1). Besides the many single songs that still retain their high popularity – *Mainacht*, *Feldeinsamkeit* and *Immer leiser wird mein Schlummer*, to mention only three – the two cycles *15 Romanzen aus Tieck's 'Magelone'* and *Vier ernste Gesänge* serve to place him beside Schubert in the ranks of lieder composers. The *Magelone* songs op.33 brought the composer sudden fame at the age of just 30. He wrote them in Münster am Stein while in the company of Clara Schumann and her children. This is his only narrative song cycle, and its music is in variation form, modified from stanza to stanza, with broad continuous interludes before and after each romance and also between the stanzas. Though the stanza principle remains it is unfolded in the wider scope of phrases and thematic groupings.

The *Vier ernste Gesänge* op.121 (see fig.13), for which Brahms himself compiled the text from passages of scripture, is one of his most sublime works. It stands in a class by itself outside the narrower category of the lied, as a set of non-denominational songs of humility and faith. It corresponds to his smaller-scale works as the *Requiem* corresponds to his larger ones. The songs are not in stanza form and are musically harsh and austere, which makes them all the more effective; Max Friedlaender's attempt to characterize them as reviving the Baroque solo cantata serves only to disguise their extreme individuality, which has neither forerunner nor successor. Brahms's stubborn refusal to allow them to be performed indicates that it is here that his deepest personal feelings are embodied.

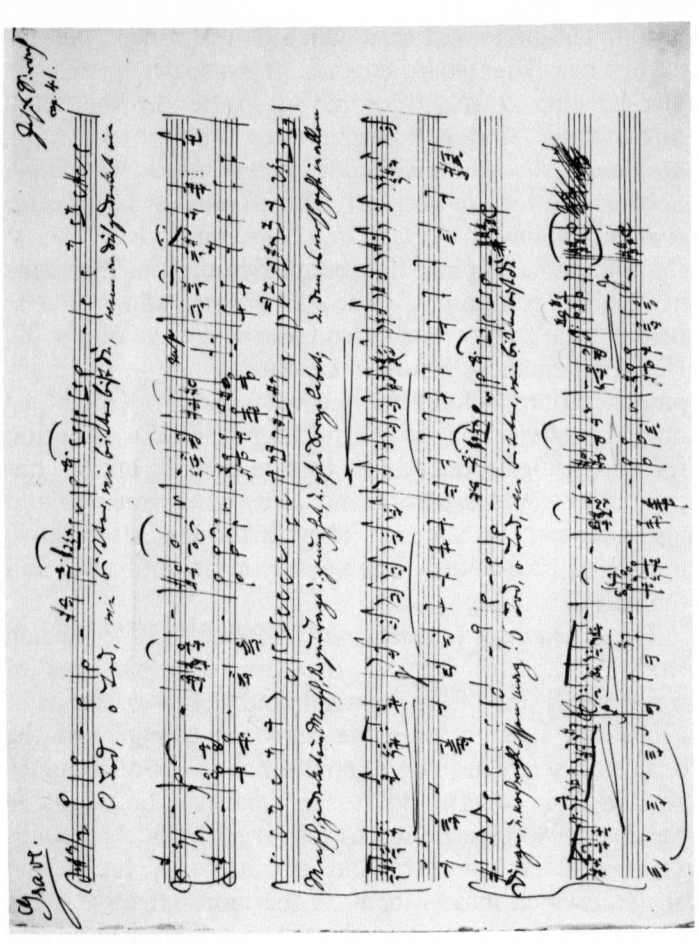

13. Autograph MS of the opening of 'O Tod, O Tod' from Brahms's 'Vier ernste Gesänge', composed 1896

VIII   Interest in earlier music

For a major composer, Brahms was unusually serious and diligent in his attention to scholarly problems and the rediscovery of early music. His interest in old music and in historical questions of musical theory was rooted in his childhood, when he went on voyages of exploration to the Hamburg city library to copy from and study its ample supply of old music manuscripts and theoretical works. His earnings as a musician enabled him to acquire rare editions from second-hand booksellers, in which he was encouraged by Schumann, who also placed his large library at Brahms's disposal. Joachim and Clara Schumann brought him back scores from their travels and other friends gave him rare works, so that his collection grew considerably over the years. His library contained the most important standard theoretical works of the 18th century, and later he acquired a valuable collection of autographs, among them those of Haydn's 'Sun' Quartets op.20, several of Schubert's songs, the original version of Mozart's Symphony in G minor K550 and, above all, works by Schumann. His rich collection of canons and a list of good and false consecutive 5ths and octaves bear witness to the care he brought to his study of counterpoint. His teacher Marxsen encouraged him in his youth to start a collection of folksongs, and in Schumann's library he found the anthologies of Kretzschmar–Zuccalmaglio and Becker, which enabled him to make a careful study and comparison of melodic variants and different versions of texts. His working copy of F. M. Böhme's *Altdeutsches Liederbuch* is covered with corrections and alterations in his own hand. He was a regular reader of the *Allgemeine musikalische Zeitung*, the *Musikalisches*

Wochenblatt and the *Vierteljahresschrift für Musikwissenschaft*.

It would not be valid to regard Brahms as a self-taught musical scholar who acquired the necessary knowledge through his innate artistic gifts, his diligence and his intuition. In fact he was in close touch with the leading music scholars of his day, including Spitta, Chrysander, Nottebohm, C. F. Pohl, Alfred Dörffel, Mandyczewski and Hanslick. Brahms exchanged views with them verbally and in writing and fully discussed technical questions, especially concerning editing and performing practice. In the dispute over transcribing the Baroque thoroughbass Brahms was in favour of using figures and of making the texture more supple by animating the middle parts. He could speak on even terms with specialists, and was among the first to challenge the declared opinion of the Bach scholar Spitta that the so-called *St Luke Passion* was authentic. He participated in many of the scholarly and practical editions, and was appointed to the commission set up by the Prussian Ministry of Culture to edit the Denkmäler Deutscher Tonkunst.

Brahms played a major part in the edition of Schumann's works, for which Clara gave permission in 1881. They often differed in their opinions, Clara feeling obliged to alter definitive versions of manuscripts wherever she remembered her husband playing the work differently. Brahms was primarily responsible for correcting the proofs, and in case of doubt he adhered strictly to the manuscript; but in the 1891 supplement to the collected edition, in which unedited works were published for the first time, he filled in gaps in the original with great artistic insight, though very much in his own style. Only recently (see Hancock) has there been any closer examination of his editorial work on earlier music and of the influence this had on his own compositions.

WORKS

Edition: *Johannes Brahms sämtliche Werke*, ed. H. Gál (i–x) and E. Mandyczewski (xi–xxvi) (Leipzig, 1926–7) [BW]

Numbers in the right-hand column denote references in the text.

ORCHESTRAL

op.	Title	Composed	Published	First performance	Remarks	BW	
							126–31
11	Serenade no.1, D	1857–8	1860/61	Hanover, 3 March 1860	orig. for small orch	iv, 1	83, 85, 126,
15	Piano Concerto no.1, d	1854–8	1861/74	Hanover, 22 Jan 1859		vi, 1	84, 85, 86, 126, 131–2, 362
16	Serenade no.2, A	1858–9, rev. 1875	1860, 2/1875	Hamburg, 10 Feb 1860	for small orch (without vns)	iv, 85	83, 85, 126
56a	Variations on a Theme by J. Haydn, Bb	1873	1874	Vienna, 2 Nov 1873	'St Anthony' Variations; theme probably not by Haydn	iii, 63	94, 127, 129
68	Symphony no.1, c	1855–76	1877	Karlsruhe, 4 Nov 1876		i, 1	95, 127
73	Symphony no.2, D	1877	1878	Vienna, 30 Dec 1877		i, 87	96, 97, 127, 238, 253
77	Violin Concerto, D	1878	1879	Leipzig, 1 Jan 1879	ded. J. Joachim	v, 1	96, 97–8, 131, 132, 133
80	Academic Festival Overture, c	1880	1881	Breslau, 4 Jan 1881	ded. U. of Breslau	iii, 1	97
81	Tragic Overture, d	1880	1881	Vienna, 26 Dec 1880		iii, 37	
83	Piano Concerto no.2, Bb	1878–81	1882	Budapest, 9 Nov 1881	ded. E. Marxsen	vi, 92	132–3
90	Symphony no.3, F	1883	1884	Vienna, 2 Dec 1883		ii, 1	100, 127
98	Symphony no.4, e	1884–5	1886	Meiningen, 25 Oct 1885		ii, 87	100, 127, 128–9
102	Concerto, a, vn, vc	1887	1888	Cologne, 18 Oct 1887		v, 67	102, 131, 133
—	Three Hungarian Dances, no.1, g, no.3, F, no.10, F	1873	1874	Leipzig, 5 Feb 1874	arr. from orig. version for pf 4 hands	iv, 143	
WoO 1							

CHAMBER

op.	Title	Composed	Published	First performance	Remarks	BW	
8	Piano Trio no.1, B	1853–4, rev. 1889	1854, 2/1891	New York, 27 Nov 1855	rev. version perf. Budapest, 10 Jan 1890	ix, 1	110, 117, 123–4
18	Sextet no.1, Bb, 2 vn, 2 va, 2 vc	1859–60	1861	Hanover, 20 Oct 1860	ded. Baron R. von Dalwigk	vii, 1	86, 88, 116, 117
25	Piano Quartet no.1, g	1855–61	1863	Hamburg, 16 Nov 1861		viii, 69	87, 121, 139
26	Piano Quartet no.2, A	1855–61	1863	Vienna, 29 Nov 1862	ded. E. Rösing	viii, 154	87, 121
34	Piano Quintet, f	?1861–4	1865	Leipzig, 22 June 1866	ded. Princess Anna of Hesse; orig. composed as str qnt; also arr. for 2 pf	viii, 1	86, 118, *122, 123*

36	Sextet no.2, G, 2 vn, 2 va, 2 vc	1864–5	1866	Boston, 11 Oct 1866	ded. J. Gänsbacher	vii, 85 — 84, 117, 362
38	Cello Sonata no.1, e	1862–5	1866	Leipzig, 14 Jan 1871		x, 96 — 100, 125
40	Trio, E♭, vn, hn/va/vc, pf	1865	1866	Zurich, 28 Nov 1865		ix, 209 — 90, 124
51	Two String Quartets, c, a	c1865–73	1873	Vienna, 11 Dec 1873 (no.1) and 18 Oct 1873 (no.2)	ded. T. Billroth	vii, 186 — 119–20
60	Piano Quartet no.3, c	1855–75	1875	Vienna, 18 Nov 1875	orig. composed in c♯	viii, 236 — 120, 121–2
67	String Quartet no.3, B♭	1875	1876	Berlin, 30 Oct 1876	ded. T. W. Engelmann	vii, 238 — 96, 125
78	Violin Sonata no.1, G	1878–9	1879	Bonn, 8 Nov 1879		x, 1 — 98, 99, 124
87	Piano Trio no.2, C	1880–82	1882	Frankfurt am Main, 29 Dec 1882		ix, 121 — 98, 99, 124
88	Quintet no.1, F, 2 vn, 2 va, vc	1882	1882	Frankfurt am Main, 29 Dec 1882		vii, 95 — 98, 99, 118
99	Cello Sonata no.2, F	1886	1887	Vienna, 24 Nov 1886		x, 124 — 100, 125
100	Violin Sonata no.2, A	1886	1887	Vienna, 2 Dec 1886		x, 31 — 100, 125
101	Piano Trio no.3, c	1886	1887	Budapest, 20 Dec 1886		ix, 171 — 100, 124
108	Violin Sonata no.3, d	1886–8	1889	Budapest, 21 Dec 1888	ded. Bülow	x, 57 — 100, 125
111	Quintet no.2, G, 2 vn, 2 va, vc	1890	1891	Vienna, 11 Nov 1890		vii, 123 — 98, 118, 119
114	Trio, a, cl/va, vc, pf	1891	1892	Berlin, 12 Dec 1891	written for R. Mühlfeld	ix, 249 — 98, 103, 119, 125
115	Quintet, b, cl, str qt	1891	1892	Berlin, 12 Dec 1891	written for Mühlfeld	vii, 152 — 103, 119, 121
120	Two Sonatas, f, E♭, cl/va, pf	1894	1895	Vienna, 11 Jan 1895 (no.1) and 8 Jan 1895 (no.2)	written for Mühlfeld	x, 153 — 103, 110
WoO 2 posth.	Scherzo, c, vn, pf	1853	1906	Düsseldorf, 28 Oct 1853	ded. Joachim; movt for a Sonata in a, collab. Schumann and A. Dietrich	x, 88 — 110, 117
—	Piano Trio, A	—	1938	—	?authentic	—

PIANO SOLO

1	Sonata no.1, C	1852–3	1853	Leipzig, 17 Dec 1853	ded. Joachim	xiii, 1 — 110–16
2	Sonata no.2, f♯	1852	1854	Vienna, 2 Feb 1882	ded. C. Schumann	xiii, 29 — 110, 111, 112, 115
4	Scherzo, e♭	1851	1854	Hanover, 8 June 1853	ded. E. F. Wenzel	xiv, 1 — 110, 111
5	Sonata no.3, f	1853	1854	Vienna, 6 Jan 1863	ded. Countess I. von Hohenthal	xiii, 55 — 110, 111, 114
9	[16] Variations on a Theme by R. Schumann, f♯	1854	1854	Berlin, 12 Dec 1879	ded. C. Schumann	xiii, 87 — 82, 110, 114, 115
10	Four Ballades, d 'Edward', D, b, B	1854	1856	Vienna, 21 March 1860 (nos.2–3) and 23 Nov 1867 (nos.1, 4)	ded. J. O. Grimm	xiv, 13 — 110, 112–3

op.	Title	Composed	Published	First performance	Remarks	BW	
WoO 3/1	Gavotte, a posth.	?1855	1979	Göttingen, 29 Oct 1855		—	
WoO 3/2	Gavotte, A posth.	?1855	1979	Göttingen, 29 Oct 1855		—	
21	[Two variation sets]					xiii, 103	114, 115
	[11] Variations on an Original Theme, D	1857	1862	Frankfurt am Main, 31 Oct 1865			115
	[13] Variations on a Hungarian Song, D	?1853		London, 25 March 1874			139
24	[25] Variations and Fugue on a Theme by G. F. Handel, Bb	1861	1862	Hamburg, 7 Dec 1861		xiii, 125	86, 114, 116
35	[28] Variations on a Theme by Paganini, a	1862–3	1866	Zurich, 25 Nov 1865	based on Caprice no.24	xiii, 147	87, 114, 116
39	[16] Waltzes	1865	1867	Hamburg, 15 Nov 1868		xiv, 33	110
76	Eight Piano Pieces 1 Capriccio, f# 2 Capriccio, b 3 Intermezzo, Ab 4 Intermezzo, Bb 5 Capriccio, c# 6 Intermezzo, A 7 Intermezzo, a 8 Capriccio, C	1878	1879	Berlin, 29 Oct 1879	ded. E. Hanslick; arr. of version for pf 4 hands no.1 composed 1871; both sets completed 1878	xiv, 61	96, 113, 114
79	Two Rhapsodies, b, g	1879	1880	Krefeld, 20 Jan 1880	ded. E. von Herzogenberg	xiv, 89	96, 110, 112
116	[7] Fantasias 1 Capriccio, d 2 Intermezzo, a 3 Capriccio, g 4 Intermezzo, E 5 Intermezzo, e 6 Intermezzo, E 7 Capriccio, d	1892	1892	Vienna, 30 Jan 1893 (nos.1–3) and 18 Feb 1893 (no.7); London, 15 March 1893 (no.6)		xiv, 105	110

op.	Title	Composed	Published	First performance	Remarks	BW	
WoO 6 Anh. IV/2	51 Exercises Study for the Left Hand, E♭	1850s–1890s —	1893 1927	— —	completed 1893 arr. of Schubert's Impromptu, D899 no.2; doubtful authenticity	xv, 126 xv, 44	103
WoO 11–15	Cadenzas to concertos by Bach (d, bwv1052), Mozart (G, k453; d, k466; c, k491) and Beethoven (G, op.58)	?1855–1861	1907, 1927	—	cadenza to Beethoven, c, op.37	xv, 101	
Anh. IV/7	Cadenza to Beethoven concerto, c, op.37	—	—		sometimes attrib. Brahms, by Moscheles	—	
			PIANO FOUR HANDS				
23	Variations on a Theme by R. Schumann, E♭	1861	1863	Hamburg, Oct 1863	ded. Julie Schumann	xii, 2	86, 114
39	[16] Waltzes	1865	1866	Oldenburg, 23 Nov 1866	ded. Hanslick	xii, 26	
52a	Liebeslieder, 18 waltzes	1874	1874	Vienna, 14 Nov 1874	arr. from orig. version for 4vv, pf 4 hands	xii, 48	
65a	Neue Liebeslieder, 15 waltzes	1875	1877	—	arr. from orig. version for 4vv, pf 4 hands	xii, 80	
WoO 1	Hungarian Dances, 21 dances in 4 bks	1868–80	1869–80	—	bks 1–2 pubd 1869, bks 3–4 pubd 1880	xii, 106	139
Anh. 1a/3	arr. of J. Joachim: Hamlet Overture	1853–4	—	—	MSS in A-Wgm	—	
			TWO PIANOS				
34b	Sonata, f	1864	1871	Vienna, 17 April 1864	ded. Princess Anna of Hesse	xii, 1	88
39	[5] Waltzes	1867	1897	Vienna, 17 March 1867	nos.1, 2, 11, 14, 15 arr. from orig. version for pf 4 hands		
56b	Variations on a Theme by J. Haydn, B♭	1873	1873	Vienna, 10 Feb 1874	'St Anthony' Variations, also composed for orch; theme probably not by Haydn	xi, 78	94, 114
Anh. 1a/4	arr. of J. Joachim: Demetrius Overture	1855–6	—	—	MSS in Wgm	—	
Anh. 1a/5	arr. of J. Joachim: Henry IV Overture	1855–6	1902	—	MSS in Wgm	—	

op.	Title, scoring	Composed	Published		BW	
122 posth.	Eleven Chorale Preludes	1896	Berlin, 24 April 1902	some may have been composed before 1896	xvi, 28	98
	1 Mein Jesu, der du mich					
	2 Herzliebster Jesu					
	3 O Welt, ich muss dich lassen					
	4 Herzlich tut mich erfreuen					
	5 Schmücke dich, o liebe Seele					
	6 O wie selig seid ihr doch					
	7 O Gott, du frommer Gott					
	8 Es ist ein Ros entsprungen					
	9 Herzlich tut mich verlangen					
	10 Herzlich tut mich verlangen					
	11 O Welt, ich muss dich lassen					
WoO 8	Fugue, a♭	1856	Leipzig, 16 April 1873		xvi, 17	
WoO 7	O Traurigkeit, O Herzeleid, chorale prelude and fugue, a	1858	Vienna, 2 Dec 1882		xvi, 22	
WoO 9–10	Two Preludes and Fugues, a, g	1856–7	Berlin, 15 Nov 1929	no.1 ded. C. Schumann	xvi, 1	

op.	Title, scoring	Text	Composed	Published	BW	
113	Thirteen Canons, 3–6 female vv		most 1859–63	1891	xxi, 179	103
	1 Göttlicher Morpheus, 4vv	Goethe				
	2 Grausam erweiset sich Amor an mir, 3vv	Goethe				
	3 Sitz a schöns Vögerl aufm Dannabaum, 4vv	trad., in A. W. von Zuccalmaglio, ed.: Deutsche Volkslieder				
	4 Schlaf, Kindlein, schlaf!, 3vv	trad., in Zuccalmaglio				
	5 Wille wille will, 4vv	trad., in Zuccalmaglio				
	6 So lange Schönheit wird bestehn, 4vv	Hoffmann von Fallersleben				
	7 Wenn die Klänge nahn und fliehen, 3vv	Eichendorff				
	8 Ein Gems auf dem Stein, 4vv	Eichendorff				

139

op.	Title, scoring	Text	Composed	Published	BW	
9 Ans Auge des Liebsten, 4vv		F. Rückert				
10 Leise Töne der Brust, 4vv		Rückert				
11 Ich weiss nicht was im Hain die Taube girret, 4vv		Rückert	1867			
12 Wenn Kummer hätte zu töten Macht, 3vv		Rückert				
13 Einförmig ist der Liebe Gram, 6vv		Rückert				
WoO 27 posth.	Spruch ('In dieser Welt des Trugs und Scheins'), 1v, va	Hoffmann von Fallersleben	1854–5	1927	xxi, 192	
WoO 28	Töne, lindernder Klang, 4vv (2 versions)	K. von Knebel	1859–60/1871	1938, 1872/1876	xxi, 156	
WoO 25	Mir lächelt kein Frühling, 4 vv	—	?1877	1881	xxi, 189	140
WoO 29 posth.	Wann? ('Wann hört der Himmel auf'), S, A	L. Uhland	?early 1870s	1885	xxi, 192	
WoO 26 posth.	O wie sanft, 4 female vv	G. F. Daumer	?late 1860s	1908	xxi, 191	
WoO 24 posth.	Grausam erweiset sich Amor, 4 female vv	Goethe	—	1927	xxi, 190	
WoO 30 posth.	Zu Rauch, 4vv (2 versions)	Harîri, trans. Rückert	?1860s–1870s	1927	xxi, 157	140

VOCAL QUARTETS

(for S, A, T, B, pf unless otherwise stated)

op.	Title	Incipit	Text	Composed	Published	First performance	BW	
31	Three Quartets							
	1 Wechsellied zum Tanz	Komm mit, o Schöner	Goethe	1859	1864	Vienna, 18 Dec 1863	xx, 17	
	2 Neckereien	Für wahr, mein Liebchen	trad. Cz., trans. J. Wenzig	1863		Vienna, 11 Jan 1864		
	3 Der Gang zum Liebchen	Es glänzt der Mond nieder		1863		Karlsruhe, 3 Nov 1865		
52	Liebeslieder, 18 waltzes, S, A, T, B, pf 4 hands; arr. for 4vv, pf 2 hands	—	from G. F. Daumer: Polydora	1868–9	1869	Vienna, 5 Jan 1870	xx, 61	137, 140
		—	—		1875	—	—	
64	Three Quartets							
	1 An die Heimat	Heimat! Heimat!	C. O. Sternau	1862–3	1874	Vienna, 7 April 1869 (1st version)	xx, 35	
	2 Der Abend	Senke, strahlender Gott	H. Schiller	1874		Vienna, 24 Feb 1875 (nos.1–2)	—	143
	3 Fragen	Mein liebes Herz	Turk., trans. Daumer	1874		Mannheim, 13 Feb 1875		

No.	Title	Incipit	Text			Première	Pages	
65	Neue Liebeslieder, 15 waltzes, S, A, T, B, pf 4 hands no.4 arr. for 1v, pf	—	from Daumer: Polydora (nos.1–14); Goethe (no.15)	1874	1875	Karlsruhe, 8 May 1875	xx, 107	137
92	Four Quartets						xx, 147	—
	1 O schöne Nacht	O schöne Nacht	Daumer	?1877	1884	Krefeld, 28 Jan 1885 Frankfurt am Main, 4 Feb 1889		
	2 Spätherbst	Der graue Nebel tropft	H. Allmers	1884				
	3 Abendlied	Friedlich bekämpfen	F. Hebbel	1884	1884	—		
	4 Warum?	Warum doch erschallen	Goethe	1884	1884	Frankfurt am Main, 4 Feb 1889		
103	[11] Zigeunerlieder		trad. Hung., trans. H. Conrat	1887–8	1888	Berlin, 31 Oct 1888	xx, 165	102, 137, 139
	1	He, Zigeuner, greife						
	2	Hochgetürmte Rimaflut						
	3	Wisst ihr, wann mein Kindchen						
	4	Lieber Gott, du weisst						
	5	Brauner Bursche führt zum Tanze						
	6	Röslein dreie in der Reihe						
	7	Kommt dir manchmal						
	8	Horch, der Wind klagt						
	9	Weit und breit schaut niemand						
	10	Mond verhüllt sein Angesicht						
	11	Rote Abendwolken ziehn						
112	Six Quartets				1891		xx, 193	139
	1 Sehnsucht	Es rinnen die Wasser	F. Kugler	?1888				
	2 Nächtens	Nächtens wachen auf die irren	Kugler	?1888				
	3 Vier Zigeunerlieder, no.1	Himmel strahlt so helle	trad. Hung., trans. Conrat	?1891				
	4 Vier Zigeunerlieder, no.2	Rote Rosenknospen	trad. Hung., trans. Conrat	?1891				
	5 Vier Zigeunerlieder, no.3	Brennessel steht an Wegesrand	trad. Hung., trans. Conrat	?1891				
	6 Vier Zigeunerlieder, no.4	Liebe Schwalbe	trad. Hung., trans. Conrat	?1891				

op.	Title	Incipit	Text	Composed	Published	First performance	BW
—	[9] Liebeslieder, arr. of op.52 nos.1–2, 4–6, 8–9, 11 and op.65 no.9 for S, A, T, B, orch	—	G. F. Daumer	1869–70	1938	—	—
—	Kleine Hochzeitskantate	Zwei Geliebte, treu verbunden	G. Keller	1874	1927	sum. 1874	xx, 226
	VOCAL DUETS						
20	Three Duets, S, A, pf				1862	Lucerne, 10 March 1864 (no.1 or 2)	xxii, 1
	1 Weg der Liebe, i	Über die Berge	from Percy: Reliques, trans. in Herder: Volkslieder	1858			
	2 Weg der Liebe, ii	Den gordischen Knoten	from Percy: Reliques, trans. in Herder	1858			
	3 Die Meere	Alle Winde schlafen	trad. It., in W. Müller: Volksharfe	1860		Munich, 30 Nov 1889	
28	Four Duets, A, Bar, pf				1863	Vienna, 18 Dec 1863 (nos.1–2) and 5 March 1869 (nos.3–4)	xxii, 17
	1 Die Nonne und der Ritter	Da die Welt zur Ruh gegangen	Eichendorff	1860			
	2 Vor der Tür	Tritt auf, tritt auf	old Ger. folksong trans. Wenzig	1862			
	3 —	Es rauscht das Wasser	Goethe	1862			
	4 Der Jäger und sein Liebchen	Ist nicht der Himmel so blau?	Hoffmann von Fallersleben	1860			
61	Four Duets, S, A, pf				1874	Vienna, 24 April 1880	xxii, 39
	1 Die Schwestern	Wir Schwestern zwei	Mörike	before 1860			
	2 Klosterfräulein	Ach, ach, ich armes Klosterfräulein	J. Kerner	1862		Merseburg, 1 Feb 1895	
	3 Phänomen	Wenn zu der Regenwand	from Goethe: West-östlicher Divan	1873–4		Basle, 5 Feb 1884	
	4 Die Boten der Liebe	Wie viel schon der Boten	trad. Cz., trans. Wenzig	1873–4		Basle, 5 Feb 1884	

op.	Title	Incipit	Text	Composed	Published	First performance	
66	Five Duets, S, A, pf						
	1 Klänge, i	Aus der Erde quellen Blumen	K. Groth	?1873	1875		xxii, 59
	2 Klänge, ii	Wenn ein müder Leib begraben	Groth	?1875			
	3 Am Strande	Es sprechen und blicken die Wellen	H. Hölty	1875		Hamburg, 13 March 1882	
	4 Jägerlied	Jäger, was jagst du die Häselein?	C. Candidus	1875			
	5 Hüt du dich!	Ich weiss ein Mädlein hübsch und fein	from Des Knaben Wunderhorn	1875		Vienna, 24 April 1880	
75	Four Ballads and Romances						
	1 Edward, A, T, pf	Dein Schwert, wie ists	trad. Scottish, from Percy: Reliques, trans. in Herder Volkslieder	1877	1878	Vienna, 17 Dec 1879	xxii, 79
	2 Guter Rat, S, A, pf	Ach Mutter, liebe Mutter	from Des Knaben Wunderhorn	1877–8		—	
	3 So lass uns wandern!, S, T, pf	Ach Mädchen, liebes Mädchen	trad. Cz., trans. J. Wenzig	1877–8		Berlin, 7 March 1880	
	4 Walpurgisnacht, 2 S, pf	Lieb Mutter, heut Nacht	W. Alexis	1877–8		Vienna, 14 Feb 1881	
84	[5] Romances and Songs, 1/2vv, pf (see under Solo songs)						

ACCOMPANIED CHORAL WORKS

op.	Title	Incipit	Text	Composed	Published	First performance		BW
12	Ave Maria, 4 female vv, orch/org	Ave Maria, gratia plena	liturgical	1858	1861	Hamburg, 1859	xix, 113	85, 134
13	Begräbnisgesang, 5vv, wind insts, timp	Nun lasst uns den Leib begraben	M. Weisse	1858	1861	Hamburg, 2 Dec 1859	xix, 124	85, 134

op	Title	Incipit	Text	Composed	Published	First performance	BW	
17	Four Songs, 3 female vv, 2 hn, harp			1860	1861	Hamburg, 15 Jan 1861	xix, 135	
	1	Es tönt ein voller Harfenklang	F. Ruperti					
	2 Lied von Shakespeare	Komm herbei, komm herbei	from Shakespeare: Twelfth Night					
	3 Der Gärtner	Wohin ich geh und schaue	Eichendorff					
	4 Gesang aus Fingal	Wein' an den Felsen	Ossian					
27	Psalm xiii, 3 female vv, org/pf, str ad lib	Herr, wie lange willst du mein so gar vergessen	biblical	1859	1864	Hamburg, 19 Sept 1864	xx, 1	134
30	Geistliches Lied, 4vv, org/pf	Lass dich nur nichts dauern	P. Flemming	1856	1864	Chemnitz, 2 July 1865	xx, 13	140
45	Ein deutsches Requiem, S, Bar, 4vv, orch, org ad lib		from the Bible, trans. Luther	1854–68	?1869	Leipzig, 18 Feb 1869	xvii, 3	86, 93–4, 96, 108, 131, 133–4, 135, 137, 145
	1 —	Selig sind die da Leid tragen	Matthew v.4; Psalm cxxvi.5–6					
	2 —	Denn alles Fleisch	1 Peter i.24–5; James v.7; Isaiah li.11					
	3 —	Herr, lehre doch mich	Psalm xxxix.5–8; Wisdom of Solomon iii.1					
	4 —	Wie lieblich sind deine Wohungen	Psalm lxxxiv.2–3, 5					92
	5 —	Ihr habt nun Traurigkeit	John xvi.22; Ecclesiasticus li.35; Isaiah lxvi.13					
	6 —	Denn wir haben hie	Hebrews xiii.14; 1 Corinthians xv.51–5; Revelation iv.11					
	7 —	Selig sind die Toten	Revelation xiv.13					
50	Rinaldo, cantata, T, 4 male vv, orch	Zu dem Strande	Goethe	1863–8	1869	Vienna, 28 Feb 1869	xviii, 92	88, 136, 137
53	Rhapsody, Alto, 4 male vv, orch	Aber abseits, wer ist's	from Goethe: Harzreise im Winter	1869	1870	Jena, 3 March 1870	xix, 1	113, 135, 136

54	Schicksalslied, 4vv, orch	Ihr wandelt droben im Licht	Hölderlin	1868–71	Karlsruhe, 18 Oct 1871	xix, 22	134, 135
55	Triumphlied, Bar, 8vv, orch	Halleluja! Halleluja!	Revelation xix	1870–71	Karlsruhe, 5 June 1872	xviii, 1	94, 106, 134, 136, 140
82	Nänie, 4vv, orch	Auch das Schöne muss sterben	Schiller	1880–81	Zurich, 6 Dec 1881	xix, 60	135, 136, 143
89	Gesang der Parzen, 6vv, orch	Es fürchte die Götter	from Goethe: Iphigenie auf Tauris	1882	Basle, 10 Dec 1882	xix, 86	98, 99, 135
93b	Tafellied, 6vv, pf	Gleich wie Echo frohen Liedern	Eichendorff	1884	Krefeld, 28 Jan 1885	xx, 218	
Anh. Ia/17	arr. of Schubert: Ellens Gesang II, D838, for S, 3 female vv, 4 hn, 2 bn; also arr. iv, wind	Jäger, ruhe von der Jagd	from Scott: the Lady of the Lake, trans. A. Storck	?1873	Vienna, 23 March 1873	xix, 153	
Anh. Ia/14	arr. of Schubert: Gruppe aus dem Tartarus, D583, for unison male vv, orch	Horch, wie Murmeln des emporten Meeres	Schiller	1862	Vienna, 8 Dec 1871	—	

UNACCOMPANIED CHORAL WORKS

139–43

22	Marienlieder, 4vv						
	1 Der englische Gruss	Gegrüsset Maria	trad., in A. W. von Zuccalmaglio, ed.: Deutsche Volkslieder	1859	Munich, 1 Dec 1873	xxi, 1	139
	2 Marias Kirchgang	Maria wollt zur Kirche gehn	trad., in Zuccalmaglio	1862	Vienna, 17 April 1864‘		
	3 Marias Wallfahrt	Maria ging aus wandern	trad., in Zuccalmaglio		Leipzig, 13 May 1874		
	4 Der Jäger	Es wollt gut Jäger jagen	trad., in L. Uhland, ed.: Alte hoch- und niederdeutsche Volkslieder		Hanover, 5 Dec 1863		
	5 Ruf zur Maria	Dich Mutter Gottes, ruf' wir an	trad., in Uhland		Vienna, 17 April 1864		
	6 Magdalena	An dem österlichen Tag	trad., in Uhland		—		
	7 Marias Lob	Maria, wahre Himmelsfreud	trad., in Zuccalmaglio		—		
	(nos.1, 2, 4–7 arr. for female vv)			—	—		
29	Two Motets, 5vv			?1860	Vienna, 17 April 1864	xxi, 11	139, 141 140, 142
	1 —	Es ist das Heil uns kommen her	P. Speratus	1864			
	2 —	Schlafe in mir, Gott	Psalm li		—		142

161

op.	Title	Incipit	Text	Composed	Published	First performance	BW
37	Three Sacred Choruses, 4 female vv		liturgical		1865	Hamburg, 26 Sept 1859 (only nos.1–2)	xxi, 159 / 139, 142
1	—	O bone Jesu		?1859			
2	—	Adoramus te, Christe		?1859			140
3	—	Regina coeli laetare		1863			
41	Five Songs, 4 male vv			1861–2	1867		xxi, 193 / 94, 139
1	—	Ich schwing mein Horn ins Jammertal	old Ger., in Uhland			Vienna, 8 Dec 1871	
2	—	Freiwillige her!	C. Lemcke			Vienna, 11 March 1893	
3	Geleit	Was freut einen alten Soldaten?	Lemcke			Vienna, 4 March 1891	
4	Marschieren	Jetzt hab ich schon	Lemcke			Vienna, 27 Nov 1867	
5	—	Gebt acht! Gebt acht!	Lemcke			Vienna, 8 Dec 1871	
42	Three Songs, 6vv				?1868		xxi, 79 / 139
1	Abendständchen	Hör, es klagt die Flöte wieder	C. Brentano	1859		Vienna, 17 April 1864	
2	Vineta	Aus des Meeres tiefem, tiefem Grunde	W. Müller	1860			
3	Darthulas Grabesgesang	Mädchen von Kola, du schläfst!	Ossian, trans. Herder	1861		Munich, 1 Feb 1874	
44	Twelve Songs and Romances, 4 female vv, pf ad lib			1859–60	1866		xxi, 164 / 84, 139
1	Minnelied	Der Holdseligen sonder Wank	J. H. Voss			Hamburg, 15 Jan 1861	
2	Der Bräutigam	Von allen Bergen nieder	Eichendorff			Hamburg, 15 Jan 1861	
3	Barcarole	O Fischer auf den Fluten	trad. It., trans. K. Witte			Hamburg, 8 Nov 1873	
4	Fragen	Wozu ist mein langes Haar	trad. Slavonic, trans. A. Grün			Basle, 4 March 1869	
5	Die Müllerin	Die Mühle, die dreht ihre Flügel	A. von Chamisso			—	

162

			Composed	Published	First performance	Pages
6 Die Nonne	Im stillen Klostergarten	Uhland			Zurich, early Feb 1868	
7 —	Nun stehn die Rosen in Blüte	from P. Heyse: Jungbrunnen			Vienna, 11 March 1885	
8 —	Die Berge sind spitz	from Heyse: Jungbrunnen			Vienna, 11 March 1885	
9 —	Am Wildbach die Weiden	from Heyse: Jungbrunnen			Vienna, 11 March 1885	
10 —	Und gehst du über den Kirchhof	from Heyse: Jungbrunnen			Basle, 4 March 1869	
11 Die Braut	Eine blaue Schürze	W. Müller			Vienna, 2 Feb 1895	
12 Märznacht	Horch! wie brauset der Sturm	Uhland			—	
(nos.5–6 arr. for mixed chorus)			—	—	—	
(no.1 arr. for 3 female vv)			—	1968	—	
(no.9 arr. for 3 female vv)			—	1952	—	
62 Seven Songs, 4–6vv						
1 Rosmarin	Es wollt die Jungfrau früh aufstehn	from Des Knaben Wunderhorn	?1874	1874	—	xxi, 95; 139
2 Von alten Liebesliedern	Spazieren wollt ich reiten	from Des Knaben Wunderhorn			Vienna, 8 Nov 1874	
3 Waldesnacht	Waldesnacht du wunderkühle	from Heyse: Jungbrunnen			Vienna, 8 Nov 1874	
4 —	Dein Herzlein mild	from Heyse: Jungbrunnen			Vienna, 8 Nov 1874	
5 —	All meine Herzgedanken	from Heyse: Jungbrunnen			Hamburg, 9 April 1886	
6 —	Es geht ein Wehen	from Heyse: Jungbrunnen			Munich, 7 Jan 1877	
7 —	Vergangen ist mir Glück und Heil	old Ger.			—	142–3
74 Two Motets, 4–6vv						
1 —	Warum ist das Licht gegeben	biblical (trans. Luther) and Luther	1877	1878	Vienna, 8 Dec 1878	xxi, 29; 139, 141
2 —	O Heiland, reiss die Himmel auf	F. von Spee	?1863–4		Hamburg, 30 Jan 1880	96, 140, 142; 142

op.	Title	Incipit	Text	Composed	Published	First performance	BW	
93a	[6] Songs and Romances, 4vv			1883–4	1884	Krefeld, 27 Jan 1885; Hamburg, 9 Dec 1884 (nos.1, 3, 5)	xxi, 105	139
	1 Der bucklichte Fiedler	Es wohnet ein Fiedler zu Frankfurt	Rhenish folksong, in Zuccalmaglio					
	2 Das Mädchen	Stand das Mädchen	trad. Serbian, trans. S. Kapper					
	3 —	O süsser Mai	A. von Arnim					
	4 —	Fahr wohl, o Vöglein	F. Rückert					
	5 Der Falke	Hebt ein Falke sich empor	trad. Serbian, trans. Kapper					
	6 Beherzigung	Feiger Gedanken	Goethe					
104	Five Songs, 4-6vv				1888	Vienna, 3 April 1889; Hamburg, 29 March 1889 (nos.2, 5)	xxi, 117	139
	1 Nachtwache, i	Leise Töne der Brust	Rückert	1888				
	2 Nachtwache, ii	Ruhn sie? ruhn sie	Rückert	1888				
	3 Letztes Glück	Leblos gleitet Blatt um Blatt	M. Kalbeck	1887				
	4 Verlorene Jugend	Brausten alle Berge	trad. Cz., trans. J. Wenzig	?1886				
	5 Im Herbst	Ernst ist der Herbst	K. Groth	1886				
109	Fest- und Gedenksprüche, 8vv		biblical	?1886–9	1890	Hamburg, 9 Sept 1889	xxi, 61	102, 139, 141
	1 —	Unsere Väter hofften auf dich						
	2 —	Wenn ein starker Gewappneter						
	3 —	Wo ist ein so herrlich Volk						
110	Three Motets, 4-8vv			1889	1890	Cologne, 13 March 1890; Hamburg, 15 Jan 1890	xxi, 47	98, 139, 141
	1 Ich aber bin elend	Ich aber bin elend	Psalm lxix.30.2 Moses xxxiv.6-7					
	2 Ach, arme Welt	Ach, arme Welt	anon.					142
	3 Wenn wir in höchsten Nöten sein	Wenn wir in höchsten Nöten sein	P. Eber (1511–69)					
WoO 20 posth.	Dem dunkeln Schoss der heiligen Erde	Dem dunkeln Schoss der heiligen Erde	Schiller: Das Lied von der Glocke	before 1864	1927		xxi, 155	

	No.	Title	Incipit					
				1926–7	1864	1854–73	1863–4	xxi, 127
WoO 34, 35 posth.		**[26] Deutsche Volkslieder, arr. 4vv**						
		Book 1						
	1	—	Von edler Art					
	2	—	Mit Lust tät ich ausreiten					
	3	—	Bei nächtlicher Weil					
	4	Vom heiligen Märtyrer, Emmerano, Bischoffen zu	Komm Mainz, komm Bayrn					
	5	Täublein weiss	Es flog ein Täublein					
	6	—	Ach lieber Herre Jesu Christ					
	7	Sankt Raphael	Tröst die Bedrängten					
		Book 2						
	8	—	In stiller Nacht					
	9	Abschiedslied	Ich fahr dahin					
	10	Der tote Knabe	Es pochet ein Knabe					
	11	—	Die Wollust in den Maien					
	12	Morgengesang	Wach auf, mein Kind					
	13	Schnitter Tod	Es ist ein Schnitter					
	14	Der englische Jäger	Es wollt gut Jäger jagen					
		additional numbers						
	15	Scheiden	Ach Gott, wie weh tut Scheiden					
	16	Wach auf!	Wach auf, meins Herzens-schöne					
	17	—	Erlaube mir, feins Mädchen					
	18	Der Fiedler	Es wohnet ein Fiedler					
	19	—	Da unten im Tale					
	20	—	Des Abends kann ich					
	21	Wach auf!	Wach auf, meins Herzens-schöne					
	22	—	Dort in den Weiden					
WoO 35 posth.								

op.	Title	Incipit	Text	Composed	Published	First performance	BW
23 Altes Volkslied	Verstohlen geht der Mond auf						
24 Der Ritter und die Feine	Es stunden drei Rosen						
25 Der Zimmergesell	Es war einmal ein Zimmergesell						
26 Altdeutsches Kampflied	Wir stehen hier zur Schlacht bereit						
WoO 17 posth.	Kyrie, 4vv, bc	Kyrie eleison		1856	1984	Vienna, 18 Oct 1983	—
WoO 18 posth.	Missa canonica, 5vv	Sanctus, Benedictus, Agnus Dei/Dona nobis		1856	1856, 1984	—	—
WoO 19 posth.	Dein Herzlein mild	from Heyse: Jung-brunnen; see op.62/4		1860	1938	—	—

143–6

SOLO SONGS

(for 1v, pf unless otherwise stated)

op.	Title	Incipit	Text	Key	Composed	Published	BW
3 Six Songs, T/S, pf							xxiii, 1
1 Liebestreu	O versenk, o versenk dein Leid	R. Reinick	e♭	1853	1853		
2 Liebe und Frühling, i (2 versions)	Wie sich Rebenranken schwingen	Hoffmann von Fallersleben	B	1853, rev. 1882	2/1882		
3 Liebe und Frühling, ii	Ich muss hinaus	Hoffmann von Fallersleben	B	1853	1853		
4 Lied aus dem Gedicht 'Ivan'	Weit über das Feld	F. Bodenstedt	e♭	1853	1853		
5 In der Fremde	Aus der Heimat	J. von Eichendorff	f♯	1852	1852		
6 Lied	Lindes Rauschen in den Wipfeln	Eichendorff	A	1852	1852		
6 Six Songs, S/T, pf							xxiii, 20
1 Spanisches Lied	In dem schatten meiner Locken	anon. Sp., trans. P. Heyse	a	1852	1853		
2 Der Frühling	Es lockt und säuselt um den Baum	J. B. Rousseau	E	1852			

145

		First line	Text source	Key			
	3 Nachwirkung	Sie ist gegangen	A. Meissner	A♭	1852		
	4 Juchhe!	Wie ist doch die Erde so schön	Reinick	E♭	1852		
	5 —	Wie die Wolke nach der Sonne	Hoffmann von Fallersleben	B	1853		
	6 —	Nachtigallen schwingen lustig	Hoffmann von Fallersleben	A♭	1853		
7	Six Songs						
	1 Treue Liebe	Ein Mägdlein sass am Meeresstrand	E. Ferrand	f♯	1852	1854	xxiii, 38
	2 Parole	Sie stand wohl am Fensterbogen	Eichendorff	e	1852		
	3 Anklänge	Hoch über stillen Höhen	Eichendorff	a	1853		
	4 Volkslied	Die Schwälble ziehet fort	trad., in G. Scherer, ed.: Deutsche Volkslieder	e	1852		
	5 Die Trauernde	Mei Mueter mag mi net	trad., in Scherer	a	1852		
	6 Heimkehr	O brich nicht, Steg	L. Uhland	b	1851		
14	Eight Songs and Romances						
	1 Vor dem Fenster	Soll sich der Mond nicht heller scheinen	trad., in K. Simrock, ed.: Die deutschen Volkslieder	g	1858	1861	xxiii, 50	84
	2 Vom verwundeten Knaben	Es wollt ein Mädchen früh aufstehn	trad., in Herder: Volkslieder	a			
	3 Murrays Ermordung	O Hochland und o Südland	from Percy: Reliques, trans. in Herder	e			
	4 Ein Sonett	Ach könnt ich, könnte vergessen sie	attrib. Count Thibault (13th century), trans. in Herder	A♭			
	5 Trennung	Wach auf, wach auf!	trad., in A. W. von Zuccalmaglio, ed.: Deutsche Volkslieder	F			
	6 Gang zur Liebsten	Des Abends kann ich nicht schlafen gehn	trad., in Zuccalmaglio	e			
	7 Ständchen	Gut Nacht, gut Nacht	trad., in Zuccalmaglio	F			
	8 Sehnsucht (no.8 arr. for 3 female vv)	Mein Schatz ist nicht da	trad., in Zuccalmaglio	e	—	1968	
19	Five Poems						
	1 Der Kuss	Unter Blüten des Mai's	L. Hölty	B♭	1858	1862	xxiii, 67	84
	2 Scheiden und Meiden	So soll ich dich nun meiden	Uhland	d			
	3 In der Ferne	Will ruhen unter den Bäumen	Uhland	d–D			
	4 Der Schmied	Ich hör meinen Schatz	Uhland	B♭			
	5 An eine Äolsharfe	Angelehnt an die Epheuwand	E. Mörike	a♭–A♭			

167

op.	Title	Incipit	Text	Key	Composed	Published	BW	
32	[9] Songs							143
	1 —	Wie rafft ich mich auf in der Nacht	A. von Platen	f	1864	1865	xxiii, 79	
	2 —	Nicht mehr zu dir zu gehen	G. F. Daumer	d				
	3 —	Ich schleich umher	Platen	d				
	4 —	Der Strom, der neben mir verrauschte	Platen	c♯				
	5 —	Wehe, so willst du mich wieder	Platen	b				
	6 —	Du sprichtst, dass ich mich täuschte	Platen	c				
	7 —	Bitteres zu sagen denkst du	Daumer, after Hafis	F				
	8 —	So stehn wir, ich und meine Weide	Daumer, after Hafis	A♭				
	9 —	Wie bist du, meine Königin	Daumer, after Hafis	E♭				
33	[15] Romances from L. Tieck's Magelone		from L. Tieck: Liebesgeschichte der schönen Magelone und des Grafen Peter von Provence				xxiii, 107	86, 145
	Set 1							
	1 —	Keinen hat es noch gereut		E♭	1861	1865		
	2 —	Traun! Bogen und Pfeil sind gut		c				
	3 —	Sind es Schmerzen, sind es Freuden		A♭				
	Set 2							
	4 —	Liebe kam aus fernen Landen		D♭	1862	1865		
	5 —	So willst du des Armen		F				
	6 —	Wie soll ich die Freude		A				
	Set 3							
	7 —	War es dir		D	before March 1864	?1869		
	8 —	Wir müssen uns trennen		G♭	before Sept 1865			
	9 —	Ruhe, Süssliebchen		A♭	before July 1868			
	Set 4							
	10 Verzweiflung	So tönet denn		c	before Dec 1866	1869		

No.	Title	First line	Source	Key	Composed	Published	Edn.
12	—	Muss es eine Trennung geben		g	early 1862	1869	
	Set 5						
13	Sulima	Geliebter, wo zaudert		E	1862		
14	—	Wie froh und frisch		G		May 1869	
15	—	Treue Liebe dauert lange		Eb		May 1869	xxiv, 1
43	Four Songs						
	1 Von ewiger Liebe	Dunkel, wie dunkel	trad. Serbian, trans. L. Haupt in Hoffmann von Fallersleben	b	1864	1868	
	2 Die Mainacht	Wann der silberne Mond	L. Hölty	Eb	1864		145
	3 —	Ich schell mein Horn ins Jammertal	old Ger., in C. F. Becker, ed.: Lieder und Weisen vergangener Jahrhunderte	Bb	1859		
	4 Das Lied vom Herrn von Falkenstein	Es reit der Herr von Falkenstein	in Uhland, ed.: Alte hoch- und niederdeutsche Volkslieder	c	1857		
46	Four Songs						
	1 Die Kränze	Hier, ob dem Eingang	Cz. and Hung., trans. Daumer	Db	1868	1868	xxiv, 18
	2 Magyarisch	Sah dem edlen Bildnis	Cz. and Hung., trans. Daumer	A	—		
	3 Die Schale der Vergessenheit	Eine Schale des Stroms	L. Hölty	E	?1864		
	4 An die Nachtigall	Geuss nicht so laut	Hölty	E	1868		
47	Five Songs						
	1 Botschaft	Wehe, Lüftchen	Daumer, after Hafis	Db	1868	1868	xxiv, 32
	2 Liebesglut	Die Flamme hier	Daumer, after Hafis	f–F	1868		
	3 Sonntag	So hab ich doch die ganze Woche	in Uhland	F	1859		
	4 —	O liebliche Wangen	Flemming	D	1868		
	5 Die Liebende schreibt	Ein Blick von deinen Augen	Goethe	Eb	1858		
48	Seven Songs						
	1 Der Gang zum Liebchen	Es glänzt der Mond nieder	anon. Bohemian, trans. J. Wenzig	e	1859–62	1868	xxiv, 48
	2 Der Überläufer	In den Garten wollen wir gehen	Des Knaben Wunderhorn	f#	1853		
	3 Liebesklage des Mädchens	Wer sehen will	Des Knaben Wunderhorn	B	before 1860		

op.	Title	Incipit	Text	Key	Composed	Published	BW
	4 Gold überwiegt die Liebe	Sternchen mit dem trüben Schein	anon. Bohemian, trans. Wenzig	e	1868		144
	5 Trost in Tränen	Wie kommt's dass du so traurig bist	Goethe	E–e	1858		
	6 —	Vergangen ist mir Glück und Heil	old Ger., in F. Mittler, ed.: Deutsche Volkslieder	d	1859–62		
	7 Herbstgefühl	Wie wenn im frostgen Windhauch	A. F. von Schack	f♯	1867		
49	Five Songs					1868	xxiv, 64
	1 Am Sonntag Morgen	Am Sonntag Morgen zierlich angetan	anon. It., trans. Heyse	e	—		
	2 An ein Veilchen	Birg, o Veilchen	G. B. F. Zappi, trans. Hölty	E	1868		
	3 Sehnsucht	Hinter jenen dichten Wäldern	anon. Bohemian, trans. Wenzig	A♭	1868		
	4 Wiegenlied	Guten Abend, gut Nacht	Des Knaben Wunderhorn, and in G. Scherer, ed.: Deutsche Volkslieder	E♭	1868		
	5 Abenddämmerung	Sei willkommen, Zwielichtstunde!	Schack	E	1867		
57	[8] Songs		Daumer		before aut. 1871	1871	xxiv, 80
	1 —	Von waldbekränzter Höhe		G			
	2 —	Wenn du nur zuweilen lächelst		E♭			
	3 —	Es träumte mir, ich sei dir teuer	Sp., trans. Daumer	B			
	4 —	Ach, wende diesen Blick		f			
	5 —	In meiner Nächte Sehnen		e			
	6 —	Strahl zuweilen auch ein mildes Licht		E			
	7 —	Die Schnur, die Perl an Perle	Ind., trans. Daumer	B			
	8 —	Unbewegte laue Luft		E			
58	[8] Songs				before aut. 1871	1871	xxiv, 109
	1 Blinde Kuh	Im Finstern geh ich suchen	anon. It., trans. A. Kopisch	g			
	2 Während des Regens	Voller, dichter tropft ums Dach da	Kopisch	D♭			

	Title	Incipit	Poet	Key	Date		Refs
	3 Die Spröde	Ich sahe eine Tigrin	anon. Calabrian, trans. Kopisch, rev. Heyse for later edns.	A			
	4 —	O komme, holde Sommernacht	M. Grohe	F♯			
	5 Schwermut	Mir ist so weh ums Herz	C. Candidus	e♭			
	6 In der Gasse	Ich blicke hinab in die Gasse	F. Hebbel	d			
	7 Vorüber	Ich legte mich unter den Lindenbaum	Hebbel	F			
59	8 Serenade	Leise, um dich nicht zu wecken	Schack	a		1873	xxiv, 134
	[8] Songs						
	1 —	Dämmrung senkte sich von oben	Goethe	g	?1871		
	2 Auf dem See	Blauer Himmel, blaue Wogen	C. Simrock	E	1873		
	3 Regenlied	Walle, Regen, walle nieder	K. Groth	f♯	1873		
	4 Nachklang	Regentropfen aus den Bäumen	Groth	f♯	1873		
	5 Agnes	Rosenzeit, wie schnell vorbei	Mörike	g	1873		
	6 —	Eine gute, gute Nacht	Daumer	a	1873		
	7 Mein wundes Herz	Mein wundes Herz verlangt	Groth	e	1873		
63	8 Dein blaues Auge	Dein blaues Auge hält so still	Groth	E♭	1873		125
	[9] Songs						
	1 Frühlingstrost	Es weht um mich	M. von Schenkendorf	A	1874		
	2 Erinnerung	Ihr wunderschönen Augenblicke	Schenkendorf	C	1874	1874	xxiv, 164
	3 An ein Bild	Was schaust du mich	Schenkendorf	A♭	1874		
	4 An die Tauben	Fliegt nur aus	Schenkendorf	C	1874		
	5 Junge Lieder, i	Meine Liebe ist grün	F. Schumann	F♯	1873		
	6 Junge Lieder, ii	Wenn um den Holunder	F. Schumann	D	1874		
	7 Heimweh, i	Wie traulich war das Fleckchen	Groth	G	1874		
	8 Heimweh, ii	O wüsst ich doch den Weg zurück	Groth	E	1874		
69	9 Heimweh, iii	Ich sah als Knabe	Groth	A	?1873	1877	xxv, 1
	Nine Songs						
	1 Klage, i	Ach, mir fehlt	anon. Bohemian, trans. Wenzig	D	1877		96, 144
	2 Klage, ii	O Felsen, lieber Felsen	anon. Slovak, trans. Wenzig	a			
	3 Abschied	Ach, mich hält der Gram	anon. Bohemian, trans. Wenzig	E♭			

op.	Title	Incipit	Text	Key	Composed	Published	BW
	4 Des Liebsten Schwur	Ei, schmollte mein Vater	anon. Bohemian, trans. Wenzig	F			
	5 Tambourliedchen	Den Wirbel schlag ich	C. Candidus	A			
	6 Vom Strande	Ich rufe vom Ufer	trad. Sp., trans. Eichendorff	a			
	7 Über die See	Über die See, fern über die See	C. Lemcke	e			
	8 Salome	Singt mein Schatz	G. Keller	C			
	9 Mädchenfluch	Ruft die Mutter	trad. Serbian, trans. S. Kapper	a			
70	Four Songs					1877	xxv, 35 96
	1 Im Garten am Seegestade	Im Garten am Seegestade	Lemcke	g	1877		
	2 Lerchengesang	Ätherische ferne Stimmen	Candidus	B	1877		
	3 Serenade	Liebliches Kind	Goethe	B	1876		
	4 Abendregen	Langsam und schimmernd	Keller	a–C	1877		
71	Five Songs					1877	xxv, 46 96
	1 Es liebt sich so lieblich im Lenze!	Die Wellen blinken	Heine	D			
	2 An den Mond	Silbermond, mit bleichen Strahlen	Simrock	b			
	3 Geheimnis	O Frühlingsabenddämmerung	Candidus	G			
	4 Willst du, dass ich geh?	Auf der Heide weht der Wind	Lemcke	d			
	5 Minnelied	Holder klingt der Vogelsang	Hölty	C			
72	Five Songs					1877	xxv, 63 96
	1 Alte Liebe	Es kehrt die dunkle Schwalbe	Candidus	g	1876		
	2 Sommerfäden	Sommerfäden hin und wieder	Candidus	c	1876		
	3 O kühler Wald	O kühler Wald	C. Brentano	A♭	1877		
	4 Verzagen	Ich sitz am Strande	Lemcke	f♯	1877		
	5 Unüberwindlich	Hab ich tausendmal geschworen	Goethe	A	1876		
84	[5] Romances and Songs, 1/2 female vv, pf					1882	xxv, 81 99
	1 Sommerabend	Geh schlafen, Tochter	H. Schmidt	d	?1881		
	2 Der Kranz	Mutter, hilf mir	Schmidt	g	?1881		
	3 In den Beeren	Singe, Mädchen, hell und klar	Schmidt	E♭	?1881		
	4 Vergebliches Ständchen	Guten Abend, mein Schatz	trad., in Zuccalmaglio	A	?1877–9		
	5 Spannung	Gut'n Abend, gut'n Abend	trad. Lower Rhenish, in Zuccalmaglio	a	?1877–9		

op.	Title	Incipit	Text	Key	Composed	Published	BW
96	Four Songs					1886	xxv, 180
	1 —	Der Tod, das ist die kühle Nacht	Heine	C	1884		
	2 —	Wir wandelten, wir zwei zusammen	Daumer	D♭			
	3 —	Es schauen die Blumen	Heine	b			
	4 Meerfahrt	Mein Liebchen, wir sassen	Heine	a			
97	Six Songs					1886	xxv, 192
	1 Nachtigall	O Nachtigall, dein süsser Schall	C. Reinhold	f	1884–5		
	2 Auf dem Schiffe	Ein Vögelein fliegt	Reinhold	A			
	3 Entführung	O Lady Judith	W. Alexis	d			
	4 —	Dort in den Weiden	trad. Lower Rhenish, in Zuccalmaglio	D			
	5 Komm bald	Warum denn warten	Groth	A			
	6 Trennung	Da unten im Tale	trad. Swabian, in Zuccalmaglio	F			
105	Five Songs, low v, pf					1888	xxvi, 1
	1 —	Wie Melodien zieht es mir	Groth	A	1886		
	2 —	Immer leiser wird mein Schlummer	H. Lingg	c♯	1886		145
	3 Klage	Feins Liebchen, trau du nicht	trad. Lower Rhenish, in Zuccalmaglio	F	?1888		
	4 Auf dem Kirchhofe	Der Tag ging regenschwer	D. von Liliencron	c	?1888		
	5 Verrat	Ich stand in einer lauen Nacht	Lemcke	b	1886		
106	Five Songs					1888	xxvi, 15
	1 Ständchen	Der Mond steht über dem Berge	F. Kugler	G	?1888		
	2 Auf dem See	An dies Schifflein schmiege	Reinhold	E	1885		
	3 —	Es hing der Reif	Groth	a	1888		
	4 Meine Lieder	Wenn mein Herz beginnt	A. Frey	f♯	1888		
	5 Ein Wanderer	Hier, wo sich die Strassen	Reinhold	f	1885		
107	Five Songs					1888	xxvi, 31
	1 An die Stolze	Und gleichwohl kann ich	Flemming	A	1886		
	2 Salamander	Es sass ein Salamander	Lemcke	a	1888		
	3 Das Mädchen spricht	Schwalbe, sag mir an	O. F. Gruppe	A	1886		
	4 Maienkätzchen	Maienkätzchen erster Gruss	Liliencron	E♭	?1886		
	5 Mädchenlied	Auf die Nacht in den Spinnstub'n	Heyse	b	?1887		

No.	Title	Text incipit	Source	Key				
							1896	98, 104, 105 145, 146
121	Vier ernste Gesänge [Four serious songs], B, pf							
1	—	Denn es gehet dem Menschen	Ecclesiastes iii.19 22	d	1896	1896	xxvi, 44	
2	—	Ich wandte mich und sahe an alle	Ecclesiastes iv.1 3	g				
3	—	O Tod, o Tod, wie bitter bist du	Ecclesiasticus xli.1–2	e				
4	—	Wenn ich mit Menschen- und mit Engelszungen redete	I Corinthians xiii	E♭				
WoO 21	Mondnacht	Es war, als hätt der Himmel	Eichendorff	A♭	1853	1853	xxvi, 62	
WoO 23	Regenlied posth.	Regentropfen aus den Bäumen	Groth	g	1872	1908	xxvi, 64	
WoO 22	Five Songs of Ophelia, S, pf ad lib		from Shakespeare: Hamlet, trans. Schlegel and L. Tieck		1873	1935	—	
1	—	Wie erkenn ich dein Treulieb		g				
2	—	Sein Leichenhemd weiss		e				
3	—	Auf morgen ist Sankt Valentins Tag		G				
4	—	Sie trugen ihn auf der Bahre bloss		F				
5	—	Und kommt er nicht mehr zurück?		d				

INDEX TO THE SONGS

The following alphabetical index includes all titles and text incipits to the works in the preceding list, and follows each with its opus number(s).

Silbermond, mit bleichen Strahlen, 71/2; Sind es Schmerzen, sind es Freuden, 33/3; Singe, Mädchen, hell und klar, 84/3; Singt mein Schatz, 69/8; So hab ich doch die ganze Woche, 47/3; Soll sich der Mond nicht heller scheinen, 14/1

Sommerabend, 84/1, 85/1; Sommerfäden hin und wieder, 72/2; Sonntag, 47/3; So soll ich dich nun meiden, 19/2; So stehn wir, ich und meine Weide, 32/8; So tönet denn, 33/10; So willst du des Armen, 33/5; Spanisches Lied, 6/1; Spannung, 84/5; Ständchen, 14/7, 106/1; Stand das Mädchen, 95/1; Steig auf, geliebter Schatten, 94/2; Sternchen mit dem trüben Schein, 48/4; Störe nicht den leisen Schlummer, 86/3; Strahlt zuweilen auch ein mildes Licht, 57/6; Sulima, 33/13

Tambourliedchen, 69/5; Therese, 86/1; Todessehnen, 86/6; Traum! Bogen und Pfeil sind gut, 33/2; Trennung, 14/5, 97/6; Treue Liebe, 7/1; Treue Liebe dauert lange, 33/15; Trost in Tränen, 48/5; Über die Heide hallet, 86/4; Über die See, fern über die See, 69/7; Unbewegte laue Luft, 57/8; Und gleichwohl kann ich, 107/1; Und kommt er nicht mehr zurück?, no op. no.; Unter Blüten des Mai's, 19/1; Unüberwindlich, 72/5

Vergangen ist mir Glück und Heil, 48/6; Vergebliches Ständchen, 84/4; Verrat, 105/5; Versunken, 86/5; Verzagen, 72/4; Verzweiflung, 33/10; Volkslied, 7/4; Voller, dichter tropft uns Dach da, 58/2; Vom Strande, 69/6; Vom verwundeten Knaben, 14/2; Von ewiger Liebe, 43/1; Von waldbekränzter Höhe, 57/1; Vor dem Fenster, 14/1; Vorschneller Schwur, 95/5; Vorüber, 58/7

Wach auf, wach auf!, 14/5; Während des Regens, 58/2; Walle, Regen, walle nieder, 59/3; Wann der silberne Mond, 43/2; War es dir, 33/7; Warum denn warten, 97/5; Was schaust du mich, 63/3; Wehe, Lüftchen, 47/1; Wehe, so willst du mich wieder, 32/5; Weit über das Feld, 3/4; Wenn du nur zuweilen lächelst, 57/2; Wenn ich mit Menschen- und mit Engelszungen, 121/4; Wenn mein Herz beginnt, 106/4; Wenn um den Holunder, 63/6; Wer sehen will, 48/3; Wie bist du, meine Königin, 32/9; Wie die Wolke nach der Sonne, 6/5; Wie erkenn ich dein Treulieb, no op. no.: Wie froh und frisch, 33/14

Wiegenlied, 49/4; Wie ist doch die Erde so schön, 6/4; Wie kommt's dass du so traurig bist, 48/5; Wie Melodien zieht es mir, 105/1; Wie rafft ich mich auf in der Nacht, 32/1; Wie schienen die Sternlein, 85/4; Wie schnell verschwindet, 33/11; Wie sich Rebenranken schwingen, 3/2; Wie soll ich die Freude, 33/6; Wie traulich war das Fleckchen, 63/7; Wie wenn im frostgen Windhauch, 48/7; Will ruhen unter den Bäumen, 19/3; Willst du, dass ich geh?, 71/4; Wir müssen uns trennen, 33/8; Wir wandelten, 96/2

FOLKSONG ARRANGEMENTS

8 Gypsy Songs, arr. of op.103 nos.1–7, 11 for 1v, pf, 1887 (1889), BW xxvi, 176

WoO 31: [15] Volks-Kinderlieder, arr. for 1v, pf, 1857 (1858), BW xxvi, 176
1 Dornröschen
2 Die Nachtigall
3 Die Henne
4 Sandmännchen
5 Der Mann
6 Heidenröslein
7 Das Schlaraffenland
8a Beim Ritt auf dem Knie ('Ull Mann wull riden')
8b Beim Ritt auf dem Knie ('Alt Mann wollt reiten')
9 Der Jäger in dem Walde
10 Das Mädchen und die Hasel
11 Wiegenlied
12 Weihnachten
13 Marienwürmchen
14 Dem Schutzengel
15 Sommerlied (unpubd)

WoO 32 posth.: 28 deutsche Volkslieder, arr. for 1v, pf, 1858 (1926), BW xxvi, 191
1 Die Schnürbrust
2 Der Jäger
3 Drei Vögelein
4 Auf, gebet uns das Pfingstei
5 Des Markgrafen Töchterlein

WoO 36 posth.: [8] deutsche Volkslieder, arr. for 3 and 4 female vv, 1859–62 (1938)
1 Totenklage / In stiller Nacht
2 Minnelied / So will ich frisch und fröhlich sein
3 Der tote Knabe / Es pochet ein Knabe
4 Ich hab die Nacht geträumet
5 Altdeutsches Minnelied / Mein Herzlein tut mir gar zu weh!
6 Es waren zwei Königskinder
7 Spannung / Guten Abend
8 Drei Vögelein / Mit Lust tät ich ausreiten

WoO 37 posth.: [16] deutsche Volkslieder, arr. for 3 and 4 female vv, 1859–62 (1964–5)
1 Schwesterlein, Schwesterlein
2 Ich hörte ein Sichlein rauschen
3 Der Ritter und die Feine / Es stunden drei Rosen
4 Ich stand auf hohem Berge
5 Gunhilde
6 Der buckliche Fiedler / Es wohnet ein Fiedler
7 Die Versuchung / Feinsliebchen, du sollst mir nicht barfuss gehn
8 Altes Minnelied / Ich fahr dahin
9 Die Wollust in den Maien
10 Trennung / Da unten im Tale
11 Der Jäger / Bei nächtlicher Weil
12 Scheiden / Ach Gott, wie weh tut Scheiden
13 Zu Strassburg auf der Schanz
14 Wach auf mein Hort
15 Der Ritter / Es ritt ein Reiter
16 Ständchen / Wach auf, mein's Herzens Schöne

WoO 38 posth.: [20] deutsche Volkslieder, arr. for 3 and 4 female vv, 1859–62 (1968)
1 Die Entführung / Auf, auf, auf!
2 Gang zur Liebsten / Des Abends kann ich nicht schlafen gehn
3 Schifferlied / Dort in den Weiden steht ein Haus
4 Gartengeheimnis / Erlaube mir, feins Mädchen

5 Schnitter Tod / Es ist ein Schnitter
6 Die Bernauerin / Es reiten drei Reiter
7 Der eifersüchtige Knabe / Es stehen drei Sterne am Himmel
8 Der Baum in Odenwald / Es steht ein Baum im Odenwald
9 Des Markgrafen Töchterlein / Es war ein Markgraf überm Rhein
10 Die Jüdin / Es war eine stolze Jüdin
11 Der Zimmergesell / Es war einmal ein Zimmergesell
12 Liebeslied / Gar lieblich hat sich gesellet
13 Heimliche Liebe / Kein Feuer, keine Kohle
14 Altes Liebeslied / Mein Herzlein tut mir gar zu weh!
15 Dauerude Liebe / Mein Schatz, ich hab es erfahren
16 Während der Trennung / Mein Schatz ist auf die Wanderschaft hin
17 Morgen muss ich fort von hier
18 Scheiden / Sind wir geschieden
19 Vor dem Fenster / Soll sich der Mond nicht heller scheinen
20 Ständchen / Verstohlen geht der Mond auf

ARRANGEMENTS OF WORKS BY OTHER COMPOSERS

Anh.1a/6: arr. of Schubert's Ländler d366 and 814, for pf (2 and 4 hands), ?1860s (1869)
Anh.1a/7: arr. of Schumann's Scherzo from Pf Qnt op.44, for pf, 1854 (1983)
Anh.1a/8: arr. of Schumann's Pf Qt op.47, for pf 4 hands, 1855 (1887)
Anh.1a/9: arr. of Bach's Chorale bwv44, figured bass (1877)
Anh.1a/10–11: arr. of Handel's 13 duets and 2 trios, figured bass (1870/1880–81)
Anh.1a/12: arr. of Schubert's An Schwager Kronos (Goethe), d369, for 1v, orch, 1862 (1933)
Anh.1a/13: arr. of Schubert's Memnon (J. Mayrhofer), d541, for 1v, orch, 1862 (1933)
Anh.1a/15: arr. of Schubert's Geheimes (Goethe), d719, for 1v, hn, str, 1862 (1933), MS in GB-Ob
Anh.1a/16: arr. of Schubert's d778, for 1v, orch, 1862 (unpubd), MS in private collection, Sussex
Anh.1a/18: arr. of Schubert's d950, piano reduction, 1865 (1865)

ARRANGEMENTS OF BRAHMS'S OWN WORKS

for orch: Hungarian Dances WoO 1/1, 3, 10

for pf with vn, vc: Double Concerto op.102, last movt

for pf, vn: Clarinet Sonatas opp.120 nos.1–2; Vn Conc. op.77

for 2 pf: Pf Conc. opp.15, 83; Syms. opp.90, 98

for pf duet: Pf Conc. op.15; Pf Qts opp.25, 26; Ovs., opp.80, 81; Requiem Op.45; Serenades opp.11, 16; Str Sextets opp.18, 36; Str Qts opp.51 nos.1, 2, op.67; Str Qnts opp.88, 111; Syms. opp.68, 73, 98 (op.90 arr. R. Keller, ed. and corr. Brahms); Triumphlied op.55

for pf: Str Sextet op.18, 2nd movt; Hungarian Dances WoO 1/1–10

for vv, pf: Liebeslieder opp.52, 65

for chorus, pf: opp.12, 13, 17, 29 nos.1–2, 42, 45, 50, 53, 54 (arr. Levi, corr. Brahms), 55, 82, 89

for chorus, orch: op.52 nos.1, 2, 4–6, 8, 9, 11, op.65 no.9

for 1v, pf: op.103 nos.1–7, 11

180

BIBLIOGRAPHY

CATALOGUES AND BIBLIOGRAPHIES

N. Simrock: *Thematisches Verzeichniss sämmtlicher im Druck erschienenen Werke von Johannes Brahms* (Berlin, 1887, 2/1897; Eng. trans., enlarged, 1956, as *Thematic Catalogue of the Collected Works of Brahms*; rev. 2/1973)

O. Keller: 'Johannes Brahms-Literatur', *Die Musik*, xii/1 (1912–13), 86

A. Seidl: 'Nachtrag zu O. Kellers Johannes Brahms-Literatur', *Die Musik*, xii/1 (1912–13), 287

A. von Ehrmann: *Johannes Brahms: thematisches Verzeichnis* (Leipzig, 1933)

O. E. Deutsch: 'The First Editions of Brahms', *MR*, xxi (1940), 123, 255

L. Koch: *Brahms-Bibliografia*, A fövárosi könytar evkönyve, xii (Budapest, 1943)

T. Quigley: 'Johannes Brahms and Bibliographic Control: Review and Assessment', *FAM* (1983), no. 30, p.207

S. Kross: *Brahms-Bibliographie* (Tutzing, 1983)

M. L. McCorkle: *Johannes Brahms thematisch-bibliographisches Werkverzeichnis* (Munich, 1984)

ICONOGRAPHIES

M. Fellinger: *Brahms-Bilder* (Leipzig, 1900, enlarged 2/1912)

V. von Miller zu Aichholz: *Ein Brahms-Bilderbuch* (Vienna, 1905)

A. Orel: *Johannes Brahms: sein Leben in Bildern* (Vienna, 1937)

E. Crass: *Johannes Brahms: sein Leben in Bildern* (Leipzig, 1957)

O. Biba: 'Ausstellung "Johannes Brahms in Wien" im Musikverein', *ÖMz*, xxxviii (1983), 254

SOURCE MATERIAL, DOCUMENTS, LETTERS

A. Dietrich: *Erinnerungen an Johannes Brahms in Briefen* (Leipzig, 1898, 2/1899; Eng. trans., 1899)

Johannes Brahms: Briefwechsel, i–xvi (Berlin, 1907–22) [Deutsche Brahms Gesellschaft edn.]

N. Bickley, ed. and trans.: *Letters to and from J. Joachim* (London, 1914)

A. Einstein: 'Briefe von Brahms an Ernst Frank', *ZMw*, iv (1921–2), 385–416

B. Litzmann: *Clara Schumann–Johannes Brahms: Briefe aus den Jahren 1853–1896* (Leipzig, 1927; Eng. trans., n.d., 2/1971)

K. Geiringer: 'Johannes Brahms im Briefwechsel mit Eusebius Mandyczewski', *ZMw*, xv (1932–3), 337–70

R. Caillet and E. Göpel: 'Ein Brahmsfund in Südfrankreich', *ZMw*, xv (1933), 371

H. Schenker, ed.: *Johannes Brahms: Oktaven und Quinten u.a.* (Vienna, 1933) [facs. edn. of a Brahms autograph MS]

K. Stephenson, ed.: *Johannes Brahms: Heimatbekenntnisse in Briefen an seine Hamburger Verwandten* (Hamburg, 1933)

O. G. Billroth: *Billroth und Brahms im Briefwechsel* (Vienna, 1935)

K. Geiringer: 'Brahms and Wagner, with Unpublished Letters', *MQ*, xxii (1936), 178

F. von Lepel: 'Ein unbekannter Brahms-Brief', *Signale*, xcvi (1938), 27

R. Litterscheid: *Johannes Brahms in seinen Schriften und Briefen* (Berlin, 1943)

E. H. Müller von Asow, ed.: *Johannes Brahms und Mathilde Wesendonck: ein Briefwechsel* (Vienna, 1943)

F. Zagiba: 'Johannes Brahms als "Dirigentenpromotor": unbekannte Briefe des Meisters', *Musikerziehung*, ix (1955–6), 238

V. Pauls: *Briefe der Freundschaft: Johannes Brahms–Klaus Groth* (Heide, 1956)

H. Barkan, ed.: *Johannes Brahms and Theodore Billroth: Letters from a Musical Friendship* (Norman, Oklahoma, 1957)

S. Djurić-Klajn: 'Correspondance inédite de Johannes Brahms', *IMSCR, vii Cologne 1958*, 88

E. Kern: 'Dokumente der Freundschaft: Johannes Brahms und Theodor Billroth', *Musica*, xii (1958), 270

R. Stöckl: 'Ein unveröffentlichter Brahms-Brief', *NZM*, cxix (1958), 647

'Ein Brief von Johannes Brahms an Friedrich Hegar', *SMz*, xcviii (1958), 202

A. L. Holde: 'Suppressed Passages in the Brahms–Joachim Correspondence, Published for the First Time', *MQ*, xlv (1959), 312

A. Spengel, ed.: *Johannes Brahms an J. Spengel: unveröffentlichte Briefe aus den Jahren 1882–97* (Hamburg, 1959)

R. Sietz: 'Johannes Brahms und Theodor Kirchner: mit ungedruckten Briefen Theodor Kirchners', *Mf*, xiii (1960), 396

K. Stephenson: *Johannes Brahms und Fritz Simrock, Weg einer Freundschaft: Briefe des Verlegers an den Komponisten* (Hamburg, 1961)

O. Jonas: 'Eine private Brahms-Sammlung und ihre Bedeutung für die Brahms-Werkstatt-Erkenntnis', *GfMKB, Kassel 1962*, 212

K. Stephenson: 'Johannes Brahms und Georg Dietrich Otten', *Festschrift Karl Gustav Fellerer* (Regensburg, 1962/*R*1972), 503

A. Greither: *Billroth im Briefwechsel mit Brahms* (Munich, 1964) [abbreviated version of O. G. Billroth (1935)]

D. Kämper: 'Ein unbekanntes Brahms-Studienblatt aus dem Briefwechsel mit Frederick Wüllner', *Mf*, xvii (1964), 57

S. Kross: 'Brahmsiana: der Nachlass der Schwestern Völkers', *Mf*, xvii (1964), 110–51

Bibliography

A. Orel: *Johannes Brahms und J. Allgeyer: eine Künstlerfreundschaft in Briefen* (Tutzing, 1964)

E. Hanslick: 'Johannes Brahms, lettere e ricordi', *Convegno musicale*, ii/3–4 (1965), 3

H. P. Schanzlin: 'Brahms-Briefe aus Basler Privatbesitz', *Basler Stadtbuch 1966*

F. Grasberger, ed.: *J. Brahms: 'Ihr habt Traurigkeit', 5. Satz aus dem Deutschen Requiem: Faksimile der ersten Niederschrift* (Tutzing, 1968)

C. Smith: 'Music Manuscripts Lost during World War II', *Book Collector*, xvii/1 (1968), 26

E. F. Flindell: 'Ursprung und Geschichte der Sammlung Wittgenstein im 19. Jahrhundert', *Mf*, xxii (1969), 298

E. R. Jacobi: '"Vortrag und Besetzung Bachscher Cantaten und Oratorienmusik": ein unbekannter Brief von Moritz Hauptmann an Johannes Brahms (15. Februar 1859)', *BJb*, lv (1969), 78

R. Heuberger: *Erinnerungen an Johannes Brahms: Tagebuchnotizen aus den Jahren 1875–97*, ed. K. Hofmann (Tutzing, 1970)

J. A. Bernstein: 'An Autograph of the Brahms "Handel Variations"', *MR*, xxxiv (1973), 272

K. Stephenson, ed.: *Johannes Brahms in seiner Familie: der Briefwechsel* (Hamburg, 1973)

K. Geiringer: 'Schumanniana in der Bibliothek von Johannes Brahms', *Convivium musicorum: Festschrift Wolfgang Boetticher* (Berlin, 1974), 79

K. Hoffmann, ed.: *Die Bibliothek von Johannes Brahms* (Hamburg, 1974)

——: *Erstdrucke der Werke von Johannes Brahms* (Tutzing, 1975)

D. and M. L. McCorkle: 'Five Fundamental Problems in Brahms Source Research', *AcM*, xlviii (1976), 253

R. Elvers: 'Die Brahms-Autographen in der Musikabteilung der Staatsbibliothek Preussischer Kulturbesitz, Berlin', *Brahms-Studien*, ii (Hamburg, 1977), 79

V. L. Hancock: 'Sources of Brahms's Manuscript Copies of Early Music in the Archiv der Gesellschaft der Musikfreunde in Wien', *FAM* (1977), no.24, p.113

P. Dedel: *Johannes Brahms: a Guide to his Autograph in Facsimile* (Ann Arbor, 1978)

H. Müller: 'Brahms' Briefwechsel mit Meiningen', *BMw*, xx (1978), 85–131

H. Gál, ed.: *Johannes Brahms: Briefe* (Frankfurt am Main, 1979)

E. Maier: 'Die Brahms-Autographen der Österreichischen Nationalbibliothek', *Brahms-Studien*, iii (Hamburg, 1979), 7

K. Hofmann: 'Ein neu aufgefundener Brief von Johannes Brahms an seine Stiefmutter', *Brahms-Studien*, iv (Hamburg, 1981), 94

O. Biba: 'Brahms-Gedenkstätten in Wien', *ÖMz*, xxxviii (1983), 245

G. S. Bozarth: 'The First Generation of Brahms Manuscript Collections', *Notes*, xl (1983), 239

——: 'Brahms's Lieder Inventory of 1859–60 and other Documents of his Life and Work', *FAM* (1983), no.30, p.98

Johannes Brahms: Briefwechsel mit dem Mannheimer Bankprokuristen Wilhelm Lindeck 1872–1882, Sonderveröffentlichung des Stadtarchivs Mannheim, no.6 (Heidelberg, 1983)

V. L. Hancock: *Brahms's Choral Compositions and his Library of Early Music* (Ann Arbor, 1983)

R. Hofmann: 'Johannes Brahms im Spiegel der Korrespondenz Clara Schumanns', *Hamburger Jb für Musikwissenschaft*, vii (Laaber, 1984), 45

RECOLLECTIONS, OTHER BIOGRAPHICAL STUDIES

A. W. Ambros: 'Wiener Chronik', *Deutsche Rundschau*, vii (1876), 146

K. Groth: 'Erinnerungen an Johannes Brahms', *Die Gegenwart*, iii (1897), 295, 307, 327; repr. in H. Miesner: *Klaus Groth und die Musik* (Heide, 1933)

J. V. Widmann: *Johannes Brahms in Erinnerungen* (Berlin, 1898, 5/1947 ed. W. Reich)

——: *Sizilien und andere Gegenden Italiens: Reisen mit Johannes Brahms* (Frauenfeld, 1898, 3/1912)

W. Hübbe: *Brahms in Hamburg* (Hamburg, 1902)

A. Door: 'Persönliche Erinnerungen an Brahms', *Die Musik*, ii/3 (1902–3), 216

R. Heuberger: 'Aus der ersten Zeit meiner Bekanntschaft mit Brahms', *Die Musik*, ii/1 (1902–3), 327

R. von der Leyen: *Johannes Brahms als Mensch und Freund* (Düsseldorf and Leipzig, 1905)

G. Henschel: *Personal Recollections of Johannes Brahms* (Boston, Mass., 1907)

G. Jenner: 'War Marxsen der rechte Lehrer für Brahms?', *Die Musik*, xii/1 (1912–13), 77

G. Ophüls: *Erinnerungen an Johannes Brahms* (Berlin, 1921)

E. Hirschmann: *Johannes Brahms und die Frauen* (Vienna, 1933)

H. Miesner: *Klaus Groth und die Musik: Erinnerungen an Joh. Brahms* (Heide, 1933)

W. Schramm: *Johannes Brahms in Detmold* (Leipzig, 1933)

K. Stephenson: *Johannes Brahms' Heimatbekenntnis* (Hamburg, 1933)

S. Stojowski: 'Recollections of Brahms', *MQ*, xix (1933), 143

K. Geiringer: 'Brahms's Family', *MO*, lx (1936), 21

Y. Lacroix-Novaro: 'De Schumann à Brahms', *ReM* (1936), no.163, p.89

T. Stettner: 'Johannes Brahms in seinen Beziehungen zu Anselm und

Bibliography

Henriette Feuerbach', *ZfM*, civ (1937), 382

K. Geiringer: 'Brahms and Chrysander', *MMR*, lxvii (1937), 97, 131, 178

A. Piovesan: 'Ritratto di Brahms', *RaM*, xiii (1940), 227

J.-C. Piguet: 'Brahms et Fauré', *SMz*, xcvi (1951), 143

L. Henning: *Die Freundschaft Clara Schumanns mit Johannes Brahms* (Zurich, 1952)

R. Rudorff: 'Johannes Brahms: Erinnerungen und Betrachtungen', *SMz*, xcvii (1957), 61, 139, 182

H. von Beckerath: 'Erinnerungen an Brahms: Brahms und seine Krefelder Freunde', *Die Heimat: Zeitschrift für niederrheinische Heimatpflege*, xxix (1958), 81

Z. Hrabussay: 'Johannes Brahms a Bratislava', *SM*, ii (1958), 209

L. Berger: *Vom Menschen Johannes Brahms* (Tübingen, 1959)

J. Matter: 'Brahms et Fauré', *SMz*, xcix (1959), 58

F. Grasberger: 'Johannes Brahms und Hugo Wolf', *ÖMz*, xv (1960), 67

W. Siegmund-Schultze: 'Chopin und Brahms', *Chopin Congress: Warszawa 1960*, 388

G. Zàccaro: 'Dialogo su Brahms', *Convegno musicale*, ii/1–2 (1965), 123

R. Fiske: 'Brahms and Scotland', *MT*, cix (1968), 1106

G. Sannemüller: 'Die Freundschaft zwischen Johannes Brahms und Klaus Groth', *Jahresgabe der Klaus-Groth-Gesellschaft 1969*, 114

V. Bickerich and N. Petri: 'Johannes Brahms in Transilvania: o informare pe bază de documente', *SM*, xii (1970), 259

J. Clapham: 'Dvořák's Relations with Brahms and Hanslick', *MQ*, lvii (1971), 241

S. Helms: Johannes Brahms und Johann Sebastian Bach', *Bach Jb 1971*, 13–81

C. Floros: 'Zur Antithese Brahms – Bruckner', *Brahms-Studien*, i (Hamburg, 1974), 59–90

H. Wirth: 'Johannes Brahms und Max Reger', *Brahms-Studien*, i (Hamburg, 1974), 91

H. Gál: 'Drei Meister, drei Welten: Brahms – Wagner – Verdi', (Frankfurt am Main, 1975)

R. McGuiness: 'Mahler und Brahms: Gedanken zu "Reminiszenzen" in Mahlers Sinfonien', *Melos/NZM*, iii (1977), 215

R. Meisner: 'Aus Johannes Brahms' Schulzeit', *Brahms-Studien*, ii (Hamburg, 1977), 85

D. S. Thatcher: 'Nietzsches Totengericht über Brahms', *Nietzsche-Studien*, vii (1977), 339

G. Fock: 'Wie Frau Celestina Truxa mit Brahms bekannt wurde: Brahms als Hausgenosse', *Brahms-Studien*, iii (Hamburg, 1979), 53

K. Hofmann: 'Brahmsiana der Familie Petersen: Erinnerungen und

Briefe', *Brahms-Studien*, iii (Hamburg, 1979), 69–105

——: *Johannes Brahms in den Erinnerungen von Richard Barth: Barths Wirken in Hamburg* (Hamburg, 1979)

K. Stahmer: 'Brahms auf Rügen: der Sommeraufenthalt eines Komponisten', *Brahms-Studien*, iii (Hamburg, 1979), 59

C. Floros: *Brahms und Bruckner: Studien zur musikalischen Exegetik* (Wiesbaden, 1980)

I. Fellinger: 'Johannes Brahms und Richard Mühlfeld', *Brahms-Studien*, iv (Hamburg, 1981), 77

W. Gerber: 'Der Brunsbüttler Brahmsstamm', *Brahms-Studien*, iv (Hamburg, 1981), 97

O.-H. Kahler: 'Billroth und Brahms in Zürich', *Brahms-Studien*, iv (Hamburg, 1981), 63

S. Kross: 'Brahms und Schumann', *Brahms-Studien*, iv (Hamburg, 1981), 7–44

——: 'Brahms and E. T. A. Hoffmann', *19th Century Music*, v (1981–2), 193

O. Biba: *Johannes Brahms in Wien* (Vienna, 1983) [exhibition catalogue, Archiv der Gesellschaft der Musikfreunde, Vienna]

I. Fellinger: 'Brahms und Mozart', *Brahms-Studien*, v (Hamburg, 1983), 141

C. Floros: 'Brahms: ein Januskopf', *Melos/NZM*, ix (1983), 4

——: Gedanken über Brahms und Bruckner', *ÖMz*, xxxviii (1983), 398

K. Kropfinger: 'Wagner und Brahms', *Musica*, xxxvii (1983), 11

H. Mayer: 'Ein Denkmal für Johannes Brahms', *Brahms-Studien*, v (Hamburg, 1983), 9

M. Musgrave: 'Brahms the Progressive: another view', *MT*, cxxiv (1983), 291

R. Pascall: 'Brahms and Schubert', *MT*, cxxiv (1983), 286

——, ed.: *Brahms: Biographical, Documentary and Analytical Studies* (Cambridge, 1983)

E. Prillinger: 'Johannes Brahms und Gmunden', *Brahms-Studien*, v (Hamburg, 1983), 181

W. G. Zimmermann: *Brahms in der Schweiz* (Zurich, 1983)

Johannes Brahms in Baden-Baden und Karlsruhe (Karlsruhe, 1983) [exhibition catalogue with numerous articles, Badische Landesbibliothek, Karlsruhe]

O. Biba: 'Brahms in Wien', *Hamburger Jb für Musikwissenschaft*, vii (Laaber, 1984), 259

K. Hofmann: 'Johannes Brahms in Hamburg', *Hamburger Jb für Musikwissenschaft*, vii (Laaber, 1984), 21

A. Horstmann: 'Die Rezeption der Werke op.1 bis 10 von Johannes Brahms zwischen 1853–1860', *Hamburger Jb für Musikwissenschaft*, vii (Laaber, 1984), 33

Bibliography

R. Pascall: 'Brahms und die Kleinmeister', *Hamburger Jb für Musikwissenschaft*, vii (Laaber, 1984), 199

P. Petersen: 'Brahms und Dvořák', *Hamburger Jb für Musikwissenschaft*, vii (Laaber, 1984), 125

B. Stockmann: 'Brahms – Reger oder Von der Legitimation des religiösen Liberalismus', *Hamburger Jb für Musikwissenschaft*, vii (Laaber, 1984), 211

H. Wirth: 'Richard Wagner und Johannes Brahms', *Hamburger Jb für Musikwissenschaft*, vii (Laaber, 1984), 147

LIFE AND WORKS

H. Deiters: *Johannes Brahms* (Leipzig, 1880–97; Eng. trans., n.d.)

P. Spitta: 'Johannes Brahms', *Zur Musik* (Berlin, 1892), 385–427

H. Imbert: *Etude sur Johannes Brahms* (Paris, 1894)

H. Reimann: *Johannes Brahms* (Berlin, 1897, 6/1922)

——: 'Johannes Brahms', *Geschichte der Musik seit Beethoven* (Berlin and Stuttgart, 1901), 742

R. Barth: *Johannes Brahms und seine Musik* (Hamburg, 1904)

M. Kalbeck: *Johannes Brahms* (Berlin, 1904–14, 3/1912–21/R1976)

H. Antcliffe: *Brahms* (London, 1905)

G. Jenner: *Johannes Brahms als Mensch, Lehrer und Künstler: Studien und Erlebnisse* (Marburg, 1905, 2/1930)

F. May: *The Life of Johannes Brahms* (London, 1905, 2/1948, rev. 3/1977)

W. Pauli: *Moderne Geister: Brahms* (Berlin, 1907)

H. C. Colles: *Johannes Brahms* (London, 1909, 2/1920)

H. Kretzschmar: 'Johannes Brahms', *Gesammelte Aufsätze aus den Grenzboten* (Leipzig, 1910), 151–207

J. A. Fuller Maitland: *Brahms* (London, 1911)

E. Evans: *Historical, Descriptive and Analytical Account of the Entire Works of Johannes Brahms* (London, 1912–38)

W. A. Thomas-San-Galli: *Johannes Brahms* (Munich, 1912, 5/1922)

L. Misch: *Johannes Brahms* (Bielefeld, 1913, 2/1922)

W. Niemann: *Johannes Brahms* (Berlin, 1920; Eng. trans.. 1929/R1969)

P. Landormy: *Brahms* (Paris, 1921, rev. 2/1948)

W. Nagel: *Johannes Brahms* (Stuttgart, 1923)

E. M. Lee: *Brahms: the Man and his Music* (London, 1925)

C. Gray: 'Johannes Brahms', *The Heritage of Music*, i, ed. H. J. Foss (London, 1927, 2/1948)

R. Specht: *Johannes Brahms: Leben und Werk eines deutschen Meisters* (Hellerau, 1928)

W. Hutschenruyter: *Brahms* (The Hague, 1929)

G. Ernest: *Johannes Brahms* (Berlin, 1930)

P. Mies: *Johannes Brahms* (Leipzig, 1930)

187

A. von Ehrmann: *Johannes Brahms: Weg, Werk und Welt* (Leipzig, 1933/*R*1974)

R. Fellinger: *Klänge um Brahms* (Berlin, 1933)

R. Hill: *Brahms* (London, 1933, 2/1941)

J. Müller-Blattau: *Johannes Brahms* (Potsdam, 1933)

W. Murdoch: *Brahms: with an Analytical Study of the Complete Pianoforte Works* (London, 1933)

J. Pulver: *Johannes Brahms* (London, 1933)

R. H. Schauffler: *The Unknown Brahms: his Life, Character and Works, Based on New Material* (New York, 1933)

E. Blom: *Johannes Brahms* (New York, 1934)

R. F. Hernried: *Johannes Brahms* (Leipzig, 1934)

K. Geiringer: *Johannes Brahms* (Vienna, 1935; Eng. trans., rev., enlarged 1947, enlarged 3/1963)

H. H. Stuckenschmidt: 'Johannes Brahms, 1833–1897', *Die grossen Deutschen*, iv, ed. W. Andreas and W. von Scholz (Berlin, 1936), 148

R. Gerber: *Johannes Brahms* (Potsdam, 1938)

K. Laux: *Der Einsame: Johannes Brahms, Leben und Werk* (Graz, 1944)

W. and P. Rehberg: *Johannes Brahms* (Zurich, 1947, 2/1963)

J. Culshaw: *Brahms: an Outline of his Life and Music* (London, 1948)

H. Eppstein: *Brahms* (Stockholm, 1948)

P. Latham: *Brahms* (London, 1948)

F. Grasberger: *Johannes Brahms: Variationen um sein Wesen* (Vienna, 1952)

G. Rostand: *Brahms* (Paris, 1954–5)

R. Goldron: *Johannes Brahms 'le vagabond'* (Paris, 1956)

R. Gerber: 'Johannes Brahms', *Die grossen Deutschen*, iv, ed. W. Andreas and W. von Scholz (Berlin, rev. 2/1957 by H. Heimpel and others), 71

N. Cardus: 'Johannes Brahms', *A Composer's Eleven* (London, 1958, 2/1970)

M. Menczigar: *Julius Epstein: sein Leben und Wirken unter besonderer Erforschung seiner Beziehungen zu Johannes Brahms* (diss., U. of Vienna, 1958)

M. Druskin: *Iogannes Brams* [Johannes Brahms] (Moscow, 1959, 2/1970)

A. Molnár: *Johannes Brahms* (Budapest, 1959)

F. Müller-Blattau: *Johannes Brahms* (Königstein, 1960)

W. Furtwängler: *Johannes Brahms, Anton Bruckner* (Stuttgart, 1963)

H. Gál: *Johannes Brahms* (Frankfurt am Main, 1961; Eng. trans., 1963/*R*1975)

Z. Hrabussay: *Johannes Brahms* (Bratislava, 1963)

J. Laufer: *Brahms* (Paris, 1963)

Bibliography

J. Bruyr: *Brahms* (Paris, 1965)

B. Delvaille: *Johannes Brahms*, Musiciens de tous les temps, xv (Paris, 1965)

W. Siegmund-Schultze: *Johannes Brahms* (Leipzig, 1966)

Y. Tiénot: *Brahms: son vrai visage* (Paris, 1968)

L. Erhardt: *Brahms* (Kraków, 1969)

K. Dale: *Brahms: a Biography with a Survey of Books, Editions & Recordings* (Hamden, Conn., and London, 1970)

J. Burnett: *Brahms: a Critical Study* (London, 1972)

W. Reich: *Johannes Brahms in Dokumenten zu Leben und Werk* (Zurich, 1975)

B. Jacobson: *The Music of Johannes Brahms* (London, 1977)

J. Chissell: *Brahms* (London, 1977)

H. A. Neunzig: *Johannes Brahms in Selbstzeugnissen und Bilddokumenten* (Reinbek, 2/1977)

K. and R. Hofmann: *Johannes Brahms: Zeittafel zu Leben und Werk* (Tutzing, 1983)

C. M. Schmidt: *Johannes Brahms und seine Zeit* (Laaber, 1983)

STYLE, HARMONY, COUNTERPOINT, FORM

H. Wetzel: 'Zur Harmonik bei Brahms', *Die Musik*, xii/1 (1912–13), 22

V. Urbantschitsch: *Die Sonatenform bei Brahms* (diss., U. of Vienna, 1925)

V. Luithlen: 'Studien zu Johannes Brahms' Werken in Variationenform', *SMw*, xiv (1927), 286–320

V. Urbantschitsch: 'Die Entwicklung der Sonatenform bei Brahms', *SMw*, xiv (1927), 265

G. Knepler: *Die Form in den Instrumentalwerken Johannes Brahms* (diss., U. of Vienna, 1930)

R. Gerber: 'Formprobleme im Brahmsschen Lied', *JbMP 1932*, 23

A. Sturke: *Der Stil in Johannes Brahms' Werken* (diss., U. of Würzburg, 1932)

F. Kurzweil: *Die Harmonik als formbildendes Element bei Johannes Brahms* (diss., U. of Vienna, 1938)

R. Kratzer: *Die Kontrapunktik bei Johannes Brahms mit besonderer Berücksichtigung der grosskontrapunktischen Formen* (diss., U. of Vienna, 1939)

H. Hautz: *Die Harmonik der Brahms'schen Soloklavierwerke* (diss., U. of Munich, 1942)

J. Fry: 'Brahms's Conception of the Scherzo in Chamber Music', *MT*, lxxxiv (1943), 105

W. Gieseler: *Die Harmonik bei Johannes Brahms* (diss., U. of Göttingen, 1949)

E. H. Alden: *The Function of Subdominant Harmony in the Works of*

Johannes Brahms (diss., U. of North Carolina, 1950)

R. Steglich: 'Zum Kontrastproblem Johannes Brahms–Hugo Wolf', *GfMKB, Lüneburg 1950*, 140

R. Hasse: *Studien zum Kontrapunktischen Klaviersatz von Johannes Brahms* (diss., U. of Cologne, 1951)

W. Siegmund-Schultze: *Untersuchungen zum Brahmsstil und Brahmsbild* (Habilitationschrift, U. of Halle, 1951)

R. Tenschert: 'Die Klangwelt von Johannes Brahms', *ÖMz*, vi (1951), 307

H. Bunke: *Die Barform im romantischen Kunstlied bei Franz Schubert, Robert Schumann, Johannes Brahms, Hugo Wolf und Felix Mendelssohn Bartholdy* (diss., U. of Bonn, 1955)

S. Kross: 'Brahms und der Kanon', *Festschrift Joseph Schmidt-Görg zum 60. Geburtstag* (Bonn, 1957), 175

L. Misch: 'Kontrapunkt und Imitation im Brahmsschen Lied', *Mf*, xi (1958), 155

H. Hirsch: *Rhythmisch-metrische Untersuchungen zur Variationstechnik bei Johannes Brahms* (diss., U. of Hamburg, 1963)

A. Mitschka: *Der Sonatensatz in den Werken von Johannes Brahms* (Gütersloh, 1963)

H. Truscott: 'Brahms and Sonata Style', *MR*, xxv (1964), 186

J. Beythien: 'Die Violinsonate in G-dur, op.78, von Johannes Brahms', *GfMKB, Leipzig 1966*, 325

W. Mohr: 'Johannes Brahms' formenschöpferische Originalität, dargestellt am ersten Satz seiner Violinsonate op.108, und seiner Rhapsodie, op.79, Nr.2', *GfMKB, Leipzig 1966*, 322

E. A. Sterling: *A Study of Chromatic Elements in Selected Piano Works of Beethoven, Schubert, Schumann, Chopin and Brahms* (diss., Indiana U., 1966)

H. Zingerle: 'Chromatische Harmonik bei Brahms und Reger', *SMw*, xxvii (1966), 151–85

J. Wetschky: *Die Kanontechnik in der Instrumentalmusik von J. Brahms* (Regensburg, 1967)

R. Pascall: *Formal Principles in the Music of Brahms* (diss., U. of Oxford, 1972)

——: 'Some Special Uses of Sonata Form by Brahms', *Soundings*, iv (1974), 58

J. Webster, 'Schubert's Sonata Form and Brahms' First Maturity', *19th Century Music*, ii (1978–9), 18; iii (1979–80), 52

O. Brusatti: 'Zur thematischen Arbeit bei Johannes Brahms', *SMw*, xxxi (1980), 191

J. Dunsby: *Structural Ambiguity in Brahms: Analytical Approaches to Four Works* (Ann Arbor, 1981)

Bibliography

W. Frisch: 'Brahms, Developing Variation, and the Schoenberg Critical Tradition', *19th Century Music*, v (1981–2), 215

H. Becker: 'Das volkstümliche Idiom in Brahmsens Kammermusik', *Hamburger Jb für Musikwissenschaft*, vii (Laaber, 1984), 87

G. Borchardt: 'Ein Viertonmotiv als melodische Komponente in Werken von Brahms', *Hamburger Jb für Musikwissenschaft*, vii (Laaber, 1984), 101

W. Frisch: *Brahms and the Principle of Developing Variation* (Berkeley, 1984)

ORCHESTRAL MUSIC

G. Jenner: 'Zur Entstehung des d-moll Klavierkonzerts von Johannes Brahms', *Die Musik*, xii/1 (1912–13), 32

R. Specht: 'Zur Brahmsschen Symphonik', *Die Musik*, xii/1 (1912–13), 3

W. Vetter: 'Der erste Satz von Brahms' e-moll-Symphonie: ein Beitrag zur Erkenntnis moderner Symphonik', *Die Musik*, xiii/3 (1913–14), 3, 83, 131

A. Orel: 'Skizzen zu Johannes Brahms' Haydn-Variationen', *ZMw*, v (1922–3), 296

E. M. Lee: *Brahms's Orchestral Works* (London, 1931)

P. A. Browne: *Brahms: the Symphonies* (London, 1933)

R. Specht: 'Brahms der Sinfoniker', *Die Musik*, xxv/2 (1933), 592

H. Feiertag: *Das orchestrale Klangbild in Brahms' Orchester-Werken* (diss., U. of Vienna, 1938)

J. A. Harrison: *Brahms and his Four Symphonies* (London, 1939)

E. Schenk: 'Zur Inhaltsdeutung der Brahmsschen Wörthersee-symphonie', *Festliche Jahresschrift des Musikvereins für Kärnten* (Klagenfurt, 1943), 38

B. Stäblein: 'Die motivische Arbeit im Finale der ersten Brahms-Sinfonie', *Das Musikleben*, ii (1949), 69

G. Gärtner: 'Das Terzmotiv, Keimzelle der 1. Sinfonie von Johannes Brahms', *Mf*, viii (1955), 332

A. Forte: 'The Structural Origin of Exact Tempi in the Brahms Haydn Variations', *MR*, xviii (1957), 138

W. Siegmund-Schultze: 'Johannes Brahms' Orchesterwerke', *Konzertbuch Orchestermusik*, i, ed. K. Schönewolf (Berlin, 1958)

J. D. Anderson: *Brass Scoring Techniques in the Symphonies of Mozart, Beethoven and Brahms* (diss., George Peabody College for Teachers, Nashville, Tenn., 1960)

C. Dahlhaus: *Brahms, Klavierkonzert Nr.1 d-moll op.15*, Meisterwerke der Musik, iii (Munich, 1965)

K. M. Komma: 'Das "Scherzo" der 2. Symphonie von Johannes Brahms', *Festschrift für Walter Wiora* (Kassel, 1967), 448

191

R. J. Rittenhouse: *Rhythmic Elements in the Symphonies of Johannes Brahms* (diss., U. of Iowa, 1967)

J. Horton: *Brahms Orchestral Music* (London, 1968)

R. Klein: 'Die konstruktiven Grundlagen der Brahms-Symphonien', *ÖMz*, xxiii (1968), 258

L. Finscher: 'Kampf mit der Tradition: Johannes Brahms', *Die Welt der Symphonie*, ed. U. von Rauchhaupt (Brunswick, 1972), 165

R. Klein: 'Die Doppelgerüsttechnik in der Passacaglia der IV. Symphonie von Brahms', *ÖMz*, xxvii (1972), 641

V. Ravizza: 'Konflikte in Brahmsscher Musik. Zum ersten Satz der c-moll-Sinfonie op. 68', *Schweizer Beiträge zur Musikwissenschaft*, ii, ed. K. von Fischer, E. Lichtenhahn and H. Oesch (Berne, 1974), 75

G. Weiss-Aigner: 'Komponist und Geiger: Joseph Joachims Mitarbeit am Violinkonzert von Johannes Brahms', *NZM*, Jg.cxxxv (1974), 232

W. Deppisch: 'Vergleichende Diskographie der Klavierkonzerte von Johannes Brahms', *Brahms-Studien*, ii (Hamburg, 1977), 47–78

G. Weiss-Aigner: *Johannes Brahms: Violinkonzert D-Dur*, Meisterwerke der Musik, xviii (Munich, 1979)

R. Pascall: 'Brahms's First Symphony Slow Movement: the Initial Performing Version', *MT*, cxxii (1981), 664

J.-J. Widmann: 'Brahms' Vierte Sinfonie', *Brahms-Studien*, iv (Hamburg, 1981), 45

D. Kerner: 'Letzter Brahms', *Das Orchester*, xxix (1981), 642

N. Geeraert: 'Johannes Brahms: Konzert für Klavier und Orchester Nr. 1 d-moll op.15', *Melos/NZM*, viii (1982), 31

M. Stegemann: 'Vor 100 Jahren: "Ein ganz kleines Klavierkonzert . . .": Zur Interpretation von Brahms' Opus 83', *Melos/NZM*, viii (1982), 11

F. Haas: 'Die Erstfassung des langsamen Satzes der ersten Sinfonie von Johannes Brahms', *Mf*, xxxvi (1983), 200

S. Kross: 'Johannes Brahms – der Sinfoniker', *Brahms-Studien*, v (Hamburg, 1983), 65–90

M. Musgrave: 'Brahms's First Symphony: Thematic Coherence and its Secret Origin', *Music Analysis*, ii (1983), 117

B. Schwarz: 'Joseph Joachim and the Genesis of Brahms's Violin Concerto', *MQ*, lxix (1983), 503

T. Seedorf: 'Brahms' 1. Symphonie: Komponieren als Auseinandersetzung mit der Geschichte', *Musik und Bildung*, xv (1983), 10

CHAMBER MUSIC

H. C. Colles: *Chamber Music of Brahms* (London, 1933/*R*1976)

D. G. Mason: *The Chamber Music of Brahms* (London and New York, 1933, 2/1950)

Bibliography

H. Düsterbehn: 'Ein Beitrag zur Entstehung der FAE-Freundschafts-Sonate', *ZfM*, ciii (1936), 284

F. Brand: *Das Wesen der Kammermusik von Brahms* (diss., U. of Berlin, 1937)

E. Bücken: 'Ein neuaufgefundenes Jugendwerk von Johannes Brahms', *Die Musik*, xxx/1 (Berlin, 1937–8), 22

F. Brand: 'Das neue Brahms-Trio', *Die Musik*, xxxi/1 (1938–9), 321

R. Fellinger: 'Ist das Klaviertrio in A-dur ein Jugendwerk von Johannes Brahms?', *Die Musik*, xxxiv (1941–2), 197

G. Jacob: 'Schoenberg and Brahms's op.25', *ML*, xxxii (1951), 252

W. G. Hill: 'Brahms' opus 51 – a Diptych', *MR*, xxxiii (1952), 110

H. F. Redlich: 'Bruckner and Brahms Quintets in F', *ML*, xxxvi (1955), 253

R. S. Fischer: *Brahms's Technique of Motivic Development in his Sonata in D minor, op.108 for Piano and Violin* (diss., U. of Arizona, 1964)

H. Hollander: 'Der melodische Aufbau in Brahms' "Regenlied"-Sonate', *NZM*, cxxi (1964), 5

I. Fellinger: 'Brahms' Sonate für Pianoforte und Violine op.78', *Mf*, xviii (1965), 11

G. L. Maas: *Problems of Form in the Clarinet Quintet of Johannes Brahms* (diss., U. of Wisconsin, 1967)

W. Czesla: *Studien zum Finale in der Kammermusik von Johannes Brahms* (diss., U. of Bonn, 1968)

K. Stahmer: *Musikalische Formung in soziologischem Bezug, dargestellt an der instrumentalen Kammermusik von Johannes Brahms* (diss., U. of Kiel, 1968)

B. Greenspan: *The Six Sonatas for Unaccompanied Violin and Musical Legacy of Eugène Ysaÿe; the Sextets by Brahms: an Analysis* (diss., Indiana U., 1969)

M. E. Hawn: *Melodic Relationships in Selected Chamber Works of Brahms* (diss., Indiana U., 1969)

C. Schmidt: *Verfahren der motivisch-thematischen Vermittlung in der Musik von Johannes Brahms dargestellt an der Klarinettensonate f-moll op.120, 1* (diss., Free U. of Berlin, 1970; Munich, 1971)

C. Dahlhaus: 'Brahms und die Idee der Kammermusik', *Brahms-Studien*, i (Hamburg, 1974), 45

I. Keys: *Brahms Chamber Music* (London, 1974)

V. Ravizza: 'Möglichkeiten des Komischen in der Musik: der letzte Satz des Streichquintetts in F dur, op.88 von Johannes Brahms', *AMw*, xxxi (1974), 137

R. Pascall: 'Ruminations on Brahms's Chamber Music', *MT*, cxvi (1975), 697

R. Häfner: *Johannes Brahms: Klarinettenquintett*, Meisterwerke der Musik, xiv (Munich, 1978)

J. Webster: 'The C sharp minor Version of Brahms's op.60', *MT*, cxxi (1980), 89

R. Wilke: *Brahms, Reger, Schönberg: Streichquartette* (Hamburg, 1980)

S. Schibli: 'Ein Johannes Brahms für jedermann: des Komponisten Kammermusik und die Willkür der Interpreten', *Musik und Medizin*, viii (1982), 65

A. Forte: 'Motivic Design and Structural Levels in the First Movement of Brahms's String Quartet in C Minor', *MQ*, lxix (1983), 471–502

H. Kohlhase: 'Brahms und Mendelssohn: Strukturelle Parallelen in der Kammermusik für Streicher', *Hamburger Jb für Musikwissenschaft*, vii (Laaber, 1984), 59

N. Meurs: 'Das verstellte Frühwerk: zum H-dur-Trio op.8 von Johannes Brahms', *Musica*, xxxvii (1984), 34

K. H. Stahmer: 'Drei Klavierquartette aus den Jahren 1875/76 Brahms, Mahler und Dvořák im Vergleich', *Hamburger Jb für Musikwissenschaft*, vii (Laaber, 1984), 113

KEYBOARD MUSIC

E. Howard-Jones: 'Brahms in his Pianoforte Music', *PMA*, xxxvii (1910–11), 117

W. Niemann: 'Johannes Brahms und die neuere Klaviermusik', *Die Musik*, xii/1 (1912–13), 38

W. Nagel: *Die Klaviersonaten von J. Brahms: technisch-ästhetische Analysen* (Stuttgart, 1915)

H. Schenker: 'Brahms: Variationen und Fuge über ein Thema von Händel, op.24', *Der Tonwille*, iv (1924), 3–46

E. Tetzel: 'Die Schumann-Variationen von Brahms', *ZfM*, xcvi (1929), 311

E. Kurzweil: *Der Klaviersatz bei Brahms* (diss., U. of Vienna, 1934)

C. Mason: 'Brahms's Piano Sonatas', *MR*, v (1944), 112

H. W. Gay: *I: Liturgical Role of the Organ in France, 757–1750, II: Selected Organ Works of Johannes Brahms* (diss., Indiana U., 1955)

O. Jonas: 'Die "Variationen für eine liebe Freundin" von Johannes Brahms', *AMw*, xii (1955), 319

K. W. Senn: 'Johannes Brahms, Elf Choralvorspiele für Orgel op.122', *Musik und Gottesdienst*, xiii (1959), 172

H. J. Busch: 'Die Orgelwerke von Johannes Brahms', *Ars organi*, xi (1963), 582

F. E. Kirby: 'Brahms and the Piano Sonata', *Paul A. Pisk: Essays in his Honor* (Austin, 1966), 163

A. C. Brandes: *The Solo Piano Variations of Johannes Brahms* (diss., Boston U., 1967)

Bibliography

W. Kirsch: 'Die Klavier-Walzer op.39 von Johannes Brahms und ihre Tradition', *Jb des Staatlichen Instituts für Musikforschung 1969*, 38–67

P. Mies: 'Zu Werdegang und Strukturen der Paganini-Variationen op.35 für Klavier von Johannes Brahms', *SM*, xi (1969), 323

V. Gotwals: 'Brahms and the Organ', *Music/The A.G.O. Magazine*, iv/4 (1970), 38

T. O. Mastroianni: *Elements of Unity in 'Fantasies', opus 116 by Brahms* (diss., Indiana U., 1970)

R. Pascall: 'Unknown Gavottes by Brahms', *ML*, lvii (1976), 404

P. J. Clements: 'Johannes Brahms: Intermezzo op.119, no.1', *CAUSM/ACEUM j.*, vii (1977), 31

B. Newbould: 'A New Analysis of Brahms's, Intermezzo in B minor, op.119 no.1', *MR*, xxxviii (1977), 33

D. Kraus: 'Das Andante aus der Sonate op.5 von Brahms: Versuch einer Interpretation', *Brahms-Studien*, iii (Hamburg, 1979), 47

D. Torkewitz: 'Die "entwickelte Zeit": zum Intermezzo op.116, IV von Johannes Brahms', *Mf*, xxxii (1979), 135

D. Kraus: 'Die "Paganinivariationen" op.35: ein Sonderfall?' *Brahms-Studien*, iv (Hamburg, 1981), 55

K. Velten: 'Entwicklungsdenken und Zeiterfahrung in der Musik von Johannes Brahms: das Intermezzo op.117 Nr.2', *Mf*, xxxiv (1981), 56

C. Floros: 'Studien zu Brahms' Klaviermusik', *Brahms-Studien*, v (Hamburg, 1983), 25–64

F. Goebels: 'Adagio h-moll: Bemerkungen zum Intermezzo h-moll op.119 Nr. 1 von Johannes Brahms', *Musica*, xxxvii (1983), 230

J. Schläder: 'Zur Funktion der Variantentechnik in den Klaviersonaten f-Moll von Johannes Brahms und h-Moll von Franz Liszt', *Hamburger Jb für Musikwissenschaft*, vii (Laaber, 1984), 171

ORIGINAL VOCAL MUSIC

G. Ophüls: *Brahmstexte* (Berlin, 1898, 2/1908)

W. Hammermann: *Johannes Brahms als Liederkomponist* (diss., U. of Leipzig, 1912)

H. Riemann: 'Die Taktfreiheiten in Brahms' Liedern', *Die Musik*, xii/1 (1912–13), 10

M. Kalbeck: *Brahms als Lyriker* (Vienna, 1921)

M. Friedlaender: *Brahms' Lieder* (Berlin and Leipzig, 1922; Eng. trans., 1929)

F. Wunsiedler: *Liederschlüsse bei Johannes Brahms* (diss., U. of Erlangen, 1922)

P. Mies: *Stilmomente und Ausdrucksstilformen im Brahmsschen Lied* (Leipzig, 1923)

F. Gennrich: 'Glossen zu Johannes Brahms' *Sonnet* op.14 Nr.4 "Ach könnt' ich, könnte vergessen sie" ', *ZMw*, x (1927–8), 129

H. Riemann: 'Brahms' Taktfreiheiten im Lied', *Die Musik*, xxv/2 (1933), 595

P. Mies: 'Das Marienlied bei Johannes Brahms', *Im Dienste der Kirche* (Essen, 1937), 139

A. H. Fox Strangways: 'Brahms and Tieck's "Magelone" ', *ML*, xxi (1940), 211

A. Kockegcy: *Brahms und Goethe* (diss., Humboldt U., Berlin, 1948)

R. Gerber: 'Das Deutsche Requiem als Dokument Brahmsscher Frömmigkeit', *Das Musikleben*, ii (1949), 181, 237, 282

W. Köser: *Johannes Brahms in seinen geistlichen Chorwerken a cappella* (diss., U. of Hamburg, 1950)

S. Drinker: *Brahms and his Women's Choruses* (Merion, Penn., 1952)

E. Rieger: 'Die Tonartencharakteristik im einstimmigen Klavierlied von Johannes Brahms', *SMw*, xxii (1955), 142–216

H. Federhofer: 'Zur Einheit von Wort und Ton im Lied von Johannes Brahms', *GfMKB, Hamburg 1956*, 97

S. Kross: *Die Chorwerke von Johannes Brahms* (diss., U. of Bonn, 1957; enlarged, Berlin, 1958, 2/1963)

M. S. Druskin: 'Vokalnaya lirika Brahmsa', *SovM* (1958), no.5, p.56

K. Giebeler: *Die Lieder von Johannes Brahms* (diss., U. of Münster, 1959)

O. Riemer: 'Zur Kritik am Deutschen Requiem', *Der Kirchenmusiker*, xii (1961), 177

K. P. Bernet Kempers: ' "Die Emanzipation des Fleisches" in den Liedern von Johannes Brahms', *SMw*, xxv (1962), 28

S. Kross: 'Rhythmik und Sprachbehandlung bei Brahms', *GfMKB, Kassel 1962*, 217

K. Stephenson: 'Der junge Brahms und Reményis "Ungarische Lieder" ', *SMw*, xxv (1962), 520

W. S. Newman: 'A "Basic Motive" in Brahms's German Requiem', *MR*, xxiv (1963), 70

I. Fellinger: 'Zur Entstehung der "Regenlieder" von Brahms', *Festschrift Walter Gerstenberg* (Wolfenbüttel, 1964), 55

H. Hollander: 'Gedanken zum strukturellen Aufbau des Brahmsschen Requiems', *SMz*, cv (1965), 326

R. Jordahl: *A Study of the Use of the Chorale in the Works of Mendelssohn, Brahms and Reger* (diss., U. of Rochester, 1965)

R. Boros: 'Petőfi – in der Vertonung von Brahms', *SM*, viii (1966), 391

F. Grasberger: 'Das Jahr 1868', *ÖMz*, xxiii (1968), 197

S. Helms: *Die Melodienbildung in den Liedern von Johannes Brahms und ihr Verhältnis zu den Volksliedern und volkstümlichen Weisen* (Bamberg, 1968)

Bibliography

B. Kinsey: 'Mörike Poems Set by Brahms, Schumann and Wolf', *MR*, xxix (1968), 257

A. Liebe: 'Zur "Rhapsodie" aus Goethes "Harzreise im Winter"', *Musa–mens–musici: im Gedenken an Walther Vetter* (Leipzig, 1969), 233

K. Reinhardt: 'Motivisch-thematisches im "Deutschen Requiem" von Brahms', *Musik und Kirche*, xxxix (1969), 13

W. Schönheit: 'Romantik in der Kirche? – Johannes Brahms', *Credo musicale . . . Festgabe zum 80. Geburtstag . . . Rudolf Mauersberger* (Berlin, 1969), 73

S. Helms: 'Johannes Brahms und das deutsche Kirchenlied', *Der Kirchenmusiker*, xxi (1970), 39

K. Blum: *Hundert Jahre Ein deutsches Requiem von Johannes Brahms* (Tutzing, 1971)

M. P. Rose: *Structural Integration in Selected Mixed a cappella Choral Works of Brahms* (diss., U. of Michigan, 1971)

M. Harrison: *The Lieder of Brahms* (London, 1972)

M. Musgrave: 'Historical Influence in the Growth of Brahms's Requiem', *ML*, liii (1972), 3

E. Sams: *Brahms Songs* (London, 1972)

P. Hamburger: 'Omkring Johs. Brahms' "Liebeslieder Walzer" op.52', *Festschrift Gunnar Heerup* (Egtved, 1973), 231

C. Jacobsen: *Das Verhältnis von Sprache und Musik in ausgewählten Liedern von Johannes Brahms* (Hamburg, 1975)

H. M. Beuerle: 'Brahms' Verhältnis zum Chor und zur Chormusik', *Melos/NZM*, ii (1976), 357

G. S. Bozarth: *The 'Lieder' of Johannes Brahms – 1868–1871: Studies in Chronology and Compositional Process* (diss., Princeton U., 1978)

B. Stockmann: 'Die Satztechnik in den Fest- und Gedenksprüchen op.109 von Johannes Brahms', *Brahms-Studien*, iii (Hamburg, 1979), 35

F. G. Zeileis: 'Two Manuscript Sources of Brahms's German Requiem', *ML*, lx (1979), 149

T. Boyer: 'Brahms as Count Peter of Provence: a Psychosexual Interpretation of the Magelone Poetry', *MQ*, lxvi (1980), 262

G. S. Bozarth: 'Brahms's Duets for Soprano and Alto, op.61: a Study in Chronology and Compositional Process', *SM*, xxv (1983), 191

——: Johannes Brahms und die Liedersammlungen von David Gregor Corner, Karl Severin Meister und Friedrich Wilhelm Arnold', *Mf*, xxxvi (1983), 177

——: 'Musikalische und dokumentarische Quellen der Lieder von Johannes Brahms: Zeugnisse eines Kompositionsprozesses',

Brahms

Johannes Brahms: Aufsätze zum 150. Geburtstag (1833–1983), ed.
C. Jacobsen (Wiesbaden, 1983)
——: 'Synthesizing Word and Tone: Brahms's Settings of Hebbel's
"Vorüber" ', *Brahms: Biographical, Documentary and Analytical
Studies*, ed. R. Pascall (Cambridge, 1983)
A. S. Garlington, jr: 'Harzreise as Herzreise: Brahms's Alto Rhap-
sody', *MQ*, lxix (1983), 527

FOLKSONG SETTINGS

M. Friedlaender: 'Brahms' Volkslieder', *JbMP 1902*, 67
R. Hohenemser: 'Brahms und die Volksmusik', *Die Musik*, ii/3 (1902–
3), 199, 422
G. von Graevenitz: 'Brahms und das deutsche Volkslied', *Deutsche
Rundschau*, xxxiii (1906), 229
J. H. Wetzel: 'Eine neue Volksliedersammlung aus Brahms' Jugendzeit',
ZMw, x (1927–8), 38
G. Döhrn: *Die Volkslied-Bearbeitungen von Johannes Brahms* (diss., U.
of Vienna, 1936)
R. Gerber: 'Brahms und das Volkslied', *Die Sammlung*, iii (1948),
652
W. Morik: *Johannes Brahms und sein Verhältnis zum deutschen
Volkslied* (diss., U. of Göttingen, 1953)
W. Wiora: *Die rheinisch-bergischen Melodien bei Zuccalmaglio und
Brahms* (Bad Godesberg, 1953)
S. Kross: 'Zur Frage der Brahmsschen Volksliedbearbeitungen', *Mf*, xi
(1958), 15
W. Moritz: *Johannes Brahms und sein Verhältnis zum deutschen
Volkslied* (Tutzing, 1965)

BRAHMS AS PERFORMER, CRITIC, HISTORIAN

H. Riemann: 'Johannes Brahms und die Theorie der Musik', *Festschrift
Erstes deutsches Brahms-Fest* (Munich, 1909), 61
W. Altmann: 'Brahmssche Urteile über Tonsetzer', *Die Musik*, xii/1
(1912–13), 46
M. Komorn: *Johannes Brahms als Chordirigent in Wien und seine
Nachfolger* (Vienna, 1928)
K. Geiringer: 'Brahms als Musikhistoriker', *Die Musik*, xxv (1932–3),
571
M. Komorn: 'Brahms, Choral Conductor', *MQ*, xix (1933), 151
K. Huschke: *Johannes Brahms als Pianist, Dirigent und Lehrer*
(Karlsruhe, 1935)
G. Fock: 'Brahms und die Musikforschung, im besonderen Brahms und
Chrysander', *Beiträge zur Hamburgischen Musikgeschichte*, vi
(Hamburg, 1956), 46

198

Bibliography

F. Bose: 'Die einzige Schallaufnahme von Brahms', *Musica Schallplatte*, i (1958)

I. Fellinger: 'Grundzüge Brahmsscher Musikauffassung', *Beiträge zur Geschichte der Musikanschauung im 19. Jahrhundert*, ed. W. Salmen (Regensburg, 1965), 113

——: 'Brahms und die Musik vergangener Epochen', *Die Ausbreitung des Historismus über die Musik*, ed. W. Wiora (Regensburg, 1969), 147

——: 'Brahms zur Edition Chopinscher Klavierwerke', *Musica scientiae collectanea: Festschrift Karl Gustav Fellerer* (Cologne, 1973), 110

K. Stephenson: 'Der Komponist Brahms im eigenen Urteil', *Brahms-Studien*, i (Hamburg, 1974), 7

K. Geiringer: 'Brahms as a Musicologist', *MQ*, lxix (1983), 463

HISTORICAL POSITION

W. Nagel: *Brahms als Nachfolger Beethovens* (Leipzig, 1892)

H. A. Harding: 'Some Thoughts upon the Position of Johannes Brahms among the Masters of Music', *PMA*, xxxiii (1906–7), 159

W. H. Hadow: 'Brahms and the Classical Tradition', *Collected Essays* (Oxford, 1928), 135

A. Schering: 'Johannes Brahms und seine Stellung in der Musikgeschichte des 19. Jahrhunderts', *JbMP 1932*, 9; repr. in A. Schering: *Von grossen Meistern der Musik* (Leipzig, 1940), 153

G. Adler: 'Johannes Brahms: Wirken, Wesen und Stellung', *SMw*, xx (1933), 6; Eng. trans., *MQ*, xix (1933), 113–42

W. Blume: *Brahms und die Meininger Tradition* (Stuttgart, 1933)

H. Osthoff: *Johannes Brahms und seine Sendung* (Bonn, 1942)

A. Orel: *Johannes Brahms: ein Meister und sein Weg* (Olten, 1948)

A. Schoenberg: 'Brahms the Progressive', *Style and Idea* (New York, 1950)

I. Fellinger: 'Das Brahms-Bild der "Allgemeinen musikalischen Zeitung" (1863–82)', *Beiträge zur Geschichte der Musikkritik*, ed. H. Becker (Regensburg, 1965), 27

C. Floros, ed.: *Brahms-Studien*, i (Hamburg, 1974)

S. Kross: 'Brahms: der unromantische Romantiker', *Brahms-Studien*, i (Hamburg, 1974), 25

N. Miller: 'Stilreinheit versus Stilvermischung: Anmerkung zu einer Brahms-Rezension von Hermann Goetz', *Musica*, xxxiv (1980), 457

O. Biba: 'Brahms, Wagner und Parteiungen in Wien: Texte und Beobachtungen', *Musica*, xxxvii (1983), 18

S. Kross: 'Kontinuität und Diskontinuität im heutigen Brahms-Bild', *ÖMz*, xxxviii (1983), 218

199

R. Pascall: 'Musikalische Einflüsse auf Brahms', *ÖMz*, xxxviii (1983), 228

G. Schubert: 'Komponisten rezipieren Brahms: Aspekte eines komplexen Themas', *Musik und Bildung*, xv (1983), 4–9

I. Fellinger: 'Brahms und die Neudeutsche Schule', *Hamburger Jb für Musikwissenschaft*, vii (Laaber, 1984), 159

C. Floros: 'Brahms: der zweite Beethoven?', *Hamburger Jb für Musikwissenschaft*, vii (Laaber, 1984), 235

——: 'Über Brahms' Stellung in seiner Zeit', *Hamburger Jb für Musikwissenschaft*, vii (Laaber, 1984), 9

M. Gregor-Dellin: 'Brahms als geistige Lebensform', *Hamburger Jb für Musikwissenschaft*, vii (Laaber, 1984), 223

OTHER STUDIES

P. Mies: 'Aus Brahms' Werkstatt', *Simrock-Jb*, i (1928), 42

——: 'Der Kritische Rat der Freunde und die Veröffentlichung der Werke bei Brahms', *Simrock-Jb*, ii (1929), 65

R. Lach: 'Das Ethos in der Musik von Johannes Brahms', *Simrock-Jb*, iii (1930), 48–84

A. Orel: 'Johannes Brahms' Musikbibliothek', *Simrock-Jb*, iii (1930–34), 18–47

R. Petzold: 'Brahms und der Chor', *Die Musik*, xxv/2 (1932–3), 578

K. Geiringer: 'Brahms as a Reader and Collector', *MQ*, xix (1933), 158

P. Mies: 'Notation und Herausgabe bei einigen Werken von W. A. Mozart, Franz Schubert und Johannes Brahms', *Festschrift Joseph Schmidt-Görg zum 60. Geburtstag* (Bonn, 1957), 213

O. Jonas: 'Brahmsiana', *Mf*, xi (1958), 286

O. E. Deutsch: 'Die Brotarbeiten des jungen Brahms', *ÖMz*, xv (1960), 522

P. Mies: 'Brahms-Bearbeitungen bei Max Reger', *Mitteilungen des Max-Reger-Instituts*, no.11 (1960), 7

I. Fellinger: *Über die Dynamik in der Musik von Johannes Brahms* (Berlin, 1961)

——: 'Zum Problem der Zeitmasse in Brahms' Musik', *GfMKB, Kassel 1962*, 219

P. Mies: 'Über ein besonderes Akzentzeichen bei Johannes Brahms', *GfMKB, Kassel 1962*, 215

O. Goldhammer: 'Liszt, Brahms und Reményi', *SM*, v (1963), 89

W. F. Korte: *Bruckner und Brahms: die spätromantische Lösung der autonomen Konzeption* (Tutzing, 1.963)

D. Kämper: 'Ein unbekanntes Brahms-Studienblatt aus dem Briefwechsel mit F. Wüllner', *Mf*, xvii (1964), 57

W. Czesla: 'Motivische Mutationen im Schaffen von Johannes Brahms', *Colloquium amicorum: Joseph Schmidt-Görg zum 70. Geburtstag* (Bonn, 1967), 64

Bibliography

F. Grasberger: 'Tradition in schöpferischer Sicht: zur Arbeitsweise von Johannes Brahms', *ÖMz*, xxii (1967), 319

S. Seiffert: *Johannes Brahms and the French Horn* (diss., U. of Rochester, 1968)

H. Braun: 'Ein Zitat: Beziehungen zwischen Chopin und Brahms', *Mf*, xxv (1972), 317

K. Stahmer: 'Korrekturen am Brahmsbild', *Mf*, xxv (1972), 152

H. Gál: *Brahms, Wagner, Verdi: drei Meister, drei Welten* (Frankfurt am Main, 1975)

W. Kirsch: 'Religiöse und liturgische Aspekte bei Brahms und Bruckner', *Religiöse Musik in nicht-liturgischen Werken von Beethoven bis Reger*, ed. W. Wiora, G. Massenkeil and K. W. Niemöller (Regensburg, 1978)

International Brahms Congress: Detroit 1980

G. S. Bozarth: 'Moderne Brahms-Forschung in Nordamerika', *ÖMz*, xxxviii (1983), 252

I. Fellinger: 'Neue Brahms-Forschung in Europa', *ÖMz*, xxxviii (1983), 248

——: 'Zum Stand der Brahms-Forschung', *AcM*, lv (1983), 131–200

K. Hoffmann: 'Marginalien zum Wirken des jungen Johannes Brahms', *ÖMz*, xxxviii (1983), 235

M. McCorkle: 'Filling the Gaps in Brahms Research', *MT*, cxxiv (1983), 284

W. Obermaier: 'Ein geplantes Brahms-Album 1922', *Brahms-Studien*, v (Hamburg, 1983), 169

H. Wirth: 'Oper und Drama im Leben von Johannes Brahms', *Brahms-Studien*, v (Hamburg, 1983), 117

ANTONÍN DVOŘÁK

John Clapham

CHAPTER ONE

Life

I Early years

Antonín (Leopold) Dvořák was born in Nelahozeves, near Kralupy, on 8 September 1841. The musical achievements of his father, František, amounted merely to an ability to play the zither and compose a few simple dances. The village schoolmaster gave Antonín his first musical instruction. Before long he was playing the violin at his father's inn, in neighbouring churches and in the village band. He left school shortly before his 12th birthday and may possibly have become an apprentice in the butchers' trade, following in the footsteps of his father and grandfather. To gain wider experience he left home a year later for Zlonice, a town in which he could learn German and which offered greater musical possibilities. He made good progress with his musical studies under the guidance of Antonín Liehmann, the school German teacher and church organist. Liehmann taught him the violin, viola, piano, organ and keyboard harmony. To improve his German, Dvořák was sent in 1856 to Česká Kamenice in northern Bohemia for a year, and while he was there he continued his musical studies under the tutelage of Franz Hancke. There are reasons for believing he did not complete his apprenticeship. František was determined that he should become a butcher; but Liehmann's pleading and an uncle's offer of financial assistance, coupled with Antonín's undisguised hatred of butchery, his intense love of music and his determination to risk following a musical career, caused František finally to relent.

In 1857 Dvořák entered the Prague Organ School, where he received the orthodox training of a church musician and had organ lessons from the principal, K. F. Pitsch. During his first year he also attended a nearby school in order to improve his German. Pitsch died in 1858 and was succeeded by Josef Krejčí, whose more modern interests extended to Mendelssohn and even Liszt. Dvořák had become a capable viola player, and was able to take part (without payment) in the St Cecilia Society concerts: their programmes included a number of contemporary works. He also played in the important golden jubilee celebrations of the Prague Conservatory, and when the Estates Theatre orchestra was augmented for performances of *Tannhäuser* and *Lohengrin*, and possibly for Meyerbeer productions as well, he almost certainly played in it. No doubt he sometimes saved enough money to attend concerts when Liszt, Bülow or Clara Schumann appeared, but he could not afford to buy scores, and there was no piano at his lodgings, so his close friendship with Karel Bendl (a third-year student and a gifted conductor and composer) was very valuable to him; Bendl allowed him to study his large collection of scores and to have free access to his piano. When Dvořák graduated in 1859 he was awarded only the second prize, and told that he was excellent but less gifted in theory than in practical work.

Dvořák's first professional post on leaving the school was with a small band, directed by Karel Komzák, which played at restaurants and for balls and which, in

1862, during the great upsurge of national culture in Bohemia, became the nucleus of the new Provisional Theatre orchestra. For the next nine years Dvořák was principal violist in the orchestra, first under J. N. Maýr and from 1866 under Smetana; when Wagner conducted a programme of his own music in Prague early in February 1863, Dvořák had the experience of playing the overture to *Tannhäuser*, extracts from *Die Meistersinger* and *Die Walküre* and the prelude to *Tristan und Isolde*. His earliest serious compositions date from this period: some chamber music, two symphonies (1865), a cello concerto, and a song cycle inspired by his unrequited love for one of his pupils, Josefina Čermáková. He had probably begun teaching in the early 1860s; his pupils included Anna Čermáková – Josefina's younger sister, his future wife. He completed his first two operas, *Alfred* and *Král a uhlíř* ('King and charcoal burner'), in 1870 and 1871, and was promised that the second, a comic opera on the Wagnerian model, would be staged at the theatre; but eventually it was declared to be 'too complicated' (Smetana had conducted the overture at a Philharmonic concert on 14 April 1872, when it was well received). At about the same time some songs and the slow movement of a piano trio were performed at the semi-private free musical evenings initiated by Ludevít Procházka; a few months later the Piano Quintet op.5 was played at a matinée. Since relinquishing his position at the theatre (1871) he had been able to devote more time to composition. But it was a struggle to make ends meet until early in 1873, when Jan Neff, a wealthy wholesale merchant, engaged him to accompany his own and his

14. Programme
of the Prague
concert
conducted by
Wagner (8
February 1863),
in which
Dvořák
played the viola

Programm
zur grossen Musikaufführung
unter persönlicher Leitung
von
Richard Wagner.
8. februar 1863.

1. Eine Faustouvertüre.
2. a) Versammlung der Meistersingerzunft. (für Orchester allein) neu.
   b) Pogners Anrede an die Versammlung, gesungen von Herrn Rokitansky, neu.
3. Vorspiel zu den „Meistersingern", neu.
4. Vorspiel zu „Tristan und Isolde".
5. Siegmunds Liebesgesang, gesungen von Herrn Bernard) neu.
6. Ouverture zu „Tannhäuser".

Sämmtliche Compositionen von Richard Wagner.

Die Herren Rokitansky und Bernard haben aus besonderer Gefälligkeit die obgenannten Partien übernommen.

Program
k velké hudební produkci
osobním řízením
Richarda Wagnera.
8. unora 1863.

1. Ouvertura k Faustu.
2. a) Shromáždění cechu mistrných pěvců. (pro orchestr samý)
   nové.
   b) Pognerovo oslovení shromáždění. nové, zpívá pan Rokitanský.
3. Předehra k „mistrným pěvcům," nová.
4. Předehra k „Tristanu a Isoldě."
5. Milostný zpěv Siegmunda, zpívá pan Bernard, nový.
6. Ouvertura k „Tannhäuseru."

Veškrz skladby Richarda Wagnera.

Pánové Rokitanský a Bernard převzali s charakterní ochoty nadzmíněné úlohy.

wife's singing and to teach the piano to their children. Dvořák relied on teaching as the main source of his income until at least 1878.

II From first recognition to international fame

Dvořák began to attract attention as a composer at the age of 31, when his patriotic cantata *Hymnus: Dědicové bílé hory* ('The heirs of the White Mountain') was performed on 9 March 1873 with striking success. Greatly encouraged, he set to work on a third symphony. A few months later *King and Charcoal Burner* was rejected; but the effect on him was salutary. It forced him to become severely self-critical, to the extent that he not only destroyed a considerable number of his early works, but in the summer of 1874 took the unusual step of resetting the libretto of the ill-fated opera using none of the original music. At the same time he was abandoning his former Wagnerian inclinations. In November 1873 he married Anna Čermáková, and three months later he became organist of St Adalbert's, Prague. It was a useful experience to hear his Third Symphony performed at a Philharmonic concert on 29 March 1874, conducted by Smetana, though he had already completed his Fourth. His second setting of *King and Charcoal Burner* was produced on 24 November.

By July 1874 Dvořák had both enough confidence and enough new works to enter 15 compositions, including his two most recent symphonies, some overtures and the Songs from the Dvůr Králové Manuscript op.7, for the Austrian State Stipendium, established to assist young, poor and talented artists. The adjudicators were Johann Herbeck (director of the Imperial Opera), Hanslick and Brahms, and Dvořák received the prize of

400 gulden. This gave him fresh encouragement: as well as some chamber music and other smaller works, he wrote a five-act grand opera, *Vanda* (rather over-ambitiously, in view of his lack of technical ability and experience), and the Symphony no.5 in F major, which represents a great advance on anything he had previously written. He competed for the stipendium several more times, winning in 1876 and 1877.

From 1873 onwards a few of Dvořák's compositions were published, almost all of them by Starý of Prague; but the firm was small, and no large sales were expected. On 30 November 1877, Hanslick wrote to inform him that he had just won 600 gulden, and told him how interested Brahms was in his music. He then added:

The sympathy of an artist as important and famous as Brahms should not only be pleasant but also useful to you, and I think you should write to him and perhaps send him some of your music. He has kept the vocal duets [the Moravian Duets] in order to show them to *his publisher* and to recommend them to him. If you could provide a good German translation, he would certainly arrange for their publication. Perhaps you might send him a copy of these and some other manuscripts. After all, it would be advantageous for your things to become known beyond your narrow Czech fatherland, which in any case does not do much for you.

Brahms wrote to Simrock on 12 December and the direct result was that the publisher accepted the duets, commissioned the Slavonic Dances, and published both works in 1878. They were favourably reviewed by Louis Ehlert in the Berlin *National-Zeitung* on 15 November that year. Simrock then went on to publish the three new Slavonic Rhapsodies, the Serenade for wind instruments, the String Sextet and String Quartet in E♭, two sets of songs, more Moravian Duets and other works, all within 12 months. Simultaneously Bote & Bock issued five of Dvořák's compositions, including the Theme and Variations for piano, the Serenade for strings and the Piano Trio in G minor.

With so much of Dvořák's music becoming available, foreign performances followed one another in rapid succession. At a time when three or perhaps four of the Slavonic Dances had been heard in Prague, Bernhard Gottlöber gave the première of the complete set of eight dances at Dresden: nos.1–4 on 4 December and 5–8 on 18 December 1878. In the following year small selections were heard at Hamburg and Nice in January, in Berlin early in February and at the Crystal Palace, Sydenham, in March. The Slavonic Rhapsody no.2 was presented at Dresden on 3 September 1879, no.3 had its world première in Berlin on 24 September, an unidentified Slavonic Rhapsody was performed at Berne on 9 October, and no.1 was performed at Münster on 8 November that year. American performances at Cincinnati, Baltimore and New York followed in February and March 1880. The Joachim Quartet, with Jacobsen and Dechert, gave the first performance of the Sextet in Berlin on 9 November 1879, and on 10 November that year the E♭ String Quartet was played at Magdeburg, five weeks before it was heard in Prague. The Serenade in D minor for wind was given at Dresden on 12 November 1879; and at Hamburg on 24 April 1880 the G minor Piano Trio, the Serenade and the Romance in F minor for violin and piano appeared in a programme devoted to Dvořák's music. Hans Richter was anxious to give the first performance of the Symphony no.6 in D in Vienna, but anti-Czech feeling prevented this (Dvořák dedicated the work to him). Paul Klengel gave its first foreign performance at Leipzig on 14 February 1882, and on 22 April Manns conducted it at the Crystal Palace. However, as a result of this rapidly awakening interest in Dvořák's music, publishers and others began to make excessive demands on the composer. Simrock acquired first option on each new work he wrote, leaving Dvořák free to offer works not completely new to Bote & Bock or Schlesinger.

At no period of his life did Dvořák allow much time to elapse without searching for a new opera libretto, composing an opera or revising one he had already written. Thus two years after *Vanda* he completed the comic opera *Šelma sedlák* ('The cunning peasant' is a more appropriate title than the customary translation 'The peasant a rogue'); and after another five years, now with a great deal more experience, he wrote a relatively successful grand opera in four acts, *Dimitrij*. By now the Prague productions of his operas were arousing interest abroad, especially those of *The Cunning Peasant* and an earlier one-act comedy, *Tvrdé palice* ('The stubborn lovers', or 'The pigheaded peasants'), both published by Simrock in 1882. The confidence of Schuch (conductor of the Dresden Opera) in the former was justified by a highly successful performance at Dresden on 24 October 1882, while a Hamburg production followed on 3 January 1883. At about this time too, Baron Hoffmann, the Generalintendant of the Vienna Imperial Opera, was trying to tempt Dvořák with a German libretto; but the composer was in no hurry to decide whether he, a Czech, would be justified in making use of one.

Brahms was the chief agent of Dvořák's success. He interested Joachim in Dvořák's music and arranged for Dvořák to visit Jauner, the director of the Imperial Opera; and his contacts with Hellmesberger (the solo violinist of the Imperial Opera) very probably led the latter to commission the Sting Quartet in C op.61. Brahms and Hanslick were both firmly convinced that it would be wise for Dvořák to move away from 'provincial Prague' to a musical centre such as Vienna, with its powerful musical tradition. As Hanslick expressed it in a letter of 11 June 1882: 'After such great initial successes, your art requires a wider horizon, a German environment, a bigger, non-Czech public'. While Dvořák was extremely grateful for his friends' assistance, he was acutely aware of the way his people had suffered under the Habsburgs, and of the continuing animosity and condescension of German-speaking people towards the Czech nation; and he found it difficult to accept the well-intentioned advice of his friends when it took this form.

The first performance of Dvořák's *Stabat mater* did not take place until 23 December 1880, three years after its completion. It was published the following year and performed by Janáček at Brno and Bellowitz at Budapest in April 1882. When Barnby presented it in London on 10 March 1883 it was given an enthusiastic welcome, which may well have contributed to the Philharmonic Society's subsequent decision to invite the composer to London to conduct some of his own music. This was Dvořák's first opportunity to conduct outside Bohemia. He had received great ovations when Richter introduced the Slavonic Rhapsody no.3 in Vienna and when *The Cunning Peasant* was performed at Dresden, but the London welcome was even warmer. At his three public appearances in March 1884 he conducted first the *Stabat mater* at the Royal Albert Hall, then his Hussite Overture, Slavonic Rhapsody no.2 and Sixth Symphony at St James's Hall, and finally his *Scherzo capriccioso* op.66 and Nocturne for strings op.40 at the Crystal Palace, where he also appeared as accompanist in two of his *Cigánské melodie* ('Gypsy melodies'). He was immediately invited to conduct the *Stabat mater* and the same symphony at the Three Choirs Festival at Worcester, and to write large choral works for the Birmingham and Leeds festivals and a new symphony for the Philharmonic Society. The prospect of a period with no financial worries made him decide to buy a cottage and some land at Vysoká, near Příbram – a welcome country retreat in which he could compose in peace.

III Vintage years

During 1884–6 preparations for visits to England were uppermost in Dvořák's mind. In late 1884 he travelled to Berlin to conduct the Berlin PO in a concert that included his Piano Concerto, played by Anna Grosser-Rilke, and the Hussite Overture; shortly afterwards Hans von Bülow, who was to become an enthusiast for this overture and for the Seventh Symphony, brought the Meiningen Orchestra to Prague, and invited Dvořák to conduct the overture *Domov můj* ('My home'). The English commissions constituted a major challenge to Dvořák, and one he was prepared to face. While working on the dramatic cantata *Svatební košile* (literally 'The wedding shift' but always known as 'The spectre's bride') for Birmingham, he grew convinced that this was his finest work; and turning to his Symphony no.7 in D minor, which he was composing for the Philharmonic Society, he resolved to make it, with God's help, 'a work which would shake the world'.

It has been suggested that the symphony owes its

15. Antonín Dvořák: photograph, c1877–8

particular noble qualities to its having been written during a period of considerable crisis. Baron Hoffmann was attempting to persuade Dvořák to write a German opera for Vienna. Having already won international fame with his orchestral, choral and chamber music, Dvořák was keen to attempt to match these achievements in the theatre. He wanted the Vienna Opera to take one of his Czech operas, but the management turned down both *The Cunning Peasant* and *Dimitrij*. The rejection of *Dimitrij* deeply wounded him, for it had been a success in Prague, and its Russo-Polish subject seemed suitable for Vienna; but he was told that the Viennese were 'rather tired of big five-act tragedies'. The main reason for Dvořák's reluctance to comply with the baron's wishes was his feeling that to do so would be to betray his fellow Czechs. Ironically, the Imperial Opera finally revoked the decision on *The Cunning Peasant* and staged it on 19 November 1885 – but at a time of intense political tension, so that there was no enthusiasm for the production and the performance was a fiasco.

With his next three visits to England Dvořák added to his reputation as one of the most important contemporary composers. The English première of *The Spectre's Bride* at Birmingham was notable for the audience's enthusiasm; and on his fifth visit the first performance of the oratorio *Svatá Ludmila* ('St Ludmilla') at Leeds on 15 October 1886 provided another triumph. However, audiences were smaller when Dvořák conducted the work at St James's Hall and the Crystal Palace in the following weeks, and provincial choral societies were discouraged from taking it up. Nevertheless, Dvořák's choral music was proving more welcome in England than anywhere else.

During this period some friction began to develop between the composer and his publisher. The first disagreement concerned the price to be paid for the Seventh Symphony; there followed an argument over Simrock's insistence on printing the titles of the works and Dvořák's first name in German. The composer demanded that the titles should be in both Czech and German and that his name should appear as 'Ant.', which would serve as an abbreviation for either the Czech 'Antonín' or the German 'Anton'; and Simrock, failing to understand how sensitive the composer was on this issue, eventually provoked Dvořák into writing on 10 September 1885:

Your last letter, in which you launched forth into national–political explanations, amused me greatly; but I am sorry you are so badly informed. All our enemies speak like that, or rather, some individual journalists are obliged to write like that, in accordance with the policy and tendencies of this or that political newspaper. But *what have we two to do with politics*; let us be glad that we can *dedicate our services solely to the beautiful art!* And let us hope that nations who represent and *possess art* will never perish, even though they may be small. Forgive me for this, but I just wanted to tell you that an artist too has a fatherland in which he must also have a firm faith and which he must love.

For a long time Simrock had been urging Dvořák to give him a second set of Slavonic Dances; but while the composer's mind was set on large-scale works, this was out of the question. A new chance came in the summer of 1886, while Dvořák was in a relaxed mood. When František Ondříček played the Violin Concerto with the Vienna PO at a Slavonic Singers' Union jubilee concert, Dvořák went there to conduct. At about this time, too, he began looking through earlier works and revising some of them to help meet the demands being made on him. It occurred to him that Richter might be interested in his Symphonic Variations, which had lain unperformed for ten years. He was right: Richter was delighted with this forgotten work, and after introducing it at a London concert on 16 May 1887 he was able to report that in his entire conducting experience no other new work had been so successful. Three months later Dvořák began work on the Piano Quintet in A op.81, and before the end of the year he was engaged on another opera, *Jakobín* ('The Jacobin'), which was not finished until a year later.

Dvořák was invited to conduct the *Stabat mater* in Budapest in March 1888, and the Fifth Symphony at Dresden a year later. In 1889 he was twice asked to join the professorial staff of the Prague Conservatory, then directed by Antonín Bennewitz; but he was not prepared to commit himself to teaching at the time, and did not accept until two years later. In June he was awarded the Order of the Iron Crown (from Austria), and a few months later he was received in audience by the emperor. He launched the Eighth Symphony in Prague on 2 February 1890.

Dvořák's visit to Russia in March 1890 was a result of his friendship with Tchaikovsky, formed during Tchaikovsky's stay in Prague in February 1888 and renewed upon his return in November. Tchaikovsky invited Dvořák to Russia on the second visit but had to wait a few weeks for a firm reply: he was delighted when Dvořák accepted but was away on a foreign tour during the whole of Dvořák's visit. In Moscow on 11 March 1890 Dvořák conducted a programme comprising his Fifth Symphony, the Adagio from the Serenade in D minor, the *Scherzo capriccioso*, Slavonic Rhapsody no.1 and the Symphonic Variations. Having had virtually no previous opportunity of hearing any of Dvořák's music, and being faced with works completely new to them (apart from the Rhapsody), many Russians left before the concert was over, and the critics were lukewarm; it was left to the Czech and German communities to lend their support. The arrangements at the Russian Musical Society concert at St Petersburg on 22 March were rather better: on this occasion Dvořák presented only two works, the Symphony no.6 and, again, the *Scherzo capriccioso*.

On his return home Dvořák was elected a member of the Czech Academy of Sciences and Arts. A few days later he left for London to introduce his Eighth Symphony at the Philharmonic Society concert (24 April 1890). During most of that year he was fully occupied with a Requiem Mass commissioned by the Birmingham Festival. There were further disagreements with Simrock, who was reluctant to offer sufficient remuneration for the new symphony, arguing that only small works made a profit: he was also very dilatory over deciding to take the small Mass in D. Since the dispute was not resolved by October, Dvořák severed his relations with Simrock and later sold both works to Novello. In November 1890 he was in Frankfurt am Main conducting the Eighth Symphony and the Hussite Overture. Two months later he began giving composition classes at the Conservatory, his pupils including Josef Suk and Oskar Nedbal. In March 1891 Prague University conferred on him an honorary PhD, and in June he went to Cambridge to receive an honorary MusD. On 15 June, the day before the ceremony, he conducted the Symphony no.8 and the *Stabat mater*, and Albani sang 'Where art thou, father dear?' from

The Spectre's Bride. Dvořák's 50th birthday was celebrated in Prague, but he preferred to remain quietly at
Vysoká. A month later, on 9 October, he conducted the
première of his Requiem at Birmingham, where it made
a much more lasting impression than *St Ludmilla* had
done at Leeds.

In June 1891 Dvořák was invited by Mrs Jeannette
Thurber to take up the directorship of the National
Conservatory of Music, New York, at a salary of
$15,000 a year. Although he found the idea attractive,
he needed to make sure that the conditions were satisfactory, and so the negotiations were not completed or the
contract signed until December. The agreement was for
him to take the post for two years from 1 October 1892.
For five months at the beginning of that year Dvořák
spent much of the time on a farewell tour of Bohemia
and Moravia with the violinist Ferdinand Lachner and
the cellist Hanuš Wihan, playing his new *Dumky* Trio at
40 concerts. At a special farewell concert in Prague on
28 April he conducted the première of his recently completed cycle of three overtures opp.91–3: *V přírodě* ('In
nature's realm'), *Karneval* and *Othello*. At the time of the
International Exhibition in Vienna, the National Theatre
company used the opportunity of visiting the city to
present two works in Czech which had never been performed there. On 1 June 1892 they performed *The
Bartered Bride* and on the following day *Dimitrij*, the
work the Imperial Opera had rejected eight years
earlier.

IV   The American period
It had been specially planned that Dvořák's arrival
in New York should coincide with the celebrations

*16. Hanuš Wihan, Dvořák and Ferdinand Lachner, who toured
together between January and May 1892 playing the 'Dumky'
Trio*

221

commemorating the fourth centenary of the discovery of America. Since Rodman Drake's poem *The American Flag* failed to reach him in time, he wrote instead a *Te Deum* for the musical programme before leaving home. Mrs Thurber's aim in inviting him was twofold: she expected him to found an American school of composition; and she wanted a figurehead, rather than an administrator, for her conservatory. She was also keen for Dvořák to write an American opera on the subject of Hiawatha, but the project never advanced beyond a few preliminary sketches. Her conservatory was run on philanthropic lines, and she controlled the finances; Dvořák was expected to teach composition and instrumentation to the most talented students three mornings a week, and on the other three mornings to conduct the choir and orchestra, and be available if necessary for business consultations with Mrs Thurber. During the first winter he conducted his *Te Deum*, Triple Overture, Symphony no.6 and Hussite Overture in New York and the Requiem at Boston, and between January and May 1893 he composed the Symphony no.9 in E minor, *Z Nového světa* ('From the New World'). Being keenly interested in the music of black Americans, Dvořák seized the opportunity of inviting a gifted black singer to sing spirituals to him. This was Harry T. Burleigh, a student at the National Conservatory, but not one of his own pupils.

Dvořák spent his summer holiday with his family at Spillville, a Czech community in north-east Iowa; during his stay there he composed his String Quartet in F and String Quintet in E♭, each known as 'The American'. He went to Chicago for the World Exhibition, and on its 'Czech Day', 12 August, he conducted the Symphony no.8, three Slavonic Dances from the op.72 set and *My Home*. He was invited to Omaha by Edward Rosewater, an American Czech newspaper proprietor, who arranged a banquet for him at the beginning of September. From there he went to St Paul to see Pastor P. J. Rynda, a Moravian, and was given another banquet by the Czechs of that city. On the return journey to New York he stopped at Buffalo and Niagara Falls. Just after his return he conducted his Hussite Overture and 149th Psalm at the Worcester Music Festival, Massachusetts, with great success. Towards the end of the year relations were resumed with Simrock, who was then able to publish the Ninth Symphony, the cycle of three overtures opp.91–3, the 'American' Quartet and Quintet and the Violin Sonatina in 1894. The Sonatina, his op.100, was dedicated to his six children. Publication was speeded up when Brahms generously offered to correct the proofs, a gesture of friendship for which Dvořák was deeply grateful. The Symphony 'From the New World' was first presented (to an eager and very enthusiastic audience) by Dvořák's friend Anton Seidl at Carnegie Hall, New York, on 16 December 1893, and the Kneisel Quartet gave the premières of the Quartet in F at Boston on 1 January and the new Quintet in New York on 12 January.

Since mid-November 1893 Mrs Thurber had been urging Dvořák to sign a new contract to take effect after their current agreement expired in the following May. He was in no hurry to do so, mainly because he was extremely worried about his financial position. Even before the full force of the 1893 American financial crisis was felt, Mrs Thurbur had fallen several months in arrears over paying Dvořák's monthly salary. The half of his salary which should have been deposited in his Prague bank account in September 1893 remained unpaid for many more months, and there was a huge gap in her monthly payments during the winter of 1893–4. Eventually a cash payment and a solemn undertaking to pay off the debts she had incurred, brought Dvořák back to the negotiating table. Finally, on 28 April 1894, he agreed to return to New York for another two years. He returned to Bohemia for the summer, and spent a quiet and happy time at his beloved country retreat. Although Mrs Thurber did not fully honour her promise, he left home in time to resume his duties as director of the National Conservatory on 1 November.

Before the end of 1893 Dvořák composed his Sonatina for violin and piano and during the extremely trying months of February and March the following year he wrote his Piano Suite in A major and the *Biblické písně* ('Biblical songs'). In April and July 1894 he revised Acts 2 and 4 of *Dimitrij*, making them in the process rather more Wagnerian, a result of his renewed interest in Wagner following discussions with Seidl. On returning to the conservatory for his third year (which in the event lasted only six months) he settled down to writing the Cello Concerto in B minor. He finished it three months later, just before he heard that he had been made an honorary member of the Gesellschaft der Musikfreunde in Vienna. In the summer he felt compelled to replace the brilliant closing bars with a long contemplative coda, reintroducing a reminiscence of his song *Lasst mich allein* (from op.82), which had already been worked into the Andante; he had just attended Josefina Čermáková's funeral and this song was a favourite of hers. He dedicated the work to Wihan.

During 1894–5 the financial situation eased considerably, but Dvořák's dislike of long spells away from home increased. He had already obtained Mrs Thurber's consent to the reduction of his fourth year in New York from eight months to six; but it was becoming increasingly obvious that the welfare and health of his six children would suffer if the family was again divided. After seeking the advice of Josef Hlávka, founder of the Czech Academy of Sciences and Arts, Dvořák decided to send Mrs Thurber his resignation. Since he had remained loyal to her during very difficult times, she was left with no alternative but to accept it. On 1 November 1895 Dvořák resumed his composition classes at the Prague Conservatory.

V Final years

Contented at being surrounded by his family again, near his friends and established in the country he loved, but deeply saddened by the death of his beloved sister-in-law, Dvořák settled down to writing two string quartets, in G and A♭, finishing the second on 30 December 1895. Next he explored some unfamiliar musical territory, the symphonic poem, and from K. J. Erben's *Kytice z pověstí národních* ('A bouquet of folk tales'), the source of *The Spectre's Bride*, he chose four more ballads: *Vodník* ('The water goblin'), *Polednice* ('The noon witch'), *Zlatý kolovrat* ('The golden spinning-wheel') and *Holoubek* ('The wild dove'); working simultaneously on the first three, he finished them in four months. After they had been privately performed at the Prague Conservatory (3 June) he made a few alterations. As soon as they had been published Richter and Henry

Wood performed them in London during October and November of the same year. By that time Dvořák was already working on *The Wild Dove*.

Dvořák visited London for the last time for the world première of the Cello Concerto, which Leo Stern played at the Philharmonic Society concert on 19 March 1896. In Vienna a few days later he visited the aging Brahms, who was most concerned about the necessity to counteract Bruckner's growing influence at the conservatory. He tried hard to persuade Dvořák to move to Vienna with his family, and even offered to place his entire fortune at his friend's disposal to make this possible. Dvořák saw him only once more, on his deathbed.

In 1897 Dvořák made extensive revisions to *The Jacobin* and composed another symphonic poem, *Píseň bohatýrská* ('Heroic song'), which has no programme. The first performance was given in Vienna by Mahler on 4 December 1898. At the end of 1897 Dvořák was appointed a judge for the Austrian State Prize. On his silver wedding day his daughter Otilje married his pupil Josef Suk. For the rest of his life, opera was his principal concern; as soon as he completed one, he began looking for a libretto for the next. *Čert a Káča* ('Kate and the Devil'), a comic opera based on an old Czech fairy tale, was followed by *Rusalka*, a tragic fairy-tale opera treated on broad symphonic lines and based on a subject derived from Hans Andersen's *Little Mermaid*, Fouqué's *Undine* and other sources. It was performed at the National Theatre on 31 March 1901 and was extremely successful: at last the composer was satisfied that he had written a stage work which had won the hearts of his countrymen. Mahler planned to present *Rusalka* in Vienna in 1902 and in May that year

18 $\frac{14}{2}$ 96

My dear friend Berger

I am sorry to announce you
that I cannot conduct
the performance of the
Cello concerto, The reason
is I have promised to my
friend Wihan - he will
play it.

If you put the concerto
into the program I could not
come at all, and will be glad
to come another time.

With kindly regards
sincerely yours

Ant Dvořák

17. *Autograph letter (14 February 1896) from Dvořák to
the secretary of the Philharmonic Society, London, object-
ing to Leo Stern being engaged to perform the world première of his Cello Concerto*

227

Dvořák signed the contract, but something went wrong; the opera was not performed there until 1910.

During these last years recognition and honours came to Dvořák from all sides. At the emperor's jubilee celebrations he was awarded a large gold medal 'per litteris et artibus', an honour that had previously been conferred on only one musician, Brahms. He was elected a member of the Austro-Hungarian House of Peers, but attended only one session. On 6 July 1901 he became the director of the Prague Conservatory, though he had no administrative duties. To commemorate his 60th birthday the National Theatre mounted a cycle of his operas and a stage version of *St Ludmilla*, and the Umělecká Besedá (Artistic Society) arranged a series of musical programmes and a banquet.

Still fascinated by opera, Dvořák spent the 17 months to August 1903 working on the well-tried subject of *Armida*. Probably in choosing this subject he was consciously making a bid for success on the international stage. It was a great blow to him that this last of his operas proved a failure, even though an inadequate production was partly to blame. During the first performance on 25 March 1904, he was forced to leave early because of a pain in his side. He was ill for five weeks and died on 1 May. He was given a national funeral and was buried at the Vyšehrad Cemetery, where the nation's leading men are laid to rest.

VI Teaching and character

Dvořák's teaching was empirical rather than systematic and included frequent references to his great predecessors' works. Josef Suk, Vítězslav Novák (who later established himself as his country's most gifted teacher of composition) and Oskar Nedbal (who conducted Dvořák's music at home and abroad) were his most talented composition pupils at the Prague Conservatory; his American pupils were much less distinguished. He encouraged them to develop a personal style, and only in their earliest music, and in the early music of Dvořák's friend Janáček, is it possible to see a close relationship with that of their teacher and friend.

While Dvořák did not identify himself with any patriotic or political group or faction, his Czech nationality was of great importance to him, and he was deeply hurt by disparaging remarks about his fellow countrymen. In his business dealings he showed both loyalty and trust, but also on occasions extreme caution, as in the lengthy negotiations leading to his first American contract, and his apparent suspicion about a successful outcome if *Rusalka* were staged in Vienna.

Dvořák was essentially a family man; his separation from his children during the American period was a cause of his nostalgia. He loved wandering in the woods and forests of his native land, and enjoyed meeting Vysoká peasants, Příbram miners and expatriate Czechs at Spillville. He bred pigeons, welcomed a game of *darda* (a card game) and took a keen interest in train spotting. He retained the simple tastes that came naturally to a man of peasant origin, and held firmly to his unquestioning religious faith. His modesty when experiencing outstanding triumphs abroad provoked comment, and he made no pretensions to be other than 'a simple Czech musician'.

CHAPTER TWO

Works

I Dvořák's style and its origins

Dvořák was neither a conservative nor a radical. He combined a profound admiration for the Classical composers with a keen interest in contemporary musical developments and succeeded in writing music that appealed equally to people with strong leanings towards tradition and to those who welcomed change. His music displays a number of influences: folk music, mainly Czech but also American; earlier composers whom he particularly admired, notably Mozart, Haydn, Beethoven and Schubert; Wagner; and his close friend Brahms.

Nationalist feelings first stirred in Bohemia shortly after the French Revolution, but no strong political movement developed until the revolutions of 1830 and 1848. Smetana was the first to channel these nationalist aspirations into music, and he alone was responsible for establishing a broadly based Czech musical style, which embraced far more than the basic elements of Czech art music and folksong but did not rely on specific folksongs. He accomplished this in his first four operas, years before Dvořák's music became strongly national in colour. Dvořák absorbed some of the essence of Smetana's style but made no attempt to imitate its characteristic personal traits. He seems to have developed a national style without a conscious effort. It flowered in

1878, the year of the Serenade for wind, the Sextet op.48 and the Slavonic Dances and Rhapsodies. Czech dance rhythms appeared more frequently in his music, and some of his scherzos – for example that of the Sixth Symphony – became *furianty*. Certain slow movements took on the character of a melancholy *dumka*, for example those of the String Quartet in E♭ op.51, the Piano Quintet op.81 and the String Sextet, in which the slow movement is presented in polka rhythm (see ex.1).

Ex.1 String Sextet op.48
Poco allegretto

Dvořák's marked preference for trochaic and dactylic (rather than iambic and anapaestic) metres can be clearly seen even in his earliest compositions, particularly the String Quartet op.2. The stress given to the initial syllable of a word or phrase in Czech speech provides justification for this, but it seems more likely that he developed it subconsciously from Czech folksong.

Dvořák also absorbed a number of characteristic melodic elements of native folksong into his musical thinking. One of these, the immediate repetition of an initial bar or figure before the normal continuation of the phrase, occurs in works from the whole of his creative life. There are two examples in the Adagio molto of the Third Symphony and another in the finale. The theme for variations in the String Quintet op.97

illustrates this practice splendidly, and there are more familiar examples among the subsidiary themes of the first movement of the Eighth Symphony, in the 'nature theme' of the three overtures opp.91–3 and in the Largo and finale of the Ninth Symphony (the second theme in each case). The motif of an initial upward leap, followed either by a leap back to the first note, as in the Slavonic Dance no.3 (the theme of which was borrowed from an authentic dance-song) and the *dumka* of the String Quartet op.51, or by a gradual descent towards the first note, as in the A major theme of the Slavonic Dance no.1 and the main theme of the Piano Quintet op.81, almost certainly emanated from folk sources. The traditional lullaby *Hajej, můj andělku*, used by Smetana in *The Kiss*, is an example of the first type; *Sil jsem proso*, a very well-known folksong twice used for variations by Smetana, is an example of the second. Dvořák used only for a limited period the so-called 'Three blind mice' figure of three descending notes, a common feature of west Slavonic folksong; it is extremely prominent in the Symphony no.8. He also made infrequent but effective use of the Lydian (augmented) 4th, which he sometimes associated with the Czech *dudy* or bagpipes; and, like Schubert, he occasionally suggested the sound of the cimbalom.

Dvořák was less audacious in his harmony than Smetana, but he showed an interest in dissonance, which he employed to produce an effect of considerable power towards the end of the Ninth Symphony (see ex.2). He did not roam from key to key, as Smetana and Wagner often did; tonality in his works thus tends to be fairly stable. He regarded modulation as a way of leading towards fresh colouring and did not, like Schubert, see it

Ex.2 Symphony no.9 op.95, 4th movt, final section

as serving the additional function of providing colour *per se*. He occasionally used a Moravian modulation, leading from a minor key to the major key a whole step lower. The influence of Smetana is evident in the structure of the opening of the 'American' Quartet and the *fortississimo grandioso* chords in C which form the climax of the Adagio in the Quartet op.106, both of which were suggested by similar passages in Smetana's String Quartet *Z mého života*.

It is impossible to gauge precisely the extent of American influence on the works Dvořák wrote in the USA. He had written pentatonic themes and used flattened 7ths in minor keys before he went there, and he was already familiar with Scotch snaps and the type of syncopation found in the spirituals of black Americans, since both of these elements occur in Slovak and Hungarian folk music. He partly foreshadowed the syncopated main theme of the first movement of the 'American' Quartet as early as 1886 in his Slavonic Dance no.9. Furthermore, the persistent dotted rhythm both of the first movement of the String Quintet op.97 and of the finale of the Violin Sonatina, both of which might be thought to have had an American Indian origin, occurred four years earlier in the Piano Quartet op.87. Yet, pentatonic themes and flattened 7ths are indeed more common in the music Dvořák wrote during his first two years in the USA, and the thematic material now is sometimes more 'primitive'. With regard to Indian music, which Dvořák heard at Spillville, it is known only that he used the melodic outline but not the rhythm of a two-bar fragment of it in the op.97 Quintet. Occasionally, as in the Largo of the Ninth Symphony and in the *Biblical Songs*, his recollection of spirituals affected what he wrote. But by the time he reached the Cello Concerto (1894–5) he appears to have tired of these exotic elements, which in any case were never more than tendencies; much of what he wrote during his years in the USA is either Czech or personal, as is clearly shown by his own continuation of a fragment of *Swing low, sweet chariot* in the G major theme in the Ninth Symphony. Nevertheless he seems not to have dismissed American influence entirely after returning home, for the element of pentatonicism and a cadence avoiding the leading note which appear in *Armida* may well owe something to it.

Unlike Smetana, Dvořák very rarely borrowed literally from folk music. The main theme of his Slavonic Dance no.7 grew out of combining two or more separate tunes (see ex.3). He tended to take only fragments of folk-tunes, as, for example, in the *Maličkosti* ('Bagatelles'), where he used the third and fourth bars of *Hrály dudy*, and in the Slavonic Dance no.11, where he used bars 9–12 of *Pod dubem, za dubem* (see ex.4). In the Slavonic Dances nos.11 and 13 he altered the character of the borrowed material by presenting it in the minor mode, in the former case in a modified tempo and with poignant chromaticism added (see ex.4).

It is well known that Dvořák had a profound admiration for Mozart, whom he described as 'sunshine' and

Ex.3

(a) *Hop škrk Helena*

(b) *U Jamolic na rohu*

(c) Slavonic Dance op.46,no.7

whose work he compared to a Raphael madonna he saw in London; both were 'so beautifully composed'. He venerated Beethoven: when a Beethoven sonata was being played in a class he was taking, he shouted to his pupils, 'Why don't you all kneel?' He owned some of Haydn's string quartets. He felt a close affinity with Schubert (about whom he wrote a long and appreciative

235

Ex.4
(a) *Pod dubem, za dubem*
Allegro

(b) Slavonic Dance op.72 no.3
Un pochettino lento

article for the *Century Illustrated Monthly* when he was in New York), and like him he delighted in changes from major to minor and vice versa. His love for these four composers, allied to the strong Classical tradition in Prague, made chamber music and the symphony natural outlets for his early music. There is a tendency to diffuseness in his early works, among which the 50-minute Cello Concerto in A is undoubtedly the least satisfactory; he probably realized this, as he did not orchestrate it.

When Dvořák succumbed to the powerful influence of Wagner he wrote amorphous string quartets, and an opera which could not be performed. He soon recognized his mistake and returned to a Classical style, but Wagner always remained a potent influence. Some passages can almost be regarded as direct borrowings from Wagner: the main theme of the Andante sostenuto of the Fourth Symphony opens with an obvious reminiscence of part of the Pilgrims' March in *Tannhäuser*; there are reminders of *Tannhäuser* and *Parsifal* in *Armida*, an echo of the Venusberg music in *Carnival* and a derivative of the 'magic sleep' motif in *Othello*. The Wagnerian character of one motif in *Rusalka* (ex.5) is unmistakable; but Dvořák wrote this kind of harmonic progression only rarely; normally his harmony was not

Ex.5 *Rusalka*, op.114

Andante sostenuto

influenced by Wagner. He came round full circle to Wagnerian methods late in his career, by which time he was well equipped to use them successfully. The revision of *Dimitrij* (1894–5) meant the loss (which he regretted) of some lyrical passages from the earlier version, but the die was cast, and the revisions of *The Jacobin* (1897) followed similar lines. He retained a good deal of lyricism and relied on the spirit of the dance in his last three operas, but he also wrote declamatory vocal lines more often, and in *Rusalka* and *Armida* he used leitmotifs fairly consistently and treated them symphonically.

Other composers who influenced Dvořák at different times include Berlioz, Schumann, Chopin, Mendelssohn, Liszt, Weber, Lortzing, Verdi and, above all, Brahms. The influence of Brahms can be observed in the style of the piano writing in the Violin Sonata and in a more general way in the D major symphony (no.6), the first and last movements of which were affected by Brahms's symphony in the same key. Although Dvořák lacked Brahms's natural inclination for contrapuntal thought, he found little difficulty in writing counterpoint. His textures, however, commonly result from a combination of lines and figures, which have distinctive characters of their own, and he frequently wrote striking counter-melodies that have a contrapuntal function. As an experienced viola player he appreciated the necessity in chamber music and the wisdom in orchestral works of providing every part, however minor, with an intrinsic interest of its own. Brahms's integrity and seriousness of purpose appear to have given him valuable moral support when he was engaged on his two most ambitious works of 1883–5, the Piano Trio op.65 and the Seventh Symphony, both of which display a greatly increased mastery of dynamic and symphonic form. Brahms's influence can also perhaps be detected in the skilful, restrained reference to the first movement in the revised coda of the finale of the Cello Concerto. As the Adagio of this work suggests, Dvořák was inclined to linger over a beautiful slow movement, reluctant to draw it to a close, but the concerto is on the whole superbly assured and demonstrates in innumerable ways his mastery of symphonic form.

II Working methods

In spite of the fact that a large number of Dvořák's sketches are lost, enough have survived to provide a valuable insight into his creative processes. He generally showed both starting and finishing dates on his sketches as well as on his scores. Using one or two staves, he normally made an extended sketch of an entire work before beginning to prepare the full score. He also made preliminary and supplementary sketches; in the former he drafted or moulded a theme, and in the latter he corrected or reshaped a passage with which he was dissatisfied. The first sketch for the first theme of the finale of the Eighth Symphony was very different from the definitive version, which emerged only with the seventh sketch and needed two more for its completion. Besides using his American sketchbooks for extended sketches, he jotted down in them many other musical ideas as they occurred to him, most of them in a rather rudimentary state. Numerous themes that went into the American works can be found here, as can the Rusalka motif, which he did not need to use for several years; there are others that he did not use at all. The earliest version of the motto theme of the Ninth Symphony was rather stiff and in F major, not the eventual E minor.

The continuous, extended sketches reveal the way Dvořák shaped and reshaped his movements. Extensive deletions show his dissatisfaction with much of what he had sketched. The Seventh Symphony, for example, caused him a great deal of trouble, and he rejected whole pages of early drafts; the scherzo was originally in 3/4 time, not 6/4, indicating that he conceived it as a *furiant*. He sketched the Largo of the Ninth Symphony in C, but later noticed that a series of chords with which he had been experimenting could be used to modulate from E, the tonic of the first movement, to D♭, the key of his earliest sketch of the english horn melody; he therefore

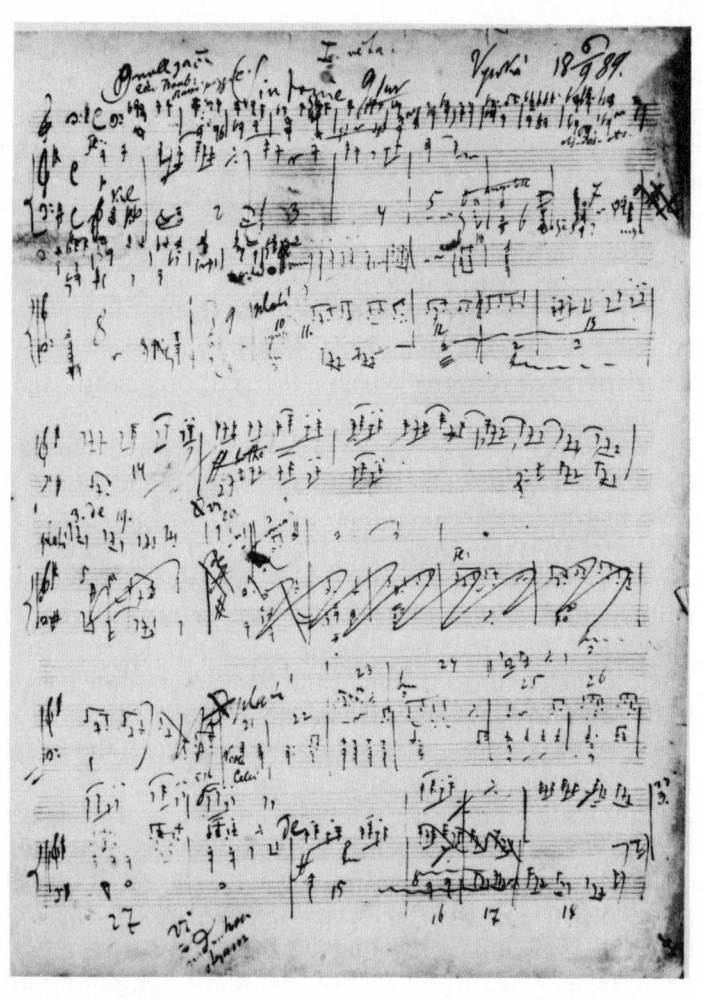

18. *Autograph sketch of the beginning of Dvořák's Symphony no.8, composed 26 August–8 November 1889*

used the chords as a bridge and rewrote the slow movement in D♭, an unusual choice of key. He had sketched and scored his Piano Trio in F minor by 31 March 1883, but a comparison with the published version reveals so many differences that it is apparent that he felt the need to revise it completely before he could allow it to be published. Other works came more easily and spontaneously than these. He always had plenty of ideas, though some of them needed polishing, and as a rule he worked relatively quickly. Although he did not find composition a straightforward matter, he had, like Schubert, the enviable gift of making his music sound as if it came naturally to him.

III Opems

Dvořák's attention was first drawn to opera during his student days and his interest was further stimulated by his participation in performances of the Italian, French, German and the few Czech operas that were in the repertory during his nine-year membership of the Provisional Theatre orchestra. When he resigned from it he was already working on his second opera. His interest in, and appreciation of, opera increased over the years, but because he lacked a natural instinct for drama it was hardly possible for him to portray characters convincingly and handle dramatic situations effectively until he had achieved, through his instrumental music, sufficient mastery in conveying a broad and comprehensive range of mood, expression and emotion. Lyrical rather than dramatic elements are thus generally more prominent in his operas. He was never able entirely to overcome his innate handicap, and it is primarily for this reason that, despite their admirable qualities and the

great affection in which *Rusalka* is held in Czecho-
slovakia, his last five operas rank lower than his finest
orchestral and chamber works.

Even though there is no spoken dialogue in any of
Dvořák's comic operas, he did not often resort to
recitative. In most of his operas the music is continuous,
although in those of the 1870s the division into numbers
is obvious enough, and even in the late works there are
some important set pieces. In his first two operas he
attempted to follow closely in Wagner's footsteps but
then moved sharply in the direction of Weber and
Lortzing, only to return, with greater success, to
Wagnerian methods when revising *Dimitrij* and *The
Jacobin* and composing his last three operas. It was
normal for him to employ a limited number of reminiscence themes in his work; in *Rusalka* and *Armida* they
can be more accurately described as leitmotifs. He often
showed the influence of Smetana, who initiated what is
acknowledged as the modern Czech musical style. But
with *Libuše* (composed 1869–72; performed 1881)
Smetana achieved his self-imposed task of providing the
Czech nation with the most strongly national of all their
operas, after which Dvořák understandably felt an
obligation to do no more than select Czech or Slavonic
subjects and compose music that inevitably possessed a
Czech flavour. In his later years he was careful, but not
always wise, in his choice of librettos, and the necessity
for substantial alterations to a work became clear to him
only after it had been performed. With experience he
was able to respond to the emotional and dramatic
demands of a libretto, but his instinctive tendency to
create a rounded piece of music characterized by
development of a symphonic nature seems to indicate

clearly that he was primarily a composer of instrumental music.

When Dvořák wrote his first two operas, Smetana's *The Brandenburgers in Bohemia*, *The Bartered Bride* and *Dalibor* had already been performed in Prague, as had operas by several lesser native composers, including František Škroup, Šebor, Bendl, Skuherský and Rozkošný, but none of these served as a real precedent for him. Notwithstanding the claims of contemporary critics, *Dalibor* contains scarcely a hint of Wagnerian tendencies. So Dvořák's *Alfred* (1870) and the earliest version of *King and Charcoal Burner* (1871) are the earliest attempts by a Czech composer to write operas in accordance with Wagner's principles. Neither was performed at the time, and they do little more than show his keen interest in the most modern techniques and the daunting task he was prepared to set himself before he had acquired the skill and experience essential for its successful completion.

The first change of style in Dvořák's operatic output came when, in 1874, he set *King and Charcoal Burner* for the second time in a simple folk style, in keeping with the origin of the libretto as a puppet play. He added a splendid ballad for the King in Act 1 for the 1881 performance, and revised the opera in 1887 after the libretto had been redrafted: he rewrote much of Act 3, and since its music became stronger, more dramatic and far more continuous, there are some inconsistencies of style. He showed growing confidence in the one-act comedy *The Stubborn Lovers* (1874) and was reasonably successful in matching a witty libretto, notable for its symmetries, with witty music. The conversational style over a continuous orchestral line which informs the two quartets and nearly all of the duet for Toník and Řeřicha was almost certainly suggested by Smetana's *The Two Widows*. The opera is dominated by the *buffo* bass Řeřicha, who has an affinity with Kecal in *The Bartered Bride*. Beneš Šumavský's libretto for the five-act opera *Vanda* (1875) is trite and its Polish subject unreasonably inflated, so the opera was doomed from the start. By giving the main musical interest to the orchestra rather than to the singers, Dvořák returned to some extent to Wagnerian methods, but the metamorphosis of the Vanda theme in various situations is reminiscent of Liszt. The plot of *The Cunning Peasant* (1877) obviously stems from *Le nozze di Figaro* and also owes something to *The Bartered Bride*. It is an exuberant work, with ample opportunities for big ensembles and dances, and the colourful score is strongly influenced by Czech folk music. Five recurring themes are associated with particular characters, most of whom, however, have no distinct, recognizable musical personality.

Until a good and really demanding text came his way, Dvořák had no real incentive to come to grips with the problem of opera, but a few weeks after completing the Sixth Symphony he received such a libretto. Although the libretto of *Dimitrij* corresponds in general outline with those of the then outmoded grand operas of Meyerbeer (and there are a few other weaknesses), it is well written, the main characters are clearly drawn and well contrasted, and it provides some strong dramatic situations. The subject forms a sequel to that of *Boris Godunov*, but Dvořák did not know Musorgsky's opera. The score of *Dimitrij*, composed in 1881–2, is rich in melody, especially in Xenia's scenes. The chorus and the big ensembles for the main characters are handled well, the conflict between the Poles and the Russians, a double chorus, being particularly vivid. There is far more assurance and musical richness here than in any of the earlier operas. Dvořák at first hesitated over setting Červinková's libretto for *The Jacobin* but warmed to the subject when he realized how strongly Benda, the schoolmaster musician, reminded him of Liehmann, his teacher at Zlonice. He composed the opera in 1887–8 but in 1897 revised and reshaped Act 3, which consequently contains the most mature music. In general a spirit of gaiety and humour prevails in Act 1, and sentimental charm informs the handling of the singing rehearsal in Act 2. The plot, however, centres on the count's intention to disinherit his son Bohuš because of his supposed revolutionary tendencies. Dvořák handled this situation with remarkable psychological insight, enhanced by the sparing use of a melodic fragment that becomes an essential part of the lullaby that Julie sings in order to revive in the count memories of his deceased wife and infant son.

Dvořák's reawakened and intensified interest in Wagner can be clearly seen in his last three operas. The last vestiges of formal recitative vanish, and there is far more continuity. Since there is little declamatory writing, these works are still essentially lyrical, and dances have a natural place in them. The leitmotifs are often concise and are used with greater consistency than before. All three of these operas turn to the world of fantasy: fairy tales form the basis of the first two, and magic is prominent in the third.

There is an abundance of animation, wit and gaiety in *Kate and the Devil* (1898–9), even though the oppres-

19. Family group at Vysoká, c1901, including Dvořák (centre), his wife Anna (centre right), and his children Aloisie and Antonín (front left and centre), Anna and Magda (back left and right)

sion of the villagers necessarily casts a deep shadow at times. Dvořák depicted his characters well, from the garrulous Kate to the quaintly comic Lucifer. An exception is the princess, who presented a problem he found difficult to solve: she is regarded with bitterness by her subjects, but she does not appear until Act 3, by which time she is frightened and already in a contrite mood. Following Smetana's example, Dvořák transformed some of his themes to make them serve several different functions. The bagpipe tune is changed to symbolize Kate's sharp tongue and becomes the basis for a waltz at the inn and some dances in Hell. Similarly the motif of Hell and the devils assumes various forms, perhaps the most striking of which accompanies the description of Lucifer's fine red castle. *Rusalka* (1900) is a spaciously and symphonically conceived work. Dvořák evidently found the spirits of river and lake and of the woods the most fascinating elements in it, for it is they, rather than the prince, the foreign princess or the comic gamekeeper and scullion, who dominate the opera. Rusalka, the frail, lovelorn heroine, her grotesque, melancholy father, ruler of the underwater kingdom, and Ježibaba, the witch, who is prepared to invoke her magic arts for Rusalka only so long as the penalties are understood, are all more real than the royal pair of humans, and their hopes and fears are expressed against a responsive and colourful backcloth of singing and dancing sprites.

Dvořák wrote his last opera, *Armida* (1902–3), when his enthusiasm for Wagner was at its height. He used in it a large number of leitmotifs, which throughout the work are constantly changed and adapted to new circumstances. The subject offered splendid opportunities for creating rounded characters. The vicissitudes of Rinaldo and his eventually achieving full stature as a Christian warrior are strongly underlined in the music, as are Armida's principal characteristics, feminine charm and determination to fight for her own cause. The powerful Ismen is vividly portrayed and is given some of the strongest music in the opera, but the lesser characters are not nearly so convincing. Vrchlický's version of the story differs from Tasso's at numerous points; Armida meets her death on the battlefield in precisely the same circumstances as Clorinda did at the hands of Tancred, and there is indeed dramatic justification for this, but the reliance on magic seems excessive and may have caused the opera to be less frequently performed than the high quality of much of the music warrants.

IV Choral works

A number of large-scale works from Dvořák's output of choral music played a significant part in his artistic development and growing reputation. The *Hymn: the Heirs of the White Mountain*, which he twice revised as the demand for his music increased abroad, brought him his first public success. The *Stabat mater* was in great demand among choral societies in several countries, and *The Spectre's Bride*, which had its first American performance at Providence, Rhode Island, only three months after its spectacular success at Birmingham in 1885, was much admired in the English-speaking world during Dvořák's lifetime. By contrast, *St Ludmilla*, on which he had laboured hard and which he considered to be one of his finest works, proved to be a failure with the public.

The *Hymn: the Heirs of the White Mountain* (1872)

showed promise for the future rather than outstanding achievement. It is a setting of seven verses of a poem by Vitězslav Hálek, the earlier part of which expresses the sorrows of the Czechs in the wake of their defeat of 1620; there follows a call for the loyalty, courage and heroism needed to bring about the rebirth of the nation. The death in September 1875 of Dvořák's second child, when two days old, prompted him to begin sketching his *Stabat mater* five months later, but possibly this was not the only reason, for he was a simple, devout Catholic who by 1892 had set all of the other major liturgical texts, with the exception of the *Magnificat*. He did not score the *Stabat mater* until late in 1877, shortly after losing two more children. His approach to the composition of this work was that of an instrumental composer: he produced a series of balanced forms and reintroduced some of the opening music in the final number but with a dramatic alteration at a climax. The first of the ten numbers is the most impressive and almost certainly the most deeply felt. It begins with rising octaves, which appear to point towards the cross, and then slow and partly chromatic descents lead towards the figure of Mary. Not all the music in other sections matches the words so well, but there are some notable passages, particularly at the end of 'Fac, ut ardeat', in the simple and charming 'Tui nati vulnerati' and in the highly individual 'Inflammatus'.

The dramatic cantata *The Spectre's Bride* (1884) came midway between the operas *Dimitrij* and *The Jacobin*. It is a setting of a ballad by K. J. Erben whose macabre subject, so characteristic of the early Romantic period, has probably discouraged performances in the 20th century. Dvořák allotted the narrative to a solo bass and the chorus, and the parts of the maiden and the demon bridegroom to a soprano and a tenor. The work is rather more stylized than his operas; as one would expect in an important work by him from this period, it is melodious, colourful and rich in invention. A prominent element is a theme announced at the beginning which helps to unify the cantata but is not used consistently in any specific context.

The oratorio *St Ludmilla*, written in 1885–6, is planned on a large scale and along monumental lines; the choruses often give strong reminders of Handelian methods. Except for the powerful chorus in Russian style at the beginning of the third part, Dvořák appears to have been less at ease in the Christian choruses than the pagan ones, the first of which is especially fine. He invariably felt a natural sympathy with his heroines, and Ludmilla is no exception, for she has the best solo arias. Her personal theme is not heard until after she has been converted; two other motifs symbolize light (both pagan and Christian) and the cross.

Dvořák composed the Mass in D for the consecration of Josef Hlávka's private chapel in 1887. It is a relatively small-scale work, expressing his direct, sincere response to the text, and it is slightly coloured with pastoral elements. The Requiem (1890) was a far greater challenge to him. A four-note chromatic, syncopated motto theme, reminiscent of the fugue subject of the second Kyrie of Bach's Mass in B minor, appears in almost all sections of the work. Given the awe and solemnity with which Dvořák approached the text, it could perhaps signify a sorrowful questioning of the mystery of life and death, but he made no attempt at the time to express in words his thoughts on the subject.

There is more than a touch of drama at appropriate moments, with splendid climaxes in the 'Quam olim Abrahae' fugue and in the Agnus Dei at the words 'Cum sanctis tuis in aeternum', after which there is an ethereal close. In general there is a strong vein of lyricism, which is specially telling in the Gradual and 'Recordare', in the quiet sections of the 'Confutatis' and above all in the Offertory. Instead of acknowledging in his *Te Deum* the three natural divisions of the canticle, Dvořák gave it four sections corresponding superficially to the four movements of a symphony. The prayer 'Dignare, Domine' has a particularly expressive melodic line for solo soprano; in several other places the basis of the music is pentatonic or tetratonic. The work opens with a joyful peal of sound over a double pedal which returns at the end of the first section and again in the final 'Alleluia'.

V Orchestral works

(*i*) *Introduction.* Dvořák's admiration for the music of Mozart and Beethoven and his great love for Schubert led him towards symphonic composition on more or less Classical lines before his emergence as a nationalist composer, and this predilection was reinforced by his warm friendship with Brahms. It was only towards the end of his career that, prompted by his sympathetic response to Czech folklore, he turned to the newer and rather more fashionable symphonic poem, which nationalist composers normally preferred. He had, however, found an outlet for his national aspirations much earlier in the Slavonic Dances, Slavonic Rhapsodies and Hussite Overture and in individual movements in the symphonies and Violin Concerto. For all the enormous, and justified, popularity of the Ninth Symphony, a work which has been accepted in areas where the rest of his music is scarcely known, there can be little doubt that the highest achievements of his creative career are the Seventh Symphony and the Cello Concerto.

(*ii*) *The symphonies*. Even though they have certain merits, Dvořák's first two symphonies, written in 1865, are unlikely to find a permanent place in the orchestral repertory. The main theme of no.1 became the principal theme of several of the piano *Silhouettes*, completed in 1879, and the finale of no.2 contains a clear anticipation of the important motif of the water sprites in *Rusalka*. Wagnerian influences are prominent in the three-movement Symphony no.3 in E♭ (1873) but are almost wholly absent from no.4 in D minor (1874), except in the Andante sostenuto, where clarinets, bassoons and brass present at the outset a theme that might almost be a direct quotation from Wagner. At this stage Dvořák had not solved the problem of form. The first movement of no.3 is unorthodox – for instance, in the definitive version the second subject is not recapitulated – but it has a splendidly broad sweep. Uncomfortable indications that the coda has already begun interrupt progress in the middle of the slow movement of no.4. The finale of no.3 is invigorating thanks to its unceasing animation, but in that of no.4 there are suggestions that too much has been attempted with the main theme. There is a thematic link between the first movement and slow movement of no.3, and the scherzo of no.4 contains a reference to the main theme of the first movement.

The Symphony no.5 in F (1875; published as no.3) provides remarkable evidence of Dvořák's growing mastery; it is significant that he found it unnecessary to alter the design of any of the quick movements when he prepared it for publication 12 years later. The key of the Andante, A minor, is of some structural importance in that the finale begins in it and avoids establishing the tonic for more than 50 bars. The drama of this movement is thus much enhanced, as it also is by a particularly powerful development section. The coda includes subtle hints of the main theme of the first movement, which eventually returns on the trombones. Dvořák wrote the Symphony no.6 in D (published as no.1) on the crest of his first nationalist phase in 1880. As has been mentioned above, the first and last movements owe something to Brahms's symphony in the same key, and Beethoven's influence is felt too, particularly in the opening of the Adagio, which recalls the slow movement of the Choral Symphony. The work is nevertheless highly characteristic of Dvořák himself: it is rich in themes, and although it is planned on classical lines it modulates freely, the second subject group of the first movement being in B minor and major. National colouring is most apparent in the scherzo, which for the first time in a symphony is a *furiant*; it is, moreover, one of Dvořák's finest.

Whereas the D major Symphony can be seen as the work of a contented and confident man with a keen enjoyment of life, the Symphony no.7 in D minor (1884–5; published as no.2) seems to be that of one who has battled with his conscience and experienced tragedy. The Piano Trio in F minor of 1883 was Dvořák's first work in an epic manner, but in the symphony he probed to even greater emotional depths, showed even greater mastery in the design and in the opinion of many

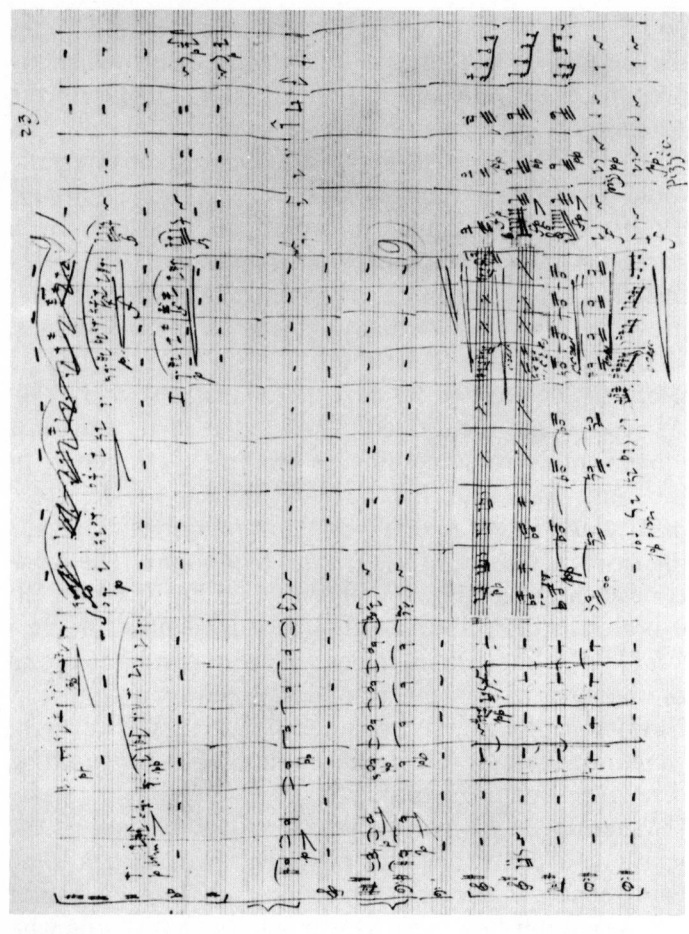

20. Autograph score of part of the first movement of Dvořák's Symphony no.9 ('From the New World'), composed 10 January–24 May 1893

254

produced his greatest work in this form. The strong, concise development, the compression of the recapitulation and the tension in the coda are particular strengths of the first movement. The tranquillity of the opening of the Poco adagio is succeeded by questioning, melancholy and a brief storm. The scherzo, though barred in 6/4 time, retains much of the character of a *furiant*, the prevailing mood of which is relieved by a charming trio. The heroic spirit that dominates the symphony is instantly apparent in the finale, and it continues almost uninterruptedly until the powerful peroration resolves on a major chord.

The Symphony no.8 in G (1889; published as no.4) is by contrast a genial and relaxed work, abounding in Czech feeling. The sombre mood of the introduction soon passes, and even though the second theme stems from it the first movement is dominated by the delightfully fresh theme announced by the flute. There are contrasts of mood and colour in the Adagio; in the C major section the descending scales suggest a cimbalom. The finale is a set of variations constructed on an experimental and not altogether satisfactory design.

While working on the Symphony no.9 in E minor, 'From the New World' (1893; published as no.5), Dvořák stated: 'The influence of America can be felt by anyone who has "a nose" '. In saying later that it was really 'a study or sketch for a longer work', he had in mind his projected composition on *The Song of Hiawatha*. The dance of Pau-Puk-Keewis lay behind the scherzo, and Minnehaha's funeral may have inspired the Largo. He explained that the title of the work simply signified 'Impressions and greetings from the New World'. Although some American influences are obvious, it is fundamentally Czech. The work is dominated by a motto theme which appears in every movement. Dvořák has been criticized for introducing into the finale a procession of themes from earlier movements, but the electrifying impact of the climax of this movement – and of the symphony – is undeniable: the motto theme reappears angrily, the introduction to the Largo 'strides over the world like Wagner's Wotan' (Tovey), the Largo and scherzo themes pair off, and the motto and the finale theme combine to produce extremely astringent harmony.

(*iii*) *Other orchestral works.* The Piano Concerto in G minor (1876) is written on commendable Beethovenian lines and has a number of attractive features but is not very successful either as a virtuoso composition for the instrument or as a work of art. The Violin Concerto in A minor (1879–80) is more rewarding. Joachim, to whom the work is dedicated, helped Dvořák with the solo part but he never played it. The concerto was a product of the nationalist enthusiasm that coloured the D major Symphony in 1880. The main theme and a subsidiary theme of the final sonata rondo are in *furiant* rhythm, and the central episode is a *dumka*. Dvořák's decision at the end of the first movement to proceed directly to the Adagio after only a few bars of recapitulation (despite having been advised not to do so) was probably unwise; for one thing it prevented the exploitation of the interesting idea of bars 78–85.

A composer normally writes a cello concerto with good cause, and in the case of his B minor concerto (1894–5) Dvořák waited many months before complying with the request for one from Wihan. His being a string player himself was an initial advantage: he had had valuable experience of problems of orchestral balance and blend and thus knew that the quiet playing of the cello in the Adagio could be tellingly supported by three trombones, which he needed elsewhere in that movement for some menacing passages in minor keys. The invention in the concerto is exceptionally rich. In the second subject of the first movement, for example, the soloist takes up the beautiful melody of the horn from the tutti, plays spiccato arpeggios on an ambiguous harmonic framework, presents a new melodious idea in F♯ as well as a bold chordal motif, and converses briefly with a trio of horns before leading up to the climax. The omission of the expected first subject and transition in the recapitulation is probably Dvořák's most brilliant and dramatic example of short-circuiting. The coda of the rondo recalls the main theme of this movement and includes a further reference to the song Josefina Čermáková admired, thus making the concerto a memorial to his sister-in-law.

The Symphonic Variations (1877) are a vivid witness to Dvořák's growing powers, imagination and resource during the years between the fifth and sixth symphonies, and the *Scherzo capriccioso* (1883) is a brilliantly successful exemplar of another of his most productive periods. The Hussite Overture from the same year makes use of two celebrated tunes, the 15th-century *Svatý Václave* ('St Wenceslas') melody and the Hussite hymn *Ktož jsú boží bojovníci* ('Those who are God's warriors'), in addition to original material which absorbs elements from them. The development section represents a battle from which the Czechs emerge triumphant, so the main theme is then recapitulated in C major instead of in the original C minor. The three overtures of 1891–2, *In Nature's Realm*, *Carnival* and *Othello*, are a manifestation of Dvořák's belief that Nature was created by the Almighty, but was in another sense also the giver of life, which can be both beautiful and ugly. A theme representing Nature appears in all three. The exhilaration and verve of *Carnival* have helped to make it one of Dvořák's most familiar works, but the strongly dramatic *Othello* in particular has not received the attention it deserves. The references in the manuscript score to several points in Shakespeare's tragedy show that he conceived the overture programmatically.

In the four symphonic poems based on Erben's ballads (1896), themes are associated with characters or other important elements in the dramas, just as in the operas. Dvořák arrived at those of *The Golden Spinning-wheel* by setting the poet's actual lines to music; following the example of Liszt and Smetana he transformed the king's theme to make it appropriate for the wicked stepmother and also for the mysterious, kindly old man, but notwithstanding such subtleties he appears to have followed the complex tale too faithfully. *The Water Goblin*, which illustrates the tale in seven short scenes and a coda, is planned in the form of a rondo. By contrast, the lengthy repetition at the beginning of *The Noon Witch* shows Dvořák temporarily rejecting a precise representation of the ballad for the sake of an initial musical balance. In the rest of the work he brings the remaining stanzas to life vividly and dramatically. *The Wild Dove*, which adheres closely to the ballad, falls naturally into four scenes and an epilogue.

There is much of interest in Dvořák's other orchestral works, from the two serenades, one for strings, the other mainly for wind, to more overtly nationalist works such as the Czech Suite and the three Slavonic Rhapsodies and the two sets of Slavonic Dances, originally written for piano duet. The latter have a special significance, because they draw attention to his great interest in his country's folk music, and the first set (1878) provided him with the opportunity of developing some important characteristics of his national and personal style. He was not particularly concerned to keep strictly to one type of dance within a single piece: the seventh dance, for instance, starts in the style of a Moravian *tetka* (dance in duple time); when it becomes more animated it resembles a *kvapík* ('galop'), and it also contains elements of the *skočná* and *vrták* (dance in a rapid 2/4). The finer second set (1886) displays a greater artistry and maturity.

(iv) Orchestration. For the most part Dvořák relied on the standard orchestra of the period but augmented it slightly from time to time. The Third, Eighth and Ninth symphonies and several other works besides require an english horn, and the Fifth includes a bass clarinet, but the double bassoon does not appear in the orchestral works until the Suite in A of 1895. He seldom wrote for the harp; but he used it in the *Scherzo capriccioso*. He did not use any of the less common percussion instruments until he reached the symphonic poems. To cite an example from outside the orchestral works, the effective use he made of Fontaine-Besson's improved double bass clarinet in the striking passage for english horn, bass clarinet, bassoons, cellos, two harps and other instruments describing the red castle in Hell in

259

Kate and the Devil is an indication that he was alive to new developments. He had an instinctive feeling for orchestral colour. He was particularly successful in his imaginative use of the flute and piccolo as can be seen in *The Golden Spinning-wheel* and the gentle, thoughtful responses made by the piccolo in the trio of the Sixth Symphony. By means of tremolos for the flutes and an oboe and rapidly reiterated notes on the harp he convincingly suggested the cooing of the bird in *The Wild Dove*. The final four-note chord for *pianissimo* divided double basses in the Largo of the Ninth Symphony is most effective, and the felicitous use of *pianissimo* strings, a muted horn (doubling the second violins) and echoes from the flute makes the 14th variation one of the most memorable in the Symphonic Variations (see ex.6).

VI Chamber music

Dvořák was strongly drawn towards chamber music, for he was a viola player and greatly admired the work of the Classical masters. It is hardly surprising, then, that his op.1 is a string quintet and his op.2 a string quartet and that he composed chamber works throughout almost the whole of his creative life. Among them are several that are imperishable and stand worthily alongside the best of his orchestral works. The finest is surely the Piano Trio in F minor, op.65, written under the shadow of his mother's death; in it he strove to give of his very best and produced one of the most outstanding of all his works. Those from his nationalist phases contain Czech dances and dance rhythms and the characteristic Dvořákian *dumka*; there are notable examples in the String Sextet, the op.51 String Quartet, the peren-

Ex.6 Symphonic Variations op.78

nially fresh Piano Quintet and the highly original *Dumky* Trio. Three works date from his American period.

Dvořák is known to have completed almost 40 chamber works for various combinations. The same kind of problems beset him here as in other areas of his work. He was unable at first to organize his material satisfactorily and avoid prolixity, and until he was able to keep Wagner's influence in check no solution seemed possible. At present the authentic, unedited score of the String Quartet in F minor op.9 (1873) is missing, so there is no evidence at this important stage in his development. But the work that followed in the same

261

year, the String Quartet in A minor op.12, appears to have been the real turning-point. He planned it in five continuous sections but decided to transform it into a conventional four-movement work and then failed to complete it. His next quartet op.16, again in A minor, is orthodox but rather uninteresting. Because of some operatic associations, its unusual textures and the casual arrangement of keys in the first movement, the String Quintet in G op.77 (1875) is rather exceptional for a chamber work; the scherzo is a delightful piece. There followed three works including piano, the first two of which also date from 1875. The piano writing in all three contains an unusually large number of parallel passages in the treble and bass, and there are frequent overtones of salon music. The Trio in B♭ op.21 is well proportioned without a single weak movement, and there is a naturalness about the musical thought. The first movement of the Quartet in D op.23 is attractive, and the plaintive variations have a simple charm, but the experimental third movement, a combination of scherzo (3/8) and finale (4/4), is poorly integrated. The prominence of minor keys in the Trio in G minor op.26 (1876) can be attributed to Dvořák's distress at the death of a daughter, further manifested in the unrest caused by the use of conflicting rhythms in the first movement; the Largo and the scherzo are the most satisfactory movements in this uneven work. There is a wistful charm in the first movement of the String Quartet in E op.80, another work affected by Dvořák's feelings of melancholy in 1876. As in other slow movements of this period, the Andante con moto suggests the mood of a *dumka*; its two themes are effec-

tively combined in the coda. Dvořák's improving crafts-
manship is more apparent in the String Quartet in D
minor op.34 (1877). The plaintive and slightly
Schubertian first movement is finely wrought, and its
development, which starts with a beautiful shift of key,
rises to an unexpected climax. In this movement and
also in the Adagio the second theme grows out of the
first, and that of the opening movement is beautifully
grafted into the coda of the Adagio. Polka rhythm and
the suggestion of a *skočná* had occurred in the finales of
the piano trios opp.21 and 26, but in this quartet
Dvořák for the first time made a whimsical polka serve
as a scherzo.

The String Sextet in A op.48 (1878) is fully representative of Dvořák's national style and was his first
chamber work to attract attention abroad. The second
movement is a highly original *dumka* in D minor with
the rhythm of a polka; the scherzo is called a *furiant*,
but it is not a very typical one. The finale is an attractive
set of variations on a theme which, surprisingly, is in B
minor, and it slips into A only towards its final cadence;
Dvořák modelled his fourth variation on one from
Beethoven's op.74 Quartet. The opening bars of the
String Quartet in E♭ op.51 (1878–9) were probably
influenced by a recollection of the beginning of
Mendelssohn's Octet, which is in the same key; they
nevertheless have a marked individuality (see ex.7).
National elements are again conspicuous. Polka rhythm
soon appears and also forms the basis of the second
subject; a contrast of moods occurs in the development
when the main theme in augmentation is accompanied
by the polka theme. The second movement, with its mel-

Ex.7 String Quartet in E♭ op.51

Allegretto ma non troppo

ancholy tone and scherzo-like interludes, is a typical Dvořákian *dumka*, and the vivacious finale shows the influence of Czech leaping dances.

In his Violin Sonata in F op.57 (1880) Dvořák reversed the normal practice by writing a yearning and questioning first subject and an animated second subject influenced by Czech dances; in the finale the dance element becomes the dominant factor. When writing the String Quartet in C op.61 in 1881 for the Hellmesberger Quartet, Dvořák may have kept national elements to a minimum because he was aware that a section of the Viennese public harboured prejudices against the Czechs; they are confined to the trio of the scherzo and the finale. This modification of his musical standpoint may have been an advantage at that time, for the quartet is one of his best. The Poco adagio, with its fascinatingly syncopated texture, was originally intended to form part of the Violin Sonata. The main theme of the first movement paves the way for a bold use of key, and Dvořák is at his most audacious in the foreshortened recapitulation, very little of which is in the tonic. The theme of the scherzo is derived from a motif from the first movement.

The Piano Trio in F minor op.65 (1883) marks a decisive step forward in Dvořák's artistic career and offers a foretaste of the epic style that he so splendidly realized two years later in the Seventh Symphony. Its intensity of feeling and seriousness of purpose are unmistakable. He had begun no previous work with a theme possessing such immense possibilities (see ex.8). After the striving development, fresh tension is engendered in the recapitulation, and in the coda a new, poignant version of the main theme is heard. A most eloquent reference to this theme occurs at the end of the Poco adagio. In the Allegretto grazioso the tendency towards pathos is ameliorated by some entrancing cross-rhythms. Even the second subject of the finale is in a minor key, though eventually yet another version of the principal theme establishes the tonic major and banishes the last vestiges of conflict.

The Terzetto in C op.74 (1887) is a modest work but beautifully written for the two violins and viola. The scherzo is a splendid *furiant*. The finale is a set of variations based on a theme with constantly shifting tonality, which leads eventually to the tonic minor. The Piano Quintet in A op.81, composed in the same year, epitomizes the quintessential features of Dvořák's music: melody and counter-melody, vital rhythm, varied and colourful scoring, a variety of moods ranging from sorrow to gaiety, and the skill of a craftsman allied to the sensitivity of an artist. In the first movement there

Ex.8 Piano Trio in F minor op.65

are characteristic changes from major to minor, and the
second subject is recapitulated in the submediant. The
Andante con moto is a particularly fine *dumka*, but the
so-called *furiant* that follows has no obvious connection
with that dance. The quintet appears to have stolen the
limelight from the scarcely less admirable Piano Quartet
in E♭ op.87 (1889). The conflict of moods between
piano and strings in the first movement is resolved
towards the end. The Lento is unusually rich in themes
and spans a wide emotional range. Following a
procedure foreshadowed in the Terzetto, the good-
humoured finale is in the tonic minor. The Piano Trio
op.90 (the *Dumky*, 1890–91) consists of a series of six
dumky, all in different keys and the majority in binary
form. Most start with a slow meditative section and
continue at a much faster pace. It was bold of Dvořák to
adopt this unique, daringly simple plan, and he executed
it with keen imagination and considerable resource, giving each *dumka* a distinct individuality and colouring.

The first of the three chamber works Dvořák wrote in the USA, all of them in 1893, is the String Quartet in F op.96 (the 'American'). Although he modelled the opening bars on the beginning of Smetana's First Quartet, he created an entirely different mood. Several of the themes have pentatonic tendencies, but few are strictly pentatonic. The crowning glory of the work is the Lento, which, with its plaintive, soaring violin melody, is a most effective foil to the animation that prevails in the rest of the work. The theme at bars 21–4 in the Scherzo is adapted from a birdsong that Dvořák heard in the Iowa woodlands. The String Quintet in E♭ op.97 also includes some 'primitive' features; for example, the motif at bars 63–4 of the first movement is a transformed fragment of Indian song. The outstanding movement is the Larghetto, a set of variations that follows Haydn's example in having a double theme, in A♭ minor and major. Dvořák had originally drafted the second one as a tune for the American national hymn, *My country, 'tis of thee*. The third work written in America is the delightful Violin Sonatina in G op.100, whose themes again tend to be 'primitive'. The Larghetto (the title 'Indian Lament' is unauthorized) is specially appealing, and so is the E major melody in the finale.

Finally there are the two string quartets that Dvořák composed in 1895 after he returned home from the USA, which are among the finest of all his chamber works. The first movement of the Quartet in G op.106 has a number of unexpected features, including a passage in B during the B♭ second subject, and the quaint transformation of the main theme when it is

21. Antonín Dvořák

recapitulated after the masterly development section. The Adagio ma non troppo, one of Dvořák's most deeply felt slow movements, is, like the slow movement of op.97, a series of variations on alternating themes, this time in E♭ major and minor. Its climax, a powerful affirmation in C, was undoubtedly suggested by the similar passage in the same key in Smetana's first quartet. The second subject of the first movement is recalled in the finale. Even if the Quartet in A♭ op.105 has no movement to compare with the Adagio of the G major Quartet, it is a particularly satisfying work as a whole. In the first movement the second limb of the theme attracts attention; it is surely no coincidence that rather similar harmony in the same key had occurred at the end of the slow movement of Smetana's E minor Quartet. The scherzo of op.105 is a superb *furiant*, whose trio makes use of two themes from the opera *The Jacobin*.

In his earlier chamber works Dvořák made no attempt to exploit the potential of the piano in more than a very limited way. By the time he reached the Violin Sonata, however, he had overcome that deficiency, and in the works that followed, the F minor and *Dumky* Trios, the Piano Quintet and the Piano Quartet in E♭, he wrote much more confidently and effectively, with a genuine understanding of keyboard idiom and an appreciation of the vast range of mood and expression of which the piano is capable. His being a viola player was a considerable advantage in that it helped him to write idiomatically for the strings. It does not, however, explain fully why his chamber works possess an indefinable quality, more apparent to the players than to the listener, which is due largely to their strikingly individual textures.

VII   Piano music

Dvořák made no claim to be more than an average pianist, but he participated in performances of his chamber music from time to time, and in particular he undertook a long tour in 1892, during which the *Dumky* Trio was invariably the central item in the programme. In his piano works he shed the salon style which is a conspicuous feature of his early chamber music with piano and eventually showed himself to be a gifted and imaginative composer for the instrument.

Dvořák favoured dances and characteristic or mood pieces in his output for piano and wrote only one longer work, the Theme with Variations in A♭ op.36, dating from 1876, the year of his first significant piano works. He took particular care over it. As is evident in the first and third variations in particular, he borrowed some ideas from the variations in Beethoven's Sonata op.26 in the same key. Since he felt there was no need for the variations to adhere strictly to the form of the theme, he was able to provide them with a natural sense of growth. The outstanding success two years later of the first set of Slavonic Dances, in their original version for piano duet, created a demand for more solo piano music; this included the 12 *Silhouettes*, in which several of the themes are drawn in rejuvenated form from the First Symphony, and an exuberant *Furiant* in D. The Eight Waltzes op.54, completed in 1880, are not intended for dancing, as the cross-rhythms of no.5 make clear, but are attractive concert pieces.

The remaining piano duets, the *Legends* (dedicated to Hanslick), *Ze Šumavy* ('From the Bohemian Forest') and the second set of Slavonic Dances appeared over the next six years. The *Legends* and Dances were soon orchestrated, but the six pieces of *From the Bohemian Forest* remained solely a keyboard work, except for one of the best of them, *Klid* ('Silent woods'), which Dvořák arranged as a cello solo with either piano or orchestra. The collection of 13 solo piano pieces *Poetické nálady* ('Poetic tone pictures') appeared in 1889, by which time he had a much greater understanding of the potentialities of the piano. There are obvious influences, for example of Brahms in the first piece and Chopin in the last, but Dvořák's lively imagination and individuality emerge strongly. *Rej skřítků* ('Goblins' dance') is perhaps the most successful; in the delightful *Na táčkách* ('Tittle-tattle') Czech characteristics are particularly strong. American influence is conspicuous in two works of 1894, the Suite in A op.98 (orchestrated in 1895) and the eight Humoresques, for many of their themes are pentatonic. The reliance in the latter on four-bar phrases becomes rather wearisome, but the seventh quickly became one of Dvořák's most internationally popular pieces. The Suite is conceived on broader lines, with its second movement, Molto vivace, possessing a splendid verve.

VIII Songs and duets
Dvořák left over 100 songs and duets written, with one late exception, between 1865 and 1895. They comprise simple, lively and tuneful settings of folk poetry, deeply felt yet simply conceived love-songs, a few settings of ballads and songs of strikingly distinctive character such as the *Cigánské melodie* ('Gypsy melodies') and the *Biblical Songs*. He showed a preference for strophic and modified strophic forms.

The most remarkable feature of the *Cypresses* song

cycle of 1865 is that it reveals an intensely romantic flowering of the composer's art at an early stage, an element completely absent from the sets of songs that followed. The cycle's 18 songs bear witness to Dvořák's deep distress when Josefina Čermáková rejected his declaration of love. The *Moravské dvojzpěvy* ('Moravian Duets', 1875–7), admired by Brahms, are all settings of Moravian folk poetry. They are delightfully fresh and often lighthearted and gay, but with occasional shadows of melancholy. Op.20 no.4 and op.32 nos.2, 9 and 10 are a few of the more successful and charming ones. The *Tři novořecké básně* ('Three modern Greek poems', 1878) are on a much more ambitious scale than any previous songs and were provided with orchestral accompaniment, now lost. The subject of the simplest of them, *Nereidy* ('Nereids'), appears to have suited Dvořák well, but *Žalozpěv Pargy* ('Parga's lament') is the most striking. Heyduk's *Gypsy Melodies*, epitomizing gypsy freedom, appealed strongly to Dvořák; they spring to life and there is hardly a weak song among them. He set the poet's German translations, as they were intended for (and dedicated to) the Austrian tenor, Gustav Walter. The set includes, as no.4, the well-known *Als die alte Mutter* ('Songs my mother taught me'). Dvořák's increasing confidence in writing for the voice is perhaps best shown in the third song, *Rings ist der Wald so stumm und still* ('All round about the woods are still'). The interesting accompaniments sometimes introduce dance elements. So completely successful a transformation of an early song after revision as is seen in *Mé srdce často v bolesti* ('Downcast am I') misleadingly published as op.2 no.3, is unusual. The set of four songs to German words, op.82 (1887–8), stands high among

Dvořák's songs and the next set, *Písně milostné* ('Love-songs'), which are again revisions of early compositions, includes such notable songs as *Kol domu se ted' potácím* ('I wander oft past yonder house'), with its attractive polka rhythm, and *Zde v lese u potoka* ('In deepest forest glade I stand').

The set *Biblical Songs* (1894), and intensely personal document, is an affirmation of faith on Dvořák's part after his friends Tchaikovsky and Hans von Bülow had died and while his own father was critically ill. All the songs are settings of verses from the Psalms taken from the Bible of Kralice. Dvořák seems to have been specially inspired by the words of *Při řekách babylon-ských* ('By the rivers of Babylon'), for the setting is truly memorable, not least for its heartfelt cry to Jerusalem. The most jubilant song, *Zpívejte Hospodinu píseň novou* ('O sing unto the Lord a new song'), is placed at the end.

Dvořák may not have penetrated quite as deeply as a Schubert or a Wolf into the heart of the poetry he set. Nevertheless in his best songs, as in his most memorable operatic and choral music, he responded acutely, sensitively and with complete sincerity and conviction to the changing moods of the text. Such songs are an expression of his intense inner feeling.

WORKS

Edition: *A. Dvořák: souborné vydání* [Complete edition], ed. O. Šourek and others (Prague, 1955–) [AD]

B – *Burghauser thematic catalogue no.*   S – *Šourek catalogue no.*

* – *completed at some time between dates given*

Numbers in the right-hand column denote references in the text.

SYMPHONIES

B	S	op.	Number	Composition	Publication	Remarks	AD	
9	—	—	no.1. c	14 Feb–24 March 1865		called 'Zlonické zvony' [The bells of Zlonice]: 1st perf. Brno, 4 Oct 1936	iii 1	207, 252, 271
12	7	4	no.2, B♭	1 Aug 9 Oct 1865	Berlin, 1911	rev. 1887: 1st perf. Prague, 11 March 1888	iii 2	207, 252
34	19	10	no.3, E♭	April 4 July 1873	Berlin, 1912	1st perf. Prague, 29 March 1874	iii 3	209, 231, 252, 259
41	22	13	no.4, d	1 Jan–26 March 1874		1st perf. Prague, 6 April 1892: listed variously as opp.18, 19, 24	iii 4	209, 252
54	32	76	no.5, F	15 June 23 July 1875	Berlin, 1888	1st perf. Prague, 25 March 1879: ded. Bülow: rev. 1887: 1st pubd as Sym. no.3: once known as op.24	iii 5	210, 218, 252, 259
112	78	60	no.6, D	27 Aug–15 Oct 1880	Berlin, 1882	1st perf. Prague, 25 March 1881: 1st pubd as Sym. no.1: formerly called op.58	iii 6	211, 213, 214, 219, 222, 231, 238, 253, 256, 260
141	94	70	no.7, d	13 Dec 1884 17 March 1885	Berlin, 1885	1st perf. London, 22 April 1885: rev. June 1885: 1st pubd as Sym. no.2	iii 7	214, 217, 238, 239, 252, 253–5, 265
163	109	88	no.8, G	26 Aug–8 Nov 1889	London, 1892	1st perf. Prague, 2 Feb 1890: 1st pubd as Sym. no.4	iii 8	218, 219, 223, 232, 239, 240, 255, 259
178	117	95	no.9, e	10 Jan–24 May 1893	Berlin, 1894	called 'Z Nového světa' [From the New World]: 1st perf. New York, 16 Dec 1893: 1st pubd as Sym. no.5	iii 9	222, 223, 232, 234, 239–40, 252, 254, 255–6, 259, 260

252–6

SOLO INSTRUMENT WITH ORCHESTRA

B	S	op.	Title	Composition	Publication	Remarks	AD	
39	20	11	Romance, f, vn	*Oct 1873–9 Dec 1877	Berlin, 1879	arr. of Andante from Str Qt B37	iii 23	214, 256
63	42	33	Piano Concerto, g	?Aug–14 Sept 1876	Breslau, 1883	1st perf. Prague, 24 March 1878	iii 10	
90	64	49	Mazurek, vn	completed 15 Feb 1879	Berlin, 1879		iii 23	
96 } 108	68	53	Violin Concerto, a	5 July Sept 1879 / 4 April–25 May 1880	Berlin, 1883	partly destroyed / revd 1882: 1st perf. Prague, 14 Oct 1883	iii 11	217, 251, 256

OTHER ORCHESTRAL section of a Dvořák works catalogue.

B	S	op.	Title	Composition	Publication	Remarks	AD	AD
181	114	94	Rondo, g, vc	16–22 Oct 1893	Berlin, 1894	arr. from B171	iii/23	
182	90	68/5	Klid [Silent woods], vc	28 Oct 1893	Berlin, 1894	arr. from B133/5	iii/23	
191	125	104	Cello Concerto, b	8 Nov 1894–9 Feb 1895	Berlin, 1896	rev. completed 11 June 1895; 1st perf. London, 19 March 1896	iii/12	224, 226, 234, 238, 252, 256

OTHER ORCHESTRAL

225, 256–9

B	S	op	Title	Composition	Publication	Remarks	AD	AD
4	—	—	Harfenice [The woman harpist], polka	?1860	—	lost	—	
5–6	3	—	Polka and Galop	1861 or 1862	—	lost; ? for orch	—	
15	7	—	Intermezzos	12 Jan–5 Feb 1867	—		iii/24	
16a	(8)	(1)	Tragic Overture (Dramatic Overture)	completed 19 Oct 1870	Berlin, 1912	ov. to Alfred (B16); also listed as op.10. op.13	i/1	
21a	12	—	Concert Overture, F	completed 20 Dec 1871	—	ov. to King and Charcoal Burner (i) (B21); also listed as op.2, op.12, op.13, op.14	i/2	
31	—	—	Three Nocturnes, no.2: Májová noc [May night]	?Oct 1872	—	nos.1, 3, lost; also listed as op.18	vii	
35	—	—	Romeo and Juliet, overture	July 1873	—	lost; also listed as op.21	—	
44	24	14	Symphonic Poem, a	Aug–12 Sept 1874	Berlin, 1912	also known as op.15, op.18, op.19	iii/18	
47	10	40	Nocturne, str, B	?Jan 1875	Berlin, 1883	rev. 1882 or 1883; arr. from Str Qt B19 and Str Qnt B49	iii/24	213
52	29	22	Serenade, str, E	3–14 May 1875	Berlin, 1879	1st perf. Prague, 10 Dec 1876; arr. pf 4 hands (Prague, 1877)	iii/16	211
70	48	78(28)	Symphonic Variations	6 Aug–28 Sept 1877	Berlin, 1888	on Já jsem huslař [I am a fiddler], B66/3; 1st perf. Prague, 2 Dec 1877	iii/22	218, 257, 260
77	53	44	Serenade, 2 ob, 2 cl, 2 bn, dbn, 3 hn, vc, db, d	4–18 Jan 1878	Berlin, 1879	1st perf. Prague, 17 Nov 1878	iii/16	210, 211, 218, 231

83	55	46	Slavonic Dances, 1st ser.	April–22 Aug 1878	Berlin, 1878	arr. from B78; 1st perf., nos.1, 3, 4, Prague, 16 May 1878; complete, Dresden, 4 Dec 1878 (nos.1–4), 18 Dec 1878 (nos.5–8)	iii/19	210, 211, 231, 232, 251
86	54	45	Slavonic Rhapsodies, 1 D, 2 g, 3 Ab	13 Feb–3 Dec 1878	Berlin, 1879	1st perf., nos.1–2, Prague, 17 Nov 1878; no.3, Berlin, 24 Sept 1879	iii/18	210, 211, 213, 218, 231, 251
88	65	54	Slavnostní pochod [Festival march]	Jan or Feb 1879	Prague, 1879	for the silver wedding of Franz Josef and Elisabeth of Austria	iii/24	
93	66	39	Česká suita, D	?April 1879	Berlin, 1881	1st perf. Prague, 16 May 1879	iii/17	
97	33	25	Vanda Overture	Aug–?Oct 1879	Leipzig, 1885	for Vanda, B55	iii/24	
99	72	–	Pražské valčíky [Prague waltzes]	? 10–12 Dec 1879	–	arr. pf (Prague, 1880)	iii/24	
100	67	–	Polonaise, Eb	20–24 Dec 1879	–	arr. pf 4 hands by J. Zubatý, rev. Dvořák (Prague, 1883)	iii/24	
105	71	54	Two Waltzes, str	?Feb 1880	Berlin, 1911	arr. of B101, nos.1, 4	iv/6	
114	(3)	53A/1	Polka 'Pražským akademikum [For Prague students], Bb	14 Dec 1880	–	arr. pf (Prague, 1882)	iii/24	
119	(3)	53A/2	Kvapík [Galop], E	?Dec 1881	Berlin, 1882	anon. arr. pf (Prague, 1882)	vii	
122	80	59	Legendy [Legends]	13 Nov–9 Dec 1881	Berlin, 1882	arr. from B117	iii/21	
125a	(83)	(62)	Domov můj [My home], overture	21–3 Jan 1882	Berlin, 1882	from Josef Kajetán Tyl, incidental music, B125; 1st perf. Prague, 3 Feb 1882	i/9	214, 223
131	88	66	Scherzo capriccioso	4 April–2 May 1883	Berlin, 1884	1st perf. Prague, 16 May 1883	iii/22	213, 219, 257, 259
132	89	67	Husitská dramatická ouvertura (Hussite overture)	?9 Aug–9 Sept 1883	Berlin, 1884	1st perf. Prague, 18 Nov 1883	iii/13	213, 214, 218, 219, 222, 223, 251, 257
147	98	72	Slavonic Dances, 2nd ser.	Nov 1886–5 Jan 1887	Berlin, 1887	arr. from B145; 1st perf., nos.9, 10, 15, Prague, 6 Jan 1887	iii/20	223, 234

B	S	op.	Title	Composition	Publication	Remarks	AD	
167	—	—	Fanfares, 4 tpt, timp				vii	
168	113	91	V přírodě [In nature's realm], concert overture	30 April 1891 31 March–8 July 1891	Berlin, 1894	b168, 169, 174 composed together as Příroda, Život a Láska [Nature, Life and Love]; 1st perf. Prague, 28 April 1892; earlier known as op.91, nos.1–3	iii/13	220, 222, 223, 232, 237, 258
169	113	92	Karneval, concert overture	28 July–12 Sept 1891	Berlin, 1894		iii/13	
174	113	93	Othello, concert overture	Nov 1891–18 Jan 1892	Berlin, 1894		iii/13	
190	121	98b	Suite, A	19 Jan after 25 April 1895	Berlin, 1911	arr. from B184	iii, 17	
195	129	107	Vodník [The water goblin], sym. poem after K. J. Erben	6 Jan–11 Feb 1896	Berlin, 1896	1st perf. London, 14 Nov 1896	iii/14	225, 258
196	130	108	Polednice [The noon witch], sym. poem after Erben	11 Jan–27 Feb 1896	Berlin, 1896	1st perf. London, 21 Nov 1896	iii/14	225, 258
197	131	109	Zlatý kolovrat [The golden spinning-wheel], sym. poem after Erben	15 Jan–25 April 1896	Berlin, 1896	1st perf. London, 26 Oct 1896	iii/14	225, 258, 260
198	132	110	Holoubek [The wild dove], sym. poem after Erben	22 Oct–18 Nov 1896	Berlin, 1899	1st perf. Brno, 20 March 1898	iii/qt	225–6, 258, 260
199	133	111	Píseň bohatýrská [Heroic song], sym. poem	4 Aug–25 Oct 1897	Berlin, 1899	1st perf. Vienna, 4 Dec 1898	iii/15	226

CHAMBER

207, 260–70

B	S	op.	Title	Composition	Publication	Remarks	AD	
7	4	1	String Quintet, a, 2 vn, 2 va, vc	begun 6 June 1861	Prague, 1943	1st perf. Prague, 15 Dec 1921	iv/8	260
8	5	2	String Quartet no.1, A	March 1862	Prague, 1948	1st perf. Prague, 6 Jan 1888; once listed as op.1	iv/5	231, 260
10			Cello Concerto, A, pf acc	completed 30 June 1865	—	orchd. by J. Burghauser (Prague, 1977) rev. G. Raphael (Leipzig, 1929)	iv/2	207, 236

14	—	Clarinet Quintet, b♭	—	*?1865–9	lost, ?destroyed: listed as ?op.5, ?op.6	—	
17	9	String Quartet no.2, B♭		*?1868–70		iv/5	
18	10	String Quartet no.3, D		*?1869–70		iv/5	
19	—	String Quartet no.4, e		? Dec 1870	once listed as op.9; Andante religioso adapted in Nocturne B48 and Str Qnt B49	iv/5	
20	11	Cello Sonata, f	—	?1870–4 Jan 1871	pf part lost; once listed as op.10	vii	
25	(13)	Piano Trio	—	?1871	lost (destroyed); listed as op.13, no.1	—	207
26	(13)	Piano Trio	—	?1871	lost (destroyed); listed as op.13, no.2	—	
28	16	Piano Quintet, A	—	?Aug 1872	1st perf. Prague, 22 Nov 1872; once listed as op.15	iv/11	207, 218
33	—	Violin Sonata, a		Jan 1873	lost (destroyed); once listed as op.19	—	
36	—	Octet (Serenade), 2 vn, va, db, cl, bn, hn, pf	—	completed Sept 1873	lost (destroyed); once listed as op.22	—	
37	20	String Quartet no.5, f	—	Sept 4 Oct 1873	rev. G. Raphael (Leipzig, 1929); once listed as op.23	iv/5	261
38	11	Romance, f, vn, pf	—	*?Oct 1873–9 Dec 1877	transcr. of Andante con moto from Str Qt B37; rev. for publication by Zubatý (Berlin, 1929)	iv/1	211
40	21	String Quartet no.6, a	—	Nov–5 Dec 1873	rev. inc.; completed by J. Burghauser	iv/5	262
40a	—	Andante appassionato, F, 2 vn, va, vc	—	?1873	once part of Str Qt B40	iv/5	
45	25	String Quartet no.7, a	Prague, 1875	?14–24 Sept 1874	1st perf. Prague, 29 Dec 1878; score (Berlin, 1894)	iv/6	262
49	27	String Quintet, G, 2 vn, va, vc, db	Berlin, 1888	?Jan–March 1875	original slow movt adapted from Andante religioso, Str Qt B19; 1st perf. Prague, 18 March 1876; definitive (4-movt) version, Boston, 25 Nov 1889; 1st listed as op.18; rev. 1888	iv/8	262

279

B	S	op.	Title	Composition	Publication	Remarks	AD	
48a	—	40	Nocturne, B, vn, pf	*?1875–83	Berlin, 1883	adapted from Andante religioso, Str Qt B19	iv/1	
51	30	21	Piano Trio, Bb	by 14 May 1875	Berlin, 1880	1st perf. Prague, 17 Feb 1877; rev. ?1880	iv/9	262, 263
53	31	23	Piano Quartet, D	24 May–10 June 1875	Berlin, 1880	1st perf. Prague, 16 Dec 1880	iv/10	262
56	34	26	Piano Trio, g	4–20 Jan 1876	Berlin, 1879	1st perf. ? Turnov, 29 June 1879	iv/9	211, 262, 263
57	35	80	String Quartet no.8, E	20 Jan–4 Feb 1876	Berlin, 1888	rev. 1888; 1st perf. Hamburg, 19 Nov 1888; 1st listed as op.27	iv/6	262
75	52	34	String Quartet no.9, d	7–18 Dec 1877	Berlin, 1880	rev. 1879; 1st perf. ?Trieste, 14 Dec 1881; ? once listed as op.43	iv/6	262
79	56	47	Maličkosti [Bagatelles], 2 vn, vc, harmonium	1–12 May 1878	Berlin, 1880	1st perf. 2 Feb 1879	iv/10	234
80	57	48	String Sextet, A, 2 vn, 2 va, 2 vc	14–27 May 1878	Berlin, 1879	1st perf. Berlin, 9 Nov 1879	iv/8	210, 211, 231, 260, 263
81	58	—	Capriccio, vn, pf	?June 1878	—	rev. G. Raphael (Leipzig, 1929); also known as Concert Rondo; variously listed as opp.24, 27; ? also arr. vn, orch, lost	iv/8	
89	64	49	Mazurek, vn, pf	Feb 1879	Berlin, 1879	arr. vn, orch as B90	iv/1	210, 211, 231, 232, 260, 263–4
92	62	51	String Quartet no.10, Eb	25 Dec 1878–28 March 1879	Berlin, 1879	1st perf. Magdeburg, 10 Nov 1879	iv/6	
94	—	—	Polonaise, A, vc, pf	?June 1879	Vienna, 1925		iv/3	
105	71	54	2 Waltzes, str, qt, ad lib db/str orch	? Feb 1880	Berlin, 1911	arr. of nos.1, 4 of B101	iv/6	
106	75	57	Violin Sonata, F	3–17 March 1880	Berlin, 1880	1st perf. ?Chrudim, 23 Sept 1880	iv/1	238, 264, 265, 270
120	—	—	Quartet Movement, F, str qt	1–9 Oct 1881	Prague, 1951	1st perf. Prague radio, 29 April 1945	iv/6	

121	82	61	String Quartet no.11, C	before 25 Oct–10 Nov 1881	Berlin, 1882	1st perf. Berlin, 2 Nov 1882	iv/7	213, 264–5
130	87	65	Piano Trio, f	before 4 Feb–?May 1883	Berlin, 1883	1st draft completed 31 March 1883; 1st perf. Mladá Boleslav, 27 Oct 1883; once listed as op.64	iv/9	238, 241, 253, 260, 265, 270
139	95	15/1	Ballad, d, vn, pf	*?Sept–Oct 1884		1st pubd in *Magazine of Music* (London, 1884), Christmas suppl.	iv/1	
148	100	74	Terzetto, C, 2 vn, va	7–14 Jan 1887	Berlin, 1887	1st perf. Prague, 30 March 1887	8v/4	265–6
149	—	75a	Drobnosti [Miniatures], 2 vn, va	? completed 18 Jan 1887	Prague, 1945	rev. as Romantic Pieces, B150	iv/4	
150	101	75	Romantické kusy [Romantic pieces], vn, pf	?20–25 Jan 1887	Berlin, 1887	rev. of Miniatures, B149	iv/1	
152	(6)	—	Cypřiše [Cypresses], 2 vn, va, vc	21 April–21 May 1887	Prague, 1921	arr. of nos.6, 3, 2, 8, 12, 7, 9, 14, 4, 16, 17, 18 from B11; nos.16, 18 unpubd	iv/7	
155	103	81	Piano Quintet, A	18 Aug–3 Oct 1887	Berlin, 1888	1st perf. Prague, 6 Jan 1888; once listed as op.77	iv/11	231, 232, 261, 266–7, 270
162	108	87	Piano Quartet, E♭	10 July–19 Aug 1889	Berlin, 1890	1st perf. Frankfurt am Main, 17 Oct 1890	iv/10	233, 267, 270
164	111	—	Gavotte for 3 vn	19 Aug 1890	Prague, 1890	pubd in Mladý houslista	iv/4	
166	112	90	Dumky, pf, vn, vc	Nov 1890–12 Feb 1891	Berlin, 1894	1st perf. Prague, 11 April 1891	iv/9	220, 261, 267, 270, 271
170	—	46/2	Slavonic Dance, e, vn, pf	? Dec 1891	—	arr. of B78 no.2	iv/1	
171	—	94	Rondo, g, vc, pf	25–6 Dec 1891	Berlin, 1894	orchd as B181; once listed as op.92	iv/3	
172	(55)	46/8	Slavonic Dance, g, vc, pf	27 Dec 1891	Berlin, 1894	arr. of B78 no.8	iv/3	
173	(90)	68/5	Klid [Silent woods], vc, pf	28 Dec 1891	Berlin, 1894	arr. of B133 no.5	iv/3	
179	118	96	String Quartet no.12, F	8–23 June 1893		'The American', 1st perf. Boston, Mass., 1 Jan 1894	iv/7	222, 223, 233, 268
180	119	97	String Quintet, E♭, 2 vn, 2 va, vc	26 June–1 Aug 1893	Berlin, 1894	'The American', 1st perf. New York, 12 Jan 1894	iv/8	222, 223, 231, 233, 234, 268, 270
183	120	100	Sonatina. G, vn, pf	19 Nov–3 Dec 1893	Berlin, 1894		iv/1	223, 224, 233, 268
192	128	106	String Quartet no.13, G	before 11 Nov 9 Dec 1895	Berlin, 1896	1st perf. Prague, 9 Oct 1896	iv/7	233, 268
193	127	105	String Quartet no.14, A♭	26 March–30 Dec 1895	Berlin, 1896	1st perf. Halle and Boston 26 Oct 1896	iv/7	270

KEYBOARD
(for pf 2 hands, unless otherwise stated)

B	S	op.	Title	Composition	Publication	Remarks	AD
1	1	—	Polka pomněnka [Forget-me-not polka], C	*?1855-6	—	trio by A. Liehmann	vii
302	—	—	Preludes and Fugues, org: 1-4, Preludes, D. G. a. B♭; 5. Prelude on a Given Theme, D; [6], Fughetta 1, D; [7], Fugue, D; [8], Fugue, g	1859	—	nos.1, [7], pubd in *Česká varhanní tvorba* (Prague, 1954)	vii
3	2	—	Polka, E	27 Feb 1860	Prague, 1873	doubtful	v/1
22	(12)	—	Potpourri from King and Charcoal Burner (i)	*?1871-3	—		vii
43	(23)	—	Potpourri from King and Charcoal Burner (ii)	*?1874-5	Prague, 1875		vii
48b	—	(40)	Nocturne, B, pf 4 hands	*?1875-83	—	adapted from Andante religioso, Str Qt B19	v/6
58	36	28	Two Minuets, A♭, F	?Feb 1876	Prague, 1879		v/1
64	43	35	Dumka, d	Dec 1876	Berlin, 1879		v/1
65	44	36	Theme with Variations, A♭	Dec 1876	Berlin, 1879		v/1 211, 271
74	50	41	Scottish Dances, d	*? Nov-Dec 1877	Prague, 1879		v/1
78	55	46	Slavonic Dances, 1st ser., pf 4 hands: C, e, A♭, F, A, D, c, g	18 March-7 May 1878	Berlin, 1878	orchd as B83	v/5 271
85	50	42	Furianty, D. F	29 May-25 Sept 1878	Berlin, 1879		v/1 271
98	70	8	[12] Silhouettes: c♯, D♭, D♭, f♯, f♯, B♭, b, B, e, A, c♯	*? Oct-Nov 1879	Leipzig, 1880	early drafts made c1870-72, known as B32	v/1 271
101	71	54	[8] Waltzes: A. a, E, d♭, g, F, d, E♭	1 Dec 1879-17 Jan 1880	Berlin, 1880	nos.1, 4 arr. str qt as B105	v/2 271
103	74	56	Eclogues: 1 Allegro non tanto (quasi polka), 2 Quasi allegretto, 3 Moderato, 4 Allegretto	24 Jan-7 Feb 1880	Prague, 1921		v/2
109a	—	—	Allegro con moto, f♯	27 May 1880	Prague, 1921		v/2
109b	—	—	Pieces without title: 1 (frag.), 2 Allegro molto, F, 3 Allegretto, G	31 May 1880	Prague, 1921 (except 1)		v/2

110	52	Piano Pieces: 1 Impromptu, 2 Intermezzo, 3 Gigue, 4 Eclogue, 5 Allegro molto, 6 Tempo di marcia	?June 1880		nos.1–4 (Leipzig, 1881), no.5 (Prague, 1921)	v/2
111	56	Mazurkas: Ab, C, Bb, d, F, b	13–?23 June 1880	Berlin, 1880	1st edn. omits no.4, incl. inc. version of Eclogue B103, no.1	v/2
116	—	Moderato, A	3 Feb 1881	Prague, 1921		v/2
117	59	[10] Legends, pf 4 hands: d, G, g, C, Ab, c#, A, F, D, bb	30 Dec 1880–22 March 1881	Berlin, 1881	orchd as B122	v/6 271
509	(62)	Domov můj [my home], overture, pf 4 hands	?1882	—		v/6
128a	—	Otázka [Question]	13 Dec 1882	—		v/2
129	86	Impromptu, d	16 Jan 1883	Prague, 1883	pubd as suppl. to *Humoristické listy*	v/3
133	90	Ze Šumavy [From the Bohemian Forest], pf 4 hands: 1 Na přástkách [At spinning time], 2 U černého jezera [By the black lake], 3 Noc filipojakubská [Witches' sabbath], 4 Na čekání [On the watch], 5 Klid [Silent woods], 6 Z bouřlivých dob [In stormy times]	?Sept 1883–12 Jan 1884	Berlin, 1884		v/6 271–2
136	12/1	Dumka, c	?Sept 1884	Prague, 1885	1st pubd in *Magazine of Music* (London, 1884), Christmas suppl.	v/3
137	12/2	Furiant, g	?Sept 1884			v/3
138	—	Humoresque, F#	1884	Prague, 1884		v/3
145	72	Slavonic Dances, 2nd ser. pf 4 hands: B, e, F, Db, bb, Bb, C, Ab	before 8 June–9 July 1886	Berlin, 1886	orchd as B147	v/5 271
156	—	Dvě perličky [Two little pearls]: 1 Do kola [In a ring], 2 Dědeček tančí s babičkou [Grandpa dances with Grandma]	?Dec 1887	Prague, 1888		v/3
158	—	Lístek do památníku [Album leaf], Eb	?1 July 1888	—		v/2

B	S	op.	Title	Composition	Publication	Remarks	AD
161	107	85	Poetické nálady [Poetic tone pictures]: 1 Noční cestou [Nocturnal route], 2 Žertem [Toying], 3 Na starém hradě [At the old castle], 4 Jarní [Spring song], 5 Selská balada [Peasant ballad], 6 Vzpomínání [Reverie], 7 Furiant, 8 Rej skřítků [Goblins' dance], 9 Serenade, 10 Bakchanale, 11 Na táčkách [Tittle-tattle], 12 U mohyly [By the tumulus], 13 Na svaté hoře [On the holy mountain]	16 April–6 June 1889	Berlin, 1889	once listed as op.84	v/3 272
303 184	— 121	— 98	Theme, for variations Suite, A	?1891 19 Feb–1 March 1894	Prague, 1894 Berlin, 1894	known earlier as op.101; orchd as B190	vii v/4 224, 272 v/4
187	123	101	[8] Humoresques: e♭, B, A♭, F, a, B, G♭, b♭	7–27 Aug 1894	Berlin, 1894		v/4
188	124	—	2 pieces: 1 Ukolébavka [Lullaby], 2 Capriccio	28 Aug–7 Sept 1894	Berlin, 1911	op. posth.	v/4

241–8

STAGE

B	S	op.	Title	Composition	Publication	Remarks	AD
16	8	—	Alfred (opera, 3, K. T. Körner)	26 May–19 Oct 1870	—	text in Ger.; 1st perf. Olomouc, Czech Theatre, 10 Dec 1938; listed both as op.1 and op.10	i/1 207, 243
21	12	—	Král a uhlíř (i) [King and charcoal burner] (comic opera, 3, B. J. Lobeský)	?April–20 Dec 1871	—	1st perf. Prague, National, 28 May 1929	i/2 207, 209, 243
42	23	(14)	Král a uhlíř (ii) (comic opera, Lobeský)	17 April–3 Nov 1874	—	1st perf. Prague. Provisional, 24 Nov 1874; with new version of ·Balada Krále Matyáše· [Ballad of King Mathias]. composed *Dec 1880–Jan 1881 (B115): rev. as B151	i/3 209
46	26	17	Tvrdé palice [The stubborn lovers] (comic opera. 1, J. Stolba)	?Sept–after 24 Dec 1874	vocal score, Berlin, 1882	1st perf. Prague. New Czech, 2 Oct 1881	i/4 212, 243

55	33	25	Vanda (opera, 5, V. B. Šumavský)	9 Aug–22 Dec 1875	—	1st perf. Prague, Provisional, 17 April 1876; rev. 1879, 1883; ov. written 1879 as B97	i/5	210, 212, 244
67	46	37	Šelma sedlák [The cunning peasant] (comic opera, 2, J. O. Veselý)	Feb–July 1877	Berlin, 1882	1st perf. Prague, Provisional, 27 Jan 1878; ov., Berlin, 1879	i/6	212, 213, 216, 244
125	83	62	Josef Kajetán Tyl (ov. and incidental music, F. F. Šamberk)	Dec 1881–23 Jan 1882	arr, pf 4 hands, Prague, 1882	1st perf. Prague, Provisional, 3 Feb 1882; arr. Zubatý for pf 4 hands; ov. pubd as Domov můj, B125a	i/9	212, 216, 220, 237, 242, 244–5, 249
127	85	64	Dimitrij (i) (opera, 4, M. Červinková-Riegrová)	8 May 1881–23 Sept 1882	vocal score, Prague, 1886	1st perf. Prague, New Czech, 8 Oct 1882; rev. 1883, 1885 [pubd version. arr. Zubatý, J. Káan]; rev. 1894–5 as B186	i/7	212, 216, 220, 237, 242, 244–5, 249
151	23	14	Král a uhlíř (iii) (comic opera, 3, Lobeský, rev. V. J. Novotný)	Feb–March 1887	vocal score, Prague, 1915	rev. of B42; 1st perf. Prague, National, 15 June 1887; pubd vocal score arr. Dvořák, R. Veselý	i/3	
159	106	84	Jakobín (i) [The Jacobin] (opera, 3, Červinková-Riegrová)	10 Nov 1887–18 Nov 1888	vocal score, Prague, 1911	1st perf. Prague, National, 12 Feb 1889; vocal score rev. K. Kovařovic, arr. Veselý; rev. as B200	i/10	218, 226, 237, 242, 245, 249, 270
186	—	64	Dimitrij (ii) (opera, 4, Červinková-Riegrová)	9 April 1894–30 Jan 1895	vocal score, Prague, 1912	rev. of B127; 1st perf. Prague, National, 7 Nov 1894; vocal score, rev. K. Kovařovic	i/8	224
200	106	84	Jakobín (ii) (opera, 3, Červinková-Riegrová, rev. with F. L. Rieger)	17 Feb–7 Dec 1897	vocal score, Prague, 1941	rev. of B159; 1st perf. Prague, National, 19 June 1898	i/10	
201	134	112	Čert a Káča [Kate and the Devil] (comic opera, 3, A. Wenig)	5 May 1898–27 Feb 1899	vocal score, Prague, 1908	based on a Cz. fairy tale; 1st perf. Prague, National, 23 Nov 1899	i/11	226, 245, 260
203	136	114	Rusalka (lyric fairy tale, 3, J. Kvapil)	21 April–27 Nov 1900	vocal score, Prague, 1905	1st perf. Prague, National, 31 March 1901; pubd score arr. J. Faměra	i/12	226, 229, 237, 242, 247
206	138	115	Armida (opera, 4, J. Vrchlický)	11 March 1902–23 Aug 1903	vocal score, Prague, 1941	after Tasso: La Gerusalemme liberata; 1st perf. Prague, National, 25 March 1904; pubd score arr. K. Šolc	i/13	228, 234, 236, 237, 242, 247

CANTATAS, MASSES, ORATORIOS

B	S	op.	Title	Composition	Publication	Remarks	AD	
2			Mass, B♭			lost (destroyed)		
27	15	30	Hymnus: Dědicové bílé hory [White Mountain] V. Hálek], chorus, orch	*?1857-9 ?May 3 June 1872	— 3rd version, London, 1885	1st perf. Prague, 9 March 1873; 1st version listed as op.4 and op.14; rev. Jan 1880 as в102; 2nd rev., completed 3 May 1884, London, 13 May 1885	ii/5	209, 248
71	38	58	Stabat mater (Jacopone da Todi), S, A, T, B, chorus, orch	19 Feb 1876- 13 Nov 1877	Berlin, 1881	1st perf. Prague, 23 Dec 1880; once listed as op.28	ii/1	213, 214, 218, 219, 248, 249
91	63	79	Psalm cxlix (Bible of Kralice), male vv, orch	13 Jan 24 Feb 1879	rev. version, Berlin, 1888	1st perf. Prague, 16 March 1879; once listed as op.52; rev. for mixed choir as в154, op.79, ?July 1887; 1st perf. Rotterdam, 14 Dec 1888	ii/6	223
135	91	69	Svatební košile [The spectre's bride] (Erben), dramatic cantata, S, T, B, chorus, orch	26 May-27 Nov 1884	London, 1885	1st perf. Plzeň, 28 March 1885	ii/2	214, 216, 220, 225, 248, 249
144	97	71	Svatá Ludmila [St Ludmila] (Vrchlický), oratorio, S, A, T, B, chorus, orch	17 Sept 1885- 30 May 1886	London, 1887	1st perf. Leeds, 15 Oct 1886; additional recit by Vrchlický, Novotný [в205], for stage perf., Prague, 30 Oct 1901	ii/3	216, 220, 228, 248, 250
153	102	86	Mass, D (S, A, T, B)/small choir, chorus, org	26 March-17 June 1887	orchd version, London, 1893	1st perf. private, Lužany, 11 Sept 1887; once listed as op.76; orchd as в175, 24 March 15 June 1892; perf. London, 11 March 1893	ii/7, 8	219, 220, 250
165	110	89	Requiem Mass, S, A, T, B, chorus, orch	1 Jan-31 Oct 1890	London, 1891	1st perf. Birmingham, 9 Oct 1891	ii/4	219, 222, 250
176	115	103	Te Deum, S, B, chorus, orch	25 June-28 July 1892	Berlin, 1896	1st perf. New York, 21 Oct 1892; once listed as op.93, op.98	ii/6	222, 251
177	116	102	The American Flag (J. R. Drake), cantata, A, T, B, chorus, orch	3 Aug 1892-8 Jan 1893	vocal score, New York 1895	1st perf. New York, 4 May 1895; once listed as op.94 and op.99	ii/5	
202	135	113	Slavnostní zpěv [Ode or Festival song] (Vrchlický), chorus, orch	?7-17 April 1900	vocal score, Prague, 1902	1st perf. private, Prague, 29 May 1900	ii/5	

OTHER CHORAL

B	S	op.	Title	Composition	Publication	Remarks	AD
59	37	29	Four Partsongs, mixed vv., unacc.: 1 Místo klekáni [Evening's blessing] (A. Heyduk), 2 Ukolébavka [Lullaby] (Heyduk), 3 Nepovím [I don't say it], 4 Opuštěný [The forsaken one]	c1876	Prague, 1879	nos.3, 4 set to Moravian folk poems	vi/4
66	45	—	Choral songs, male vv. unacc.: 1 Převozníček [The ferryman], 2 Milenka travička [The beloved as poisoner], 3 Huslař [The fiddler] (Heyduk)	12–16 Jan 1877	Prague, 1921	nos.1, 2 set to Moravian folk poems	vi/4
72	45	41	Kytice z českých národních písní [Bouquet of Czech folksongs], male vv., unacc.: 1 Zavedený ovčák [The betrayed shepherd], 2 Úmysl milenčin [The sweetheart's resolve], 3 Kalina [The guelder rose], 4 Český Diogenes [Czech Diogenes]	?Nov 1877	nos.1–3 Prague, 1877	set to Cz. and Moravian folk poems; nos.1–4 (Prague, 1921), with B 66	vi/4
73	—	—	Píseň Čecha [The song of a Czech] (F. J. Vacek-Kamenický), male vv. unacc.	?Nov 1877	Prague, 1921	inc.	vi/4
76	51	43	Z Kytice národních písní slovanských [From a bouquet of Slavonic folksongs], male vv, pf: 1 Žal [Sorrow], 2 Divná voda [Miraculous water], 3 Děvče v háji [The girl in the woods]	21 Dec 1877 6 Jan 1878	Prague, 1879	nos.1, 3. Slovak folk poems: no.2 Moravian folk poem: arr. pf 4 hands by Zubatý for publication	vi/4
87	61	27	Five Partsongs, male vv., unacc.: 1 Pomluva [Village gossip], 2 Pomořané [Dwellers by the sea], 3 Přípověď lásky [The love promise], 4 Ztracená ovečka [The lost lamb], 5 Hostina [The sparrows' party]	completed 12 Dec 1878	Prague, 1890	Lithuanian folk poems. trans. F. L. Čelakovský; once listed as op.30	vi/4
107	—	32	Moravian Duets, female vv. unacc.	?18–19 March 1880		transcr. of B60, 62, nos.6, 10, 13, 2, 3	vi/4

B	S	op.	Title	Composition	Publication	Remarks	AD
126	84	63	V přírodě [In nature's realm] (Hálek). mixed vv, unacc.: 1 Napadly písně v duši mou [Music descended to my soul], 2 Večerní les rozvázal zvonky [Bells ring at dusk], 3 Žitné pole, žitné pole [The rye field], 4 Vyběhla bříza běličká [The silver birch], 5 Dnes do skoku a do písničky! [With dance and song]	24–27 Jan 1882	Leipzig, 1882		vi/6
143	96	28	Hymna českého rolnictva [Hymn of the Czech peasants] (K. Pippich), mixed vv, orch	13 Aug 1885	vocal score, Prague, 1885	pubd score arr. Zubatý, rev. Dvořák	ii/5

272–4

SONGS AND DUETS
(for 1v, pf, unless otherwise stated)

B	S	op.	Title	Composition	Publication	Remarks	AD
11	6	—	Cypřiše [Cypresses] (G. Pfleger-Moravský): 1 Vy vroucí písně [Sing fervent songs], 2 V té sladké moci [When thy sweet glances], 3 V tak mnohém srdci mrtvo jest [Death reigns], 4 Ó duše drahá jedinká [Thou only dear one], 5 Ó byl to krásný zlatý sen [Oh, what a perfect golden dream], 6 Já vím, že v sladké naději [I know that on my love], 7 Ó zlatá růže, spanilá [O charming golden rose], 8 O naší lásce nekvete [Never will love lead us], 9 Kol domu se teď potácím [I wander oft], 10 Mne často týrá pochyba [Tormented oft by doubt], 11 Mé srdce často v bolesti [Downcast am I], 12 Zde hledím na ten drahý list [Here gaze I], 13 Na horách ticho a v údolí ticho [Everything's still], 14 Zde v lese u potoka [In deepest forest glade], 15 Mou celou duši zádumně [Painful emotions pierce my soul], 16 Tam stojí stará skála [There stands an ancient rock], 17 Nad krajem vévodí lehký spánek [Nature lies peaceful], 18 Ty se ptáš proč moje zpěvy bouří [You are asking why]	10–27 July 1865	—	nos.1, 5, 9, 8, 13, 11 rev. as B123; nos.1, 5, 11, 13 rev. as B124; nos.8, 3, 9, 6, 17, 14, 2, 4, rev. as B160; nos.6, 3, 2, 8, 12, 7, 9, 14, 4, 16, 17, 18 arr. str qt as B152; no.10 pubd in *Dvořákova čítanka* (Prague, 1929); English translations by J. Clapham, provided to replace the composer's faulty declamation in setting the Czech text	vii

207, 272

B	S	op.	Title	Composition	Publication	Remarks	AD
61	40	3; 9,3; 9,4; 31	Večerní písně [Evening songs] (Hálek): 1 Ty hvězdičky tam na nebi [The stars that twinkle in the sky], 2 Mně zdálo se žes umřela [I dreamed last night], 3 Já jsem ten rytíř z pohádky [I am that knight], 4 Když Bůh byl nejvíc rozkochán [When God was in a happy mood], 5 Umlko stromů šumění [The soughing of the trees], 6 Přilítlo jaro z daleka [The spring came flying], 7 Když jsem se díval do nebe [When I was gazing], 8 Vy mali, drobni ptáčkové [You little tiny singing birds], 9 Jsem jako lípa košatá [Just like a lime tree], 10 Vy všichni, kdo jste stísněni [All you with burdens], 11 Ten ptáček, ten se nazpívá [That little bird sings], 12 Tak jak ten měsíc v nebes báň [Thus as the moon]	*June–July 1876		nos.1–4 rev., pubd as op.3 (Leipzig, 1881); nos.5, 6 rev., pubd in Ger. as nos.3, 4 of 4 Lieder. op.9 (Berlin, 1880): nos.7–11 rev., pubd as op.31 (Prague, 1883); no.12 unpubd; nos.2–3 orchd as B128	vi/1
68	(69)	19b	Ave Maria (sacred), A/Bar, org	23–4 July 1877	Prague, 1883	pubd with B95	vi/1
69	47	38	Moravské dvojzpěvy [Moravian duets], S, A, pf: 1 Možnost [Hoping in vain], 2 Jablko [Greeting from afar], 3 Věneček [The crown], 4 Hoře [The smart]	?Aug 1877	Berlin, 1879	Moravian folk poems; 1st pubd in Ger. and Eng.; pubd in Cz. (Prague, 1913)	vi/3
82	59	—	Hymnus ad laudes in festo Sanctae Trinitatis (sacred), 1v, org	14 Aug 1878	Prague, 1911	pubd version rev. J. Suk	vi/1
84a	(60)	(50)	Tři novořecké básně [3 modern Greek poems] v, orch, lost	?1878			—
84b	60	50	Tři novořecké básně [3 modern Greek poems] (trans. V. B. Nebeský): 1 Koljas (Píseň kleftská) [Klepht song], 2 Nereidy [Nereids], ballad, 3 Žalozpěv Pargy [Parga's lament], heroic song	completed 22 Aug 1878	Breslau, 1883		vi/1 273
95A	(69)	19b	Ave maris stella (sacred), 1v, org	4 Sept 1879	Prague, 1883	pubd with B68	vi/1
95B(a)	69	19a	O sanctissima dulcis virgo Maria (sacred), A, Bar, org	6 Sept 1879	Prague, 1883	arr. S, A, [org] as B163a. 28 May 1890	vi/3
95B(b)	(69)	19a	O sanctissima dulcis virgo Maria (sacred), S, A, (org)	28 May 1890	—	voice parts only	vi/3
104	73	55	Zigeunermelodien (Heyduk): 1 Mein Lied ertönt, ein Liebespsalm, 2 Ei, wie mein Triangel wunderherrlich läutet, 3 Rings ist der Wald so stumm und still, 4 Als die alte Mutter, 5	? 18 Jan ?23 Feb 1880	Berlin, 1880	composed to Ger. trans. by Heyduk	vi/1 273–4

			Reingestimmt die Saiten, 6 In dem weiten, breiten, luf¹gen Leinenkleide, 7 Horstet hoch der Habicht auf den Felsenhöhen				
113	79	—	Dětská píseň [Child's song] (Š. Bačkora), 2vv unacc.	14 Nov 1880		pubd in *Hudební výchova* (1956)	vi/3
118	81	—	Na tej našej střeše laštověčka [There on our roof a swallow carries], S, A, pf	*?March–?May 1881	Prague, 1882	Moravian folk poem; pubd in Album of Umělecká beseda	vi/3
123	(6)	—	6 Songs (Pfleger-Moravský)	*?1881–2	—	rev. of B11 nos.1, 5, 9, 8, 13, 11	vi/2
124	(6)	2	4 songs (Pfleger-Moravský)	*?1881–2	Prague, 1882	rev. of B11 nos.1, 5, 11, 13	vi/2
128	—	3	Večerní písně [Evening songs] (Hálek), 1v, orch	24 Nov 1882	—	orch of B61, nos.2, 3	ii/5
140	—	—	Kačena divoká [The wild duck]	Sept/Oct 1884	—	folk poem, lost; once listed as op.15/?2	—
142	—	—	Two songs: Schlaf, mein Kind, in Ruh', 2 Seh' ich dich, mein liebes Mädchen	1–2 May 1885	Prague, 1921	Cz. folk poems; composed to Ger. trans.	vi/2
146	99	73	V národním tónu [In folk tone]: 1 Dobrú noc, má milá [Good-night, my darling], 2 Žalo dievča, žalo trávu [When a maiden was a-mowing], 3 Ach, není, není tu, co by mě těšilo [Nothing can change], 4 Ej, mám já koňa faku [I have a faithful mare]	completed 13 Sept 1886	Berlin, 1887	nos.1, 2, 4 Slovak folk poems; no.3 Cz. folk poem	vi/2
157	105	82	Vier Lieder (O. Malybrok-Stieler): 1 Lasst mich allein, 2 Die Stickerin, 3 Frühling, 4 Am Bache	?22 Dec 1887–5 Jan 1888	Berlin, 1889	composed to orig. Ger.	vi/2	224
160	(6)	83	[8] Písně milostné [Love-songs] (Pfleger-Moravský)	Dec 1888	Berlin, 1889	rev. of B11, nos.8, 3, 9, 6, 17, 14, 2, 4	vi/2
185	122	99	[10] Biblické písně [Biblical songs] (Bible of Kralice): 1 Oblak a mrákota jest vůkol Něho [Clouds and darkness], 2 Skrýše má a paveza má Ty jsi [Thou art my hiding-place], 3 Slyš, ó Bože, slyš modlitbu mou [Give ear to my prayer], 4 Hospodin jest můj pastýř [The Lord is my shepherd], 5 Bože! Bože! Píseň novou [I will sing a new song], 6 Slyš, ó Bože, volání mé [Hear my cry], 7 Při řekách babylonských [By the rivers of Babylon], 8 Popatřiž na mne a smiluj se nade mnou [Turn thee unto me], 9 Pozdvihuji očí svých k horám [I will lift up mine eyes], 10 Zpívejte Hospodinu píseň novou [O sing unto the Lord a new song]	5–26 March 1894	Berlin, 1895	nos.1–5 orchd as B189, 4–8 Jan 1895, pubd for S. orch (Berlin, 1929) with nos.6–10, arr. orch by V. Zemánek	vi/2	224, 234, 272, 274

B		Title	Arranged	Publication	Remarks	AD
194	126 —	Ukolébavka [Lullaby] (F. L. Jelínek)	20 Dec 1895	Prague, 1896	pubd in *Květy mládeže*, suppl.	vi/4
204	137 —	Zpěv z Lešetínského kováře [Song from The smith of Lešetín] (S. Čech)	5–6 Aug 1901	Berlin, 1911	op.posth. inc., rev. J. Suk	vi/2

ARRANGEMENTS

B	Title	Arranged	Publication	Remarks	AD
601	Dvě irské písně [2 Irish songs], male vv unacc: 1 Můj Konnor má váře jak červená růže [Oh my Connor], 2 Nuž zdobte se kvitím, ať zaplane zář [Ho! adorn yourself with flowers]	24 Oct 1878	—	no.2 from the Irish song 'Contented am I' ('Noch bonin shin doe'), later known as 'The Battle Eve of the Brigade'	vii
602	Brahms: Hungarian Dances nos.17–21, arr. orch	29 Oct–6 Nov 1880	Berlin, 1881		vii
603	Ruské písně [Russian songs], 2 vv, pf: 1 Povylétla holubice pode stráni (Viletala golubina), 2 Čím jsem já tě rozhněvala (Chem tebya ya gorchila?), 3 Mladá, pěkná krasavice (Belolitsa, kruglolitsa), 4 Cožpak, můj holoubku (Akh, chto zh tí, golubchik), 5 Zkvětal, zkvětal v máji květ (Tsveli, tsveli tsvetiki), 6 Jako mhou se tmí (Akh, kak pal tuman), 7 Ach, vy fíčky šumivé (Akh, rechenki, rechenki), 8 Mladice ty krásná (Molodka, molodaya), 9 Po mátušce, mocné Volze (Vniz po matushke po Volge), 10 Na políčku bříza tam stála (Vo pole beryoza stoyala), 11 Vyjdu já si podle fíčky (Vyjdu ya na rechenku), 12 Na tom našem náměstí (Kak u nas na ulitse), 13 Já si zasíl bez oráni (Ya noseyal konopelku), 14 Oj, ty luční kačko malá (Akh, utushka lygovaya), 15 V poli zrají višně (Gey, u poli vishnya), 16 Oj, kráče havran černý (Oy, kryache, chernenky voron)	?March 1883	Prague, 1951	2nd voice added and acc. rev. to songs in M. Bernard: Pyeseni ruskoga naroda (St Petersburg, 1866)	vii
604	J. Lev: Ha, ta láska [Ah, that love], 1v, orch	*?1880–84	—		vii
605	S. Foster: Old Folks at Home, arr. S. B. chorus, orch	*?Dec 1893, Jan 1894			vii
606	Vysoká polka, arr. pf	11 June 1902	—		vii

BIBLIOGRAPHY

CATALOGUES

O. Šourek: *Dvořák's Werke: ein vollständiges Verzeichnis* (Berlin, 1917)

J. Burghauser: *Antonín Dvořák: thematický katalog, bibliografie, přehled života a díla* [Thematic catalogue, bibliography, survey of life and work] (Prague, 1960)

SOURCE MATERIAL

A. Dvořák: 'Antonín Dvořák on Negro Melodies', *New York Herald* (25 May 1893)

——: 'Franz Schubert', *Century Illustrated Monthly Magazine*, xlviii (New York, 1894), 341; repr. in J. Clapham: *Antonín Dvořák, Musician and Craftsman* (London, 1966)

Anon.: 'How Dr. Dvořák Gives a Lesson', *New York Herald* (14 Jan 1894), §3, p.5 [mostly interview]; repr., abridged, in *Musical Standard*, new ser., xxxii (17 Feb 1894), 147

A. Dvořák: 'Music in America', *Harper's New Monthly Magazine*, xc (New York, 1895), 428; repr., abridged, in *Composers on Music*, ed. S. Morgenstern (New York, 1956)

W. Altmann: 'Antonín Dvořák im Verkehr mit seinem Verleger Fritz Simrock', *Die Musik*, x (1910–11), 259–92, 346–53; rev. in *Simrock-Jb*, ii (Berlin, 1929), 84–151

V. H. Jarka: 'Příspěvek k vídeňské korrespondenci Antonína Dvořáka' [A contribution to Dvořák's Vienna correspondence], *HR*, vii (1913–14), 376 [letters to Mandyczewski]

R. Newmarch: 'The Letters of Dvořák to Hans Richter', *MT*, lxxiii (1932), 605, 698, 795

O. Šourek: *Dvořák ve vzpomínkách a dopisech* (Prague, 1938, 9/1951; Eng. trans., 1954, as *Antonín Dvořák: Letters and Reminiscences*)

P. Stefan: 'Why Dvořák would not return to America', *Musical America*, lviii (25 Feb 1938), 34

O. Šourek: *Antonín Dvořák přátelům doma* [Dvořák to his friends at home] (Prague, 1941)

A. Špelda: *Dr Antonín Dvořák a Plzeň* (Plzeň, 1941)

O. Šourek: *Antonín Dvořák a Hans Richter* (Prague, 1942)

——: 'Z neznamých dopisů Antonína Dvořáka nakladateli Simrockovi' [From Dvořák's unknown letters to the publisher Simrock], *Smetana*, xxxvii (1944), 119, 131

O. Fric: *Antonín Dvořák a Kroměříž* (Kroměříž, 1946)

H. G. Farmer: *Cavaliere Zavertal and the Royal Artillery Band* (London, 1951) [incl. 6 Dvořák letters, some facs.]

A. Hořejš: *Antonín Dvořák: the Composer's Life and Work in Pictures* (Prague, 1955)

293

Dvořák

V. A. Kiselev: 'Perepiska A. Dvorzhaka s V. I. Safonovim'
[Correspondence of Dvořák with Safonov], *Kratkiye soobshcheniya*
(Moscow, 1955), no.17, p.57

J. Burghauser: *Král a uhlíř* (Prague, 1957) [critical edn. of lib]

J. Clapham: 'Dvořák and the Philharmonic Society', *ML*, xxxix
(1958), 123

——: 'Dvořák at Cambridge', *MMR*, lxxxix (1959), 135

J. Burghauser: *Dimitrij* (Prague, 1961) [critical edn. of lib]

J. Clapham: 'Dvořák's Visit to Russia', *MQ*, li (1965), 493

M. R. Aborn: *The Influence on American Culture of Dvořák's Sojourn
in America* (diss., U. of Indiana, Ann Arbor, 1966) [incl. letters and
contracts]

E. Herzog: *Antonín Dvořák v obrazech* [Dvořák in pictures] (Prague,
1966)

J. Clapham: 'Dvořák's Musical Directorship in New York', *ML*,
xlviii (1967), 40

B. Geist: 'Dva nezámé Dvořákovy dopisy' [Two unknown Dvořák
letters], *HV*, v (1968), 316; vii (1970), 497

V. A. Kiselev, ed.: 'Pis'ma A. Dvorzhaka iz Moskvi', *Puti razvitiya i
vzaymosvyazi russkovo i cheshkoslovatskovo iskusstva* (Moscow,
1970), 183 [incl. facs. letters]

J. Clapham: 'Dvořák's Relations with Brahms and Hanslick', *MQ*,
lvii (1971), 241; Cz. trans., *HV*, x (1973), 213 [incl. orig. Ger. text of
letters]

J. Burghauser: Commentary on facs. edn. of *IX Symfonie E moll Z
nového světa, op.95* (Prague, 1972)

K. Honolka: *Antonín Dvořák in Selbstzeugnissen und Bilddokumenten*
(Reinbek, 1974)

J. Clapham: 'Dvořák's Unknown Letters on his Symphonic Poems',
ML, lvi (1975), 277; Ger. trans., *ÖMz*, xxxi (1976), 645 [incl. orig. Ger.
text of letters and facs.]

——: 'Dvořák's First Contacts with England', *MT*, cxix (1978), 758

——: 'Dvořák's Musical Directorship in New York: a Postscript',
ML, lix (1978), 19

J. Clapham: 'Dva neznámé Dvořákovy dopisy E. Hanslickovi'
[Two unknown Dvořák letters to E. Hanslick], *HV*, xvii (1980),
154

M. Kuna: 'Transkripční problematika Dvořákovy korespondence'
[The transcriptional problems of Dvořák's correspondence], *HV*,
xviii (1981), 3

J. Slavíková: 'K charakteristice jazyka Dvořákovy korespondence
[Syntax a slovní zásoba]' [Characterization of the language of
Dvořák's correspondence: syntax and vocabulary], *HV*, xviii
(1981), 27

M. Kuna: 'Nová východiska ve dvořákovském bádání' [New

294

Bibliography

opportunities in Dvořák research], *HRo*, xxxvii (1984), 250

——: 'Z Dvořákovských dokumentů) [From Dvořák's documents], *HV*, xxi (1984), 85 [incl. illustrations of diplomas etc]

J. Clapham: 'Dvořák's Visit to Worcester, Massachusetts', *Slavonic and Western Music: Essays for Gerald Abraham* (Ann Arbor and Oxford, 1985), 207

MEMOIRS

J. Michl: 'Rok u Dvořáka' [A year with Dvořák], *HR*, vi (1912–13), 169

——: 'Z Dvořákova vyprávění' [From what Dvořák related], *HR*, vii (1913–14), 400, 440

——: 'Vzpomínky na Antonína Dvořáka' [Reminiscences of Dvořák], *HR*, x (1916–17), 293

J. M. Thurber: 'Dvořák as I knew him', *Etude*, xxxvii (1919), 693

R. Evans: 'Dvořák at Spillville', *The Palimpsest*, xi (Iowa City, 1930), 113

H. G. Kinscella: 'Dvořák and Spillville, Forty Years After', *Musical America*, liii (25 May 1933), 4

J. J. Kovařík: 'Dr. Antonín Dvořák', *Kalendář Katolik*, xl (Chicago, 1934), 156

J. Bachtík: *Antonín Dvořák dirigent* (Prague, 1940)

K. Leitner: 'Antonín Dvořák jak učil' [How Dvořák taught], *New-yorkské listy* (7 Sept 1941); pubd separately (New York, 1943)

BIOGRAPHICAL AND CRITICAL STUDIES

E. Hanslick: 'Concerte', *Neue freie Presse* (Vienna, 23 Nov 1879); repr. in Hanslick: *Concerte, Componisten und Virtuosen* (Berlin, 1886, 4/1896); Eng. trans. as 'Anton Dvořák', *Musical Review*, i/9 (New York, 11 Dec 1879), 141; *Dwight's Journal of Music*, xl (3 Jan 1880), 2; *Musical Standard*, new ser., xviii (1880), 58

L. Ehlert: 'Anton Dvořák', *Westermanns illustrirte deutsche Monatshefte*, lxviii (Brunswick, 1880), 232

H. Krigar: 'Anton Dvorak', *Musikalisches Wochenblatt*, xi (1880) 3, 15, 39, 67, 79, 91

M. Schütz: 'Regentage in Ischl', *Pester Lloyd* (Budapest, 19–20 Oct 1880)

J. Bennett: 'The Music of Anton Dvořák', *MT*, xxii (1881), 165, 236

J. Zubatý: *Ant. Dvořák: eine biographische Skizze* (Leipzig, 1886)

S. Taylor: 'Dvořák', *Cambridge Review*, xii (1891), 381

W. H. Hadow: 'Antonín Dvořák', *Studies in Modern Music*, 2nd ser. (London, 1895, 12/1930s/*R*1970)

F. J. Sawyer: 'The Tendencies of Modern Harmony as Exemplified in the Works of Dvořák and Grieg', *PMA*, xxii (1895–6), 53

H. E. Krehbiel: 'Anton Dvořák', *The Looker-on*, iii (New York, 1896), 261

Dvořák

Dvořákův sborník [Dvořák memorial volume], *HR*, iv (1910–11), 409–96 [28 articles by Šourek and others, incl. L. Janáček: 'Za Antonínem Dvořákem', repr. in *Musikologie*, v (1958), 353, ed. B. Štědroň]

Antonín Dvořák: sborník statí o jeho díla a životě [Dvořák memorial volume: essays on his work and life] (Prague, 1912)

J. Bartoš: *Antonín Dvořák: kritická studie* (Prague, 1913)

L. Bráfová: *Rieger, Smetana, Dvořák* (Prague, 1913)

O. Šourek: *Život a dílo Antonína Dvořáka* [Life and work of Dvořák] (Prague, 1916–33; i–ii, 3/1954–5; iii–iv, 2/1956–7)

K. Hoffmeister: *Antonín Dvořák* (Prague, 1924; Eng. trans., 1928)

O. Šourek: *Antonín Dvořák* (Prague, 1929, 3/1947; Eng. trans., 1952)

——: *Dvořákova čítanka: články a skadby* [Dvořák reader: articles and works] (Prague, 1929)

O. Šourek and P. Stefan: *Dvořák: Leben und Werk* (Vienna, 1935; Eng. trans., 1941/R1971, as *Anton Dvořák*)

H. Sirp: *Anton Dvořák* (Potsdam, 1939)

V. Fischl, ed.: *Antonín Dvořák: his Achievement* (London, 1942)

J. M. Květ: *Mládí Antonína Dvořáka* [The youth of Dvořák] (Prague, 1943, 3/1944)

A. Robertson: *Dvořák* (London, 1945, rev. 2/1974)

I. Belza: *Antonin Dvorzhak* (Moscow, 1949, 2/1954)

O. Šourek: *Z Dvořákovy cesty za slávou* [Dvořák's path to fame] (Prague, 1949)

H. Boese: *Zwei Urmusikanten: Smetana – Dvořák* (Vienna, 1955)

R. Smetana: *Antonín Dvořák: o misto a význam Dvořákova skladatelského díla v českém hudebnim vývoji* [Dvořák: the place and meaning of Dvořák's compositions in the development of Czech music] (Prague, 1956)

K. B. Jirák: *Antonín Dvořák: 1841–1961* (New York, 1961)

A. Hetschko: *Antonín Dvořák* (Leipzig, 1965)

J. Burghauser: *Antonín Dvořák* (Prague, 1966; Eng. trans., 1967)

J. Clapham: *Antonín Dvořák, Musician and Craftsman* (London, 1966)

——: 'Dvořák and the American Indian', *MT*, cvii (1966), 863

L. S. Ginzburg, ed.: *Antonin Dvorzhak: sbornik statyei* [Dvořák: a collection of articles] (Moscow, 1967)

J. Berkovec: *Antonín Dvořák* (Prague, 1969)

Z. Sádecký: 'Dvořákova tónina dur a moll: oblast diatonicky I', *HV*, viii (1971), 152, 318

R. Gerlach: 'War Schönberg von Dvorák beeinflusst? Zu Arnold Schönbergs Streichquartett D-Dur'. *NZM*, cxxxiii (1972), 122

Z. Gulinskaya: *Antonin Dvorzhak* (Moscow, 1973)

J. Bajer and L. S. Ginsburg, eds.: *Ceská hudba světu svět česke hudbě* (Prague, 1974) [incl. M. Černý: 'K periodizaci tvorby A. Dvořák', 87; V. Yegorova: 'O některých společných rysech Dvořákova a Čajkovského symfonismu', 105]

Bibliography

J. Clapham: 'Dvořáks Aufstieg zum Komponisten', *Mf*, xxx (1977), 47
M. Kuna: 'Antonín Dvořák a Rusko', *HRo*, xxx (1977), 386
J. Clapham: *Dvořák* (Newton Abbot and London, 1979)
B. Štědroň: 'Dvořák a Janáček', *HRo*, xxxii (1979), 282
J. Clapham: 'Dvořák on the American Scene', *19th Century Music*, v (1981–2), 16
———: 'The Dissemination Abroad of Czech Music towards the end of the 19th Century', *Hudba slovanských národů* (Brno, 1981), 119
J. Burghauser: 'Některé tvůrčí aspekty Dvořákovy komorní tvorby' [Several creative aspects of Dvořák's chamber music], *Acta Dvořákiana* (Prague, 1983), 25
M. Černý: 'Komorní hudba Ant. Dvořáka, její vyznam a ohlas ve vývoji české hudby' [Dvořák's chamber music, its meaning and reception in the development of Czech music], *Acta Dvořákiana* (Prague, 1983), 7
J. Clapham: 'Nové dvořákovské objevy' [New Dvořák discoveries], *HRo*, xxxvi (1983), 138
OM, xv/3 (1983) [special Dvořák number] incl. J. Fukač: 'Kam směřuje dvořákovské vědění' [Where knowledge of Dvořák is leading]; J. Volek: 'Harmonické "lahůdky" Antonína Dvořáka' [Dvořák's harmonic 'titbits']; A. Čubr: 'Dvořákova hudebně dramatická díla v kritické edici' [Dvořák's musico-dramatic works in the critical edition]; R. Kvapil: 'Zamyšlení nad klavírním dílem Antonína Dvořáka' [Thoughts on the piano works of Dvořák]; J. Vysloužil: 'Proč Anton Bruckner a Antonín Dvořák?' [Why Bruckner and Dvořák?]
M. Kuna: 'Od matčiny písně k Dvořákovu Jakobínu' [From the origin of song to Dvořák's *Jacobin*], *HV*, xxi (1984), 32
P. Petersen: 'Brahms und Dvořák', *Hamburger Jb für Musikwissenschaft*, vii (Laaber, 1984), 147
H.-H. Schönzeler: *Dvořák* (London, 1984)
J. Slavíková: 'Ohlasy Dvořákova díla v Paříži [1880–1904]' [The reception of Dvořák's work in Paris, 1880–1904], *HV*, xxi (1984), 70
J. Clapham: *Dvořák: Man and Artist* (in preparation)

SPECIFIC WORKS

L. Ehlert: [on Slavonic Dances and Moravian Duets], *National-Zeitung* (Berlin, 15 Nov 1878)
A. Naubert: 'Anton Dvořák, Op.33, Concert für Pianoforte und Orchester', *NZM*, lxxxi (1885), 129, 141
———: 'Geisterbraut', *NZM*, lxxxii (15 Jan 1886), 25
L. Janáček: 'České proudy hudební' [Czech musical currents], *Hlídka*, ii (Brno, 1897), 285, 454, 594, iii (1898), 277, repr. in *Musikologie*, v (1958), 342–52, ed. B. Štědroň [analyses of *The Water Goblin, The*

Dvořák

Noon Witch, The Golden Spinning-wheel and The Wild Dove]
O. Šourek: Dvořákovy symfonie (Prague, 1922, 3/1948; Eng. trans. in The Orchestral Works of Antonín Dvořák, 1956)
D. Tovey: Essays in Musical Analysis (London, 1935–9, 2/1972)
O. Šourek: Dvořákovy skladby komorní (Prague, 1943; Eng. trans., abridged, 1956, as The Chamber Music of Antonín Dvořák)
——: Dvořákovy skladby orchestralní (Prague, 1944–6; Eng. trans., abridged, 1956, as The Orchestral Works of Antonín Dvořák)
H. Kull: Dvořáks Kammermusik (Berne, 1948)
M. Očadlík: 'Antonín Dvořák', Svět orchestru [The world of the orchestra], ii (Prague, 1953), 243–335
Introductions to works in A. Dvořák: souborné vydání [Dvořák complete edition], ed. O. Šourek and others (Prague, 1955–)
J. Clapham: 'The Evolution of Dvořák's Symphony "From the New World" ', MQ, xliv (1958), 167
J. Burghauser: Orchestrace Dvořákových Slovanských tanců (Prague, 1959)
M. Černý: 'Smyčcový kvartet D dur Antonína Dvořáka' [Dvořák's String Quartet in D major], Živá hudba, i (1959), 85
J. Clapham: 'Blick in die Werkstatt eines Komponisten: die beiden Fassungen von Dvořáks Klaviertrio f-moll', Musica, xiii (1959), 629
A. Sychra: Estetika Dvořákovy symfonické tvorby [The aesthetics of Dvořák's symphonic works] (Prague, 1959; Ger. trans., 1973)
V. Tausky: 'Dvořák's "Rusalka" ', Opera, x (1959), 76
J. Clapham: 'Dvořák's Symphony in D minor – the Creative Process', ML, xlii (1961), 103
——: 'The National Origins of Dvořák's Art', PRMA, lxxxix (1962–3), 75
J. Harrison: 'Antonín Dvořák', The Symphony, i, ed. R. Simpson (Harmondsworth, 1966, 2/1972)
J. Zich: 'Instrumentace dechové serenády Antonína Dvořáka' [The instrumentation of Dvořák's wind serenade], Živá hudba, iv (1968), 65
M. Černý: 'Zum Wort-Ton-Problem im Vokalwerk Antonín Dvořáks', Music and Word: Brno IV 1969, 139
J. Clapham: 'Indian Influence on Dvořák's American Chamber Music', Musica cameralis: Brno VI 1971, 174 [music exx., 525]
D. Beveridge: 'Sophisticated Primitivism: the Significance of Pentatonicism in Dvořák's American Quartet', CMc (1977), no.24, p.25
J. Smaczny: 'Armida-Dvořák's Wrong Turning?' Zpráva, iii/5 (London, 1977), 10
R. Layton: Dvořák Symphonies and Concertos (London, 1978)
J. Clapham: 'Dvořák's Cello Concerto, a Masterpiece in the Making', MR, xl (1979), 123

Bibliography

V. Yegorova: *Simfoniy Dvorzhaka* (Moscow, 1979)

K. Mikysa: 'Klavírní trio f moll op.65 Ant. Dvořáka', *Acta Dvořákiana* (Prague, 1983), 35

J. Trojan: 'Zač děkují Moravě Slovanské tance' [What the Slavonic Dances owe to Moravia], *OM*, xv (1983), 91

A. Stich: 'O libretu Dvořákova Dimitrije' [About the libretto of Dvořák's *Dimitrij*], *HV*, xxi (1984), 339

J. Volek: 'Tektonické ambivalence v symfoniích Antonína Dvořáka' [Tectonic ambivalence in the symphonies of Antonín Dvořák], *HV*, xxi (1984), 3

HUGO WOLF

Eric Sams

CHAPTER ONE

Life

I Formative years

Hugo Filipp Jakob Wolf was born on 13 March 1860 in Windischgraz, Styria (now Slovenj Gradec, Yugoslavia), a German-speaking enclave of a Slovene region. His mother Katharina (1824–1903) was of Slovene yeoman stock (her paternal grandfather's name was Orehovnik, which he changed to its German equivalent Nussbaumer; her maternal grandfather's name was Stank or Stanko). According to a family tradition, she also had some Italian antecedents. She was strong-willed and energetic, four years older than her husband Philipp Wolf, whom she married in 1852. His family was German in origin; he inherited the leather business established in Windischgraz in the 18th century by his grandfather Maximilian. Philipp Wolf (1828–87) was a gifted musician who taught himself the piano, violin, flute, harp and guitar. His trenchant and colourful letters reveal him as the thwarted artist, moody and introspective. These gifts and temperament seem to have been inherited by Hugo, the fourth of six children (two others died in infancy). As he later recorded appreciatively, he was given piano and violin lessons by his father at a very early age. At the village primary school from 1865 to 1869 he was taught the piano and theory by Sebastian Weixler, who also played the viola in the Wolf household orchestra (Philipp first violin, Hugo second, brother Max cello, an uncle as horn player).

In 1868 Hugo saw his first opera (Donizetti's *Belisario*), which made an overwhelming impression. In September 1870 he was sent to the regional secondary school in Graz (where he was remembered as speaking German with a Slovene accent) but left after only one term with the general report 'wholly unsatisfactory', though with some praise for his musical gifts. In September 1871 he began two years as a boarder at the Benedictine abbey of St Paul, where he excelled as a musician, playing the violin and organ for school services and the piano in a trio (with a repertory including Italian and French opera arrangements). But he lagged at the compulsory Latin; and in the autumn of 1873 he was transferred to the secondary school at Marburg (now Maribor, Yugoslavia). There he absorbed the classical repertory in score or performance, including Beethoven and Haydn symphonies in piano duet arrangement. But again he left after only two years. His wilful and passionate nature spurned compromise; he had time and energy only for music. His father received two placatory dedications, that of op.1, a piano sonata begun in April 1875, and that of the Variations op.2. It was decided that Wolf should go and live with an aunt in Vienna that September and study at the Vienna Conservatory.

At first all went well. He studied the piano with Wilhelm Schenner and harmony and composition first with Robert Fuchs and then with the strict and pedantic Franz Krenn. He made many friends, including the young Gustav Mahler. The first fruits were an unfinished 'violin concerto' (in piano score) and more piano sonatas, as well as songs and choruses. Now Wolf began regular opera-going: Meyerbeer's *Les Huguenots* was a special favourite. But his deepest devotion was reserved for Wagner, then (November 1875) in Vienna for performances of *Tannhäuser* and *Lohengrin*. Wolf attended both, and became (as he told his dismayed parents) a dedicated Wagnerian – a term then synonymous with avant-garde turbulence. In December he visited Wagner, bringing his piano pieces, which he explained were in the style of Mozart. Wagner was indulgent and affable; he gravely agreed that it was best to model oneself on the classics, and counselled patience and practice. When he next went to Vienna, he said, he would look forward to being shown larger-scale works.

This encounter inspired Wolf, always a passionate hero-worshipper and famished for encouragement. He duly attempted larger-scale works, notably a Lenau setting for accompanied male-voice chorus, *Die Stimme des Kindes*. But the part-writing went awry, a blemish pointed out by Hans Richter, then director of the Vienna Opera, whom Wolf had also buttonholed and blandished. Technical shortcomings recur in further choruses written in 1876; but in one Goethe setting, *Mailied*, the contours of coming mastery are discernible in rhythmic verve and harmonic vitality. Also from this period date orchestral essays (an arrangement of the 'Moonlight' Sonata), various chamber music fragments and sketches and a piano *Rondo capriccioso* which later became a symphonic finale. No doubt many of these were set as academic exercises, but their style testifies to a growing independence. Soon Wolf was again in conflict with authority. In later life he would explain that he resigned from the conservatory in protest at its entrenched conservatism. But he was also officially dismissed for 'breach of discipline'; and his cause was not helped by the prank of a fellow student who sent the director a threatening letter, signed 'Hugo Wolf'. By March 1877 Wolf was home again in disgrace.

There he worked on a symphony and composed the earliest song that he thought worthy of publication, *Morgentau*. He was allowed back to Vienna in November to earn his own living as a music teacher. On the journey he lost the score of his symphony. That start was symptomatic. Wolf never had the teacher's gift or temperament. His talents needed (and his charm secured) the patronage of generous households, such as those of the actor Ludwig Gabillon and Freud's early collaborator Josef Breuer.

Wolf was already known in other cultured circles, notably that of the composer Adalbert von Goldschmidt (which included the critics Gustav Schönaich and Hans Paumgartner, and the conductor Felix Mottl). They adopted the young Wolf, took him to concerts and operas, lent him books, music and money. But this fostering may also have proved fatal. For it was Goldschmidt who (according to Alma Mahler) took Wolf to a brothel; and there is no doubt that Wolf's insanity in 1897 and death in 1903 were among the sequelae of a syphilitic infection assignable with fair certainty to 1878. It was then, as members of the Gabillon and Breuer families later recalled, that he began to avoid their dinner tables and their company (eating only such food as could be conveyed direct to the mouth, and refusing to travel in the same railway carriage as his hosts). Such conduct then seemed merely eccentric or boorish; but Dr Breuer later came to believe that it was founded on medical advice and consideration for others.

The phase of sexual initiation and stimulus was also a time of spontaneous songwriting, the first signs of an intuitive mode of creativity that would later characterize Wolf's greatest work. Early in 1878 he was in love with Vally Franck, a relative of the Lang family, who were among his most generous benefactors. He later said that in that year he had written 'at least one good song every day'. This seems exaggerated (unless the works were atypically destroyed); but it testifies to a wealth of feeling in that year. Romantic love and 'Weltschmerz' are explicit in the choice of 1877–8 song texts from such sources as Heine, Lenau, Chamisso, Rückert, Hoffmann von Fallersleben and Goethe's *Faust*.

After the Schumannesque Heine settings of May and June 1878 a new and agonized note is sounded in the Faust setting of *Gretchen vor dem Andachtsbild der Mater Dolorosa*, begun on 22 August. The confession of sin and prayer for forgiveness, novel and uncharacteristic themes in Wolf, are expressed in anguished chromatics. He next wrote settings of gloomy and life-abnegating texts (also perhaps related to the inevitable if temporary separation from Vally Franck), closely followed by the first movement of the D minor String Quartet with its outbursts of impassioned declamation. The Grave introduction is prefixed by the words 'Entbehren sollst du, sollst entbehren' ('You must renounce, renounce'), spoken by Faust when sealing his pact with the Devil and renouncing human life and love. Both this movement and the Scherzo (Resolut) bear the date January 1879.

It was no doubt in a dejected mood that Wolf had called on Brahms early in that year. He was kindly received and given the same advice as Wagner's, namely to extend his musical horizons. From the blunt Brahms this seemed an affront, especially when coupled with the suggestion of counterpoint lessons from Nottebohm. The fee was well beyond Wolf's means; and the idea was dismissed as 'north German pedantry'. This note of antipathy soon swelled to an enduring diapason. As in Shaw's contemporary London, the younger musicians tended to brand Brahms as reactionary and hail Wagner as progressive. Wolf's immediate circle, a Bohemian fraternity comparable to the first Schubertians, were all fanatical Wagnerites, following their master to the point of becoming vegetarians – as Wolf did for a year or two, partly also perhaps because that diet was cheaper. His meagre earnings were eked out by parcels of food and clothes sent from home. He was constantly changing lodgings (on occasion sharing with Mahler, with whom he had remained on affable terms) in search of seclusion or economy. Life was hard, but intellectually and socially formative. Goldschmidt and Schönaich in particular continued to be generous with help and introductions: the circle of Wolf's friends and admirers gradually widened. In April 1879 he first met Melanie Köchert (née Lang), who later became his mistress and protectress. Her sister Henriette and her brother Edmund Lang also became close friends. Meanwhile Wolf's love for their quasi-cousin Vally Franck was rekindled; but the two were separated most of that year by her absence on holiday. Wolf's letters and music are alike passionate, as three Lenau songs testify. But his penury and misfortune kept the lovers parted if not estranged. His patterns of cyclic mood swing and unpredictably sporadic creativity were already clearly delineated. By 1880 his depression and illness were both apparently abating. Sweetness and serenity return to the song music, especially in *Erwartung* and *Die Nacht*, two Eichendorff settings inscribed to Vally and thought worthy of publication in the later songbook. The slow movement of the D minor Quartet, begun in July, has overtones of healing (recalling Beethoven's *Heiliger Dankgesang*) and redemption that suggest a mood of regeneration and thanksgiving, enhanced by an idyllic summer holiday in Mayerling. There Wolf's mature songwriting style continued its slow burgeoning, nurtured by studies and transcriptions of Wagner. Two paraphrases (of *Die Meistersinger* and *Die Walküre*), probably made at this time, were presented to the lawyer Joseph Heitzes, another of Wolf's benefactors, whose Mayerling home was rented to the Preyss family. They willingly agreed to look after Wolf and give him the tranquillity and independence he needed. By now he was sufficiently recovered to take his meals *en famille*. His high spirits and manifest genius captivated not only the Preyss family but their own summer visitors, including the Werners, especially the seven-year-old Heinrich, who became wholly devoted to Wolf and later served his cause well as editor, critic and biographer.

Summertime in Mayerling, then and later, brought out the radiant side of Wolf's nature, including his love of children and of the countryside. His small stocky figure, fair hair, and dark brown eyes fitfully lit by hilarity, were well described by a later friend, Edmund Hellmer, who added that to know him really well one had to hear him laugh and see him in the open air. But the sunshine regularly faded, and a darker side supervened; then the Wolfian moods turned first to a daunting wildness of speech and mien and thence sometimes

to snapping and snarling, even at his devoted benefactors.

Before Wolf's 21st birthday Vally Franck had broken
off their attachment and returned to her native France.
Despair resounded in the *Sechs geistliche Lieder*, choruses to words by Eichendorff; again secular human
feeling was presented in the guise of spiritual agony. As
ever when wounded Wolf sought refuge in Windischgraz, composing a further Eichendorff song of soulful
separation, *In der Fremde I*. Once again he was helped
by the devoted Goldschmidt, who in November 1881
found him a post as second conductor at Salzburg. As
before, Wolf's musicianship was applauded but there
were jarring personal notes. He resented the trivial
tedium of operetta rehearsal and quarrelled violently
with the director. Again he left under a cloud; early in
1882 he was back in Vienna. His unhappy father
compared himself, with some justice, to a Sisyphus
forever doomed to push the same heavy stone uphill and
behold it rolling ineluctably back, this time perhaps with
crushing and fatal effect. For a time father and son were
estranged. Wolf, though contrite, was helpless to govern
the forces that determined his life and fate. It was
apparently early in this year that he was conscripted for
a short time into military service, then compulsory at
20. For unknown reasons, whether the influence of
friends, or his own ill-health, or unstable temperament,
or small stature (5′ 1½″), he was neither called up in
1880 nor long retained in 1882. His diary records this
as the year of a 'terrible moral hangover'. But as usual the
arid tracts were diversified by occasional oases,
including the Mörike setting of *Mausfallensprüchlein*,
the fruit of another summer spent with the Preyss and

22. Hugo Wolf

Werner families in Mayerling. There was a further remission in late 1882 and early 1883 with a group of generally serene and sunny Reinick and Eichendorff songs. This time, when the darker mood returned, composition continued. It was as if two strands (bright and dark, lyric and dramatic, simple and complex, Schumannian and Wagnerian) were beginning to interweave in a new and essentially Wolfian pattern. His tense and dramatic Kerner setting *Zur Ruh, zur Ruh!* of June 1883 may have been his threnody on the death of Wagner four months earlier. In August he saw *Parsifal* in Bayreuth; then again he was at a standstill.

II Years of uncertainty

The trail Wolf should follow was not clear to him or his family or friends. Hanslick had admired his songs, and thought them worth publishing. But first Schott and then Breitkopf rejected them, though in affable terms. Perhaps he was not destined to be a songwriter after all? At this impasse came his third encounter with a great composer, this time Liszt, at a meeting (again engineered by the faithful Goldschmidt) in April 1883. Although impressed with the songs Wolf showed him, which included *Die Spinnerin*, Liszt (like Wagner and Brahms) counselled further composition in the larger forms. This again chimed with Wolf's own mood. That winter he had drafted the libretto of a Spanish opera. Now he instantly began work on a symphonic poem based on Heinrich von Kleist's *Penthesilea*, a drama which (like *Faust*, and perhaps for the same reason) had long been an obsession of his; its theme is the injuries inflicted by women on men through sexual passion. In Lisztian style it seeks to develop and integrate small-scale motifs into the orchestral tone poem frame. Wolf went again to Bayreuth for *Parsifal*; he spent an agreeable holiday in Rinnbach visiting the Köcherts. But then the tides of inspiration again receded, leaving a barren and featureless shore. He found a new friend and admirer, the writer Hermann Bahr. But by the end of 1883 another depressive phase had set in. There are more sad stories of recrimination and parting, offence given and taken. Wolf quarrelled with his friends the Breuers because of his immoderate language about women. He stormed out of the hospitable house of the industrialist Fritz Flesch because his host passed him a pear on a toothpick – not a trifling matter to a sensitive and fastidious syphilitic who had scrupulously spent his infectious phase in enforced isolation.

The outbursts and estrangements of these and later years have to be viewed in the perspective of Wolf's artistic frustration, his mental and physical case history and the enduring love and solicitude shown by faithful friends. Supreme among them was Melanie Köchert, whom Wolf had been teaching and adoring since 1881. Her husband Heinrich Köchert was the Vienna court jeweller, and had influential friends. Under his aegis Wolf was appointed music critic of the fashionable Sunday *Wiener Salonblatt*. But there was nothing merely modish in Wolf's writing or in his readership, the new and growing public for music criticism fostered by Hanslick yet left dissatisfied by the latter's intransigent anti-Wagnerism. Into this vacuum Wolf rushed headlong. Notoriously, he did Wagner more than justice, and Brahms less. But it would be wrong to see his outspoken critiques as merely partisan or their anti-Brahmsian thrust as merely retaliatory. They are not

313

only a literate and lively mirror of the age; they have a special interest for the Wagner scholar, for there can hardly have been anyone at the time who was more articulately knowledgeable about the operas. Above all, they afford significant insights into Wolf's own creative mind.

The three-year spell of criticism was useful as a vocation and a discipline, but it inhibited composition. Although Wolf took a long summer holiday in each of the three years 1884 to 1886, his comparative quietude was not matched by comparable peace of mind. The sardonic turbulence of his prose is well matched in his only song of this period, the Mörike setting *Die Tochter der Heide*, written during a sojourn with the Köcherts at Rinnbach in July 1884. It was probably at this time that he and Melanie Köchert avowed their mutual love. The last movement of the D minor Quartet was also sketched in the same summer. Some fragmentary sketches for another Kleist play, *Prinz Friedrich von Homburg*, about the conflicts between love and duty, convention and temperament, date from August, when Wolf was visiting his sister Modesta and her husband Josef Strasser at Oblarn; this time love is a saving grace, not the destructive force of *Penthesilea*. On an outing with Strasser Wolf met the folk poet and singer Johann Kain, and was entranced by his songs. By October 1884 Wolf was back in Vienna writing reviews and vainly striving to arrange performances or publication of his own works. He resolved to devote the coming summer to completing, for submission to the Philharmonic Orchestra, his *Penthesilea* and *Prinz Friedrich von Homburg* music. The latter remained fragmentary, but in September he called on Richter with the score of

Penthesilea and was promised a trial later that year.

Wolf felt he was at last gaining a foothold, and indeed he had been making a name for himself as a critic. Sadly, it was a hated name. Among those Wolf had mauled was Sigismund Bachrich, whose pretensions as an opera composer had been pointedly deflated. But Bachrich was the viola player of the famed Rosé Quartet; so Wolf was naive in submitting his D minor Quartet to them for a hearing. It was returned with a woundingly worded note signed by Bachrich on behalf of his colleagues. Worse still, *Penthesilea* was put on trial in every sense. Its rehearsal on 15 October 1885 was (whether or not with Richter's connivance) a fiasco. Bachrich was in the orchestra, and Richter made some disparaging remarks (which Wolf overheard) about people who dared to criticize so great a master as Brahms. Such comments were wholly predictable and unsurprising. It was Wolf's turn to be lacerated. His critiques continued with unabated vigour; but his own music was aborted or stillborn. It was not until October 1886 while on holiday with the Strassers (now living at Murau) after some embarrassing contretemps, including a grave eye injury sustained while playing with the children's toys, that he completed his next viable work, the Intermezzo in E♭ for string quartet. At the turn of the year he began work on *Christnacht*, a setting of Platen for soloists, chorus and orchestra. Wolf himself described it as uniting two aspects of the Christ child: naive and childlike, yet conquering and redemptive. Again the impulse seems intuitively self-expressive. Similarly all three songs of 1886 (*Der König bei der Krönung, Der Soldat II, Biterolf*) and the first three of 1887 (*Wächterlied auf der Wartburg, Wanderers*

315

Nachtlied, Beherzigung) have texts relating to various aspects of staunchness and resolution in the face of adversity. At last the music affirms a confident sense of purpose and vocation. Finally in 1887 Wolf attained a new plateau near the summit of mastery. The impetus was provided by a change of route from subjectivity towards the sonorous re-creation of imaginative literature, a concept frequently cited by Wolf the critic as a touchstone of excellence. So it proved for Wolf the composer. From March to May 1887 he was inspired by the vitality of Eichendorff's poetry about lightness in love (*Der Soldat I*) or the bewitching power of women (*Die Kleine, Die Zigeunerin, Waldmädchen*) and of nature (*Nachtzauber*). Between these last two songs he composed the highly original *Italienische Serenade* for string quartet (2–4 May). Its relaxed and amused irony may also have owed its conception to Eichendorff, whose novella *Aus dem Leben eines Taugenichts* offers many a textual correspondence with Wolf's life and music and includes an Italian serenade.

There could now be no further doubt in Wolf's mind about the fact of his gift, though its actual nature remained unclear to him. He had written his first masterpiece, and his last critique. At that moment his father was suddenly taken ill, and died on 9 May, thus being denied his son's later triumphs but spared the final tragedy. Hugo, summoned by telegram, was a solace at the end, but then became himself inconsolable. Hardly another word was written or another note composed in that year. He needed affectionate support and encouragement; a mainstay had gone. Help came from Friedrich Eckstein, whose library and conversation had enriched and influenced the young Wolf in his earlier

Vienna days and who now performed the further signal service of persuading a publisher (perhaps with some financial inducement) to bring out two volumes of Wolf's songs. From among his manuscripts of many years Wolf selected six women's songs and six for male voice, to be inscribed respectively to his mother and to his father's memory. The project induced a tumultuous creative euphoria.

III Mastery and fame

Wolf instinctively sought solitude. The Werners offered him the use of their holiday home in Perchtoldsdorf, near Vienna. He took with him the poems of his favourite Mörike, whose lyrics had no doubt been germinating in his musical mind for many years. Now came a sudden spontaneous flowering of song music that in its profusion and variety matched the Schubert of 1814–15 and the Schumann of 1840–41. The biographical parallels with the latter are especially clear. Wolf too had just emerged from some years of activity as a critic and was celebrating a long-lasting love affair (by 1888 Wolf and Melanie Köchert were lovers, though they could meet only with difficulty and by stealth). Wolf too found himself moving in the song medium with a new and surprising assurance (with characteristic irony he compared the process to the final undoing of a frequently and frustratingly fumbled button). Finally, he too was disconcerted by the violence of his musical creativity, though overjoyed by its profusion. On 22 February for example he wrote to Edmund Lang, 'I have just put a new song on to paper [*Der Knabe und das Immlein*]. A song for the gods, let me tell you! . . . My cheeks are glowing with excitement like molten iron; and this state

317

of inspiration is more a delicious torment to me than an unalloyed pleasure'. But that was only a beginning. Far finer songs grew and proliferated, at the rate of two or even three a day. Again to Edmund Lang, on the same day, 'Hardly was my letter dispatched than I took up my Mörike and wrote another song [*Jägerlied*]' PS . . . I have succeeded in a third song, and *how*! [*Ein Stündlein wohl vor Tag*]. This is an eventful day'.

A month later he was still composing at the same pitch and writing in the same strain. To Josef Strasser. 23 March: 'I'm working at 1000 horsepower from early morning until late at night, without respite. What I am now putting on to paper, dear friend, is also being written for posterity. They are masterpieces. . . . When I tell you that [despite several unavoidable visits to Vienna] I have, since 22 February, written 25 songs, each better than the last, about which connoisseurs agree that there has been nothing like them since Schubert, Schumann, etc, you'll readily gather what kind of songs they are'. Earlier Wolf had written modestly to Edmund Lang, 'I wonder what the future may hold in store for me? This question torments me, perturbs and preoccupies me waking or sleeping. Am I called? or perhaps even chosen?' By March he knew. By mid-May (after 43 songs) he needed rest. He took a holiday with the Strassers; he visited Bayreuth. In September the spate of song resumed. This time Wolf sought sanctuary with the Eckstein family at Unterach, where he wrote (again perhaps using some earlier ideas) 13 Eichendorff settings. Then Mörike settings resumed with another nine in the first fortnight of October, including some with a deep spiritual content (Wolf had again been much moved by *Parsifal*). Then came a return to Vienna, and an outburst even more sustained than ever. By 13 February 1889 Wolf had finished the 51 songs of the Goethe songbook, except for one incomplete sketch (*Die Spröde*) which dissatisfied him and was later recomposed.

Again the connoisseurs could recognize masterpieces, this time directly challenging comparison with the Goethe settings of Schubert and Schumann. The word soon spread from old friends to new converts. It was only on 2 March 1888 that any Wolf song had been publicly performed (by Rosa Papier, Hans Paumgartner's wife). By 23 March Wolf was playing and singing his latest Mörike settings to the Wagner-Verein. Among its more influential members Josef Schalk and Ferdinand Löwe, both professors at the conservatory, were powerfully impressed. So was the tenor Ferdinand Jäger (who had sung Parsifal at Bayreuth) when, on 8 November, he heard three of the Mörike songs from a soprano of the Vienna Opera accompanied by Schalk. Jäger was soon to Wolf as Vogl was to Schubert, a lifelong devotee and partner. Their Wolf concert on 15 December was the composer's first public appearance as an accompanist. This and subsequent recitals were received with acclaim.

In May 1889 Wolf returned to Perchtoldsdorf with his mind still ringing with plaudits. The prospect of public success again focussed his attention on large-scale forms, both operatic and orchestral. (Two settings from *A Midsummer Night's Dream* date from this month as well as two orchestrations of songs from the Mörike volume, which had meanwhile been published.) After summer holiday visits to Bayreuth and to his mother who was in Windischgraz, Wolf returned to

Perchtoldsdorf at the end of October 1889 and instantly began work on his Spanish songbook. Thoughts of opera often suggested Spain or Italy to his mind (from this summer also dates the draft of a few dreamy bars of string quartet music intended as a slow movement for the *Italienische Serenade*). This impulse, together with his established penchant for characterization and description, his strong sense of national feeling and local colour, and a mood of mysticism perhaps induced or fostered by the Bayreuth visits, led to a choice of translations from the Spanish by Heyse and Geibel (a source earlier used by both Schumann and Brahms). By April 1890 the 44 Spanish songs (including translations from Camoens, Cervantes, Lope de Vega and others, as well as anonymous lyrics) were completed. Meanwhile the thrust towards stage music continued: a sketched theme of December 1889 is headed 'Introduction to Hamlet'. Two more Reinick settings (one with orchestra on a patriotic theme) and six Keller songs in June 1890 (again including characterization and mysticism) bring to an end this great creative period, in which 174 songs, including many acknowledged masterpieces, had been composed within two and a half years.

Meanwhile the reverberations of Wolf's fame were spreading outside Austria. The first critical article was by Heinrich Rauchberg, an early friend; his 'Neue Lieder und Gesänge' (about the Mörike and Eichendorff songbooks) appeared in the November–December issue of the *Österreichisch-ungarische Revue*. Far more influential, however, was Josef Schalk's 'Neue Lieder, neues Leben' in the *Münchener allgemeine Zeitung* for 22 January 1890. This gave rise to widespread interest and correspondence. Wolf heard from the Tübingen

music director Emil Kauffmann (whose father had been
a friend of Mörike's) and the Mannheim judge Oskar
Grohe. Both became close friends. Gustave Schur of the
Wagner-Verein was able to negotiate with the well-
established firm of Schott in Mainz to supplement or
replace the small Viennese publishers Wetzler (already
on the point of bankruptcy) and Lacom.

Within Austria Jäger had given another very successful Wolf recital to the Graz Wagner-Verein on 12
April. It was heard by Heinrich Potpeschnigg, a dentist
and amateur pianist, who soon became a close friend
and helper. In Vienna Wolf's name was steadily gaining
ground, but also meeting some resistance. Richard
Heuberger recalled a talk with Brahms and Richter in
November 1890, about 'the Wagnerians and in particular Hugo Wolf, whom they now praised as a great
songwriter, the inventor of the "symphonic song",
whereas Schubert, Schumann and Brahms are said to
have written songs as if with guitar accompaniment'.
The partisan note is clear; and there was some resent-
ment even within the Wagner societies. But the general
reaction was favourable; and this wave of recognition
carried Wolf to a further crest of enthusiasm for opera.
In 1890, with his mind very much on Spanish themes,
he had been offered a libretto on Alarcón's *El sombrero
de tres picos*, by the feminist and journalist Rosa
Mayreder. This was rejected, together with other suggestions such as *The Tempest* and the story of
Pocahontas (proposal and counter-proposal between
Wolf and the poet Detlev von Liliencron, whose attention had been drawn to Wolf by Josef Schalk, and who
composed a verse-eulogy of the songs). Among other
topics mooted, the life of Buddha and the *Golden Ass* of

321

23. Hugo Wolf, 1895

Apuleius might be said to typify Wolf's contrasting spiritual and secular aspects. But when he received a commission from the Burgtheater to compose incidental music for a production of Ibsen's *The Feast at Solhaug*, Wolf's zest sharply diminished. He found the assigned task irksome and uncongenial; he was dilatory and uninspired; he scored for too large an orchestra; and his procrastination delayed the opening night until 21 November 1891, when the reception was lukewarm. His recalcitrance was enhanced by some fresh song inspiration from Heyse's polished translations of anonymous Italian poems in a courtly style and tradition dating from the 16th century or earlier (hardly folk poems, as is sometimes claimed). Seven such settings were completed in October and November 1890 despite the distraction of another visit to Germany to complete the negotiations with Schott. On his itinerary Wolf met the conductor Hermann Levi and the singer Eugen Gura in Munich and called on his new friends Kauffmann and Grohe.

But now bodily and mental exhaustion supervened, with some ominous signs. Apart from the Ibsen commission and the orchestration of a Mörike song Wolf was barren for most of 1891. The tedium of inactivity was alleviated by a further visit to Germany to hear *Christnacht* under Weingartner at Mannheim. There he met Humperdinck, who as Schott's reader had recommended Wolf's songs; but they did not take up the option on *Christnacht*, in which Wolf could recognize defective scoring. A depressive phase ensued. He suffered from insomnia and malaise; he despaired of writing another note. But at the end of December he composed (or perhaps completed) another 15 Italian songs, again full of masterly invention. Then darkness fell again, more impenetrable than ever. The long fallow period was again put to good use in tours and concerts in Germany.

The first Wolf recital in Berlin on 3 March 1892, with the local tenor Grahl (replacing the indisposed Jäger) and the mezzo-soprano Friedrike Mayer, was enthusiastically received, though it was not a financial success. Wolf made many new friends including his patron Baron Lipperheide, the chorus master Siegfried Ochs, the critic Richard Sternfeld (who wrote his laudatory article 'Ein neuer Liedesfrühling' on 12 March), the opera singer Emilie Herzog-Welti (who gave a successful Wolf recital on 12 April) and the librettist Richard Genée. As a suitable opera text for Wolf he recommended Alarcón's *Il niño de la bola*, translated into German as *Manuel Venegas*. This project preoccupied Wolf to the last.

On his return from Berlin Wolf again fell victim to the feverish throat inflammation (no doubt a symptom of secondary syphilis) to which he had been prone since 1891. He was cared for, as so often, by the Köcherts. Perhaps it was the presence of Melanie, his shy and reticent mistress (who was never seen among the social circle of Wolf's musical friends), that prompted him to orchestrate his great song on the theme of covert and illicit love, *Geh, Geliebter, geh jetzt*, from the Spanish songbook. He scored the *Italienische Serenade* for small orchestra, with some slight but perplexing thematic changes; he sporadically sketched or planned some additional movements. Otherwise he was barren and listless. In the three years 1892 to 1894 he wrote not a single note of viable original music. As before, he sought distraction in continued travel and concert tours. Thus in January 1894 he attended a very successful performance of his Shakespeare *Elfenlied* and the choral version of his Mörike song *Der Feuerreiter* under the direction of Siegfried Ochs in Berlin. On the same programme was the *Te Deum* of Bruckner, also present in person; he and Wolf were on affable terms. In Mannheim Wolf met another disciple and benefactor, the barrister and amateur tenor Hugo Faisst of Stuttgart. In Darmstadt he became infatuated with the soprano Frieda Zerny of the Mainz opera, and formed wild plans of emigrating with her to the USA. This brief liaison somehow became known to Melanie Köchert, to her distress and Wolf's embarrassment. He renewed his allegiance to her; and the summer months of 1894 were spent first at her country home in Traunkirchen, and later with the Lipperheides near Brixlegg in the Tyrol.

With the success of Humperdinck's *Hänsel und Gretel* in December Wolf's opera fever reached a new crisis. The Alarcón story of the three-cornered hat began to dominate his mind. He rejected a version prepared by Franz Schaumann, chairman of the Wagner-Verein and enthused instead over the previously despised libretto of Rosa Mayreder, entitled *Der Corregidor*. Its merits are disputable; but this text indubitably now began to fertilize Wolf's long-dormant creative genius. As before, there was a period of winter gestation followed by springtime labour. Early in April 1895 Wolf again sought solitude in Perchtoldsdorf. There the Mörike drama was re-enacted: he began to compose daily from dawn to dusk. In May he left for the more comfortable Lipperheide château in Brixlegg. By 9 July the whole four-act opera was complete in piano score; the orchestration occupied the rest of the year. The opera was offered, unsuccessfully, to Vienna, Berlin and Prague and was eventually accepted (with some help from Grohe) for performance at Mannheim. The rehearsals were prolonged and tense because of inaccuracies in the copied parts and fluctuations in Wolf's own mental state; he continued to be plagued by insomnia. The first performance (7 June 1896) under Hugo Röhr was a great success, with curtain calls for the composer, but the enthusiasm abated in later performances, with the gradual departure of Wolf's friends and admirers; the opera has still not reached the general repertory or the wider public.

Meanwhile Wolf in a further access of creative fervour returned to Perchtoldsdorf and composed (or completed) the final section of the Italian songbook, with 24 songs in the five weeks between 25 March and 30 April. He then returned to Vienna to occupy – for the first time in his life – his own home. Ever since his arrival there he had been living either in penury or else as a guest. The Köcherts had always been generous; the Lipperheides and Grohe had provided a stipend; now Faisst and other friends found and furnished a flat in the Schwindgasse. There, for most of 1896 and the beginning of 1897, he revised (with the devoted help of Potpeschnigg) the score and parts of *Der Corregidor*, influenced *inter alia* by Johann Fuchs, Kapellmeister of the Vienna Opera, who advised that revisions (notably a cut in the last act) were mandatory. In autumn 1896 he wrote two settings of Byron and one of Reinick.

IV   Breakdown and terminal illness

In March 1897 Wolf composed his last songs, to sonnets by Michelangelo in German translation – the

24. *Hugo Wolf, with his nurse in the background*

Christmas gift of Paul Müller, the founder of the Berlin
Hugo Wolf-Verein. In April 1897 a Vienna Wolf-Verein
was inaugurated by the university professor Michael
Haberlandt, a staunch support in Wolf's declining years.
Meanwhile Wolf had pursued his plans for a second
Alarcón opera on the story of Manuel Venegas.

The theme is sexual jealousy and revenge, as in *Der
Corregidor*, but with dark overtones of violence and
tragedy. Perhaps Wolf's mind in its depressive phase
was reverting to a febrile subjectivism. The
Michelangelo songs, fine though they are, have evident
personal application. By 1897 Wolf was clearly a very
sick man, whose always unpredictable behaviour was
now causing distress and alarm. A medical examination
in the previous year had disclosed (though the knowledge was withheld from Wolf himself) a characteristic
loss of pupillary reflex, symptomatic of the incipient
general paralysis of tertiary syphilis. Nevertheless he
was again ready to compose at fever-heat. A *Manuel
Venegas* libretto prepared by Rosa Mayreder was sum-
marily rejected. Moritz Hoernes (a colleague of Michael
Haberlandt) produced an alternative version which
seemed to the sick Wolf to have a truly Shakespearean
quality. In September 1897 he was again sequestered in
his apartment working from dawn to dusk on the new
opera. He completed some 60 pages of piano score in
three weeks; then his mind gave way. He claimed to
have been appointed director of the Vienna Opera;
thenceforth only his own works (mostly unfinished or
unwritten) would be performed. No doubt his madness
took this turn because of a recent visit from his old
friend Mahler, who had just been appointed opera
Kapellmeister and who according to Wolf had promised

to do his utmost to stage *Der Corregidor* in the coming season. The stress of the ensuing excitement, or perhaps the disappointment of a later change of plan, finally unhinged Wolf's already wrenched reason. He called a meeting of his sympathizers, played them his *Venegas* fragments, told them of his new appointment and his plans for dismissing Mahler and taking over. He was removed under restraint to the asylum of Dr Wilhelm Svetlin. His letters announce grandiose plans for world tours of his own operas with the support of the Weimar theatre. His overheated brain boiled over with insipid music. Some remission ensued and he was discharged on 24 January 1898. He paid inconsequential and disconsolate visits to various resorts and centres (including Semmering, Graz, Cilli and Trieste) accompanied by his sister and the devoted Melanie Köchert. On 6 March he returned to Vienna, to a new home in the Mühlgasse. That summer he stayed with the Köcherts at Traunkirchen. In October he was seized by another gust of madness and tried to drown himself in the Traunsee. He entered the Lower Austrian provincial asylum in Vienna on 4 October 1898. There his sufferings were alleviated by the love and loyalty of Melanie, whose frequent and regular visits continued unflinchingly until the day of his death on 22 February 1903. Then she gave way to remorse and a slow melancholy. On 21 March 1906 she fell to her death from the fourth-floor window of her Vienna home.

Wolf inscribed all his song manuscripts to her, as the one who understood him and his music best of all. She lies in the family grave at Hietzing. He is buried in the Vienna Central Cemetery beside Schubert and Beethoven.

CHAPTER TWO

Works

I Early vocal works

At the beginning of his career, Wolf had little inkling
of his goal. He was even misdirected by his own refrac-
tory temperament and a preoccupation with large-
scale forms. As compensation, his extremes of mood
commanded an analogously wide range of expression,
while his obsession with opera concentrated his mind on
musical techniques of characterization and atmosphere.
Further, his self-willed and poetic nature constrained
him to voice and keyboard rather than to such social or
academic disciplines as chamber music or orchestration.
So his strengths were early if unwittingly bent towards
the compression of large-scale forms and ideas into the
lyric frame. The essences of grand opera, tone poem and
expressive symphony – as exemplified by Wagner, Liszt
and Bruckner, Wolf's three most admired masters – were
to be distilled and concentrated into song.

Not surprisingly, Wolf's early attempts to cultivate
what he later called 'the infertile ground of absolute
music' (*Musikalische Kritiken*, p.50) proved fruitless or
abortive. Even his native ground of musico-poetic expression had to be prepared by deep reading. Goethe
and Heine lyrics led him to their settings in Schubert
and Schumann and thence to a study of expressive techniques in piano music as well as songwriting. Wolf ex-
perimented by crossing all these strains into new hyb-

rids. Thus his Heine setting *Wenn ich in deine Augen seh* (1876) has a piano part derived from a Schubert impromptu, while *Ich stand in dunkeln Träumen* (1878) uses the Brahmsian device of a vocal line related to the piano theme by augmentation or diminution. But the main influence was Schumann. Wolf's early works for piano (sonatas and variations) soon yielded place to Schumannesque genre pieces (*Humoreske*, 1877). At the same time he was composing equally Schumannesque piano songs, that is, a lyric piano solo the melody of which serves as vocal line. This style proved quickly viable, as in *Morgentau* (1877). Yet the influence was sometimes inhibiting. Thus a marginal note on the unfinished manuscript of *Was soll ich sagen?* (1878; a Chamisso text also set by Schumann) reads 'Zu viel Schumannisch; deshalb nicht vollendet'. The essential lesson was soon learnt, by Wolf as by Schumann: the addition of a declamatory vocal line to an independent piano part yields a new stock of expressive device. For example the piano can depict a convivial scene, the protagonist's isolation from which is expressed in the voice part (*Sie haben heut Abend Gesellschaft*, 1878; cf Schumann's *Das ist ein Flöten und Geigen*). The vocal lines themselves are keenly expressive of poetic stress, cadence and significance. From the first Wolf's wordsetting has recitative inflections with touches of cadential pointing and plainsong repetition perhaps not uninfluenced by his background of church school and choir. This thrust towards verbal expressiveness led him to explore choral writing for mixed- or male-voice chorus, accompanied or *a cappella*, at the same time as the earliest songs. Linear independence and significance are sometimes taken to the point of ungrammatical over-

331

lapping (e.g. in *Die Stimme des Kindes*, 1876). There are also deliberate contrasts of texture, for example, of solo with half-chorus (*Grablied*, 1876) or full chorus (*Letzte Bitte* from the *Sechs geistliche Lieder*, 1881, the culmination of Wolf's work in this genre). Here too the basic idea is a quasi-dramatic presentation; voices in three and four parts are used as accompanimental background for a solo voice, again with effects of isolation and contrast. One corollary is that the piano part of a song can be quasi-vocal; and this is another highly original and fertile source of expressive effect. Even the earliest songs (e.g. *Du bist wie eine Blume*, 1876) can show traces of the four-part (almost four-voice) texture that later became a staple style – as acknowledged by Wolf himself; a letter to Melanie Köchert of 7 July 1897 announces the discovery that the piano part of *Führ mich, Kind, nach Bethlehem* is in effect a four-part chorus. This texture too may reflect the early environment of the boy organist; it appears electively in songs of devotion, whether sacred (as in that example) or secular. Another possible influence was Robert Franz, who acknowledged his own indebtedness to the Protestant chorale. Any early imprinting would have been strongly reinforced by the strict grounding in four-part harmony that Wolf received at the Vienna Conservatory, and then by the simultaneous impact of Wagner's operas. Even without Wagner, Wolf's own bold linear independence of melody would have led him to poignant discords, striking modulations and fluctuating tonalities, as well as to effects of counterpoint and canon and other such melodic interplay whether between voice and accompaniment or within the four-part keyboard texture.

At first all these devices tended to be used for their own sake, or for self-expressive purposes. But gradually they served to illustrate and enact a poetic mood. For example in *In der Fremde I* (1881) the contrasting melodic lines in voice and piano enhance the poet's theme of separation, as in some forms of operatic duet. The task of distilling an operatic essence into voice and keyboard was dramatically eased by the techniques of piano reduction used by Karl Klindworth and others, in their vocal scores of Wagner operas. Wolf's own Wagner paraphrases (*c*1880) presage the piano parts of his later songs, both in their part-writing and in their transcription of orchestral effects such as string runs or tremolandos. He could also call upon the melodic and harmonic vocabulary of French or Italian opera, or the popular styles of folksong or student song, all familiar to him from his own early music-making. Further, even the early songs already show abundant evidence of an innate and developing capacity for inventing vivid motivic equivalents for poetic ideas and using them constructionally, in the Schubertian lied tradition, as the building-blocks of the song form.

But these apprenticeship years were far richer in promise and potential than in actual achievement. By Wolf's own stringent but not unjust criteria only a dozen of the 100-odd songs he wrote before 1887 were worth publishing. There is of course much to admire, as in the Reinick and Eichendorff songs of 1882–3; but the early works tend to be fallible both in form (e.g. the overemphatic postlude of *Andenken*) and in content (sometimes obviously derivative). Such flaws can be traced to a failure of objective concern for the poem as such. The outpouring of personal emotion often fails to

333

fit easily into the miniature form. Wolf was more likely to succeed in larger-scale instrumental music, where the link with words, though still vital, was not a criterion of excellence. In this respect too he had much to learn which would later be of service to him as a song-writer.

II Instrumental works

Wolf's instrumental compositions are brilliant concep-tions rather than finished works of art, and hence present difficulties of appreciation, evaluation and per-formance. The first was the D minor Quartet, begun in 1878. Wolf had recently contracted syphilis; his score bears the Faustian epigraph 'Entbehren sollst du, sollst entbehren', which the opening motifs seem to declaim. The Beethoven influence is so manifest (e.g. *Grosse Fuge* in the powerful leaps and dissonance of the histrionic Grave introduction, and the Allegro assai vivace ma serioso of the F minor Quartet op.95 in the Scherzo, marked 'Resolut') and so unusual (it recurs only in the 1888 Mörike song *Der Genesene an die Hoffnung*, sig-nificantly about recovery from mortal sickness) as to suggest that this too is a consciously expressive device. It is as if Beethoven were being deliberately invoked, as another Faustian archetype of the suffering hero. (The claim, now largely discounted, that Beethoven was syph-ilitic would have been a recent talking-point among musicians in Vienna.) Wolf's lyrical slow movement (dated 1880) begins with a Wagnerian symbol of re-demption, an overt homage to the 'pardon' motif in *Tannhäuser*, as if the work were further designed as a pilgrimage through despair by way of faith and fortitude to final recuperation. On that assumption the much lighter

last movement of 1884 with its touches of ironic in-
souciance is musically anticlimactic yet humanly convincing. The music was written as the experience was
lived. By that time Wolf was 24 and had regained his
composure and (as he thought) his health. On this autobiographical interpretation the right order of movements in performance would be the logical time-
sequence: Grave – Leidenschaftlich bewegt; Resolut;
Adagio; and Sehr lebhaft (not, as in earlier editions, with
the second and third movements transposed). Thus considered, this extended and complex work has the unity
and novelty which, as absolute music, it might be held to
lack. On any analysis the genuine (if sporadic) power
and expressiveness of its thematic details are undeniable.

The composition of this quartet overlapped with the
even more ambitious orchestral work *Penthesilea*,
begun in 1883, which also displays, though in differing
proportions, the same admixture of derivation, self-
expression, originality and poetic inspiration. This time
the last of those qualities is paramount, and the music
verges on greatness. There is ample testimony to Wolf's
obsession with Heinrich von Kleist's drama of the
Amazon queen who leads her warrior-maidens to Troy,
becomes enamoured yet jealous of Achilles, and finally
avenges her subjection to him, in both love and war, by
inciting her war-hounds to tear him to shreds. Under the
smooth classical surface of Kleist's blank verse rages an
erotic turbulence. The appeal to subconscious motive
anticipates Freud. Wolf at the time still had reason to be
preoccupied with the idea of male vulnerability to the
traumata of love. His scoring, including four horns, four
trumpets, three trombones, tuba and harp as well as a

full complement of wind, strings and percussion, aims to re-create the epic scale of the conflict as well as the heroic stature of protagonist and antagonist. The music creates panorama (extremes of orchestral pitch and dynamics, with antiphonal trumpets on each side of the orchestra, like battle signals) as well as character, situation and emotion (motifs for the passionate Penthesilea, the noble Achilles, war marches, love-feasts and snarling hounds, interspersed with pleading recitative).

Wolf had given much thought to the structural problems of the tone poem. He ardently admired the symphonic poems of Liszt, who had inspired this work both by personal suggestion and by example. Wolf felt (*Kritiken*, p.52) that unity in this new genre was to be attained by deriving form as well as content from the poetic source. It is not immediately clear how this end is best subserved by Wolf's chosen structure. The two short preludes ('Departure of the Amazons for Troy'; 'Penthesilea's Dream of the Love-festival') presumably depict the dual nature of the heroine, ferocious yet tender; their contrasting motifs derive from the same basic theme. There follows a long final development section ('Conflicts, Passions, Madness and Destruction') in which all the themes are freely metamorphosed, developed and confronted so as to present the elements of the drama both collectively as mood-painting and consecutively as narrative. The work may thus be considered as an opera without words, condensed into an overture. Against the background of Kleist's drama re-enacted in Wolf's imagination the music can appear not only powerful but profound. Otherwise its construction may seem diffuse and even obscure (for example the main theme of the last movement is not heard in its entirety until bar 832), and its instrumentation (as Wolf himself came to acknowledge) not wholly secure. These factors could account for its rejection in both rehearsal and repertory and also help to explain, if not extenuate, the prodigious and unauthorized cuts imposed by its first editors.

Much the same characteristics might have been predicted of Wolf's projected incidental music to Kleist's better-known drama *Prinz Friedrich von Homburg*, where the conflict lies among love, duty and individual self-fulfilment, which again were questions much in Wolf's mind at the time. This music remained fragmentary; but the *Penthesilea* patterns are again discernible in the completed work *Christnacht* for soloists, chorus and orchestra. Here Wolf (as he wrote to Oskar Grohe, 26 February 1891) aimed to symbolize the duality of the Incarnation – innocent child, triumphant hero. Again there may be some element of sub-conscious self-portraiture; little enough of such searching themes can be inferred from Platen's poem about the night of the Nativity, with its chorus of angels and shepherds. Wolf adds a chorus of believers, for good measure. The handling of such large choral and orchestral forces (the latter much the same as for *Penthesilea*, but with the percussion scaled down to timpani only) is rather beyond Wolf's technical competence (again, as he later conceded), despite his natural flair for orchestration; the published score contains revisions by Reger and Foll. The formal structure, however, is clearer than in *Penthesilea* because the words provide the necessary frame of reference. The music is again highly original in conception; and this time the Lisztian or Wagnerian influences are better assimilated. The work is Wolfian in its colourful interweaving of solemnity and simplicity. The latter is effectively symbolized by a traditional carol melody, recalled from a provincial boyhood, which is scored and presented with a lightness of touch that suggests a corresponding lightness of mood. By 1886, when the main thematic material of *Christnacht* was conceived, the sombre canvases of Wolf's creative imagination were being replaced by bright miniatures, beginning with the Intermezzo in E♭ for string quartet. Its main theme had been sketched in 1882 and left to germinate in a sunnier climate of mood. In summer 1886 it grew into a rondo with episodes and varied restatements all so cunningly derived from the main theme as to suggest different aspects of the same characters linked by dialogue or colloquy with a hint of dance-measure. Nothing is known of any literary background, though a verbal source would seem *prima facie* plausible. The effect is of expressive music written to an unknown programme; one clue is Wolf's later reference to his 'Humoristisches Intermezzo'. A comparison with his contemporary songwriting suggests Mörike as a possible source for this slight but spirited and engaging piece.

The next instrumental work, also for string quartet, was the Serenade in G (later called by Wolf 'an Italian Serenade'; letter to Kauffmann of 2 April 1892). With this work Wolf at last attained expressive if not formal mastery. As with the Intermezzo, there is no avowed literary source. But the *Italienische Serenade* (2–4 May 1887) was composed during a phase of Eichendorff settings (7 March–24 May). It is thematically related to the first of them, *Der Soldat I*, about love for a lady who lives in a castle. The Eichendorff novella *Aus dem*

Leben eines Taugenichts has that same theme; central to its plot is an Italian serenade. The novella contains a lyric (*Heimweh*) which Wolf had certainly set by the following year, and perhaps sketched at this time. Its hero is a young musician, a violinist, who leaves his country home and his grumbling father, to seek his fortune. He soon charms everyone with his gifts, or antagonizes them with his inconsequence. Wolf could hardly have found a more congenial or compelling self-portrait in all German literature. The novella also contains a serenade played by a small orchestra, for which Wolf later arranged his work. The original string quartet however is preferable in the transparent lightness and delicacy of its texture; and though it is not without technical problems (e.g. of ensemble at the required tempo) the string writing is far more relaxed and assured than in the early D minor Quartet. The Serenade too, like the other instrumental works, is novel in both content and form. Its rather diffusely episodic rondo structure with ironic quasi-recitative passages gently parodying romantic love, again in conformity with the Eichendorff style, suggests an unspecified programme. Again there is a strong sense of motivic writing deliberately presented and developed so as to suggest character (the dominance of the solo violin), speech (the recitative passages), colloquy (the duetting melodies), scene-painting (the conspiratorial assembling and tuning in the prelude), gesture (the sweeping fiddle flourishes) and instrumentation (the thrumming guitar imitations). It may not be coincidence that Wolf's own description (to Oskar Grohe, 28 June 1890) of the kind of opera he would one day wish to write (the strumming of guitars, sighs of love, moonlit nights, champagne banquets) is closely paralleled in Eichendorff's *Aus dem Leben eines Taugenichts* (chap.8). This in turn may account for Wolf's ten-year preoccupation with the arrangement and development of his *Italienische Serenade* music, in close parallel to his preoccupation with opera.

In 1887 this dramatic lyricism brings Wolf's music in the Serenade and the Eichendorff settings on to a new and high plateau close to the summit of songwriting. The upward thrust may have two sources of impetus. First, the music seems to derive directly from words and ideas without any serious subjective intervention. Second (and perhaps the point is related), Wolf's two basic creative moods merge into a balanced integration. They may be described as gravity and levity or (as in *Christnacht*) sublimity and naivety; their tutelary deities are Wagner and Schumann. The early songs had tended to one extreme or the other, sombre or sparkling (compare *Ein Grab* with *Mädchen mit dem roten Mündchen*, both 1876, or *Zur Ruh, zur Ruh!*, 1883, with *Mausfallensprüchlein*, 1882). A similar dichotomy is discernible in the instrumental music where the contrasts of mood are linked by monothematic techniques which later appear in the songs. The polarities are separately exemplified in *Wo wird einst* and *Gesellenlied*, both written on 24 January 1888. Thus these two strong currents converge only three weeks before the Mörike song outburst.

III Mature songs

The outstanding quality of Wolf's Mörike songs was their originality. All the contemporary critiques had the word 'new' in their titles – new springtime, new life, new songs. Wolf himself wrote of the novel aspects of his musical language. Yet he did not define them; and the evidence suggests that their essential originality was not wholly grasped, perhaps not even by their creator, much of whose songwriting is manifestly in the main lied tradition. He and his audiences felt that he was continuing the line of Schubert and Schumann, without radical departure. Wolf himself thought it worth pointing out (letter to Emil Kauffmann, 21 May 1890) that even his boldest harmonies were justifiable by reference to accepted theory. Much of his mature work uses folk or popular song. His well-known solicitude for the choice and treatment of words is by no means invariable and in any event represents a difference of degree rather than kind from the practice of his predecessors. Well over half his texts have no pretension to poetic greatness or even excellence. Even the rest can be treated cavalierly: thus the accentuation can go astray (e.g. 'Leib*röss*lein' in *Der Gärtner*) and the subtler declamatory effects are quite often second thoughts inserted at proof stage. *Er ist's* has repeated phrases and *Das verlassene Mägdlein* uses an unauthentic text, no doubt under the influence of Schumann in both instances. On occasion Wolf could repeat a whole strophe without textual justification (*Benedeit die sel'ge Mutter*) or tacitly omit one (*Geh, Geliebter, geh jetzt*). He could embellish his texts with his own insertions or inventions (*Die Zigeunerin*) or simply mistranscribe them (there are several textual errors in the manuscripts or even in the first editions). He could deliberately add a new meaning unintended by the poet (*Wer rief dich denn?*). Even his practice of calling his songbooks 'Gedichte von' Eichendorff, Mörike or Goethe was anticipated and perhaps prompted by Schumann. The same applies to his choice of translations, for example, from the Spanish. Finally Wolf's notable spontaneity of composition was hardly different in kind from that of, say, Schubert in 1815 and Schumann in 1840. All three composers no doubt planned and sketched beforehand and revised afterwards.

Nevertheless Wolf was original, and in four main ways. First, he seems to have planned in advance the contents of each volume (e.g. the Spanish songbook: letter of 12 November 1889 to his sister Käthe), rather as if the artistic unity is not the poem as such but the songbook considered as representative of the poet or source. Secondly, it was his practice to preface a performance of each song by a recital of the text: the words were separately acknowledged as a vital part of the artwork's content as well as its form. Thirdly, Wolf was reluctant to set a poem which he considered had already been successfully composed – a view which presupposes that a musical setting is more like a translation or objective critique than a personal commentary. His songbooks are thus perhaps designed as anthologies, as homage, and also as critiques or translations. They make no sense, have no being, apart from the text which has breathed its life and essence into the music. Fourthly, this essence is dramatic.

It follows that Wolf's art is a means of framing, embodying, presenting, enacting, the life of words. As a corollary, the piano has a more important role than with previous songwriters; and melody does not necessarily predominate. It is in this sense that Wolf compressed Wagnerian music drama, leitmotif, orchestra and declamation into voice and keyboard. Perhaps it was this feeling of historical mission that led to his lifelong

25. Opening of the autograph sketch for Wolf's 'Mignon' ('Kennst du das Land'), completed 17 December 1888

obsession with large-scale composition even though the appropriate forms and techniques were among his own acknowledged weaknesses. He even felt himself stifled by Wagner – with whom he was never in serious contention. He began to resent the title of songwriter. At the very moment when his true genius was first revealed to himself and the world he could still write (letter to Strasser, 28 March 1888): 'For the moment they are admittedly only songs'. On the very day when that inspiration had at last begun, he could still be preoccupied (to Lang, 22 February 1888) with extemporizing a comic opera at the keyboard. Even with three great songbooks completed he could still lament (to Grohe, 1 June 1891) 'I'm beginning to think that I have reached the end of my life. I can't go on writing songs for another 30 years'. Next (again to Grohe, 12 October 1891) comes the astoundingly anguished cry 'I really and truly shudder at the thought of my songs. The flattering recognition as "songwriter" disturbs me down to the very depths of my soul. What does it signify but the reproach that songs are all I ever write, that I am master of what is only a small-scale genre?' Finally Wolf's eventual madness took the form of, and was probably provoked by, a megalomaniac obsession with operatic composition and performance.

There are perhaps three main reasons for this fixation. Songs were still generally held to be an inferior art form; Wolf as an expressive composer craved the maximal audiences attainable only through opera and symphony; his genius was in fact for dramatic music, though in a condensed form. No wonder he aggregated his songs into composite volumes comprehensive enough to yield extended recitals and programmes of

344

planned contrasts, with at least a potential appeal to a mass audience. Further, each major songbook contains linking motifs designed to relate the single songs to a larger conceptual scheme, as with Eichendorff songs 9–10, Mörike songs 2–3, Goethe songs 39–40, Spanish sacred songs 8–10, Italian songs 42–3.

The songbook is thus itself the large-scale dramatic form. With the 20 Eichendorff songs (mentioned first because nearly half of them were written before 1888) Wolf lifted the curtain on his singing theatre of the imagination. There everything is made of music – construction, action, character, plot and sub-plot, narrative, gesture, mime, dance and song, costume, scenery, and even stage properties and effects, including lighting. Piano preludes set the scene or delineate character. The songs are conceived as *tableaux vivants* viewed through the proscenium arch of the song form. As Wolf told Emil Kauffmann, he always imagined a background to each of his songs, and the examples he gave (the goddess sitting on a reef in the moonlight, playing her harp, in *Gesang Weylas*; a chorus of wise men joining in the refrain of *Cophtisches Lied I*) go well beyond anything described in the text. So his submission to poetry was far from slavish. Yet the verse does in fact give each song a formal framework which the instrumental music is sometimes felt to lack. In a sense therefore Wolf's structural sense has certain defects which the poetry is called upon to redress. On the other hand the musical response is so varied and flexible that Wolf might as justly be hailed as a master of form. The poems are more often strophic than their settings, which strive towards free evolution and development. Even in strophic song, unchanged repetition is rare; more typically the melody, for example, is varied to highlight a particular word, such as 'süsser' in *Um Mitternacht*. Unity is usually attained by the main factor common to music and poetry, namely rhythm. This may reflect either the metre or the theme of the poem: thus in *Jägerlied* the rare trochaic pentameter appears as 5/4 time, while in *Fussreise* the piano maintains a steady walking rhythm.

A repeated rhythmic figure may suggest an obsessive character or gesture (*Rat einer Alten*; *Mühvoll komm ich und beladen*) while changes of basic rhythm serve to imply (as it were by modulation) a change of mood or meaning (*Agnes*; *Grenzen der Menschheit*). A piano melody or figuration may suggest words by its rhythmic shape (postlude to *Komm, Liebchen, komm!*). Regular piano rhythms can provide a patterned lattice for vocal melodies to curve and stray around, anticipating certain words or syllables, lingering over others, with the effect of a written-out rubato (e.g. 'stumm' or 'heilig' in *An die Geliebte*), whether, as there, to enhance the poetic meaning or, as often in the Italian songs, to create a new one. Occasionally too Wolf would prolong a word that especially pleased him (e.g. 'geflügelt' in *Die ihr schwebet*). Such devices are to be distinguished from their operatic or Wagnerian counterparts. The Wolfian vocal line conveys a current of poetic feeling, deriving character from verbal inflection and not vice versa. His melodies vary from complex nuance to straightforward singability in folk or popular style, as the context requires. The counterpoints of voice against piano, already noted in the earlier songs, are greatly developed from 1888 onwards. A typical example is *Lied eines Verliebten*, where the isolated left-hand melody is a symbol of separation. This image is further intensified in such songs as *Mein*

Liebster singt am Haus, where the independence of the piano part embodies the excluded lover. Thus Wolf could create not only décor (by distinguishing foreground from background) but also dramatic irony (by presenting two different levels of involvement simultaneously, as in *Bei einer Trauung*). Autonomy in the piano part also permits a quasi-symphonic motivic development reflecting the changing moods of a poem (*Auf einer Wanderung; Im Frühling*). Piano interludes can link contrasting sections of a song and so suggest continuous action, whether in narrative or ballad forms (*Ritter Kurts Brautfahrt*) or, more rarely, in lyric modes (e.g. in *Fussreise*, where a modulating piano interlude leads back to the original theme).

Similarly Wolf's harmonic usages are attuned to his texts, whether as single words or whole poems. An example of the former is at 'froh und traurig' in *Alles endet, was entstehet*, where a major and a minor inflection speak respectively of joy and sorrow. Again, augmented 5ths mean increasing intensity (*Das verlassene Mägdlein*) even to the point of parody (*Nimmersatte Liebe*), while second inversions at cadence points give an impression of peroration ('da bin' in *Wohl denk ich oft*). But such short-range or local effects are comparatively rare. More generally, Wolf's harmonic procedures provide a framework isomorphic with that of the poem, within which particular aspects can be highlighted; for example, successive mediant modulations convey the idea of increasing lightness, as in *In der Frühe* and *Morgenstimmung*. This is the sense in which it was important for Wolf that his harmonic language should remain, as he said, traditional. He needed chromaticism and dissonance in order to create new expressive intensity. At the same time the constraints of his song form require such effects to be readily relatable (whether in terms of affinity or contrast) to some recognizable tonal centre. Thus the modal harmony of *Auf ein altes Bild* sets that song apart from the rest of the Mörike volume and from contemporary music generally; the music is as it were seen, like the poem, through a haze of time. Within that song, the single acute dissonance at 'Kreuzes Stamm' throws that phrase into high relief, again in parallel with the poetry. Conversely, chromatics or dissonance can be relieved by touches of diatonic harmony (as in *Mir ward gesagt*, among many examples) yielding effects of relaxation from tension, or simplicity within complexity. More specifically, the introduction or recurrence of the tonic major can be delayed, so that its eventual arrival brings a sensation of repose and fulfilment (*Wir haben beide lange Zeit geschwiegen*); or the major form of a minor tonic can restate an idea in a brighter mode (*Ob der Koran von Ewigkeit sei?*). Such contrasts and juxtapositions are the essence of Wolf's songwriting, as of his mentor Schumann's. Among the corollaries are personal verbal associations with certain keys. Thus in Wolf extreme flat or sharp keys express nervous tension, in contrast with the bluff plainness of C major (*Gesellenlied*); A major suggests springtime (*Frühling übers Jahr*), and so on. Of course there are exceptions; but such associations, usual in all songwriting, are especially manifest and significant in Wolf, and a study of them is relevant to interpretation and performance (for example, the desirability of transposition).

Such effects shade into overt musical depiction, at which Wolf was also adept. Examples abound, ranging from imaginative embroidery to frank onomatopoeia. Widely spaced chords suggest hollowness and reverberation (*Der Feuerreiter*); upward chromatic runs and bare 5ths convey disappearance into thin air (*Der Rattenfänger*); glissandos and other flourishes depict extravagant gesture (*Der Schreckenberger*); acciaccaturas mean laughter (*Rat einer Alten*). There is a lute in *Nachruf*, a harp in *Gesang Weylas*, a violin in *Wie lange schon*, a guitar in the Spanish and serenading songs. One hears a spinning-wheel in *Die Spinnerin*, gunfire in *Unfall* or *Der Jäger*, a carillon in *Zum neuen Jahre* or *St Nepomuks Vorabend*, whips in *Gesellenlied* and *Selbstgeständnis*, a donkey's bray in *Lied des transferierten Zettel*, birdsong in *Das Vöglein*, bees in *Der Knabe und das Immlein*, horses' hooves in *Der Gärtner* and perhaps *Auf einer Wanderung*, and so on.

In all this a major share of expression inevitably falls to the pianist, not only in the ballad tradition of pictorial interludes, in which Wolf was no doubt influenced by Loewe, but also in the newer vein of grandiloquent quasi-orchestral device found in Wagner transcriptions. The piano equivalents of string tremolandos express a pulsating intensity or a rapport with the moods of Nature (the thunder in *Prometheus* or *Der Jäger*). In general the upper reaches of the piano symbolize lofty thoughts, spiritual aspirations, the starry sky (*An die Geliebte*), while the low notes of the left hand sound out the depths of darkness or despair (*Neue Liebe*). Such symbolism is in the lied tradition of Schubert. Wolf's allusions are further enriched by directly Wagnerian resonances, sometimes deliberate (the affectionate allusions to *Die Meistersinger* in *Gesellenlied*), sometimes perhaps less so. An example of the latter is *Die Geister am Mummelsee*, where the poem speaks of a funeral procession ('Totengeleit'); and the piano part is evocative of the cortège of Titurel ('Geleiten wir') in *Parsifal*. But far more characteristic and ubiquitous is the new-minted motif, again usually entrusted to the piano part, which serves both to express a poetic idea (e.g. sadness, love, isolation, mystery, freedom, sleep, among many others) and to create musical structure.

Examples are manifold; none is wholly typical; each belongs inseparably to its context. The following illustration exemplifies not only the Wolfian motif but also perhaps a connection between his creative inspiration and his personal experience. For many years he suffered from insomnia; and poetry about solitary wakefulness and movement at night evoked a definable though varied musical response. A repeated figuration in the piano right hand is underlined by a left-hand theme in single notes. This motif first appears in the Körner *Ständchen* of 1877. The opening words describe the silence of the night; lovers' thoughts alone are awake. At the following idea of being surrounded by nocturnal phantoms ('mich umschleichen . . . nächtliche Gespenster') the left-hand single notes surround the repeated right-hand chords, on both sides. In the 1888 song *Auf eine Christblume I*, Mörike's description of deer grazing at twilight evokes the analogue shown in ex.1. The same music, decorated and transposed an octave higher, later depicts the activities of an elf at midnight. In *Gutmann und Gutweib* this motivic idea recurs at the words 'Im Bette liegen beide nun'. The old folk are lying in bed, deliberately keeping awake. In *Lied eines Verliebten* the whole song is about staying awake at night; the entire piano part assumes the basic shape described. The same is true of *Alle gingen,*

Ex.1 *Auf eine Christblume I* (Mörike)

Herz, zur Ruh. The association persists in Act 2 of *Der Corregidor* (1895) as Frasquita keeps her nocturnal vigil (scene iii) or as Manuela gropes her way in the dark (scene x). The same Gestalt underlies each example. By such means (characteristic of the lied) Wolf could express a wide-ranging diversity of mood, scene and character. Human feeling is symbolized either directly or through images of external nature (the so-called 'pathetic fallacy').

This is also the essence of Wolf's first source of inspiration, Eichendorff, whose works contain all the necessary elements of scenes and characters (soldiers, sailors, students, musicians) with their good or bad humour or fortune and their happy or unhappy loves, whether for God, man, nature or fatherland. Wolf's

351

selection from these texts is, perhaps intentionally, more broadly representative than the nature- or love-poems already set by Schumann. A further constraint was Wolf's determination not to use poems which had already, in his view, been definitively set to music. Mörike's complex quasi-symbolic style and imagery needed a correspondingly advanced musical language; so Wolf's settings had few precedents and no rivals. His choice was accordingly unfettered; but again it concentrated on themes of people and places conceived as actors and scenes. The difference is one of degree: Mörike's characters and landscapes are drawn with far more depth and definition than Eichendorff's (whose art Wolf later came to regard as somewhat superficial; cf his letter to Kauffmann of 7 March 1894). In particular the themes of humour, both broad and sophisticated, and the supernatural, whether in the context of orthodox religion or of fairy tale and folklore, are far more fully developed in the Mörike songs. The music is correspondingly more intense and diversified, for example with evocations of folksong (*Das verlassene Mägdlein*) and other popular strains (student song in *Nimmersatte Liebe*; Viennese waltz in *Abschied*). Styles and forms are more ambitious and panoramic, with Wagnerian as well as Schumannesque components, especially in religious songs (*Karwoche*; *Wo find ich Trost*). Some of the piano accompaniments seem orchestral in range and scope (*Neue Liebe*; *Der Feuerreiter*). Elsewhere, themes and structures are designed to convey a sense of movement through vistas both spatial (*Auf einer Wanderung*) and temporal (*In der Frühe*).

This sense of extended musical frontiers and horizons

26. Autograph MS of the opening of the second orchestral version of Wolf's 'Anakreons Grab' ('Wo die Rose blüht'), dated 13 November 1893

is even more manifest in the Goethe settings. The lyric style is just as intense (*Blumengruss*; *Gleich und Gleich*); but the ballad style has become more diffuse (*Ritter Kurts Brautfahrt*) and the piano writing even grander in conception (*Prometheus*; *Mignon*: 'Kennst du das Land'). Further, Goethe's poem offers a new rich source of quasi-dramatic background and effect. Both Eichendorff and Mörike had incorporated their lyrics into their novels; Wolf set several such examples. But these poems are separable entities, whereas the interspersed lyrics in Goethe's *Wilhelm Meister* are integrally related to plot and character, so that Wolf's music designedly sets context as well as text. Much the same is true of the *Westöstlicher Divan* poems. The characters of Hatem and Suleika are not merely costume parts assumed by the poet and his mistress; they also inhabit a whole secondary world, a notional orient peopled with other characters from cupbearers to sultans. From that world it is no great journey to the Spanish songbook, which not only contains fine poetry (e.g. by Cervantes, Lope de Vega and Camoens) in skilled translation (by Heyse and Geibel) but also offers the elements of national character and local colour that Wolf increasingly needed for his musico-dramatic projections.

In consequence his own musical style is again in transition. Wolf had now exhausted German poetry of the necessary quality and quantity, and the translations to which he turned were no longer, despite their technical excellence, the source of direct verbal inspiration. With the Spanish songbook, therefore, it is not the lyric as such but its substructure of ideas and concepts that serves as the foundation for musical setting. The result (already foreshadowed by some of the *Westöstlicher*

Divan songs, such as *Was in der Schenke waren heute*)
was a new autonomy for the composer, who now
became less dependent on an intuitive response to
poetry. Wolf the partial poet was gradually supplanted
by Wolf the complete musician. Rhythmical motifs,
dance patterns, accompaniment figures, recurrent
refrains, formal structures, begin to dominate the
musical expression. Folk music, nature studies,
humorous songs, ballads, all disappear. The themes and
styles that persist in the Spanish volume are the
religious (the first ten songs) and the erotic (almost all
the rest); and these become more personal and more
intense.

The six Keller songs of 1890 revert to the earlier
themes of character study and psychology, with occasional symbolic allusions to nature (as in *Wandl ich in
dem Morgentau*): here, as before, poetry is the main
source of inspiration. But in these songs Wolf was working against the grain of his own development, which
may account for the sometimes perceptible effort
entailed in their composition. With the Italian songbook,
begun at the end of the same year, the established trend
was resumed with increasing momentum. All the lyrics
are anonymous; all have the same translator, Paul
Heyse (as compared with only about two thirds of the
Spanish songbook, in each respect). Wolf was now confronted with a polished and uniform poetic style with
no creative personality of its own; the lyrics were thus
a blank page on which to inscribe his own knowledge of human feeling. There are no religious themes
as such; all the poems are in some sense love-songs. In
consequence the style becomes totally unified and integral. Previous songbooks had contained the separately

identifiable strains described above as Wagnerian and Schumannesque. This still applies in part to the Spanish volume (thus *Bedeckt mich mit Blumen* is Tristanesque, while the lighter songs, as well as the textual source as a whole, recall Schumann's Spanish vein). In the Italian songs all such sources merge into Wolf's basic four-part style. The forms are further concentrated by the brevity and metrical pattern of the lyrics. Here Wolf finally succeeded in compressing the universal picture into the miniature frame; so these songs are the epitome of his art.

Wolf may well have sketched in 1890 many more of them than he then completed. The Italian settings of 1896 maintain the same style; perhaps not all were newly composed in that year. The manuscripts of two of them, *Gesegnet sei das Grün* and *O wär dein Haus durchsichtig*, bear the marginal annotations 'Phönix no.1' and 'Phönix no.2' respectively, suggesting that these at least were new inspirations. Other late songs however seem lacking in fresh invention. Thus the Michelangelo songs of 1897, though they contain much fine music, are in part palpably indebted to earlier songs (compare for example the postlude of *Fühlt meine Seele* with those of *Peregrina I* and *II*); texts and treatment alike suggest that despite the ostensible character-drawing Wolf was reverting to the self-expressive subjectivism of his early songs. His mental breakdown and terminal illness (1897–1903) were only six months away.

Wolf completed some 20 separate song orchestrations as well as two for incorporation in *Der Corregidor*. The form is intermediate between what might be called the compressed opera of his songbooks and the expanded songbooks of his operas. The hybrid

356

27. Autograph MS of the opening of the third song ('*Fühlt meine Seele*') of Wolf's '*Drei Gedichte von Michelangelo*', dated 22–8 March 1897

has not proved fertile: the works are rarely performed. Yet Wolf himself thought them important; and most of them date from 1890, one of his most prolific songwriting years. Their purpose was not only to reach a wider public but also to deploy even greater expressive power and device, whether to broaden the scene-painting (e.g. the thunder and lightning effects in *Prometheus*) or to brighten the sound-painting (e.g. the chromatic runs in *Der Rattenfänger*). But Wolf also invoked the orchestra for depth of feeling. Thus even the tiny but intense lyric by Lenau, *Scheideblick* (?1876–7), was sketched in an orchestral version. Similarly *Gesang Weylas* remains lyrical in conception even when scored: its added horn counterpoints aim at enhanced intensity. But in general Wolf's aim was to convert his miniatures into oil paintings suitable for wider exhibition, whether in the concert hall or (in his own works) the opera house. The transition is perhaps most convincing in static tableaux such as *Prometheus* or *Auf ein altes Bild*. Where motion is to be depicted, the heavier textures tend to slow down the action: thus in *Der Feuerreiter* the articulation of added voices both choral and orchestral, at the required speed, presents grave problems of ensemble. Similarly the grace and fire of the *Italienische Serenade* are harder to achieve in the orchestral version.

IV Stage music

Analogous difficulties to those that are found in the orchestral works are inherent in Wolf's music for the stage. The brilliant pictorial writing of his first completed work of incidental music, the *Elfenlied* (a setting of 'You spotted snakes' from *A Midsummer Night's Dream* in German translation), aroused acclaim at its first performance, about which Wolf wrote (to Kauffmann, 11 January 1894) that the orchestration 'so glittered and glowed in moonbeams that you could forget to hear for sheer seeing'. The Ibsen play *The Feast at Solhaug* (again in German translation, as *Das Fest auf Solhaug*) presented fewer opportunities for quasi-visual effects, and the music was commissioned in an otherwise fallow phase; but the processional entrances and choruses are typically evocative. Whatever the quality of Wolf's invention, his stage music, like his song orchestrations, suggests the deliberate extension or enlargement of a smaller-scale original inspiration.

The operas are no different. As Wolf told Potpeschnigg (9 July 1895) the piano score as it stood served as the orchestral sketch for *Der Corregidor*. Further, the Wagnerian texture and scoring (Wolf's orchestra is larger than that of *Die Meistersinger*, without which, as he wrote to Rosa Mayreder on 1 June 1895, his *Corregidor* music could not have been written) are possibly too inspissated for the sunny mood and milieu of the well-known story *El sombrero de tres picos*. Wolf told Ferdinand Löwe that Bizet's task in *Carmen* was far easier because of the comparative lack of orchestral polyphony; and perhaps a lighter texture would have worn better. In Wolf's treatment, the three-cornered hat is not only a symbol of universal authority but also has overtones of the eternal triangle (for instance when the power of the Corregidor's motif is heard dominating that of the supposedly cuckolded Tio Lukas). Wolf's well-documented obsession with themes of sexual jealousy and tension, which darken to stark tragedy in *Manuel Venegas*, may well have been highly personal in origin. The motivic techniques of *Der*

359

Corregidor seem to reflect that obsession in their insistent repetition. The Wolfian lied motif inevitably becomes obtrusive when used as a Wagnerian leitmotif, serving narrative and dramatic ends as well as the lyric purposes for which it was designed. Thus the five-note Tio Lukas theme is heard nearly 100 times in Act 1, serving variously as character study, stage direction, cross-reference or general background. It is relevant that Wolf himself in rehearsal took little interest in stagecraft or décor: even in the operas, his musical world remains that of inward imagination rather than visual presentation. It is thus not surprising that the dramatic structure of *Der Corregidor* has been much criticized, and with some plausibility: for example most of Act 4 is recapitulation of themes and events already familiar. Nor is the musical material always of the finest, perhaps partly by design (e.g. the Alcalde's banal motif may be intended as character-drawing), partly because not all the libretto was equally inspiring, and partly because of Wolf's deteriorating health.

Such objections have far more force when levelled at the 600-bar fragment of *Manuel Venegas* than at the completed *Der Corregidor*. But the latter is rarely performed, and has never belonged to the standard opera repertory. It has been excluded because of disparity rather than inferiority; and it might more rationally be regarded as a success in a new genre than as a failure in an old one. Thus the often striking discrepancy (to which Frank Walker has drawn attention) between the characters as embodied in the music and as observed on the stage becomes both meaningful and effective when considered as a Wolfian equivalent for dramatic irony. The musical style too is novel. As always it derives from the German text, and is hence less complex and intense than the generality of Wolf's songwriting. The prototypes are the two songs orchestrated specially for inclusion (*In dem Schatten meiner Locken*; *Herz, verzage nicht geschwind*) in a sweetened but refreshing dilution of the lighter Spanish songbook essence. Whatever the defects of dramatic structure, each separate scene has a songlike vividness of invention.

There are thus grounds for supposing that Wolf, had he lived, might have evolved new forms intermediate between song and opera. Both his operas are based on short stories; he could profitably have continued his exploration of Eichendorff, Mörike and Goethe by quasi-dramatic presentations of their novellas for voices with piano solo or duet or with chamber orchestra; *Der Corregidor* too might prove viable in such a guise. Conversely, Wolf might have extended his Spanish or Italian songs on similar lines, benefiting from the example already set by Schumann (e.g. in his op.138). Alternatively Wolf might have returned to songbooks inspired by the dramatic or plastic qualities of original German poetry (by Rilke for example), although in the light of Wolf's known views and traceable development this seems less plausible.

V Critical writings
In the role of music critic, Wolf shared with his contemporary Bernard Shaw the deliberately provocative and partisan stance of the standard-bearer. Both were notoriously fervent advocates of Wagner and browbeaters of Brahms; both have lasting value as the spokesmen and interpreters of their own musical times and trends. Prose was not a creative medium for Wolf,

and he resisted republication of his reviews on the ground of their stylistic shortcomings. But his writing has enough of the trenchancy and immediacy of his music to render it readable and often memorable, affording further insights, both for him and his readers, into the nature of his art. First, regular reviewing and concert-going gave him much-needed discipline and experience, as well as a new understanding of the nature of language and its relation to music, including his own. His critiques reveal *inter alia* his own attitudes and criteria. Style and content alike are indebted to Schumann, whose conception of music as mood- or scene-painting ('Seelengemälde' or 'Tongemälde') Wolf wholeheartedly endorsed and adopted. Wolf envisaged music as essentially a transitive mode of expression using symbolic equivalents for human thought and feeling, whether directly or as reflected in external nature. Both these latter aspects unite in Wolf's intuitive depiction of music in terms of organic life and growth. For him, absolute music was a waste ground choked with academic works like weeds. He hated any hint of the cerebral or the contrived (as in fugues and pedal points). Bodily malfunction or discomfort are recurrent metaphors for musical unacceptability. The following (on Brahms's First Piano Concerto) is typical – 'The air that blows through this composition is so icy, dank and foggy that it could easily freeze your heart up and snatch your breath away; you could catch a cold from it. Unhealthy stuff!' Good music, however (including some by Brahms, such as the G major Sextet), is as regularly compared with nature, springtime, fresh founts of healing and many another such symbol of wholesome emotive life.

362

Further detailed criteria are inferable from other *obiter dicta*. Wolf had a deep sense of commitment to his own time and place, his own society, class and nationhood (German rather than Austrian). He manifested a passionate concern for human values, as vested not only in individuals but in the whole nexus of social function and interrelation. The musical equivalent is opera, especially Wagner and Mozart. Wolf's criticism fastens on all aspects of stage spectacle and presentation considered as parts of the total musical artwork – action, costume, gesture, speech and stage-effects. Every page testifies to the visualizing and dramatizing mind at work in his own songwriting, in a ceaseless quest for vividness and immediacy of effect. His ancillary absorption in language is evidenced by his unselfconscious recourse to metaphor and quotation from modern and classical literature. Finally Wolf's critical insight into his own expressive mode of music is predictably penetrative; thus he noted (*Kritiken*, p.52) that the forms and contents of the greatest symphonic poems (those of Liszt, in this context) are, no less than their thematic material, derived from the literary works that inspired them.

That *aperçu* defines Wolf's own achievement. It was his mission as he saw it to compose in a new musical language expressing the closest imaginable relation to words and their gamut of visual, auditory or other symbolism. In this endeavour his declared aim was truth to life; as he wrote to Emil Kauffmann (5 June 1890) 'For me the sovereign principle in art is rigorous, harsh and inexorable truth, truth to the point of cruelty'. Here is the link between his four years as a critic and his lifetime as an artist. He expressed the truth about the human condition as he apprehended it, as keenly and as stringently as he could. It was his assigned task (letter to Schmid, 14 June 1891) to cultivate that gift to the furthest limit of his powers. When he could no longer compose, as he told Rosa Mayreder, he was fit only for the dung-heap.

His sense of purpose and mission gave Wolf's life and art their fierce concentration, their characteristic burning intensity of expression. His vision was limited by its close focus on those points where words and music intersect or coincide. But within that specialized lyric field he has claims not only to greatness but to supremacy.

WORKS

Editions: *H. Wolf: Sämtliche Werke*, ed. H. Jancik and others (Vienna, 1960–) [WW]
H. Wolf: Lieder aus der Jugendzeit, ed. F. Foll (Leipzig, 1903) [LJ]
H. Wolf: Nachgelassene Werke, ed. R. Haas and H. Schultz (Leipzig and Vienna, 1936) [NW]
Numbers in the right-hand column denote references in the text.

SONGS: UNPUBLISHED OR POSTHUMOUSLY PUBLISHED
(including orchestral and/or choral arrangements; incipit given if different from title)

No.	Title	Incipit	Text	Key	Composed	Publication or MS
1	Das taube Mütterlein, frag.				c1875	lost
2	Soldatenlied, frag.				c1875	lost
3	Der Morgen, frag.				c1875	lost
4	Die Sterne, voice part only				c1875	lost
5	Gebet, voice part only	Leise, leise	F. Kind	B♭	c1875	lost
6	untitled duet, S, Bar, inc.	Du wirst ja blass			c1875	*A-Wst*
7	Nacht und Grab, op.3 no.1	Sei mir gegrüsst	H. Zschokke	c	1875	WW vii/3
8	Sehnsucht, op.3 no.2	Was zieht mir das Herz so	Goethe	E	1875	WW vii/3
9	Der Fischer, op.3 no.3	Das Wasser rauscht	Goethe	c	1875	WW vii/3
10	Wanderlied, op.3 no.4	Von dem Berge zu den Hügeln	Goethe	G	1875	WW vii/3
	arr. chorus, op.4 no.1				1875	lost
11	Auf dem See, op.3 no.5	Und frische Nahrung	Goethe	A	1875	*Wst*
	arr. chorus, op.4 no.2				1875	Alto in *Deutsche Nachrichten* (Zagreb, 23 March 1940)
12	Der Raubschütz, op.5, inc.	Der alte Müller Jakob	N. Lenau	c	1875–24 June 1876	*Wst*
13	Frühlingsgrüsse, op.6, 2 versions, 1st inc.	Nach langem Frost	Lenau	G/E	3 Jan 1876	WW vii/3
14	Meeresstille, op.9 no.1	Sturm mit seinen Donnerschlägen	Lenau	e	Jan 1876	WW vii/3
15	Liebesfrühling, op.9 no.2	Ich sah den Lenz einmal	Lenau	G	29 Jan 1876	WW vii/3
16	Erster Verlust, op.9 no.3	Ach, wer bringt	Goethe	E♭	30 Jan 1876	WW vii/3
17	Abendglöcklein, op.9 no.4	Des Glöckleins Schall	V. Zusner	c♯	18 March–24 April 1876	WW vii/3
18	Mai, op.9 no.5, 2 inc. versions	Leichte Silberwolken schweben	Goethe	F	25 April–1 May 1876	*Wst*
19	Der goldene Morgen, op.9 no.6	Golden lacht und glüht		B	1 May 1876	WW vii/3
20	Perlenfischer	Du liebes Auge	O. Roquette	A♭	3 May 1876	WW vii/3
21	Mailied, inc.	Willkommen, lieber schöner Mai	L. C. H. Hölty	F	13 June 1876	*Wst*

No.	Title	Incipit	Text	Key	Composed	Publication or MS	
22	Stille Sicherheit	Horch, wie still es wird	Lenau	d/F	cDec 1876	WW vii/3	
23	Scheideblick orch version, frag.	Als ein unergründlich Wonnemeer	Lenau	g	cDec 1876 c1877	WW vii/3	358
24	Ein Grab	Wenn des Mondes bleiches Licht	P. Peitl	g	8-10 Dec 1876	NW i, WW vii/2	340
25	Mädchen mit dem roten Mündchen		H. Heine	F	17 Dec 1876	NW ii, WW vii/2	340
26	Du bist wie eine Blume		Heine	Eb	18 Dec 1876	NW ii, WW vii/2	332
27	Wenn ich in deine Augen seh		Heine	Bb	21 Dec 1876	NW ii, WW vii/2	331
28	Bescheidene Liebe	Ich bin wie andre Mädchen nicht		G	?1876-7	LJ	
29	Abendbilder	Friedlicher Abend	Lenau	Db	4 Jan-24 Feb 1877	NW ii, WW vii/2	350
30	Ständchen	Alles wiegt die stille Nacht	T. Körner	F	5 March-12 April 1877	NW i, WW vii/2	
31	Andenken	Ich denke dein	F. von Matthisson	E	23-5 April 1877	NW i, WW vii/2	333
32	An*	O wag es nicht	Lenau	d	27 April-8 May 1877	LJ	
33	Wanderlied	Es segeln die Wolken	anon.	G	14-15 June 1877	LJ	
34	Die Verlassene, inc.	Hört Ihr dort drüben		eb	19 June 1877	facs. in R. Batka and W. Nagel: *Allgemeine Geschichte der Musik*, iii (Stuttgart, c1915), 252	
35	Der Schwalben Heimkehr	Wenn die Schwalben heimwärts ziehn	K. Herlossohn	Ab	Aug-29 Dec 1877	NW i, WW vii/2	
36	Das Lied der Waise, inc.	Einsam steh ich und alleine	F. Steinebach	a	10 Oct 1877	Wst	
37	Wunsch, inc.	Fort möcht ich reisen weit	Lenau	a	26 Nov 1877	Wst	
38	Traurige Wege	Bin mit dir im Wald gegangen	Lenau	eb	22-5 Jan 1878	LJ	
39	So wahr die Sonne scheinet		F. Rückert	Ab	8 Feb 1878	WW vii/3	
40	Ich sah die blaue unendliche See, frag.		H. Hoffmann von Fallersleben	F	15 Feb 1878	Wst	
41	Nächtliche Wanderung	Die Nacht ist finster	Lenau	c	19-21 Feb 1878	LJ	
42	Auf der Wanderschaft 1st version 2nd version	Wohl wandert ich aus	A. Chamisso	e/E e/E	20 March 1878 23 March 1878	WW vii/3 WW vii/3	
43	Was soll ich sagen?, inc.	Mein Aug ist trüb	Chamisso	g	1 April-4 May 1878	Wst; facs. in Werner (Regensburg, 1921) and Grasberger (1960)	331

No.	Title	First line	Poet	Date	Key	Source	Page
				1878			
44	Geschiedensein	Frau Amme, Frau Amme	F. Hebbel			lost	
45	Das Kind am Brunnen	Vom Berg der Knab	Hebbel	16-27 April 1878	G	LJ	
46	Knabentod		Heine	3-6 May 1878	♯♭	NW i, WW vii/2	331
47	Sie haben heut Abend Gesellschaft		Heine	18-25 May 1878	G	ed. (Cologne, 1927)	331
48	Über Nacht		J. Sturm	23-4 May 1878	E♭	LJ	
49	Ich stand in dunkeln Träumen		Heine	26-9 May 1878	A♭	LJ	
50	Das ist ein Brausen und Heulen		Heine	31 May 1878	f	LJ	
51	Wo ich bin, mich rings umdunkelt		Heine	3-4 June 1878	e	LJ	
52	Aus meinen grossen Schmerzen		Heine	5 June 1878	g	LJ	
53	Mir träumte von einem Königskind		Heine	16 June 1878, rev. 20 Jan 1881	C	ed. (Cologne, 1927)	
54	Mein Liebchen, wir sassen beisammen		Heine	?June 1878	f♯	ed. (Cologne, 1927)	
55	Es blasen die blauen Husaren		Heine	22 June 1878	A	ed. (Cologne, 1927)	
56	Manch Bild vergessener Zeiten, inc.		Heine	24 June 1878	c♯	Wst	
57	Frühling, Liebster, inc.	Ich sass an einem Rädchen	Rückert	20 July 1878	e	Wst	
58	Liebesfrühling	Wie oft schon	Hoffmann von Fallersleben	9 Aug 1878	F	NW i, WW vii/2	
59	Auf der Wanderung	Über die Hügel und über die Berge	Hoffmann von Fallersleben	10 Aug 1878	C	NW i, WW vii/2	352
60	Ja, die Schönst! ich sagt es offen		Hoffmann von Fallersleben	11 Aug 1878	A	NW i, WW vii/2	
61	Gretchen vor dem Andachtsbild der Mater Dolorosa	Ach neige, du Schmerzenreiche	Goethe	22 Aug–9 Sept 1878	f	NW i, WW vii/2	307
62	Nach dem Abschiede	Dunkel sind nun alle Gassen	Hoffmann von Fallersleben	31 Aug–1 Sept 1878	e/G	NW i, WW vii/2	
63	Die Nachtigallen schweigen, frag.		Hoffmann von Fallersleben	10 Sept 1878	e♭	Wst	
64	Es war ein alter König		Heine	4 Oct 1878	g	LJ	
65	Mit schwarzen Segeln		Heine	6 Oct 1878	d	NW ii, WW vii/2	
66	Spätherbstnebel		Heine	7 Oct 1878	a/A	NW ii, WW vii/2	
67	Ernst ist der Frühling		Heine	13-17 Oct 1878	A♭	LJ	
68	Schön Hedwig		Hebbel	?1878		lost	
69	Der Kehraus		J. von Eichendorff	?1878		lost	
70	Das zerbrochene Ringlein		Eichendorff	?1878		lost	

No.	Title	Incipit	Text	Key	Composed	Publication or MS	
71	Der traurige Jäger		Eichendorff		?1878	lost	
72	Eight songs from Des Knaben Wunderhorn				?1878	lost	
73	Der schwere Abend		Lenau		?1879	lost	
74	Verschwiegene Liebe, 1st setting, sketch	Über Wipfel und Saaten	Eichendorff	G	?1879	Wst	
75	Herbstentschluss	Trübe Wolken, Herbstesluft	Lenau	g	8 July 1879	NW ii, WW vii/2	
76	Frage nicht	Wie sehr ich Dein	Lenau	Db	21 July 1879	NW ii, WW vii/2	
77	Herbst	Nun ist es Herbst	Lenau	f♯	24 July 1879	NW ii, WW vii/2	
78	Herbstklage, inc.	Holder Lenz, du bist dahin	Lenau	f	11 Sept 1879	Wst	
79	Wie des Mondes Abbild zittert		Heine	Eb	13 Feb 1880	NW ii, WW vii/2	
80	Der kriegslustige Waffenschmied, frag.	Spritze Funken, Säbel klinge	Lenau	D	28 May 1880	Wn	
81	Nachruf	Du liebe treue Leute	Eichendorff	Ab	7 June 1880	NW iii, WW vii/2	349
82	Nachgruss, inc.	Wie kühl schweift sich's	Eichendorff	Eb	2 Nov 1880	Wst	
83	Sterne mit den goldnen Füsschen		Heine	E	26 Nov 1880	NW ii, WW vii/2	
84	Das gelbe Laub erzittert, frag.		Heine	eb	7 Dec ?1880	Wst	
85	Suschens Vogel	Ich hatt ein Vöglein	E. Mörike	C	24 Dec 1880	NW iii, WW vii/2	310, 333
86	An die Wolke, frag.		Lenau	f	7 Jan 1881	Wn	
87	In der Fremde I	Da fahr ich still im Wagen	Eichendorff	F	27 June 1881	NW iii, WW vii/2	
88	In der Fremde II, 1st setting, frag.	Ich geh durch die dunklen Gassen	Eichendorff	g	3 Feb 1882–1 Jan 1883	Wn	
89	Wohin mit der Freud?	Ach, du klarblauer Himmel	R. Reinick	G	31 Dec 1882	NW iv, WW vii/2	
90	Rückkehr	Mit meinem Saitenspiele	Eichendorff	F♯	12 Jan 1883	NW iv, WW vii/2	
91	Ständchen	Komm in die stille Nacht!	Reinick	Db	19 Jan 1883	NW iv, WW vii/2	
92	Nachtgruss	In dem Himmel ruht die Erde	Reinick	Ab	24 Jan 1883	NW iv, WW vii/2	
93	In der Fremde VI	Wolken, wälderwärts gegangen	Eichendorff	g	30 Jan 1883	NW iii, WW vii/2	
94	Frühlingsglocken	Schneeglöcken tut läuten!	Reinick	D	19 Feb 1883	NW iv, WW vii/2	
95	Liebesbotschaft	Wolken, die ihr nach Osten eilt	Reinick	Ab	18 March 1883	NW iv, WW vii/2	
96	Liebchen, wo bist du?	Zauber bin ich	Reinick	F	12 April 1883	NW iii, WW vii/2	
97	In der Fremde II, 2nd setting	Ich geh durch die dunklen Gassen	Eichendorff	g♯	3 May 1883	NW iii, WW vii/2	314
98	Die Tochter der Heide	Wasch dich, mein Schwesterchen	Mörike	E	11 July 1884	NW iii, WW vii/2	316
99	Die Kleine	Zwischen Bergen, liebe Mutter	Eichendorff	E	8 March 1887	NW iii, WW vii/2	319
100	Die Spröde, frag.		Goethe	A	13–14 Feb 1889	Wn	
101	Dem Vaterland	Das ist ein hohes helles Wort	Reinick	C	12 May 1890	copy, Wst; orig. MS lost; facs. 1st page, Newman (Ger. trans., 1910), 198	

arr. male vv, orch					
1st version				May–4 June 1890	
2nd version				May–June 1894, rev. 1897, 1898	
102 Frohe Botschaft	Hielt die allerschönste Herrin	Reinick	E	25 June 1890	*Wn* vocal score (Mainz, 1895), full score (Mannheim, 1902)
103 Irdische und himmlische Liebe	Zur Schönheit meine Blicke suchend	Michelangelo, trans. W. Robert-Tornow		March–April 1897	NW iv, WW vii/2 destroyed by Wolf

SONGS: PUBLISHED BY THE COMPOSER
(including orchestral and/or choral arrangements)

Title	Incipit	Text	Key	Date	Publication or MS	
Sechs Lieder für eine Frauenstimme						
1 Morgentau	Der Frühhauch hat gefächelt	? A. Reinhold	D	6–19 June 1877	(Vienna, 1888)	
2 Das Vöglein	Vöglein vom Zweig	Hebbel	E	2 May 1878		306, 331
3 Die Spinnerin	O süsse Mutter	Rückert	a	5–12 April 1878		349
4 Wiegenlied im Sommer	Vom Berg hinabgestiegen	Reinick	F	17 Dec 1882		349
5 Wiegenlied im Winter	Schlaf ein, schlaf ein	Reinick	A♭	20 Dec 1882		
6 Mausfallensprüchlein	Kleine Gäste, kleines Haus	Mörike	F	18 June 1882	(Vienna, 1888)	310, 340
Sechs Gedichte von Scheffel, Mörike, Goethe und Kerner						
1 Wächterlied auf der Wartburg arr. male vv, orch, frag.	Schwingt euch auf, Posaunenchöre	J. V. von Scheffel	E♭	24 Jan 1887 1894		315
2 Der König bei der Krönung	Dir angetrauet am Altare	Mörike	E	13 March 1886	sketch, *Wn*	315
3 Biterolf	Kampfmüd und sonnverbrannt	Scheffel	F	26 Dec 1886		315
4 Beherzigung	Feiger Gedanken	Goethe	g/G	1 March 1887		316
5 Wanderers Nachtlied	Der du von dem Himmel bist	Goethe	G♭/B	30 Jan 1887		315
6 Zur Ruh, zur Ruh!		J. Kerner	A♭	16 June 1883		312, 340, 345
Gedichte von Eduard Mörike					(Vienna, 1889); WW i	
1 Der Genesene an die Hoffnung	Tödlich graute mir der Morgen	Mörike	f♯/G♭	6 March 1888		334
2 Der Knabe und das Immlein	Im Weinberg auf der Höhe		g/G	22 Feb 1888		317, 349
3 Ein Stündlein wohl vor Tag	Derweil ich schlafend lag		g	22 Feb 1888		318

Title	Incipit	Text	Key	Date	Publication or MS	
4 Jägerlied	Zierlich ist des Vogels Tritt		A	22 Feb 1888		318, 346
5 Der Tambour	Wenn meine Mutter hexen könnt		E	16 Feb 1888		341
6 Er ist's	Frühling lässt sein blaues Band		G	5 May 1888		
orch version				20 Feb 1890	(Leipzig, 1904); WW ix	
7 Das verlassene Mägdlein	Früh, wann die Hähne krähn		a	24 March 1888		341, 347, 352
8 Begegnung	Was doch heut Nacht ein Sturm		E♭	22 March 1888		
9 Nimmersatte Liebe	So ist die Lieb		A♭	24 Feb 1888		347, 352
10 Fussreise	Am frischgeschnittnen Wanderstab		D	21 March 1888		347
11 An eine Äolsharfe	Angelehnt an die Efeuwand		E	15 April 1888		
12 Verborgenheit	Lass, o Welt, o lass mich sein		E♭	13 March 1888		347
13 Im Frühling	Hier lieg ich		f♯	8 May 1888		
14 Agnes	Rosenzeit, wie schnell vorbei		f	3 May 1888		347, 349
15 Auf einer Wanderung	In ein freundliches Städtchen		E♭	11–25 March 1888		
16 Elfenlied	Bei Nacht im Dorf der Wächter rief		F	7 March 1888		325, 358
17 Der Gärtner	Auf ihrem Leibrösslein		D	7 March 1888		341, 349
18 Zitronenfalter im April	Grausame Frühlingssonne		a/A	6 March 1888		346
19 Um Mitternacht	Gelassen stieg die Nacht		c♯	20 April 1888		
20 Auf eine Christblume I	Tochter des Walds		D	26 Nov 1888		350
orch version, inc.				25 Sept 1890		
21 Auf eine Christblume II	Im Winterboden schläft		F♯	21 April 1888	Wst	
22 Seufzer	Dein Liebesfeuer		e	12 April 1888		
orch version				28 May 1889	(Leipzig, 1904); WW ix	
23 Auf ein altes Bild	In grüner Landschaft Sommerflor		f♯	14 April 1888		348, 358
orch version				28 May 1889	(Leipzig, 1904); WW ix	
24 In der Frühe	Kein Schlaf noch kühlt das Auge		d/D	5 May 1888		347, 352
orch version				6 May 1890	(Leipzig, 1904); WW ix	
25 Schlafendes Jesuskind	Sohn der Jungfrau		F	6 Oct 1888		
orch version				28 May 1889	(Leipzig, 1904); WW ix	
26 Karwoche	O Woche! Zeugin heiliger Beschwerde		A♭	8 Oct 1888		352
orch version				29 May 1889	(Leipzig, 1904); WW ix	

Title	Incipit	Text	Key	Date	Publication or MS
Gedichte von Joseph v. Eichendorff		Eichendorff			(Vienna, 1889); WW ii
1 Der Freund	Wer auf den Wogen schliefe		E	26 Sept 1888	345, 351
2 Der Musikant	Wandern lieb ich		A	22 Sept 1888	
3 Verschwiegene Liebe	Über Wipfel und Saaten		g	31 Aug 1888	
4 Das Ständchen	Auf die Dächer		D	28 Sept 1888	315, 338
5 Der Soldat I	Ist auch schmuck nicht mein Rösslein		C	7 March 1887	315
6 Der Soldat II	Wagen musst du		c	14 Dec 1886	316, 341
7 Die Zigeunerin	Am Kreuzweg, da lausche ich		a	19 March 1887	316
8 Nachtzauber	Hörst du nicht die Quellen rauschen		F#	24 May 1887	349
9 Der Schreckenberger	Aufs Wohlsein meiner Dame		G	14 Sept 1888	
10 Der Glücksritter	Wenn Fortuna spröde tut		C	16 Sept 1888	
11 Lieber alles	Soldat sein ist gefährlich		G	29 Sept 1888	
12 Heimweh	Wer in die Fremde will wandern		Eb	29 Sept 1888	
13 Der Scholar	Bei dem angenehmsten Wetter		a	22 Sept 1888	
14 Der verzweifelte Liebhaber	Studieren will nichts bringen		g	23 Sept 1888	349
15 Unfall	Ich ging bei Nacht		d	25 Sept 1888	
16 Liebesglück	Ich hab ein Liebchen		E	27 Sept 1888	
17 Seemanns Abschied	Ade, mein Schatz		F	21 Sept 1888	
18 Erwartung	Grüss euch aus Herzensgrund		E	26 Jan 1880	309
19 Die Nacht	Nacht ist wie ein stilles Meer		f#	3 Feb 1880	309
20 Waldmädchen	Bin ein Feuer hell		G	20 April 1887	316
Gedichte von J. W. v. Goethe		Goethe			
1 Harfenspieler I orch version	Wer sich der Einsamkeit ergibt		g	27 Oct 1888 / 2 Dec 1890	(Vienna, 1890); WW iii
2 Harfenspieler II orch version	An die Türen will ich schleichen		c	29 Oct 1888 / 4 Dec 1890	(Leipzig, 1904); WW viii
3 Harfenspieler III orch version	Wer nie sein Brot mit Tränen ass		f	30 Oct 1888 / 4 Dec 1890	(Leipzig, 1904); WW viii
4 Spottlied aus Wilhelm Meister	Ich armer Teufel, Herr Baron		F	2 Nov 1888	(Leipzig, 1904); WW viii
5 Mignon I	Heiss mich nicht reden		F	19 Dec 1888	
6 Mignon II	Nur wer die Sehnsucht kennt		g	18 Dec 1888	
7 Mignon III	So lasst mich scheinen		a	22 Dec 1888	
8 Philine	Singet nicht in Trauertönen		A	30 Oct 1888	

Title	Incipit	Text	Key	Date	Publication or MS
37 Sie haben wegen der Trunkenheit			g	18 Jan 1889	355
38 Was in der Schenke waren heute			d	16 Jan 1889	
39 Nicht Gelegenheit macht Diebe			F	21 Jan 1889	
40 Hochbeglückt in deiner Liebe			B♭	23 Jan 1889	
41 Als ich auf dem Euphrat schiffte			A	24 Jan 1889	
42 Dies zu deuten, bin erbötig			A	24 Jan 1889	
43 Hätt ich irgend wohl Bedenken			A♭	26 Jan 1889	346
44 Komm, Liebchen, komm!			f	25 Jan 1889	
45 Wie sollt ich heiter bleiben			c	23 Jan 1889	
46 Wenn ich dein gedenke			A	25 Jan 1889	
47 Locken, haltet mich gefangen			A	29 Jan 1889	
48 Nimmer will ich dich verlieren			d	30 Jan 1889	
49 Prometheus	Bedecke deinen Himmel, Zeus			2 Jan 1889	349, 354, 358
orch version				12 March–cApril 1890	(Mannheim, 1902); WW viii
50 Ganymed	Wie im Morgenglanze		D	11 Jan 1889	lost
orch version				1890	
51 Grenzen der Menschheit	Wenn der uralte heilige Vater		a	9 Jan 1889	(Mainz, 1891); WW iv
Spanisches Liederbuch, nach Heyse und Geibel					346
Geistliche Lieder					356
1	Nun bin ich dein	J. Ruiz, trans. P. Heyse	F	15 Jan 1890	345
2	Die du Gott gebarst, du Reine	N. Nuñez, trans. Heyse	a	5 Nov 1889	
3	Nun wandre, Maria	Ocaña, trans. Heyse	e	4 Nov 1889	346
4	Die ihr schwebet	Lope de Vega, trans. E. Geibel	E	5 Nov 1889	
5	Führ mich, Kind, nach Bethlehem	anon., trans. Heyse	A	15 Dec 1889	332
6	Ach, des Knaben Augen	L. de Úbeda, trans. Heyse	F	21 Dec 1889	
7	Mühvoll komm ich und beladen	M. del Rio, trans. [?Geibel]	g	10 Jan 1890	346
8	Ach, wie lang die Seele schlummert	anon., trans. Geibel	E♭	19 Dec 1889	
9	Herr, was trägt der Boden hier	anon., trans. Heyse	e	24 Nov 1889	
10	Wunden trägst du, mein Geliebter	J. de Valdivielso, trans. Geibel	b	16 Dec 1889	

Weltliche Lieder

No.		First line	Text	Key	Date	Notes	Ref
1		Klinge, klinge, mein Pandero	A. F. de Almeida, trans. Geibel	g	20 Nov 1889		
2	orch version	In dem Schatten meiner Locken	anon., trans. Heyse	B♭	17 Nov 1889 by mid-Aug 1895	in Der Corregidor; WW ix	361
3		Seltsam ist Juanas Weise	anon., trans. Geibel	g	14 Nov 1889		
4		Treibe nur mit Lieben Spott	anon., trans. Heyse	g	15 Nov 1889		
5		Auf dem grünen Balkon	anon., trans. Heyse	A	12 Dec 1889		
6	orch version	Wenn du zu den Blumen gehst	anon., trans. Heyse	A	1 Nov 1889 5–6 Dec 1897	for inclusion in Manuel Venegas (Vienna, 1937); WW ix	
7	orch version	Wer sein holdes Lieb verloren	anon., trans. Geibel	f♯	28 Oct 1889 1–4 Dec 1897	for inclusion in Manuel Venegas (Vienna, 1937); WW ix	
8		Ich fuhr über Meer	anon., trans. Heyse	b	31 Oct 1889		
9		Blindes Schauen, dunkle Leuchte	R. Cota, trans. Heyse	b	26 Nov 1889		
10		Eide, so die Liebe schwur	anon., trans. Heyse	b	31 March 1890		
11	orch version	Herz, verzage nicht geschwind	anon., trans. Heyse	e	19 Nov 1889 early Oct 1895	in Der Corregidor; WW ix	361
12		Sagt, seid ihr es, feiner Herr	anon., trans. Heyse	G	19 Nov 1889		
13		Mögen alle bösen Zungen	anon., trans. Geibel	D	3 April 1890		
14	(Preciosas Sprüchlein gegen Kopfweh)	Köpfchen, Köpfchen, nicht gewimmert	Cervantes, trans. Heyse	B♭	31 Oct 1889		
15		Sagt ihm, dass er zu mir komme	anon., trans. Heyse	b	4 April 1890		
16		Bitt ihn, o Mutter	anon., trans. Heyse	g	26 Nov 1889		
17		Liebe mir im Busen zündet	anon., trans. Heyse	a	2 April 1890		
18		Schmerzliche Wonnen und wonnige Schmerzen	anon., trans. Geibel	A	29 March 1890		
19		Trau nicht der Liebe	anon., trans. Heyse	a	28 March 1890		
20		Ach, im Maien wars	anon., trans. Heyse	A	30 March 1890		
21		Alle gingen, Herz, zur Ruh	anon., trans. Geibel	F	2 Nov 1889		
22		Dereinst, dereinst, Gedanke mein	C. de Castillejo, trans. Geibel	f	11 April 1890		350–1

Title	Incipit	Text	Key	Date	Publication or MS	
23	Tief im Herzen trag ich Pein	Camoens, trans. Geibel	c	12 April 1890		
24	Komm, o Tod, von Nacht umgeben	Escriva, trans. Geibel	D♭	14 April 1890		356
25	Ob auch finstre Blicke glitten	anon., trans. Heyse	b	16 April 1890		
26	Bedeckt mich mit Blumen	? M. Doceo, trans. Geibel	A♭	10 Nov 1889		
27	Und schläfst du, mein Mädchen	G. Vicente, trans. Geibel	E♭	17 Nov 1889		
28	Sie blasen zum Abmarsch	anon., trans. Heyse	B♭	13 Dec 1889		
29	Weint nicht, ihr Äuglein	Lope de Vega, trans. Heyse	b	29 March 1890		
30	Wer tat deinem Füsslein weh?	anon., trans. Geibel	A	5 Dec 1889		
31	Deine Mutter, süsses Kind	Luis el Chico, trans. [?Heyse]	f♯	2 April 1890		
32	Da nur Leid und Leidenschaft	anon., trans. Heyse	b	20 April 1890		
33	Wehe der, die mir verstrickte	Vicente, trans. Heyse	a	27 April 1890		
34	Geh, Geliebter, geh jetzt	anon., trans. Geibel	F♯	1 April 1890	lost; sketches, *Wn*	341
orch version				1892	(Mainz, 1891)	324
						355
Alte Weisen: sechs Gedichte von Keller		G. Keller				
1 Tretet ein, hoher Krieger			D	25 May 1890		
2 Singt mein Schatz wie ein Fink			A	2 June 1890		
3 Du milchjunger Knabe			a	16 June 1890		355
4 Wandl ich in dem Morgentau			A	8–23 June 1890		
5 Das Köhlerweib ist trunken			d	7–23 June 1890		
6 Wie glänzt der helle Mond			g	5–23 June 1890		
Italienisches Liederbuch, nach Paul Heyse, i		anon. It. poems, trans. Heyse			(Mainz, 1892); *WW* v	323, 345, 355
1 Auch kleine Dinge			A	9 Dec 1891		
2 Mir ward gesagt			e	25 Sept 1890		348
3 Ihr seid die Allerschönste			A♭	2 Oct 1890		
4 Gesegnet sei, durch den die Welt			E♭	3 Oct 1890		
5 Selig ihr Blinden			E♭	4 Oct 1890		
6 Wer rief dich denn?			F	13 Nov 1890		341
7 Der Mond hat eine schwere Klag			e♭	13 Nov 1890		

No.	First line	Source	Date	Key	Page
8	Nun lass uns Frieden schliessen		14 Nov 1890	E♭	
9	Dass doch gemalt		29 Nov 1891	F	
10	Du denkst mit einem Fädchen		2 Dec 1891	B♭	349
11	Wie lange schon		4 Dec 1891	f	
12	Nein, junger Herr		7 Dec 1891	G	
13	Hoffärtig seid Ihr, schönes Kind		8 Dec 1891	f♯	
14	Geselle, woll'n wir uns in Kutten hüllen		5 Dec 1891	D	
15	Mein Liebster ist so klein		3 Dec 1891	F	
16	Ihr jungen Leute		11 Dec 1891	C	
17	Und willst du deinen Liebsten sterben sehen		4 Dec 1891	A♭	
18	Heb auf dein blondes Haupt		12 Dec 1891	A♭	348
19	Wir haben beide lange Zeit geschwiegen		16 Dec 1891	E♭	
20	Mein Liebster singt am Haus		12 Dec 1891	g	346–7
21	Man sagt mir, deine Mutter		23 Dec 1891	a	
22	Ein Ständchen euch zu bringen		10 Dec 1891	C	
	Italienisches Liederbuch, nach Paul Heyse, ii	anon. It. poems, trans. Heyse			
23	Was für ein Lied soll dir gesungen werden?		30 April 1896	B♭	323–4, 35; (Mannheim, 1896); WW v
24	Ich esse nun mein Brot		25 March 1896	e♭/E♭	
25	Mein Liebster hat zu Tische		26 March 1896	F	
26	Ich liess mir sagen		28 March 1896	c	
27	Schon streckt' ich aus im Bett		29 March 1896	A♭	
28	Du sagst mir, dass ich keine Fürstin		30 March 1896	E♭	
29	Wohl kenn ich Euren Stand		9 April 1896	C	
30	Lass sie nur gehn		30–31 March 1896	g	
31	Wie soll ich fröhlich sein		12 April 1896	g	
32	Was soll der Zorn, mein Schatz		20 April 1896	c	
33	Sterb ich, so hüllt in Blumen		13 April 1896	A♭	
34	Und steht Ihr früh am Morgen auf		3–4 April 1896	E	
35	Benedeit die sel'ge Mutter		21 April 1896	E♭	341
36	Wenn du, mein Liebster		24 April 1896	G♭	
37	Wie viele Zeit verlor ich		2 April 1896	g	
38	Wenn du mich mit den Augen		19 April 1896	G	
39	Gesegnet sei das Grün		13 April 1896	A	356

Title	Incipit	Text	Key	Date	Publication or MS	
40	O wär dein Haus durchsichtig		a	12 April 1896		356
41	Heut Nacht erhob ich mich		d	25 April 1896		
42	Nicht länger kann ich singen		a	23 April 1896		
43	Schweig einmal still		e	23 April 1896		
44	O wüsstest du, wie viel ich deinetwegen		d	26 April 1896		
45	Verschling' der Abgrund		d	29 April 1896		
46	Ich hab in Penna einen Liebsten		F	25 April 1896		
Drei Gedichte von Robert Reinick		Reinick			(Mannheim, 1897)	340, 348, 349
1 Gesellenlied	Kein Meister fällt von Himmel		C	24 Jan 1888		347
2 Morgenstimmung	Bald ist der Nacht		E	8 Sept – 23 Oct 1896		
arr. chorus, orch as Morgenhymnus				12-17 Dec 1897	rev. W. Kähler (Leipzig, 1910)	
3 Skolie	Reich den Pokal mir		B	1 Aug 1889	(Mannheim, 1897)	
Drei Gesänge aus Ibsens Das Fest auf Solhaug		Ibsen, trans. E. Klingenfeld				
1 Gesang Margits	Bergkönig ritt durch die Lande		g	7–23 Jan 1891		
2 Gudmunds erster Gesang	Ich wandelte sinnend allein		G	30 Oct 1891, rev. 12 Nov 1896		
3 Gundmunds zweiter Gesang	Ich fuhr wohl übers Wasser		a/A	7 March 1891	(Mannheim, 1897)	
Vier Gedichte nach Heine, Shakespeare und Lord Byron						
1 Wo wird einst		Heine	F	24 Jan 1888		340
2 Lied des transferierten Zettel	Die Schwalbe, die den Sommer	Shakespeare, trans. Schlegel	a	11 May 1889		349
3 Sonne der Schlummerlosen	Sonne der Schlummerlosen	Byron, trans. O. Gildemeister	c♯	29-31 Dec 1896		
4 Keine gleicht von allen Schönen	Keine gleicht von allen Schönen	Byron, trans. Gildemeister	B	18 25 Dec 1896		
Drei Gedichte von Michelangelo		Michelangelo, trans. Robert-Tornow			(Mannheim, 1898)	356
1 Wohl denk ich oft			g/G	18 March 1897		347
2 Alles endet, was entstehet			c♯	20 March 1897		347
3 Fühlt meine Seele			e/E	22 - 8 March 1897		356, 357

The following index gives titles and (in quotation marks) incipits of the works listed above, indicating (with the sigla below) the place of each in the list.

Abendbilder, UP 29; Abendglöcklein, UP 17; Abschied, Mö 53; 'Ach, des Knaben Augen', SG 6; 'Ach, du klarblauer Himmel', UP 89; 'Ach, im Maien wars', 3G 2; 'Ach neige, du Schmerzenreiche', UP 61; 'Ach, was soll der Mensch verlangen?', G 18; 'Ach, wer bringt', UP 16; 'Ach, wie lang die Seele schlummert', SG 8; 'Ade, mein Schatz', E 17; Agnes, Mö 14; 'Alle gingen, Herz, zur Ruh', SW 21; 'Alles endet, was entstehet, Mi 2; 'Alles wiegt die stille Nacht', UP 30; 'Als ein unergründlich Wonnemeer', UP 23; Als ich auf dem Euphrat schiffte, G 41

'Als ich noch ein Knabe war', G 23; 'Am frischgeschnittnen Wanderstab', Mö 10; 'Am Kreuzweg, da lausche ich', E 7; An *', UP 32; Anakreons Grab, G 29; 'An dem reinsten Frühlingsmorgen', G 26; Andenken, UP 31; An den Schlaf, Mö 29; 'Anders wird die Welt', Mö 37; An die Geliebte, Mö 32; 'An die Türen will ich schleichen', G 2; An die Wolke, UP 86; An eine Äolsharfe, Mö 11; 'Angelehnt an die Efeuwand', Mö 11; 'Auch kleine Dinge', It 1; 'Auf dem grünen Balkon', SW 5; Auf dem See, UP 11; Auf der Wanderschaft, UP 42

Auf der Wanderung, UP 59; 'Auf die Dächer', E 4; Auf ein altes Bild, Mö 23; Auf eine Christblume I, Mö 20; Auf eine Christblume II, Mö 21; Auf einer Wanderung, Mö 15; 'Auf ihrem Leibrösslein', Mö 17; 'Aufs Wohlsein meiner Dame', E 9; Auftrag, Mö 50; Aus meinen grossen Schmerzen, UP 52; 'Bald ist der Nacht', R 2; 'Bedecke deinen Himmel, Zeus', G 49; 'Bedeckt mich nit mit Blumen', SW 26; Begegnung, Mö 8; Beherzigung, G 18; Beherzigung, 6G 4; 'Bei dem angenehmsten Wetter', E 13; 'Bei dem Glanz der Abendröte', G 27.

Bei einer Trauung, Mö 51; 'Bei Nacht im Dorf der Wächter rief', Mö 16; 'Benedeit die sel'ge Mutter', It 35; 'Bergkönig ritt durch die Lande', 3G 1; Bescheidene Liebe, UP 28; 'Bin ein Feuer hell', E 20; 'Bin jung gewesen', Mö 41; 'Bin mit dir im Wald gegangen', UP 38; Biterolf, 6G 3; 'Bitt ihn, o Mutter', SW 16; 'Blindes Schauen, dunkle Leuchte', SW 9; Blumengruss; G 24, Cophtisches Lied I, G 14; Cophtisches Lied II, G 15; 'Da fahr ich still im Wagen', UP 87; Dank des Paria, G 30; 'Da nur Leid und Leidenschaft', SW 32

'Das Beet, schon lockert sich's', G 28; Das gelbe Laub erzittert, UP 84; Das ist ein Brausen und Heulen, UP 50; 'Das ist ein hohes helles Wort', UP 101; Das Kind am Brunnen, UP 45; Das Köhlerweib ist trunken, K 5; Das Lied der Waise, UP 36; 'Dass doch gemalt', It 9; Das Ständchen, E 4; Das taube Mütterlein, UP 1; Das verlassene Mägdlein, Mö 7; Das Vöglein, 6L 2; 'Das Wasser rauscht', UP 9; Das zerbrochene Ringlein, UP 70; 'Deine Mutter, süsses Kind', SW 31; 'Dein Liebesfeuer', Mö 22

Dem Vaterland, UP 101; Denk es, o Seele!, Mö 39; 'Der alte Müller Jakob', UP 12; 'Der du von dem Himmel bist', 6G 5; 'Dereinst, dereinst, Gedanke mein', SW 22; Der Feuerreiter, Mö 44; Der Fischer, UP 9; Der Freund, E 1; 'Der Frühhauch hat gefächelt', 6L 1; Der Gärtner, Mö 17; Der Genesene an die Hoffnung, Mö 1; Der Glücksritter, E 10; Der goldene Morgen, UP 19; Der Jäger, Mö 40; Der Kehraus, UP 69; Der Knabe und das Immlein, Mö 2; Der König bei der Krönung, 6G 2

Der kriegslustige Waffenschmied, UP 80; 'Der Mond hat eine schwere Klag', It 7; Der Morgen, UP 3; Der Musikant, E 2; Der neue Amadis, G 23; Der Rattenfänger, G 11; Der Raubschütz, UP 12;

Der Sänger, G 10; Der Schäfer, G 22; Der Scholar, E 13; Der Schreckenberger, E 9; Der Schwalben Heimkehr, UP 35; Der schwere Abend, UP 73; Der Soldat I, E 5; Der Soldat II, E 6; 'Der Spiegel dieser treuen', Mö 33; 'Der Strauss, den ich gepflücket', G 24; Der Tambour, Mö 5; Der traurige Jäger, UP 71; Der verzweifelte Liebhaber, E 14

'Derweil ich schlafend lag', Mö 3; 'Des Glöckleins Schall', UP 17; 'Des Schäfers sein Haus', Mö 48; 'Des Wassermanns sein Töchterlein', Mö 45; Die Bekehrte, G 27; 'Die du Gott gebarst, du Reine', SG 2; Die Geister am Mummelsee, Mö 47; 'Die heiligen drei König', G 19; 'Die ihr schwebet', SG 4; Die Kleine, UP 99; Die Nacht, E 19; Die Nachtigallen schweigen, UP 63; 'Die Nacht ist finster', UP 41; 'Die Schwalbe, die den Sommer', 4G 2; Die Spinnerin, 6L 3; Die Spröde, G 26, UP 100

Die Sterne, UP 4; Dies zu deuten, bin erbötig, G 42; Die Tochter der Heide, UP 98; Die Verlassene, UP 34; Die Zigeunerin, E 7; 'Dir angetrauet am Altare', 6G 2; 'Drei Tage Regen fort und fort', Mö 40; 'Du bist Orplid, mein Land', Mö 46; Du bist wie eine Blume, UP 26; 'Du denkst mit einem Fädchen', It 10; 'Du liebes Auge', UP 20; 'Du liebe treue Laute', UP 81; Du milchjunger Knabe, K 3; 'Dunkel sind nun alle Gassen', UP 62; 'Du sagst mir, dass ich keine Fürstin', It 28; 'Du wirst ja blass', UP 6; 'Eide, so die Liebe schwur', SW 10

'Ein Blumenglöckchen vom Boden', G 25; 'Eine Liebe kenn ich', Mö 31; Ein Grab, UP 24; 'Einmal, nach einer lustigen Nacht', Mö 49; 'Einsam steh ich und alleine', UP 36; 'Ein Ständchen euch zu bringen', It 22; Ein Stündlein wohl vor Tag, Mö 3; 'Ein Tännlein grünet wo', Mö 39; Elfenlied, Mö 16; Epiphanias, G 19; Er ist's, Mö 6; Ernst ist der Frühling, UP 67; Erschaffen und Beleben, G 33; Erster Verlust, UP 16; Erstes Liebeslied eines Mädchens, Mö 42; Erwartung, E 18; Es blasen die blauen Husaren, UP 55

'Es segeln die Wolken', UP 33; Es war ein alter König, UP 64; 'Es war ein fauler Schäfer', G 22; 'Feiger Gedanken', 6G 4; 'Fort möcht ich reisen weit', UP 37; Frage nicht, UP 76; Frage und Antwort, Mö 35; 'Fragst du mich', Mö 35; 'Frau Amme, Frau Amme', UP 45; Frech und froh I, G 16; Frech und froh II, G 17; 'Friedlicher Abend', UP 29; Frohe Botschaft, UP 102; 'Frühling lässt sein blaues Band', Mö 6; Frühling, Liebster, UP 57; Frühlingsglocken, UP 94; Frühlingsgrüsse, UP 13

Frühling übers Jahr, G 28; 'Früh, wann die Hähne krähn', Mö 7; 'Fühlt meine Seele, Mi 3; 'Führ mich, Kind, nach Bethlehem', SG 5; Fussreise, Mö 10; Ganymed, G 50; Gebet (Kind), UP 5; Gebet (Mörike), Mö 28; 'Geh! gehorche meinem Winken', G 15; 'Geh, Geliebter, geh jetzt', SW 34; 'Gelassen stieg die Nacht', Mö 19; Genialisch Treiben, G 21; Gesang Margits, 3G 1; Gesang Weylas, Mö 46; Geschiedensein, UP 44; 'Gesegnet sei das Grün', It 39; 'Gesegnet sei, durch den die Welt', It 4; Gesellenlied, R 1

'Geselle, woll'n wir uns in Kutten hüllen', It 14; Gleich und Gleich, G 25; 'Golden lacht und glüht', UP 19; 'Grausame Frühlingssonne', Mö 18; Grenzen der Menschheit, G 51; Gretchen vor dem Andachtsbild der Mater Dolorosa, UP 61; 'Grosser Brahma!', G 30; 'Grüss euch aus Herzensgrund', E 18; Gudmunds erster Gesang, 3G 2; Gudmunds zweiter Gesang, 3G 3; Gutmann und Gutweib, G 13; 'Ha, ich bin der Herr der Welt', G 31; 'Hans Adam war ein Erdenkloss', G 33; Harfenspieler I, G 1; Harfenspieler II, G 2

Harfenspieler III, G 3; Hätt ich irgend wohl Bedenken, G 43; 'Heb auf dein blondes Haupt', It 18; Heimweh (Mörike), Mö 37; Heimweh (Eichendorff), E 12; 'Heiss mich nicht reden', G 5; Herbst, UP 77; Herbstentschluss, UP 75; Herbstklage, UP 78; 'Herr! schicke was du willt', Mö 28; 'Herr, was trägt der Boden hier', SG 9; 'Herz, verzage nicht geschwind', SW 11; 'Heut Nacht erhob ich mich', It 41; 'Hielt die allerschönste Herrin', UP 102; 'Hier lieg ich', Mö 13; Hochbeglückt in deiner Liebe, G 40

'Hoffärtig seid Ihr, schönes Kind', It 13; 'Holder Lenz, du dist dahin', UP 78; 'Horch, wie still es wird', UP 22; 'Hörst du nicht die Quellen rauschen', E 8; 'Hört ihr dort drüben', UP 34; 'Ich armer Teufel, Herr Baron', G 4; 'Ich bin der wohlbekannte Sänger', G 11; 'Ich bin meiner Mutter einzig Kind', Mö 52; 'Ich bin wie andre Mädchen nicht', UP 28; 'Ich denke dein', UP 31; 'Ich esse nun mein Brot', It 24; 'Ich fuhr über Meer', SW 8; 'Ich fuhr wohl übers Wasser', 3G 3; 'Ich geh durch die dunklen Gassen', UP 88, 97; 'Ich ging bei Nacht', E 15

'Ich hab ein Liebchen', E 16; 'Ich hab in Penna einen Liebsten', It 46; 'Ich hatt ein Vöglein', UP 85; 'Ich liess mir sagen', It 26; 'Ich sah den

Lenz einmal', UP 15; Ich sah die blaue unendliche See, UP 40; 'Ich sass an einem Rädchen', UP 57; Ich stand in dunkeln Träumen, UP 49; 'Ich wandelte sinnend allein', 3G 2; 'Ihr jungen Leute', It 16; 'Ihr seid die Allerschönste', It 3; Im Frühling, Mö 13; 'Im Weinberg auf der Höhe', Mö 2; 'Im Winterboden schläft', Mö 21; 'In aller Früh', Mö 43; 'In dem Himmel ruht die Erde', UP 92

'In dem Schatten meiner Locken', SW 2; In der Fremde I, UP 87; In der Fremde II, UP 88, 97; In der Fremde VI, UP 93; In der Frühe, Mö 24; 'In ein freundliches Städtchen', Mö 15; 'In grüner Landschaft Sommerflor', Mö 23; 'In poetischer Epistel', Mö 50; Irdische und himmlische Liebe, UP 103; 'Ist auch schmuck nicht mein Rösslein', E 5; Ja, die Schönst! ich sagt es offen, UP 60; Jägerlied, Mö 4; 'Kampfmüd und sonnverbrannt', 6G 3; 'Kann auch ein Mensch', Mö 30; Karwoche, Mö 26

Keine gleicht von allen Schönen, 4G 4; 'Kein Meister fällt vom Himmel', R 1; 'Kein Schlaf noch kühlt das Auge', Mö 24; 'Kennst du das Land', G 9; 'Kleine Gäste, kleines Haus', 6L 6; 'Klinge, klinge, mein Pandero', SW 1; Knabentod, UP 46; 'Komm in die stille Nacht!', UP 91; Komm, Liebchen, komm!, G 44; 'Komm, o Tod, von Nacht umgeben', SW 24; Königlich Gebet, G 31; 'Köpfchen, Köpfchen, nicht gewimmert', SW 14; 'Lasset Gelehrte', G 14; 'Lass, o Welt, o lass mich sein', Mö 12; 'Lass sie nur gehn', It 30

Lebe wohl, Mö 36; 'Lebe wohl! Du fühlest nicht', Mö 36; 'Leichte Silberwolken schweben', UP 18; 'Leise, leise', UP 5; 'Lichtlein schwimmen auf dem Strome', G 20; Liebchen, wo bist du?, UP 96; Lieber alles, E 11; 'Liebe mir im Busen zündet', SW 17; Liebesbotschaft, UP 95; Liebesfrühling (Lenau), UP 15; Liebesfrühling (Hoffmann von Fallersleben), UP 58; Liebesglück, E 16; 'Liebesqual verschmäht mein Herz', G 17; Lied des transferierten Zettel, 4G 2; Lied eines Verliebten, Mö 43; Lied vom Winde, Mö 38; Locken, haltet mich gefangen, G 47; 'Mädchen mit dem roten Mündchen', UP 25

Mai, UP 18; Mailied, UP 21; Manch Bild vergessener Zeiten, UP 56; 'Man sagt mir, deine Mutter', It 21; Mausfallensprüchlein, 6L 6; Meeresstille, UP 14; 'Mein Aug ist trüb', UP 43; Mein Liebchen, wir sassen beisammen, UP 54; 'Mein Liebster hat zu Tische', It 25; 'Mein Liebster ist so klein', It 15; 'Mein Liebster singt am Haus', It 20; Mignon, G 9; Mignon I, G 5; Mignon II, G 6; Mignon III, G 7; Mir träumte von einem Königskind, UP 53; 'Mir ward gesagt', It 2

'Mit des Bräutigams Behagen', G 12; 'Mit Mädchen sich vertragen', G 16; 'Mit meinem Saitenspiele', UP 90; Mit schwarzen Segeln, UP 65; 'Mögen alle bösen Zungen', SW 13; Morgenstimmung, R 2; Morgentau, 6L 1; 'Mühvoll komm ich und beladen', SG 7; Nach dem Abschiede, UP 62; 'Nach langem Frost', UP 13; Nachruf, UP 81; Nachtgruss (Eichendorff), UP 82; Nachtgruss (Reinick), UP 92; 'Nacht ist wie ein stilles Meer', E 19; Nächtliche Wanderung, UP 41; Nacht und Grab, UP 7; Nachtzauber, E 8; 'Nein, junger Herr', It 12

Neue Liebe, Mö 30; Nicht Gelegenheit macht Diebe, G 39; 'Nicht länger kann ich singen', It 42; Nimmersatte Liebe, Mö 9; Nimmer will ich dich verlieren, G 48; Nixe Binsefuss, Mö 45; 'Nun bin ich dein', SG 1; 'Nun ist es Herbst', UP 77; 'Nun lass uns Frieden schliessen', It 8; 'Nun wandre, Maria', SG 3; 'Nur wer die Sehnsucht kennt', G 6; 'Ob auch finstre Blicke glitten', SW 25; Ob der Koran von Ewigkeit sei?, G 34; 'O süsse Mutter', 6L 3; 'O wag es nicht', UP 32; 'O wär dein Haus durchsichtig', It 40

'O Woche! Zeugin heiliger Beschwerde', Mö 26; 'O wüsstest du, wie viel ich deinetwegen', It 44; Peregrina I, Mö 33; Peregrina II, Mö 34; Perlenfischer, UP 20; Phänomen, G 32; Philine, G 8; Prometheus, G 49; Rat einer Alten, Mö 41; 'Reich den Pokal mir', R 3; Ritter Kurts Brautfahrt, G 12; 'Rosenzeit, wie schnell vorbei', Mö 14; Rückkehr, UP 90; 'Sagt ihm, dass er zu mir komme', SW 15; 'Sagt, seid ihr es, feiner Herr', SW 12; St Nepomuks Vorabend, G 20

'Sausewind, Brausewind', Mö 38; Scheideblick, UP 23; 'Schlaf ein, schlaf ein', 6L 5; Schlafendes Jesuskind, Mö 25; 'Schlaf! Süsser Schlaf!', Mö 29; 'Schmerzliche Wonnen und wonnige Schmerzen', SW 18; 'Schneeglöckchen tut läuten!', UP 94; Schön Hedwig, UP 68; 'Schon streckt ich aus im Bett', It 27; 'Schweig einmal still', It 43; 'Schwingt euch auf, Posaunenchöre', 6G 1; Seemanns Abschied, E 17; 'Sehet ihr am Fensterlein', Mö 44; Sehnsucht, UP 8; 'Sei mir gegrüsst', UP 7; Selbstgeständnis, Mö 52; 'Selig ihr Blinden', It 5

'Seltsam ist Juanas Weise', SW 3; Seufzer, Mö 22; 'Sie blasen zum Abmarsch', SW 28; Sie haben heut Abend Gesellschaft, UP 47; Sie

movt (Scherzo: Presto); D, sketch, 8 March 1894, *Wn* [45 bars]; Finale (Tarantella), C, inc., 2 Dec 1897, *Wst* [40 bars]; incipits in *MR*, viii (1947), 171

Dritte Italienische Serenade, C/E, 18 Dec 1897, sketch, *Wn* [190 bars]; incipits in *MR*, viii (1947), 171

Tarantella, on Funiculì, funiculà, frag., C/E, 28 Dec 1897, ed. in *MR*, xiii (1952), 127

Transcr.: Beethoven: Pf Sonata, c♯, op.27 no.2, orchd 1876 [3rd movt inc.]

CHAMBER

String Quartet, D, 9 March 1876, *Wst* [32 bars]   309, 315, 334, 339, 358

Piano Quintet, frag., 13 Sept–18 Oct 1876, lost   338

Violin Sonata, g, 10 Nov 1877, frag. (Leipzig and Vienna, 1940) [pubd with Sym., 1876–7]   316, 320, 324, 339, 340

String Quartet, d, 1878–84 (Leipzig, 1903); WW xv/1

Intermezzo, E♭, str qt, April–Oct 1886; WW xv/2

Serenade (Italienische Serenade), str qt, G, 2–4 May 1887 (Leipzig, 1903); WW xv/3

Serenade movt (Langsam), frag., E♭, 15 May 1889, ed. in *MR*, viii (1947), 170   331

PIANO

(for 2 hands unless otherwise stated)

Sonata, E♭/D, op.1, c April 1875, inc., *Wst*   304

Variations, G, op.2, 1875; WW xviii   304

Variations, E/A, frag., c1875, *Wst*

Sonata, D, op.7, 1875, inc., *Wst*

Sonata, G, op.8, Jan–Feb 1876, inc.; WW xviii

Fantasia, B♭, op.11, 1876, inc., *Wst* [22 bars]

March, E♭, 4 hands, op.12, Feb 1876, *Wst* [trio missing]

Sonata, g, op.14, March–April 1876, inc., *Wst*

Rondo capriccioso, B♭, op.15, 4 April–4 June 1876, ed. (Leipzig and Vienna, 1940) [pubd with Sym., 1876–7]; WW xviii   305

Wellenspiel, D, Jan 1877, inc., lost [c60 bars; no.1 of projected set, 6 Charakterstücke]

Verlegenheit, frag., a, 23 Feb 1877, *Wst* [4 bars; from 6 Charakterstücke]

Humoreske, g, 9–26 Sept 1877; WW xviii   331

Schlummerlied (Aus der Kinderzeit, no.1), G, 20 May 1878, ed., with added text, as Wiegenlied (Mainz, 1910); WW xviii

Scherz und Spiel (Aus der Kinderzeit, no.2), G, 20 May 1878; WW xviii

Fantasie über Lortzings Zar und Zimmermann, c1878, lost

Reiseblätter nach Gedichten von Lenau, c1878–9, lost

Fantasia, c, 1878, lost

Sonata, f♯, ?1879, lost

Paraphrase über Die Meistersinger von Nürnberg von Richard Wagner, G, c1880; WW xviii

Paraphrase über Die Walküre von Richard Wagner, e, c1880; WW xviii

Albumblatt [rev. of Schlummerlied], 1880; WW xviii

Canons, C, c1882, ed. E. Werba, *ÖMz*, xxv (1970), 110; WW xviii

WRITINGS

ed. R. Batka and H. Wolf: *Musikalische Kritiken* (Leipzig, 1911/*R*1976; Eng. trans. 1979)   330, 336, 363

BIBLIOGRAPHY

CATALOGUES, BIBLIOGRAPHIES

P. Müller: *Hugo Wolf: Verzeichnis seiner Werke, mit einer Einführung* (Leipzig, 1908)

F. Walker: 'Hugo Wolf: a Bibliography – principally Biographical', 'Wolf's Compositions', *Hugo Wolf: a Biography* (London, 1951, enlarged 2/1968; Ger. trans., enlarged, 1953)

F. Grasberger: *Hugo Wolf: Persönlichkeit und Werk* (Vienna, 1960) [centenary exhibition catalogue]

ICONOGRAPHY

A. Ehrmann: *Hugo Wolf: sein Leben in Bildern* (Leipzig, 1937)

LETTERS

E. Hellmer, ed.: *Hugo Wolf: Briefe an Emil Kauffmann* (Berlin, 1903)

M. Haberlandt, ed.: *Hugo Wolf: Briefe an Hugo Faisst* (Stuttgart, 1904)

'Hugo Wolfs Briefe an schwäbische Freunde', *Süddeutsche Monatshefte* (Munich, 1904), May

P. Müller, ed.: 'Ungedruckte Briefe von Hugo Wolf an Paul Müller', *JbMP 1904*, 69–100

H. Werner, ed.: *Hugo Wolf: Briefe an Oskar Grohe* (Berlin, 1905)

E. Hellmer, ed.: *Hugo Wolf: Familienbriefe* (Leipzig, 1912)

H. Werner, ed.: *Hugo Wolf: Briefe an Rosa Mayreder, mit einem Nachwort der Dichterin des 'Corregidors'* (Vienna, 1921)

——: *Hugo Wolf: Briefe an Henriette Lang, nebst den Briefen an deren Gatten, Prof. Joseph Freiherr von Schey* (Regensburg, 1922)

H. Nonveiller, ed.: *Hugo Wolf: Briefe an Heinrich Potpeschnigg* (Stuttgart, 1923)

K. Geiringer: 'Hugo Wolf and Frida von Lipperheide: some Unpublished Letters', *MT*, lxxvii (1936), 701, 793

F. Grasberger, ed.: *Hugo Wolf: Briefe an Melanie Köchert* (Tutzing, 1964)

R. Schaal, ed.: 'Ungedruckte Briefe von Hugo Wolf', *DJbM*, xiii (1968), 115

E. Werba: 'Briefe Hugo Wolfs an seine Schwester Adrienne', *ÖMz*, xxvii (1972), 263

MEMOIRS
(many including letters)

M. Haberlandt: *Hugo Wolf: Erinnerungen und Gedanken* (Leipzig, 1903, enlarged 2/1911)

H. Werner: *Hugo Wolf in Maierling: eine Idyll* (Leipzig, 1913)

E. Hellmer: *Hugo Wolf: Erlebtes und Erlauschtes* (Vienna, 1921)

H. Werner: *Der Hugo Wolf-Verein in Wien* (Regensburg, 1921)
H. Werner, ed.: *Gustav Schur: Erinnerungen an Hugo Wolf, nebst Hugo Wolfs Briefen an Gustav Schur* (Regensburg, 1922)
H. Werner: *Hugo Wolf in Perchtoldsdorf* (Regensburg, 1924)
R. Kukula: *Erinnerungen eines Bibliothekars* (Weimar, 1925)
H. Werner: *Hugo Wolf und der Wiener Akademische Wagner-Verein* (Regensburg, 1927)
F. Eckstein: *Alte unnennbare Tage* (Vienna, 1936)
M. Klinckerfuss: *Aufklänge aus versunkener Zeit* (Urach, 1947)

BIOGRAPHY

E. Decsey: *Hugo Wolf* (Berlin and Leipzig, 1903–6)
E. Schmitz: *Hugo Wolf* (Leipzig, 1906)
E. Newman: *Hugo Wolf* (London, 1907/*R*1966; Ger. trans., 1910, incl. additional facs. and photographs)
Z. Jachimecki: *Hugo Wolf* (Kraków, 1908)
M. Morold: *Hugo Wolf* (Leipzig, 1912)
R. Prati: *Hugo Wolf* (Turin, 1914)
E. Decsey: *Hugo Wolf: das Leben und das Lied* (Berlin, 1919, 2/1921)
K. Grunsky: *Hugo Wolf* (Leipzig, 1928)
B. Benevisti-Viterbi: *Hugo Wolf* (Rome, 1931)
G. Abraham: 'Hugo Wolf', *Lives of the Great Composers*, ed. A. L. Bacharach (London, 1935)
H. Schouten: *Hugo Wolf: mens en componist* (Amsterdam, 1935)
R. Litterscheid: *Hugo Wolf* (Potsdam, 1939)
F. Walker: 'New Light on Hugo Wolf's Youth', *ML*, xx (1939), 399
W. Rauschenberger: *Ahnentafel des Komponisten Hugo Wolf* (Leipzig, 1940)
M. Hattingberg-Graedener: *Hugo Wolf: vom Wesen und Werk des grössten Liedschöpfers* (Vienna and Leipzig, 1941, rev. 2/1953)
A. Orel: *Hugo Wolf* (Vienna, 1947)
F. Walker: 'Hugo Wolf's Vienna Diary 1875–6', *ML*, xxviii (1947), 12
——: *Hugo Wolf: a Biography* (London, 1951, enlarged 2/1968; Ger. trans., enlarged, 1953 [incl. additional MS facs.])
N. Loeser: *Hugo Wolf* (Antwerp, 1955)
R. Stephan: 'Hugo Wolf', *Die grossen Deutschen*, iv (Berlin, 1958)
D. Lindner: *Hugo Wolf* (Vienna, 1960)
F. Walker: 'Conversations with Hugo Wolf', *ML*, xli (1960), 5
F. Grasberger: 'Hugo Wolf und Melanie Köchert', *ÖMz*, xix (1964), 61
E. Werba: 'Hugo Wolfs Lebens- und Schaffensstationen in Niederösterreich', *ÖMz*, xxv (1970), 107
——: *Hugo Wolf oder der zornige Romantiker* (Vienna, 1971)
W. Schuh: 'Hugo Wolf im Spiegel eines Tagebuchs', *SMz*, cxii (1972), 11, 73

Bibliography

F. Schachermayer: 'Der "private" und der "öffentliche" Hugo Wolf',
ÖMz, xxviii (1973), 438

PSYCHOPATHOLOGY

G. Vorberg: 'Lenau, Nietzsche, Maupassant, Wolf', *Zusammenbruch:
pathographische Abhandlung*, i (Munich, 1922)
Berichte aus dem Irrenhaus (Vienna, 1924)
W. and B. Leibbrand: 'Hugo Wolf und seiner Geisteskrankheit', *Die
medizinische Welt*, xvii (1930), 615
H. Hécaen: *Manie et inspiration musicale: le cas Hugo Wolf* (Bordeaux,
1934)
K. Eickemeyer: *Der Verlauf der Paralyse Hugo Wolfs* (diss., U. of
Jena, 1945)
E. Slater and A. Meyer: 'Contributions to a Psychography of the
Musicians', *Confinia psychiatrica*, iii (1960), 132

MUSICAL AND RELATED STUDIES

Gesammelte Aufsätze über Hugo Wolf (Berlin, 1898–1900) [incl. J.
Schalk: 'Neue Lieder, neues Leben'; P. Müller: 'Ein neuer
Liederkomponist'; vol.i repr. from various publications]
Die Musik, ii (1902–3), 411–48 [Hugo Wolf issue]
P. Müller: *Hugo Wolf*, Moderne Essays, xxxiv–xxxv (Berlin, 1904)
K. Heckel: *Hugo Wolf in seinem Verhältnis zu Richard Wagner*
(Munich, 1905) [repr. from *Süddeutsche Monatshefte* (Munich,
1905), June]
K. Grunsky: *Hugo Wolf-Fest in Stuttgart: Festschrift* (Gutenberg,
1906)
R. Rolland: 'Hugo Wolf', *Musiciens d'aujourd'hui* (Paris, 1908; Eng.
trans., 1915)
F. Austin: 'The Songs of Hugo Wolf', *PMA*, xxxviii (1911–12), 161
W. Salomon: *Hugo Wolf als Liederkomponist* (diss., U. of Frankfurt
am Main, 1925)
W. Jarosch: *Die Harmonik in den Liedern Hugo Wolfs* (diss., U. of
Vienna, 1927)
Musical Courier (New York, 1928), Feb [Hugo Wolf issue]
E. Newman: *Notes* (London, 1932–8) [for vols.i–vi of Hugo Wolf
Society recordings]
H. Hinghofer: *Hugo Wolf als Liederkomponist* (diss., U. of Vienna,
1933)
W. Ford: *The Heritage of Music* (Oxford, 1934)
K. Varges: *Der Musikkritiker Hugo Wolf* (Magdeburg, 1934)
G. Bieri: *Die Lieder von Hugo Wolf* (Berne, 1935)
——: 'Hugo Wolfs Lieder nach verschiedenen Dichtern', *SMz*, lxxv
(1935), 401

F. Kuba: 'Hugo Wolfs Musik zu Kleists Schauspiel Prinz Friedrich von Homburg', *Jb der Kleist-Gesellschaft*, xvii (1937)

A. Breitenseher: *Die Gesangstechnik in den Liedern Hugo Wolfs* (diss., U. of Vienna, 1938)

A. Aber: 'Hugo Wolf's Posthumous Works', *MR*, ii (1941), 190

W. Legge: 'Hugo Wolf's Afterthoughts on his Mörike-Lieder', *MR*, ii (1941), 211

F. Walker: 'Hugo Wolf's Spanish and Italian Songs', *ML*, xxv (1944), 194

A. Tausche: *Hugo Wolfs Mörike-Lieder* (Vienna, 1947)

F. Walker: 'The History of Wolf's Italian Serenade', *MR*, viii (1947), 161

E. Stahl: *Die Jugendlieder Hugo Wolfs* (diss., U. of Göttingen, 1950)

G. Mackworth-Young: 'Goethe's Prometheus and its Settings by Schubert and Wolf', *PRMA*, lxxviii (1951–2), 53

A. Orel: 'Hugo Wolfs Musik zu Ibsens "Fest auf Solhaug" und ihre ungeschriebene Ouvertüre', *SMz*, xci (1951), 485

H. Redlich and F. Walker: 'Hugo Wolf and Funiculì, Funiculà', *MR*, xiii (1952), 125

ÖMz, viii (1953), 45–65 [Hugo Wolf issue]

U. Sennhenn: *Hugo Wolfs Spanisches und Italienisches Liederbuch* (diss., U. of Frankfurt am Main, 1955)

S. Eisold: *Der Gehalt der Lyrik Mörikes in der Vertonung von Hugo Wolf* (diss., U. of Berlin, 1956)

P. Hamburger: 'The Interpretation of Picturesque Elements in Wolf's Songs', *Tempo* (1958), no.48, p.9

ÖMz, xv (1960), 49–112 [Hugo Wolf issue, incl. F. Racek: 'Hugo Wolfs erste Chorversuche', 55]

S. Martinotti: 'Hugo Wolf, musicista mediterraneo', *Musica d'oggi*, iv (1961), 104

E. Sams: *The Songs of Hugo Wolf* (London, 1961; rev., enlarged 2/1983)

E. Kravitt: 'The Influence of Theatrical Declamation upon Composers of the Later Romantic Lied', *AcM*, xxxiv (1962), 18

R. Egger: *Die Deklamationsrhythmik Hugo Wolfs in historischer Sicht* (Tutzing, 1963)

M. Shott: *Hugo Wolf's Music Criticisms* (diss., Indiana U., 1964)

V. Levi: 'L'Italienisches Liederbuch di Hugo Wolf', *RIM*, ii (1966), 203

C. Rostand: *Hugo Wolf* (Paris, 1967)

J. Stein: 'Poem and Music in Hugo Wolf's Mörike Songs', *MQ*, liii (1967), 22

P. Boylan: *The Lieder of Hugo Wolf* (diss., U. of Michigan, 1968)

B. Campbell: *The Solo Sacred Lieder of Hugo Wolf* (diss., Columbia U., 1969)

Bibliography

H. Seelig: *Goethe's Buch Suleika and Hugo Wolf* (diss., U. of Kansas, 1970)

H. Thürmer: *Die Melodik in den Liedern von Hugo Wolf* (Giebing, 1970)

I. Fellinger: 'Die Oper im kompositorischen Schaffen von Hugo Wolf', *Jb des Staatlichen Instituts für Musikforschung Preussischer Kulturbesitz 1971*, 87

ÖMz, xxviii (1973), 433–67 [Hugo Wolf issue, incl. L. Spitzer: 'Rosa Mayreders Textbuch zu Hugo Wolfs "Manuel Venegas" ', 443; H. Jancik: 'Hugo Wolfs Eichendorff-Chöre', 452; W. Legge: 'Hugo Wolf in England', 457]

E. Sams: 'Literary Sources of Hugo Wolf's String Quartets', *Musical Newsletter*, iv (1974), 3

E. Busse: *Die Eichendorff-Rezeption im Kunstlied: Versuch einer Typologie anhand von Kompozitionen Schumanns, Wolfs und Pfitzners* (Tutzing, 1975)

H. Jancik: 'Die Hugo Wolf-Autographen in der Musiksammlung der Österreichischen Nationalbibliothek', *Beiträge zur Musikdokumentation: Franz Grasberger zum 60. Geburtstag* (Tutzing, 1975), 115–54

P. Cook: *Hugo Wolf's Der Corregidor* (London, 1976)

M. Carner: *The Songs of Hugo Wolf* (London, 1982)

H. Eppstein: 'Zu Hugo Wolfs Liedskizzen', *ÖMz*, xxxix (1984), 645

——: 'Zum Schaffensprozess bei Hugo Wolf', *Mf*, xxxvii (1984), 4

Index

391

Index

Index

Index

Index

Index